SPORT

A CULTURAL HISTORY

RICHARD D. MANDELL

COLUMBIA UNIVERSITY PRESS

NEW YORK

Library of Congress Cataloging in Publication Data

Mandell, Richard D.
Sport: A cultural history.

Bibliography: p.
Includes index.
1. Sports—Social aspects—History.   2. Social history.
I. Title.
GV706.5.M36 1984   306'.483   83-20017
ISBN 0-231-05470-X (alk. paper)

Columbia University Press
New York   Guildford, Surrey

Printed in the United States of America

c 10 9 8 7 6 5 4 3

p 10 9 8 7 6 5 4 3 2
Book design by Ken Venezio

To my parents,
Harry and Norma

CONTENTS

SPORT
A CULTURAL HISTORY

LIST OF
ILLUSTRATIONS

PREFACE

This book is about sport in the lives of all people. Putting aside for a time the problem of defining just what sport is, practices resembling the individual or recreational or theatrical activities we now call "sport" have existed in most societies. These activities have differed over time, place and social class. More important, however, are the continuities, or constants in forms of society and in forms of sport. A cultural history of this kind should be therefore more than a collection of stories. It should illuminate persistent themes in human nature, such as man's relations with his fellows and the uses men make of their power over others.

These special areas of human creativity have rarely been surveyed and (I am assuming) never satisfactorily concluded. The significance or at least ubiquitousness of sport in the twentieth century is almost burdensomely obvious. Sports education, sports equipment, sports architecture, sports journalism and sports theater are large enterprises in every modern nation. Just to touch on a subject that will receive due attention later in this history, sport in our newspapers occupies more space and is the object of more passionate reader concern than domestic and international politics combined. The ways or extent in which sport occupies the symbolic inner life of modern man must remain a subject of conjecture. However, proportional representation in the printed and electronic media and the extent to which our sports are socially sanctioned conversational subjects all suggest that the participatory and spectator sports in the western world now offer more objects for men's spiritual concerns than all the formal religions combined.

In writing this book I have been forced to make some lightly supported claims. Formal and, even more so, informal recreation have left little evidence for the historian. In cultures less literary and with a less precisely compartmentalized conception of time than our own, play, games and ritualized competitions are far more difficult to be certain about than the sports of our recent past or our present. Nevertheless, it is worthwhile to examine what we know about developed, sophisticated societies aside from our own.

In addition to the chronology of a standard survey of western culture, I also look at some cultures that flourished apart from that chronology. The sports of various societies in Asia and in pre-Columbian America were no less integrated into their respective societies and were particular adaptions to particular economic and political realities. It might be argued that the bull dancers schematically shown on a small carved stone from ancient India, a Persian miniature of a princely polo game, or a Japanese wood cut of wrestlers are pretty relics worth attention only from the esthete or the antiquarian. However, all of these things and many more traces left by peoples long since gone must be examined by a historian who seeks constants in human nature that transcend the boundaries of time and place.

When we look outside the modern sports tradition (which, as we shall see, is itself so young and so dynamic as to make inappropriate the word "tradition"), we must be skeptical. If we come across an ancient Chinese stone relief of a human figure kicking a ball, we cannot assume that he is a precursor of the modern football player. The existence of pottery statuettes of two Peruvian wrestlers do not mean that the ancient inhabitants of the Andes had rounds, referees, weight classes, or even victors. Lots of activities in the past that *look* like our sports were in practice and in principles quite different from our own. Artists tend to preserve the unusual occurrence.

On the other hand institutionalized play, games, and competitions have been so common and well-integrated into cultural life as to be ignored by artists and chroniclers. In the records of most literate societies one may read more about two-headed calves than about target shooting, foot races, and the scoring of ball games. Even in our own times, when the stars of sport receive vast amounts of attention, we still know but little regarding what our sports mean to performers and spectators and what roles our sports are playing in the development of culture as a whole.

Certain activities we may call sport are general in most cultures. Examples are foot races, wrestling, tests of strength, contests in accuracy with projectiles, and demonstrations of dexterity with a ball. But within these broad categories we discover differences. For children a footrace most often is a playful sprint. But in some instances (as in the classical Greek Olympic games) a footrace could be a cult activity serving oracular purposes or (as in the modern Marathon race) an elaborate, perhaps monstrous celebration of the industrial age's achievement principle. Wrestling can be a spur-of-the-moment romp. But formal (that is, announced in advance with invited spectators) wrestling matches rarely take place except in quasi-religious clan gatherings and must be viewed as much like formal dance and formal theater. Public lifting or heaving of a great weight has perhaps always been used to select employees for difficult work. The strong man will have prestige. But the benefits to be gained by that prestige vary greatly. Accuracy with a boomerang, sling, bow and arrow, or firearm has promoted efficiency in hunting or war and thus is a practical attribute. But ball games are a different matter. With ball games we encounter a dizzying variety of activities encompassing individual and group juggling, apparatus (aside from the balls themselves which may or may not be spherical) ranging from all sorts of rackets and wickets to the use of mounts such as horses and camels. At a sports meet the relationship between performers and spectators may be so close as to make them interchangeable, as in the ball games of Europe's peasants and the townspeople of Italy in Medieval times. In American professional ice hockey and in European football, the spectators are separated from the players by purposefully impenetrable fences or glass partitions and, sometimes, by cordons of police.

How have athletes viewed what they were doing? In the past,

like many today, they may have been ordinary euphoric youths taking some time out for a happy, pointless dash across a meadow. Or, they may have been professionals—freaks like the Sumo wrestlers or the giants who drop the ball through the hoop in basketball games. He (rarely she, incidentally) may have played (or competed) as a joke of the moment, as the summit performance of a life of preparation, or as a drugged cult functionary going through rehearsed motions in a trance.

This book will dwell only briefly on athletes as personalities. After all, the mists of time have hidden from us much of what we would like to know about athletes of the past, and the athletes of recent times are concealed behind popular myths. Athletes are interesting mostly because of their skills and because of the importance a culture assigns to their performances. Sports techniques and outstanding performances are only incidental subjects of this book. We will observe athletes in social settings. If sports and games are used to serve broadly conceived educational purposes, we will be more interested in the intentions of the organizers than in the equipment, tactics, and rules. If sport is entertainment, we will be more concerned with the theatrical setting and what the spectators wished to experience when they appeared for the performance. When athletes have inspired artists, we will be most interested in the products that resulted than in the acts and individuals that inspired them.

Having embarked on the task, I am intimidated, but not subdued, by its size. I will discuss sport from what we may assume are the beginnings, basing the conclusions on descriptions of animal behavior, archaeological evidence, and the observations of ethnologists. I will agree with the anthropologists' assumption that, ultimately and essentially, man as the anthropologists study him is much like prehistoric man and that both are, in turn, very much like me and my readers. I shall assume that many of the elements in human nature or in society upon which our sports are based or from which they spring are persistent and perhaps constant.

Like most univeral histories, the narrative will dwell on the culture of the classical Greeks. The Greeks produced the most original and dazzling of the world's golden ages and most historians regret not having been there to participate. There are additional reasons for discussing Greek sport. We know a lot about it. The sports of the Greeks were essential elements in much of their cultural originality. But I must also counter some popular assumptions about ancient sports (particularly about the Olympic Games) that have justified some aspects of modern physical education and the theatrical presentation of some modern sports festivals.

There will be a chapter on the athletic contests and games of some high cultures, such as those of China and Japan, which are apart from the Western tradition. This survey will be separate from the chronological order of the book as a whole. Sport in Europe will be treated rather sketchily and in broad strokes until we arrive at the Anglo-Saxon world in the seventeenth and eighteenth centuries. During this period Englishmen made decisive and influential innovations in social and economic organization and in politics as well. Not uncoincidentally, many Englishmen also began to examine, reject, and refine forms of play or recreation which had been common in comparable social classes all over Europe. In England there evolved some new and broadly based attitudes toward games and competitions and athletes and their performances. These new notions favoring equal (sporting) opportunity, fair play, codified rules, training, transregional leagues, and referees had striking analogues in English social and economic life, which were being transformed. Few historians have noticed that modern sport has characteristics that are distinctive and that modern sport has its origins in precisely those social circumstances that fostered rationalized industrial production. For a while, industrial production and modern sport were uniquely regnant in England and both, subsequently, have spread over much of the world.

Historians actually have large, if fragmented, amounts of detailed evidence about games and competitions in the past. We believe that there were professional wrestlers in ancient Egypt. We know how the sprinters in ancient Olympia started their races in unison. We know how ice skates looked in seventeenth-century Holland and what the amateur records were for the broad jump in English colleges in the 1860s. But often the information we possess provokes more than it satisfies. We yearn to go behind the details. The elements in human character or in society that lead to particular sports cannot be stated with confidence. Part of our problem is that modern sport is still much in process. Sport is even now being invented. Something so richly dynamic naturally offers us no firm place to stand in order to observe it.

Considering that sport as we know it more or less was invented by Englishmen (though they were scarcely aware of it at the time) and then grandly elaborated by Americans, it is remarkable that so few comprehensive or serious studies of sport have appeared in English. One might conclude (as I have) that Anglo-Saxon sport arose, grew, and continues to evolve naturally without the presiding help of intellectuals as leaders or even observers. Such a chasm between the creative dynamism of sport and the people who work with ideas has not been the case in Central and Eastern Europe where recreational activities—whether designed as physical education, popular gymnastics, paramilitary training, or the preparation of national teams—have long been a matter for informed debate and, subsequently, purposeful direction. Sport has been regarded earnestly east of the English channel for almost two hundred years. This earnestness and the historical literature that is a byproduct of it have been helpful for the production of this volume. A novel characteristic of this book in English on sport history is that it is based on literature in several languages, but most especially German.

As stated before, much of the book will be a conventional, chronological survey. But I will not be able to put aside some nettlesome problems that have bothered all others who have surveyed this subject or large parts of it. The speculative or analytical problems will be most apparent in the first and in the last two chapters. The most serious problem is the linch-pin word which appears in the book's title and which I have already used many times in this introduction. "Sport" covers vastly too much. The word came to English from medieval French. For centuries "sport" in England meant mostly hunting. Then in the twentieth century, along with the conquest of the world by a number of formalized competitions and contests loosely called "sport" in English, the word has been appropriated by most of the world's languages and subsequently incorporated into nouns, verbs, and adjectives to apply to activities that are various indeed. Sport historians before me have regularly used the word to describe or encompass many activities that existed for millennia before the word did. This broad coverage in both diversity and time makes precision in writing difficult. Modern sport has evolved and spread much too fast for our languages to adapt to its fads, subtleties, and regional variations. It is imprecise to refer to certain activities of the ancient Greeks, the Tokugawa Japanese, and the German philanthropists all as "sport." No contemporary observers of those activities used the word "sport." But, since all my predecessors have used "sport" rather broadly and I intend this book for the general as well as the specialist reader, I feel far more would be lost than gained if I imposed a new terminology of my invention. In almost all cases the reader should know what I mean.

However, I believe I must insert a tentative definition of sport that will be elaborated in the course of the chapters. It is meant to provide a basis for inclusion and exclusion. Sport will here encompass competitive activity of the whole human body according to sets of rules for purposes ostensibly or symbolically set apart from the serious, essential aspects of life. I will consider as sport all team games, track-and-field events, gymnastics, wrestling, fencing, speed swimming, cycling, rowing, and skating. The book is cultural history, not an encyclopedia. Many particular sports may not even be mentioned. I must ignore jai-alai and Chinese golf and slight two of my own favorite recreational activities: bicycle touring and body surfing. Excluded are board games like chess, card games, and almost all spectator viewing of fighting animals. Except where they may lend parallel historical background to parts of the narrative, I will also exclude sledding, sailing, and auto racing—in short, those activities where the technical apparatus dominates the human performer. I will include mat gymnastics, figure skating, and springboard diving, all of which are now much like dance. It is worth noting here that at various times in the past dance has been competitive. On the other hand many competitions in societies before our own were highly estheticized. There will be frequent references to the hunt, for in hunting as well as in preparation for war lay impulses that were the basis for formal recreations and pacific contests.

The book's first outline excluded the horse sports, since they did not deal with the "whole body" of my working definition. But in the course of my collecting and pondering of information I had to conclude that the sporting horse had always had immense symbolic importance in identifying and ornamenting the politically dominant class. This is particularly so for two societies, those of classical Greece and Georgian England, which have been seedbeds for international sport. The early chapters will include some descriptions of Roman festivals and of the medieval tournaments because they provide structural and suggestive comparisons with sports such as professional football (both American and international) which are now, when viewed in their cultural settings, more theatrical and festive than athletic.

I have chosen illustrations that, when possible, meet three criteria: they come from the period under discussion, they demonstrate claims made in the text, and they are (or were) of artistic merit. Artists, particularly those in the Western tradition, have used athletes as ideal types. Athletes enjoy their physical supremacy. Our observations of athletes rouses in us a yearning for physical euphoria that is elusive. The performing athlete similarly stimulates the artist and, the artist hopes, his audience will be analogously stimulated. Artistically viewed and transmuted, the athlete tends to concretize an epoch's ideals of beauty and pleasure.

When artists choose athletic contests and games as subjects they are only one kind of intellectual attempting to load the performers with ideological baggage. High-performance athletes are rarely artists or intellectuals themselves—a matter, incidentally, worth pondering. Still, there exists enough work to demonstrate the connection between sport and art.

The reader will observe that the twentieth century is represented only sparsely. I feel that the essential qualities of sporting art—a precious moment, sublimated voyeurism, familiar harmonies, optimistic health—are almost antithetical to the dominant ideologies of twentieth-century art. However, sports photographers, particularly some Americans and Germans of recent decades, are maintaining and extending a grand tradition as they innovate.

I have used a bibliographical system that is intended to ease the progress of the general reader. In the chapters of the running text I have used a few content footnotes and a minimum of bibliographical citations. Little of the book is based on primary sources, so at the end of each chapter, after introducing them with a short critical essay, I will list the monographs or other works used. Readers who wish to read further should not assume that the books and articles listed after each chapter are of comparable quality. The only periods in sport history that have received respectable attention are classical Greece and (much less so) England in the nineteenth century, recent North America, and the modern Olympic Games. The only team sports of any age that have attracted good historians are American baseball and British football. No one has yet published a scholarly respectable, comprehensive, sports bibliography. The world still awaits a book living up to the title *Joe Louis (or Max Schmeling or Sonja Henie) and His (or Her) Times.* Whether on-the-spot or retrospective, sports writing has almost always been hasty, hyperbolic, chauvinistic, venal, or some combination of the above.

I have tried to write an objective, explanatory narrative. But, of course, I am not without prejudices—some of which ought to be revealed early. I am one kind of athlete: a mediocre, middle-aged, long-distance runner. When possible, I train with friends in order to converse, but more often I run alone. Almost always I tend to be suspicious of sporting competitions or games that are staged for people or groups that are other than the athletes themselves. I am nearly convinced that sport for adult participators is and has been a special taste. It seems to me that the capacity for pleasure in athletic competition might be confined to such special and incommunicable tastes as those for community dancing and pleasure in experiencing art music. It also seems that the capacity for pleasure in athletic competition might be confined to no more than 10 percent of any population. Probably all societies have had competitions and ceremonialized games, yet none (excepting, naturally, the children in them) have had large proportions of the population who spontaneously participated for fun. Participation (excepting, of course, physician-prescribed gymnastics and military training) may in fact be a demonstration of a certain residual childishness—suggesting that the performer has compartmentalized his life so that a part of him is not fully grown up. Yet it also seems that in many societies certain observed performers have been given a grandly earnest, ponderous symbolic importance.

Though the impulse to participate may be uncommon, the appeal of regular public festivals and the enclosed theater are broader—perhaps so broad as to be one of the definers of social life. And ever more, our sports are excuses for some vital theatrical innovations of our age. As I will show, most of the sports of our time share characteristics that are particular for our age and did not exist before. These particular characteristics of modern times and of modern sports may have been present rudimentarily or not at all in the formal games and competitions of epochs before our own. On the other hand theatrically presented competitions among horses and among actors, dancers, and athletes (the distinctions among these last three classes of entertainers should not be too sharply made) have for millennia excited and satisfied certain social desires. These desires may be more capable of being roused now because of the prevalence of leisure in many modern societies.

But enough! I have, I think, responsibly stated my claims and exposed my doubts and anxieties in this preface. As a summary, then, this book is a history of the cultural importance of the sports of all people. The employed definition of "sport" is restricted. The narrative is based almost entirely on previously existing scholarship, much of it in German.

Though I am responsible for the book's organization, theoretical positions, and errors, I could not have written it if I had not received a Fulbright-Hayes award in the years 1973–1974 in Germany. My protector throughout was Professor Hajo Bernett of the *Sportwissenschaftliches Institut* of the University of Bonn. Other helpful scholars were Professors Manfred Lämmer and Wolfgang Decker of the *Historisches Seminar* of the *Sporthochschule* in Cologne. Those who guide the destinies of the University of South Carolina granted me leaves—some of them paid—so I could do the actual writing with a minimum of interruptions.

Richard D. Mandell
JANUARY 1984

SPORT
A CULTURAL HISTORY

[1]

SPORT BEFORE
HIGH CULTURE

When did sport begin?

If sport is, in essence, play, the claim might be made that sport is much older than mankind for, as we all have observed, the beasts play. Dogs and cats wrestle and play ball games. Fishes and birds dance. The apes have simple, pleasureable games. Frolicking infants, school children playing tag, and arm wrestlers in a bar are demonstrating strong, trans-generational and trans-species bonds with the universe of animals—past, present and future. Young animals, particularly, tumble, chase, run, wrestle, mock, imitate, and laugh (or so it seems) to the point of delighted exhaustion. Their play, and ours, appear to serve no other purpose than to give pleasure to the players, and apparently, to remove us temporarily from the anguish of life in earnest.

Some philosophers have claimed that our playfulness is the most noble part of our basic nature. In their generous conceptions, play harmlessly and experimentally permits us to put our creative forces, fantasy, and imagination into action. Play is release from the tedious battles against scarcity and decline which are the incessant, and inevitable, tragedies of life. This is a grand conception that excites and provokes. The holders of this view (most influentially, Johan Huizinga in his *Homo ludens*, 1938 and Roger Caillois in his *Man, Play and Games*, 1958) claim that the origins of our highest accomplishments—liturgy, literature, and law—can be traced to a play impulse which, paradoxically, we see most purely enjoyed by young beasts and children. Our sports, in this rather happy, non-fatalistic view of human nature, are more splendid creations of the nondateable, trans-species play impulse.

An orthodox Marxist historian, working from the assurance of a rigidly monist position (that is, the substance of the universe, including man, is basically one—in this case, matter) sees man's nature as dynamically pliable, though the course of life for a particular person may be fixed. Man's existing social or cultural forms and activities depend upon the existing state of material use or technology. To the Marxists, man is essentially a worker. From these assumptions a Marxist sport historian (Gerhard Lukas, *Die Körperkultur in frühen Epochen der Menschenentwicklung*, 1969) has determined that the first sport was spear throwing. The argument is impressive.

To become good at using the spear, one had to practice. The would-be, confident spear tosser had to master and perform a here-there kind of thinking that was sharply different from the hunting techniques of non-tool using beings whose play, relaxation, and exercise was not much different from that of the beasts. According to the Marxist, sport separates men from beasts. Sport is a cultural manifestation but is not play. Sport is only preparation for work and a reflection of the needs of a creative animal to survive and progress.

One traditional view of the origins of sport bases its assumptions on some sentimental currents of the last century and still has a few evangelists in the committees governing the modern Olympic Games. They suggest that sport somehow appeared gloriously and spontaneously during the golden age of classical Greece and then suddenly and tragically disappeared, waiting to be brought to life again in our own times. They assumed that the noble Greeks practiced sport from morning to night. And in their sports and their attitudes toward sports we all can (it is suggested) find explanations for the Grecian accomplishments in art, philosophy, and education. The Greek athlete was an embodiment of classical ideas; the ancient Olympic Games their festive climaxes. The ancient Games, which began precisely in 776 B.C., if they had been more enthusiastically maintained might have saved the classical Greeks from the political irrascibility that led to their downfall. This view is the one that is the least based upon good evidence.

A critical and rather challenging view of sport sees our sports as not at all ancient in their origins and scarcely at all culturally uplifting. The critics (Bero Rigauer, *Sport und Arbeit*, 1969; Henning Eichberg, *Der Weg des Sports in die industrieller Gesellschaft*, 1973; Allen Guttmann, *From Ritual to Record*, 1978) of our "achieving society" have gathered evidence to show that modern sport is a unique adaption to modern life. Some of them claim that sport is not merely work. It can be disguised, demoralized work. Bero Rigauer lists some characteristics of modern sport: discipline, authority, competition, accomplishment, skill, purposeful rationality, organization, and bureaucracy. Rigauer, then, sees sport as mirroring and supporting the central assumptions of industrial capitalism.

The person who is a participating athlete, a physical educator, or a sports fan may be expected to shudder at so bleak a depiction of activities that give him exceptional health, career satisfaction, or theatrical pleasures. Yet the historian has to be impressed that some of the essential aspects of sport as we know it (and not necessarily only those general traits named above) first appeared in England when that society, and not merely coincidentally, was beginning to undergo the Industrial Revolution. Modern sports, therefore, are particular adaptions to modern economic, social, and political life—a provocative thesis I will devote a great deal of attention to.

Our sports may be the creative impulses and products of inventions yet more recent than those claimed by any of these theories. We may cite the invention of such banal items as the stop watch, rubber balls, mass market newspapers, television, and steel ball bearings. All have influenced and have been influenced by our sports. Or we can raise more weighty social inventions such as constitutional theory (which preceded codified rules for games) and international expositions (which preceded international athletic contests, including the modern Olympic Games). Certain broad social attitudes deserve mention as well: for example, equality of opportunity and patriotism or even more specific social novelties that may be determinants for the peculiar characteristics of modern sport. Some of these are compulsory universal education, mass leisure, and the scientific analysis of human behavior.

The theories briefly outlined above give us peeks at some venerable and enchanting philosophical problems. For example: if one accepts the belief that sport antedates man, implicit is the suggestion that man himself may be in essence a beast and not a unique and utterly separate creation of God. Theological and moral implications here! Everyone knows that children play much more and perhaps very differently than adults do. We must ask then, "What is a child? Is he a miniature adult or a separate variety of being with very special needs?" Deep educational implications! Or further: the Marxists ask us to decide whether man is a worker or a player or, if neither, which mixture of the two. Does man stand alone in the universe? Is he a creation of his own, of fate, or of an interested supreme being? To what extent is each of us a product of momentums established in the past and to what extent are we creations of our independent wills?

Sports historians have usually written from an advocate's point of view. Most often sport historians seek and assemble evidence to suggest not only that the sport they cherish existed always, but also that it existed most vigorously in some golden age. Yet, despite the constancy of play and a variety of games, competitions, and festivals that defy enumeration and classification, sports before our times and at present are activities that are not easily separated from social life for description and analysis. Being interested only in exceptional events, the chroniclers of early ages kept few records of sport and gave everyday play no notice. Those activities we call sport are too common. Strong and agile players and their performances were noticed either when they struck outsiders by their oddness or when the performances were outstanding. Almost all our feeble knowledge of premodern and, most especially, prehistoric sport is inferred (perhaps too cleverly) from a pitifully small collection of artifacts.

From what we have been able to ascertain, it appears that aspects of man's life in society, those activities that appear to resemble our games and contests, have been closely connected with those areas of life that are governed by magic or the sacred. Sporting competitions in almost all societies before our own were integral parts of or adjuncts of religious observations. Formal games and contests were like the dance and the theater. Indeed, in a historical description of sport, we may be making artificial separations if we remove sport very far from ritual, the dance, and the theater.

Here might be a good place to make some partially repetitious statements about sport which would probably find wide agreement. Activities which we regard as play or—stretching our terms—informal physical education, served selective or evolutionary purposes among social animals, including men. Those practiced and skilled in playful running, swimming, leaping, or mock battle (e.g. wrestling) were better prepared for these activities when energetic action was required in earnest for defense, attack, or the struggle against scarcity. We may assume that early man—whose origins we now place in southern Africa roughly some 500,000 years ago—played and practiced rather variously. We can assume that early man lifted and tossed when not urgently required to do so. Some exceptionally adept individuals were the first entertainers who, like the first singers, juggled, did acrobatics, or lifted great stones for the amusement of others and for their own heightened self-esteem. We can only guess when the first men wrestled or otherwise had person to person combat with someone who was not an enemy. May we not assume that there were rules (as there are among cats and dogs) to protect the eyes and genitals of the competitors? Some of us know that it is not necessary to have a surfboard to ride a foaming wave as it rushes toward the beach. Our own practiced bodies permit us to revel in that kind of ecstasy. Another kind of sensuous trance can be approached by the dancer. When early man danced, is it not likely that some of them strenuously competed for attention, thereby placing their dancing close (as it almost always has been) to sport? One way to define society is in terms of the restraints put on its members. These restraints are well known by the participants in wrestling as well as by the spectators. For a society requires stern rules against maiming one's fellows. Wrestling, which permits shifts in rank without inflicting crippling injury, existed or exists in almost all societies. We can assume, I believe, that pre-civilized men practiced these and other sports with and against their fellows for stakes that may not have, but most likely did affect their intratribal prestige.

Some philosophers of sport have focused on various elements in human nature: among others, the pleasure or compulsion to move one's body, the struggle for social status, and social approbation. The classical Greeks used the terms *agón* (the compulsion to compete) and *arete* (the yearning for recognition of excellence) to describe the athlete's preoccupations. The terms described personal characteristics outside of athletes as well. Whether or not these terms and what they describe are universal may not be learned here, but they may be used or kept in mind when one considers the amazing richness of invention regarding amusements, games, and competitions in societies blithely called "primitive" or "simple."

To return to history and sport: the life-forms of prehistoric man can be deduced only from the traces they have left us. Examples are the hammerheads, other stone tools, and those first spearheads from which the orthodox Marxist dates the origin of sport. Our deductions about the nature of prehistoric society from the evidence in graves or piles of animal bones are buttressed by the accounts of travelers and ethnographers of the past several centuries in Asia, Africa, America, and Australasia. The historians of prehistoric man more or less go along with the anthropologist's assumption that basically and intrinsically, mankind is one and, furthermore, that we are legitimate in guessing about the behavior of unobservable prehistoric societies when we work from careful observations of preliterate, recent, or existing societies.

In any case, with the invention of tools and weapons came the need to practice with them. Besides spears, the first specifically man-made projectiles, there were darts, blowguns, and the bow and arrows. This last was a major invention that figures prominently in the paintings found in Europe and Africa. The attention given the bow in prehistoric art suggests that its mastery was a dramatic leap forward, a miraculous accomplishment, a beneficence of the gods. Significantly, the practice of archery was ceremonialized and practiced in ritualized forms in China and Japan (where certain competitions are still ceremoniously observed) and very likely in other societies as well.

If we read the observations of the ethnologists, we come across a variety of recreational activities that are bewildering in number, but familiar in classification. So various is recreation that these observations tend to weaken the Marxist equation, sport equals work. Non-Western, non-modern varieties of recreation suggest rather that the creative fantasy seems to invent ever new means of achieving distinction when no work is available or when work is shunned. How can we explain the accounts of stilt walkers among the nonliterate peoples in the Middle East and in Africa? Or the exhilarating practice of swinging at the end of a line suspended from a tall pole as was done by the Maoris in order to launch themselves for a soaring plunge into deep water? Various Central American people swing from ropes around tall poles in masks and costumes to the cheers of delighted spectators. The Hawaiian Aborigines invented and used the surfboard for rides of longer duration than the trips obtainable by the outstretched body. The North American Aborigines devised snowshoes in order to cross otherwise seasonally impassable territory, but they also had races and danced in snowshoes. We possess a stone-age cave drawing of three skiers who hunt with bow and arrow and who (curiously) are strikingly phallic.

If one claims that acrobatics and juggling predated written history or indeed any records at all he is, to be sure, on insecure ground, but then, he can be sure no skeptic will produce evidence demonstrating the contrary. We do have traveler's reports and pictorial evidence that the Eskimos have used certain kinds of gymnastic apparatus including a stretched leather cord that was employed something like the modern high bar. We also have ethnographical records of log rolling, tree climbing and hurling of almost infinitely various objects for distance and/or accuracy. The proliferation or variety of combative sports such as wrestling or boxing among non-Western societies has been vast and includes exquisite distinctions regarding the allowable holds, protective padding, definitions of a fall, and the behavior of the referees and audiences. All of the above could be practiced and indeed was practiced before the transforming inventions of agriculture and the domestication of animals—from which we date the beginnings of civilization.

With these momentous developments—which occurred nearly simultaneously about 10,000 B.C. in the valleys of the Indus, Nile, Tigris, and Euphrates rivers—the possibilities for new social forms, new tools, and consequently new sports were broadened. However, just as the invention of agriculture and the domestication of the dog, cow, goat, sheep, and horse may have increased the potential recreations, so, paradoxically, was participation restrained and particularized. With the establishment of dense populations and definite social hierarchies, the fierce joys of pursuing scarce and distant game were thereafter available only to the arms-bearing class which had the necessary freedom of movement. In order to stultify any nascent ambitions among the agricultural laboring classes, the masses were kept legally fixed in their places of residence and denied any sort of weapons. When time and the overlords permitted, the agricultural laborers were likely to practice dancing, wrestling, board games, and many kinds of juggling which were harmless and which early became and remained class and locality specific. Priests would be likely to devise for themselves dances or theatrically presented rituals that were intended to be publicly performed in handsome costumes. Their recreations (if indeed they were that) were likely to be rehearsed in advance and overlaid with arcane symbolism that tended to affirm to the masses below them and to the temperamentally dangerous classes above them the beauty, indispensability, and incomprehensibility of the priests' functions in society. More so than with other classes, among the priests it became and remained difficult to separate formal dances and games from sacred dance and ritual sacrifices. In a stable society, the supreme ruler might have his own sports peculiar to him alone in which his unapproachable supremacy would be demonstrated in public ceremonies or, if he was a languid weakling, in descriptions of his supremacy composed by propagandists dependent upon his favors and his staying in place.

The domestication of animals was a marvelous accomplishment. But always the beasts that lived among men retained some of the danger and magic of the wild animals who were still in the forests and on the steppes. The large and potent bull, especially, came to acquire a mythic and exalted position in many early cultures from the Indus to Crete. The ceremonial bull might be bred for great size and speed. He was groomed for the public demonstrations of acrobatics against his menace or for drawn-out ritual slaughter. If the breeding bull was dangerous, the castrated bull was tamable and was rather easily put to work or cut into tasty portions. Oxen may dependably pull a sledge or a wagon or plow, but their ponderous movements are the opposite of the controlled vertigo sought by the sportsman.

The horse is another matter! The ancestors of our present sport horses were much smaller beasts, who were caught, tamed, and selectively bred for flesh, milk, and for work as draft animals—in all of which classifications they are inferior to cattle. Horse technology is sufficiently complex that it had to be slow to develop, but it was probably begun around 4000 B.C. somewhere in the steppes of Persia. The war chariot was momentously effective. It was so stunning a weapon that often even the sight of warriors with chariots was enough to intimidate their opponents into submission. Where chariots were introduced into the Middle East they were destabilizing, and it became necessary for fixed cities to adopt new fortifications and the chariot itself in order to survive. Innovations in cavalry technique also required that stable societies as well as barbarian nomads become breeders and trainers of horses. Equine technology is especially costly for a fixed agricultural society. Large numbers of horses require good pasture or great quantities of forage to maintain their combat readiness. The harnesses and chariots are dear. Military horses with their drivers require regular, disciplined exercise. To be sure, horse racing and various tournaments have typically taken on lives of their own, but until modern times they basically were portentous theater intended to prove the fitness and readiness of the splendid and fearsome animals for more earnest tasks.

For millennia the most splendid and terrifying spectacle the world had to offer was the light two-wheeled cart, drawn by two or four horses with a bellowing driver at the reins. They were fast, dazzling equipages. Their splendor (suggesting wealth, and sudden punishment) was heightened by gilding and trailed ribbons.

The finest chariots were so awesome to see in movement that much of their effect in battle, on parade, or in a race was due to the intimidation of those who had no chariots or who had only drab ones. Military and sport horses (the distinction would be indistinct until recent times) became essential for the preservation of the political independence and maintenance of order in almost all complex societies in Eurasia. Those people without military horses, whatever the level of sophistication in other areas of endeavor, became pushovers for those using them. The chariot team was an essential element for political control from about 2000 B.C. until the appearance of the giant horse or cataphract in about 500 A.D. (a matter to which we will return). The horse was less essential in very rough terrain (which did not support important agricultural wealth anyway) or along seacoasts protected at their rear by rough terrain. Nevertheless, even where horses could not be used to best advantage, they became imbued with such an aura of power, wealth, and terror that even in ancient Greece, where grazing land was especially scarce, the ruling classes were partly defined as those who owned, bred and raced horses.

Superior domesticated animals were favored for selective breeding. There must have been informal races to select the superior animals. When informal contests became formal we cannot know, but we may assume that among groups of mounted hunters or the owners of teams there were publicly observed races and, in the light of the attachment of owners to their animals, the stakes could be large. A defeat suffered by a socially ambitious and boastful horse owner could signify a severe loss in prestige and perhaps a fall from grace as well. On the other hand, a victory in a race might be seen by the victor and those who watched him as an augury, an indication of favor by the gods.

The discussions above about auguries, the gods, social prestige, and political position lead to further matters of importance. We must make attempts to view empathetically people who perceived the universe and their positions in it differently than we do. In almost all the societies we shall discuss, life was more rigidly and mysteriously compartmentalized than our lives are. We moderns have dispelled mysteries that gave meaning to billions of people whose lives preceded our own. Our predecessors yearned to learn more about the intentions of their cruel and fickle gods by means of the signs given by nature. Only recently and then rather selectively have the players of various board and court games come to regard the progress and outcomes of the games as the products of mathematical probability, memory, and tactics. The ethnologists have told us that the North American Indians played their myriad, almost infinitely various, board and dice games in quasi-sacred circumstances and that the outcomes—victory, loss, or something indeterminate—were interpreted as signs of the players' status with the omnipotent, but obfuscatory deities. We may assume that all but the most playful, informal games and contests also took place in a well-observed atmosphere of portents, symbols, and theatrical earnestness.

The above observations regarding board games apply as well to other activities, posing competitive forces on a prescribed territory for an unforseeable result. With the help of anthropologists and ethnologists we must turn to the earliest ball games. Almost all our indications that there were ball games before the modern age come from archeological traces. This purely visual evidence tempts observers to construct parallels with our various modern ball and court games. But we probably err if we assume that these games were entered into with the informality of the youths of American college fraternities or other rival sport clubs which have as their object to determine objectively which is the best team. Among non-Western people or among our ancestors some dozens of generations back, the *practice* for ball games, like among us, may have been disjointed and lighthearted, but the actual performances were not. The participant in a ball game endured (perhaps enjoyed) the utter subjugation of his individuality into a temporary sacred community. The ball games (if indeed they were that) would be preceded by processions of priests and accompanied by musicians and dancers. Participators and spectators entered into a temporary, earnest, sacred community perhaps in some ways comparable to a modern theater or ballet audience. Indeed, certain aspects of twentieth-century dance—the ascetic preparation of the performers according to various arcane and mutually exclusive schools, the selfless subjection of actor or dancer to director or choreographer, the adaption by some "players" of costumes and masks to indicate their sharp removal from every day life—suggest parallels. The formal court games were more like rituals than a soccer match of the present. We have many ethnological reports showing that participators in games and in theater (the clear distinction we make between sporting competitions and the theater may be a scheme *we* have imposed on public festivities) might be in trances induced by rhythmic dance, breath control, drugs, or hypnotic suggestion. Certainly the progress and results of the ball games were interpreted oracularly. Winners could be grandly celebrated as the favorites of the gods; the losers punished or even sacrificed.

All the descriptions we have of prehistoric sport are of necessity based on dubious archaeological evidence buttressed by observations of varying dependability of modern pre-literate societies. It would profit us little to survey the fragmentary literature describing the sports of all the people—the New Guineans, the Balinese, the West Sumatrans, the Bushmen, the Nuba, the Bedouins, the Kalmuks, the Lapps, and others. Most of the evidence attests to both the variety of recreational pursuits and the extent to which these games are integrated in the world view of the people who enjoy them.

We do have an especially detailed survey done by a close observer and meticulous collector which may be used to establish the point regarding the playful inventiveness of mankind in a natural state. Stewart Culin (1858–1929), a young archaeologist and ethnologist, was asked in 1891 to prepare, for the 1893 Chicago World's Fair, an exhibit of the games of the peoples of the world. Culin embarked on the task, but quickly determined that he did not have enough time to organize that show. The subject was too vast. He eventually decided to concentrate on the aborigines of North America and subsequently spent more than 15 years collecting and organizing specimens, previous reports, and his own observations. The result was *The Games of the North American Indians* published in 1907 as an annual report of the Smithsonian Institution. The book has 846 pages of small print and 1112 illustrations in addition to the plates and charts.

Culin tried valiantly to organize what he had assembled and concluded. He divides "Games of Chance" into dice games (over which there was a great deal of gambling) and guessing games.

"Games of Dexterity" cover over 232 pages of text and more than 400 pictures. They include archery, hoops and sticks, rings and pins, and an amazing variety of ball games, for which some of the balls, rackets, and players are illustrated. Many of the ball games would now seem more readily classifiable as running races, since the object was for several contestants to hustle a kicked ball for very long distances. The inadequacy of Culin's classification scheme is apparent in his "Minor Amusements," which covers shuttle-cock, quoits, shuffleboard, bean shooters, cat's cradle and many, many other activities. Culin stresses that these games are not de-rived from the Europeans (he has a separate short section on these). His style is scientific and cooly comprehensive.

The book has been much praised and used by subsequent social scientists. It was reprinted in 1974. So various and fetching are these hundreds of written descriptions and pictures that some writers have concluded that the North American Indians were the most imaginative and devoted players the world has ever known. They fail to notice that the Chippewas' counting sticks, the Zunis' feathered darts, the Blackfoots' gaming rings, and the balls of the Passamaquoddy, Penobscots and Cherokees (all of which exist in preserved examples) were made of wood, leather, or other perish-able materials. The mesolithic Britons, the pre-Etruscan Italians, the neolithic Chinese may all have had such playthings, which would perish without a trace. All these peoples and others like them have also left but little evidence of their lives behind them. They may have been as inventive as the North American Indians, but they did not have a respectful Stewart Culin to observe them.

The thesis offered here is that it is idle to look for the precur-sors of the competitions and games of modern industrial society by tracing the history of these activities themselves. The human imagination is a rich constant and may always have invented ways to gamble, juggle, race, and interpret outcomes of organized con-tests. Mankind's fantasy may have been far more productive than we are prepared to acknowledge. More difficult (and more rele-vant) is for us to attempt to determine who participated and who watched and what meaning was given by those present at the pro-ceedings.

It is essential to summarize some of Culin's conclusions about the variety of play he had so devotedly observed and pondered: he saw both superficial and deep similarities in the games of all the tribes. He believed that while the games' object "appears to be purely a manifestation of the desire for amusement or gain, they are performed also as religious ceremonies, as rites pleasing to the gods." After he surveyed the games of the North American Indians he concluded that "In part they agree in general and in particular with certain widespread ceremonial observances found in other continents, which observances, in what appear to be their oldest and most primitive manifestations, are almost exclusively divinatory" (p. 809).

To return to and to repeat some basic points: So-called primitive men lived complex lives, many subtleties of which are likely to remain hidden or misinterpreted by modern analytical eyes. All societies, including our own, require self-discipline, the suppression of aggression, and widely accepted justifications of the social order. There have always been social or professional classes to interpret the random happenings of the universe and otherwise to maintain by propaganda and by force the existing political order. To stabilize its social order further, a society will have a mythic version of its origins and its destiny that affirms the correctness of the existing order. The prevailing interpretation of the cosmic order or theology, in order to be made manifest or given concrete visual or otherwise perceivable form to the society as a whole, requires symbolically presented, well-observed, public performances or festivals. Participants and spectators (here again, rarely, if ever has this separation been as great as it is in our own day) enjoy during the festival a heightened sense of personal worth, a welcoming of community solidarity, and a vivid perception of the power of the deities.

I have emphasized here the creative flexibility of mankind in a social setting. Some of mankind's creative activity has been devoted to inventing games, contests, and apparatus that suggest some comparisons with the activities we now summarize (with too few distinctions) as sport. Using archeological artifacts and ethnographical evidence, we can be sure that a great variety of athletics and spectators, sports, and sports festivals existed long before the founding of the great empires from which we date the beginnings of civilization. New technologies and new political organizations regularly resulted in new varieties of class-specific and broadly sanctioned recreations or theatrically presented contests that symbolically affirmed the correctness of the social order that fostered them.

[2]

SPORT BEFORE
THE GREEKS

As well as we are able to determine, the first people to direct the building of cities were outsiders who imposed their rule upon some farming villages between the Tigris and Euphrates rivers about 3500 B.C. Urban life required the keeping of written records, and with a sustained burst of creative activity these Sumerians invented a form of writing, a calendar and a system of weights and measures. They also had some trade with India and Egypt. As with the other earliest civilizations in Egypt, China, and India, the economic basis was the management of rivers so as to provide for large-scale irrigation. Irrigation permitted a previously unknown regularity and richness in farming production.

To manage a whole river required the steady discipline of a large population. It seems likely that slavery may have begun as a makeshift control over small numbers of people, but eventually, with the hardening of social discipline, the slaves became the majority of the population. As they settled down to rule, the unprecedented wealth of the Sumerians was an attraction to the envious tough nomadic tribes (much like the Sumerians themselves had been some generations before) who were never far from the rich farms and the glittering cities. To maintain their power internally and externally, the Sumerians formed appropriate political, religious, and military institutions and established the bureaucracies necessary to run them.

Judging from the written records and the art the Sumerians have left us, their originality and their wealth did not make them cheerful. Perhaps with good reason, the Sumerians may have felt that their civilization had too many envious enemies near at hand. No matter how careful the priests were in their rituals and how generous their sacrifices to the gods, the gods seemed capable at any time of punishing the people with droughts, floods, or earthquakes which wrecked the splendid engineering works and the monumental architecture. The possibilities of slave revolt were another source of anxiety. The valleys through which their rivers flowed were exposed to the conscienceless marauders from the mountains and slopes to the north and east.

The political history of the Middle East, because of the frequency of invasion, was uncertain and unstable. Over the centuries raiders or restive underlings were occasionally triumphant, bringing with them new instruments for maintaining supremacy, for advancing knowledge, and for making beautiful things. The language of the ruling class changed. More effective techniques in agriculture, administration, and military hegemony let the area of high Mesopotamian civilization spread far beyond the original river valleys to include what is now Syria and Israel, much of the land around the Persian Gulf and even near to Egypt. The whole area came under Persian control in 539 B.C.

The literary and archaeological remains of the succeeding dynasties in the Near East are, necessarily, the creations of the literate, ruling classes alone. To settle at last on the topic of this book, these traces of the past provide some scant indications of the nature of the games and competitions of that influential society which flourished for almost 3000 years.

The intention of all public Mesopotamian art was to demonstrate, to those who would see it, the skill and fierceness of the ruling class, and thus to intimidate potential enemies of that class. We must, of course, assume that when released from the struggle to survive, children and some adults of all classes played and that there were always informal contests of strength or skill. In Mesopotamia (as in almost all the societies of the past) unofficial sport left no traces. The accidents of time have preserved a few things that suggest that sport was an exclusive property of the ruling class. Official sport served only military or paramilitary purposes.

We have a low relief showing three Assyrian swimmers, two using floats and one apparently doing a crawl stroke, but it is clear that the swimmers are a part of an army attacking a moated fort. An ancient statue of two wrestlers wearing (for reasons that cannot have contributed to their success) hats, and another of two boxers ready to start slugging, demonstrate what we can assume—that these sports were known and practiced. Many pictures of battle scenes show poised Assyrian or Hittite archers. But what are depicted are ferocious warriors and not the abstracted contests of sporting competitions. These pictures of warriors are for public viewing and demonstrated to the masses of the people and to visitors to the cities the power of the kings who were presumably masters of armies. The lively depictions on low reliefs or in ceramic tiles of war and of equally strenuous hunting scenes of dying lions and other big game can be interpreted as admonitions to the arms-bearing classes to stay fit and at the ready. Members of the political caste must not succumb to the temptations of easy riches to be earned in trade or in banking. The successive decay of political elites had repeatedly instructed that it was dangerous for the aristocrats to become lax and pacific in the face of their enemies within or without the city walls.

Significantly the horse appears often in Mesopotamian art and literature. The Sumerian armies probably fought only on foot. Some early dynastic regimes in the Near East, however, used the ass as a draft animal and there is some evidence that they sometimes also rode the domestic horse, which for thousands of years had been used only for milk and meat. A major invention—indeed one of the most politically significant inventions of all time—was the chariot. It was the two-wheeled chariot's ability to inspire terror of the marauding nomads that permitted these less civilized warriors to seize and then, once in power, be seduced by the superior cultures they had overcome.

We have a training manual for horses from approximately 1360 B.C. The series of tablets called the "Kikkulis text" outlines in some detail how horses were to be fed and exercised. The book contains some discussion of race preparation, but we must not be tempted to see evidence of sport as we know it here. The breeding, care, and use of horses to pull chariots were all vital in the area of national defense. The cavalry horse came into use much later and, consequently, was shown in pictorial representations as the mount for King Ashurbanipal (669–627 B.C.) and other great nobles as they hunted lions.

Aside from what has been mentioned above we have little concrete evidence of what we might call sport in the ancient Middle East. We have no suggestions of ball games or of anything more elaborate than the simplest kinds of dance. In the processions and festivals that punctuated the year in the Near East, if there were a variety of lighthearted sports, there are no records. In summary we might conclude that those sports which left traces for us to mull over were paramilitary and aristocratic. Sport was intended to preserve the fitness of the dominant classes and to proclaim as propaganda their menacing power.

We need not be so hesitant when surveying the ancient Egyptians. Indeed there is a temptation to conclude that in Egypt there were many more sports among more classes of people and that there was much more pleasure in participating and observing these sports. Though our records are hardly conclusive, it appears that the official ideology of the ancient Near East opposed playful competitions. The contrary was true along the Nile even though these two seminal civilizations had comparable economic and political origins.

Some time about 3000 B.C. a strict administrative order was quickly imposed on a settled agricultural population along the Nile and its delta. Control and diversion of the long river's flow vastly increased the area cultivated and the land's productivity. Population and wealth grew, but, as usual, luxury accrued to the thin layer of overseers, priests, and nobles who used their control to develop a culture of remarkable variety, elegance, and durability.

All the evidence we have from ancient Egypt suggests that the tone of life was different from that of Mesopotamia. The Nile Valley is 750 miles long as the river flows and, except near the delta in the north, never more than 13 miles wide. The natural barriers of the desert and the sea were inhospitable to envious outsiders who almost always had to remain distant and harmless.

Under the initial impetus of the more sophisticated Sumerians to the North and East, upper class Egyptian life styles matured amazingly quickly. By the third and fourth dynasty of the Old Kingdom (2780–2280 B.C.) Egypt had its system of divine king-ships, its funeral cults, its canons of art and architecture, its hier-oglyphics and cursive script, and had already advanced knowledge of science, engineering, and mathematics. It was also during this early period that the colossal pyramids of Gizeh were built.

So appealing were these first creations that later generations of the ruling classes were content to enjoy and alter but slightly the accomplishments of their forebearers. For all except the slaves (of whom we have little definite information) life was pleasant even though it was ritualized (and possibly boring) to an extent not approached by any other culture. The obsession with the afterlife, the tombs, embalming, funeral equipment, wall frescoes, inscrip-tions and bric-a-brac accompanying the entombed are all evidence that the wealthy people were eager to prolong forever the plea-sures they knew while living.

The various palace revolts, the establishment of new dynasties by obstreperous generals, the expanding and contracting empire, the period of the Hyksos usurpers—all of these disturbances oc-curred over many centuries and should not obscure the remark-able stability (one might almost say the rigidity) of Egyptian soci-ety.

Egyptian pleasures also became ritualized and estheticized quickly. Rich men competed in display and opulence—possibly because there were few socially sanctioned areas allowing for more open, aggressive rivalry. Those who could, indulged in imported delicate foods and ceremonial barge trips along the Nile. The rul-ers commissioned commemoratory obelisks covered with plates of hammered gold, and encouraged the staging of grand religious cel-ebrations designed to impress upon the whole population the riches, and therefore the power, of the royal house.

Our evidence for Egyptian sport also demonstrates the ceremonial elegance and complexity of upper-class life. Those sports most often portrayed in surviving Egyptian pictorial records are of various kinds of person-to-person combat. One completed fresco (a wall painting done on wet plaster) from the tomb of a prince of the eleventh dynasty (2100–2000 B.C.) shows two wrestlers demonstrating 122 different positions and holds. In order to clarify the strategy and counter-strategy of the opponents, the artist has painted one dark brown and the other a brighter, reddish brown. That these sports were already formal and had some of the stylized prettiness that characterized so much of Egypt's culture is shown by the lack of gouging and the absence of referees who would be necessary to impose the decorum essential for a combat to be maintained as a sport and not in earnest. That wrestling was so highly regarded as to be pursued by some professionals is suggested by a fresco dating from some six hundred years later, showing a marching group of stocky light-heavyweight wrestlers in loincloths. The last of their number carries a small standard upon which is a picture of a wrestler—the symbol of their trade.

But if these men are professionals, we see in Egyptian art no evidence that wrestling was so ceremonialized as to require the cumbersome costumes and apparatus that wrestlers have worn in other cultures—for example, those of pre-Columbian Central America. We see no ear guards, heavy belts, or jock straps. The wrestlers are most often near-naked, slender youths whose standards of etiquette very likely prevented severe injury. Boxers also use a minimum of equipment. The youths wear a short skirt and swing at each other with bare fists. But we have no pictures of a boxer's fist actually doing damage to his opponent. The mayhem one expected in imperial Rome or in nineteenth-century America is missing.

Another combative sport that appears often in early Egyptian pictures is a sort of fencing with sticks or wooden poles. The sticks, which are about a meter long, were swung with the right hand, the left arm being shielded. Some stick fighters wore a light helmet to protect their faces and ears. We also have depictions of a kind of formal battle where the unprotected battlers have long sticks, presumably for attack or for defense, in either hand. The Greek traveler, Herodotus, who visited Egypt in 450 B.C., described stick fighting as part of a cult ceremony. Even today in some parts of Egypt stick fighting with somewhat longer poles is a form of ritualized recreation.

We possess a long relief from a tomb of the twentieth dynasty (about 1160 B.C.) which shows groups of elegantly dressed spectators at a display of seven pairs of wrestlers and groups of stick battlers. In this relief are two of the few pictures we have of defeat. But the losers are not Egyptians: one is a Negro; the other is a Semite. These cosmopolitans in an athletic tableau where the other contestants all look like stylized Egyptians has led to the claim that this scene is the earliest one of an international sports meet.

The scenes of sporting battle in Egyptian art (we have only the scantiest written records) are more likely to give us the shiver of esthetic pleasure rather than the sports spectator's shivers of suspense or fright. Indeed, the lightly clad, graceful wrestlers, boxers, and stick fighters closely resemble the surviving pictures of nubile gymnasts, acrobats, and dancers who were also on hand to provide entertainment for cultivated spectators. The varieties of pretty recreations seen in Egyptian art is almost endless. Men carry happy children on their backs as they walk on their hands and knees. Boys play tag and tug-of-war. They practice long- and high-jumping. Others chase hoops, carry chums on their shoulders, or perform balancing acts. Some hoist bags of sand in what may be weight lifting contests. A limestone relief of the Old Kingdom shows some youths in what is clearly the yoga "lotus" position. Another relief shows a youth standing on his head with his arms folded behind his back.

Since for the Egyptians the Nile was central for existence it is natural to expect a variety of recreations in and on the water. The management of the great river's gifts was the basis of Egypt's security and its pleasures. Swimming was therefore not only a pleasure for the playful, but also a necessity in case of an accident on the water. We have frescoes of slender girls swimming below the surface to catch water birds unawares. Several museums have statuettes of silver or of wood in the form of girl swimmers who hold in their outstretched arms a container for ointments or salves. Some documents suggest that swimming instruction was obligatory for royal princes. That swimming was regularly taught is also suggested by many depictions of the crawl stroke—a form of swimming that is not natural to man and which was re-invented for competition less than a century ago.

Naturally the Egyptians painted pictures of rowers in large and small boats. Stick fencing was also done from the bows of boats. The object was to land one's opponent in the water. The contest appears to be the same as the one now regularly displayed at Canadian logging festivals.

Common objects found in the tombs of children are balls made of pieces of colored leather holding packed straw. Other balls were made of wood or of baked clay. Informal (and therefore not worth recording) ball play was probably very ordinary. Some frescoes show girl jugglers doing routines in which they toss many balls from one to another in rhythms that suggest the performances were dance. Sometimes there are whole groups of jugglers. Though it is likely that some jugglers trained to give virtuoso demonstrations, it seems that the object of their performances was to arouse the pleasure of esthetes and connoisseurs. I do not think it is correct to see here parallels of the team ball games that had deep ritual and cult implications for the North American aborigines or the violent competitions of the medieval European peasants. Many Egyptian athletes are best viewed as comparable to our circus performers.

But perhaps the picture of Egypt and, consequently that of Egyptian sport, as merely decorative and playful has been overstressed. It is worthwhile here to bring up the curious incident of the Hyksos in Egyptian history. The Hyksos were a group of warriors from the Near East who infiltrated, overran, and for a while ruled Egypt. They damaged some temples, burned some fields, and were disrespectful to a lot of aristocrats who for generations had been accustomed to delicate handling. Naturally they appear in the chronicles as being despicable. The fifteenth dynasty, that of the Hyksos, lasted for 108 years, until 1580 B.C., when the founders of the New Kingdom expelled them.

The foreigners performed for the Egyptians the beneficial service (though it was not viewed so at the time) of wrecking forever the assumptions of unassailable superiority that had heretofore guided Egyptian military policy. The temporary (by Egyptian standards) success of the Hyksos led generals of the New Kingdom to adopt improved daggers and swords, stiffer and more powerful bows, and the horsedrawn chariot.

With the recognition that the new techniques of warfare and the preparations for them were now essential for the maintenance of stability, new and more earnest recreations and competitions came into the culture and public life of the Egyptian upper classes. The horses that the Egyptians felt required to raise were small (under 13 hands high), spirited, and (because of the scarcity of grazing areas) costly to breed and maintain. Nevertheless, it became a military and a propaganda necessity for the nobles and the royal house to keep harness and riding animals and to perform for the populace with them. With the establishment of new paramilitary recreations and the resulting new political propaganda that was intended to assure all levels of the populace that foreigners would never come again, we have evidence of new sports in Egypt.

The kings of the New Kingdom had new socially stabilizing roles to play. In addition to establishing reputations as divinely inspired statesmen and strategists, they had to advertise themselves as supreme athletes and especially vigorous hunters. For centuries it was politically necessary to nurture the public myth that the king was unassailably supreme as an athlete. To do this, each king was required to surpass the publicized performances of his predecessors in order to demonstrate that he was the most powerful being yet produced in the universe. Even constitutionally indolent rulers after the Hyksos episode accepted as their kingly duty the construction of their legends as big game hunters. Whether the athletic reputations of the rulers of the New Kingdom were based on real accomplishments or were the inspired creations of the priest-propagandists, we can never know for sure. But we must be suspicious.

A ceremonial summit performance for the athlete-kings of the eighteenth dynasty (1580–1350 B.C.) was a unique type of mounted archery combining the use of the awe-inspiring chariot and powerful bows with bronze-tipped arrows. For these displays the usual targets of wood or reed were replaced by thick plates of copper used only by the Pharaohs. "In the presence of the whole army," so a source of the time states, Tuthmosis III (1503–1450 B.C.) shot an arrow deeply into a metal plaque which was later displayed in a temple as demonstration of his unsurpassable power."

Naturally his son had to surpass him. From his glittering chariot going at full speed Amenophis II (1450–1425 B.C.) shot four successive arrows at four copper targets spaced about 35 feet apart. Each arrow struck and passed through the plates, which were three inches thick. A granite relief from Karnak shows Amenophis II performing such a stunt. The accompanying inscription says: "His majesty performed this act of athleticism in sight of all the land." Another inscription claims that no member of the Egyptian army or even one of the tough chieftains of Syria could even draw the bow of Amenophis II "because his strength is so much greater than that of any other king who ever existed."

An Egyptian might acquire great prestige by feats of rowing that were performed apart from the utilitarian transporting of freight or passengers. The tomb of a great army officer states that he first attracted his king's attention because of his exceptional rowing of the royal ship of state at a public festival. As might be expected, the Pharaohs themselves were celebrated as the very best rowers. At a purported performance of the royal athlete, Amenophis II, that hero outlasted 200 other oarsmen. In addition to the victory, the performance produced another desired result, for "all faces were joyful at watching him."

The Egyptian kings left many inscriptions that immortalized them as hunters. In the Old Kingdom, the aristocrats merely waited in blinds for beaters to drive previously penned animals toward them. But with the adoption of the mobile chariot and the new bows, hunters could take excursions across the plains of the upper Nile region and chase down large beasts. Big game hunting became paramilitary training and a propagandistic obligation among the highest nobility. These same leaders were the ones who managed the campaigns that for a while expanded the Egyptian empire north and east into Asia and south into Nubian Africa.

It is from a record of the Syrian campaign of Tuthmosis I (1530–? B.C.) that we first hear of an elephant hunt. Half a century later one of his successors, Tuthmosis III, claimed that he had slaughtered 120 of the enormous beasts. On one occasion, a soldier,

Amenemheb, saved the Pharaoh from calamity by cutting off the trunk of a threatening elephant. We have lots of relief carvings, tomb paintings, and commemorative scarabs that celebrate the hunting down of rhinoceros, wild cattle, and crocodiles. One of the prettiest pieces of Egyptian painting to survive is a fresco showing the Pharaoh Tutankhamen (1361–1352 B.C.) hunting lions from a light chariot. The two prancing horses have feathered headdresses. The king's stretched bow is ready to let loose a long arrow. Just below the horses is a magnificent male lion deeply impaled with three of the king's shafts. One of the king's hunting dogs is atop the trophy. Several younger males, a couple of heavy titted suckling females and some cubs are also in various stages of their death agonies. The eight lions, the dog, the horses, the keen profiled hunter, his attendants bearing plumed fans at the end of long poles, and the flowers filling the otherwise spare spaces of the composition all make a grand ensemble that must be acknowledged as an ambitious artistic exercise and not reportage.

Frequent pictures of the chase in temple reliefs and on small objects are scenes of the kings harpooning hippopotamuses. The kings stand in papyrus-reed boats. The accompanying inscriptions testify to the superior strength of the royal arms. Wolfgang Decker, the leading scholar of Egyptian sport, explains the frequent appearance of the hunted hippopotamus in Egyptian art. Long ago, the voracious hippopotamus ranged all along the Nile and was a looming threat to the crops near wetlands. Since, as has always been the case, the peasants could not bear arms, the enormous beasts could raid almost at will. The hideous and destructive animal had for ages been seen as the representative of Seth, traditionally the enemy of Horus, son of Osiris, who was the king's ally in guaranteeing the order of the universe. Simply stated, the artistic depictions of royal personages harpooning hippopotamuses or slaughtering other great beasts are actually allegorical reassurances to his subjects that the king is the essential protector against chaos.

Decker suggests, then, that all the pretty pictures and hyperbolic tales of royal prowess are propaganda. We cannot know what the actual activities and preferences of the kings were. It may be reasonable to assume that they, as most people born and raised in isolation and sycophantic luxury, were more likely to be devoted to the charms of the harem and the table rather than to target practice and the hunt. Yet for public consumption, the Pharoah was always represented as possessing the strongest arm, the truest eye, and the bravest heart in all the world. The king's qualities as athlete, hunter, and hero were essential elements in the cosmic (and deliberately maintained) view that was critical for the maintenance of Egypt's stability. High-performance sport was therefore affirmative and socially stabilizing propaganda. The myth of the all-powerful king remained central in Egyptian political theory well into Roman times.

Despite grave robbers, earthquakes, and other human and natural depredations, we have immense quantities of written and pictorial records of Egyptian life over a period of more than 3000 years. Consequently we have lots of evidence for what I have several times loosely called sport in Egyptian life. It might be tempting to conclude that the Egyptians were the most athletic people before our times. The conclusions drawn from this evidence should be more modest. We also know a lot about Egyptian cookery, burial customs, architecture, and water navigation. For the other high civilizations of other epochs, we have much more fragmentary information regarding all these and other aspects of life. Since the people of the comparably complex civilization of ancient India built their monuments and kept their records with perishable materials in a damp climate, we know little of their cuisine, their architecture, or burial customs. Nevertheless, we must assume that their arts and recreations were elaborate and well-suited to maintaining the wealth, class system, and political myths which characterized that society. Until proven wrong we might well assume that if a society provides leisure, some stability, and the materials to work with, the people in that society will run, leap, climb, swim, wrestle, and play ball. Furthermore we might assume there will be informal as well as ceremonial competitions in these activities. It may not be hazardous to assume also that "standing" or prestige was to be gained or lost in many or most cultures by the public demonstration of superiority in these skills.

The politically unstable civilization of Mesopotamia and the more rigid culture of Egypt were already a thousand years old when another sophisticated society arose which has left us sufficient evidence that permits—indeed obliges—us to discuss its sport. On Crete, a large island in the eastern Mediterranean, the first palaces were erected about 2000 B.C. A rather complex and novel society flourished for about 600 years. By Egyptian standards this period is short, but it is of longer duration than the present political and social forms of the whole Western hemisphere. Ancient Cretan or Minoan (so-called because of the legendary King Minos of Crete wealth was extracted from the soil by agricultural slaves. Minoan merchants and sea captains carried their products all over the Mediterranean. Unlike most trading peoples it appears that the Minoans were trusting, secure people. Evidence for this claim is that their administrative and cult centers were not fortified and their burial sites have revealed little evidence of chariots, armor, or weapons. Perhaps the Minoans assumed that their ships and sailors were adequate to guard against piracy or invasion. When earthquakes destroyed the cities they were quickly rebuilt. The usual explanation for the sudden and utter end of their civilization about 1380 B.C. is that the people of Crete renounced their power to the implacably more energetic and aggressive Myceneans of the Greek mainland.

Like the aristocrats of old Egypt before them and the nobles of Ming China after them the Minoan upper classes were delicately refined and isolated—perhaps almost immune—to the influences from the cultures around them. It seems strange, for example, that the astonishing elegance of some of the Minoan art and entertainment, including what we must assume was a rich bardic and poetic tradition, never led to the adoption of a form of writing that would encapsulate and broaden the culture. Had they wished, the Minoans might have learned from the Mesopotamians or the Egyptians, with whom they had trading contacts, how to preserve literature. But their writing was rudimentary, *sui generis*, and responses only to commercial and administrative needs.

Cretan literary records are therefore useless for the historian of sport. However, the pictorial records of ancient Cretan sport have the appeal of being concrete, instructive, and lovely. Alas, these tantalizing relics are few in number and offer suggestions only about boxing, a kind of acrobatic bull fighting, and some dances which may have been performed competitively. Alas also, we cannot draw assured conclusions as to the role that even these activities played in the culture as a whole.

The most useful scene of boxers is from a steatite vase of about 1600 B.C. found at the archaeological site called Hagia Triada on the island. On three bands of the four-banded frieze of the vase are posed males—some wearing helmets, some with full heads of heavy curls. Two boxers have fallen while most of the nine others have taken lively poses. Unlike the suave Egyptian pictures, the Minoan boxers reveal the tense striations of effort along their rib cages and hips. Their costumes consist of calf-high boots, necklaces, and thick, tight belts giving them the wasp-waisted look that is shared by most humans in Cretan art. In all the pictures, the male boxers of Crete wear a kind of jock strap or loin cloth which pulls up the genitals to clasp them for display against the stomach. Analogously, most of our pictures of Cretan women show them bare breasted or they wear corsets which raise the breasts for easier admiration. We also have pictures—our earliest of the sort—of Cretan boxers with fists bound with thongs to protect the hands of the battlers and so present more forceful blows.

A favorite topic for Minoan artists was the ceremony of acrobatic bull leaping. In certain places in the Mediterranean the bull had long been a creature of oracular or semi-sacred importance. One band of the aforementioned Hagia Triada vase has two splendid bulls cavorting in unison at full gallop. There may have been several kinds of bull fighting or baiting. We have the remains of a magnificent fresco from Knossos showing two white skinned girls and a dark skinned boy in various stages of a vault through and over the horns of an enormous, charging bull. The acrobats land onto his back for a handspring to the ground in back of the bull. This maneuver must have demanded considerable courage to carry off with grace and, if perfectly done, surely was breathtaking to observe. It seems that the whole performance was indeed intended to be observed, for we have frescoes of well dressed, made-up ladies in what has to be a spectators' box and sketched representations of many heads to represent crowds of other observers. In their daring and the general setting, the actions seem strikingly like some rodeo events in America and comparable, as well, with bull fighting at present in Spain or Mexico. Indeed, we have another picture of a bull captured by a lasso and another of a Cretan (cowboy?) using a bull's horns to wrestle him to the ground. It may be that enthusiasm for observing the leaping over the backs of bulls had to be cultivated and was highly aestheticized. As well as we can tell, in Crete, the general desire was for a kind of choreographed showy daring rather than the climaxing death at the modern Plaza de Toros. On the other hand, we do know that, as elsewhere in the Mediterranean, bulls were commonly sacrificed. Their spilled blood was offered to the gods for the expected reward of fertile land or other blessings.

We must resist the temptation to see the standardized abstractions of modern competitive gymnastics in the sports with bulls, or to assume from the frequency of the surviving pictures that such sports were central in the lives of all Minoans. The preservation of many scenes of acrobatics with bulls may be an archaeological accident, but the prominence of the bull, pictorial or sculpted, and his athletic attendants in royal or cult surroundings suggests that for the upper or priestly classes the performances were essential aspects of sacred ritual and that the results of the performances and sacrifices may have had oracular importance.

Various kinds of dance were also adjuncts of what we may assume were passionately attended, aestheticized rites of the Cretans. In almost all societies—our own being the outstanding exception—the combination of simple rhythmic movements and subtly varied music with a simple beat is used to induce socially affirmative, ecstatic dances. From ancient Crete we have many pictures of female dancers, their busts raised, their eyes mascaraed, their long arms and fingers decked out with gold jewelry, their waved hair swinging about their bodies and limbs. The poses and surroundings suggest a trance-like, sensual joyousness.

It should also be mentioned here that there are indications that the Cretans were devoted to hunting on foot in their hilly country. At the Olympic Games much later, Cretans had the reputation for being especially swift runners.

There is a section in the *Odyssey* which describes the participation of Odysseus, the hero, in the after dinner games of the Phaecians. The hero, we remember, comes by accident to the land of these mysterious people (scholars still cannot determine who the Phaecians were, but agree that they were not Greeks). They invite Odysseus to observe their athletic skills. There follows an impromptu sports meet consisting of foot races, with a field of 16 entries, wrestling, and the putting of weights. The pleasures of the assembled athletes and the "innumerable company" of spectators fail to stir the seated Odysseus from his brooding and his homesickness. Aroused by the festive atmosphere, the Phaecians taunt their sad guest while observing his brawny and sinewy thighs, arms, and neck which appear to be rather coarse for their ideal of athletic beauty. A well-born youth also tells Odysseus that "there is no greater glory for a man while he yet lives, than that which he achieves by hand and foot." Another rebukes Odysseus for his greedy and confined sea captain's life which is so deleterious for one's physical fitness.

Stung, Odysseus explains in shouts why he appears to be so unfit and then rushes over to lift and toss a huge stone which is at the site just for demonstrations of that sort. He heaves the stone much farther than the weight had ever gone before. The crowd is agreeably astonished and then all listen as Odysseus convinces them of his excellence in sports, including wrestling, the use of the polished bow and the spear. The aging and tired traveler confesses that the nimble Phaecians could very likely outstrip him in foot races. Whereupon the host of the festival reassures Odysseus of his good will and confesses

For we are not perfect boxers, nor wrestlers, but speedy runners and the best of seamen: and dear to us ever is the banquet, and the harp, and the dance and changes of raiment and the warm bath and love and sleep.

The party goes on with singing, some competitive tossing and catching of a purple ball thrown high into the air, some juggling, and some enthusiastic dancing—all of which Odysseus observes with pleasure. He admits to his host, "Thou didst boast thy dancers to be the best in the world, and lo, thy words are fulfilled. I wonder as I look upon them."

In the passages just summarized and quoted, we see two different attitudes toward sport: one forthright and based on egoism and raw power; the other where superiority is aestheticized and communalized. The Phaecians treasure dexterity and grace. Now, as we know, the long poems of Homer (to which we shall return in the next chapter) deal with the artistically transmuted and mythologized adventures of a people who predated, by centuries, the classical Greeks who treasured these epics. Carefully studied, the *Odyssey* and the *Iliad* reveal a lot about the pre-golden-age Greeks, including their attitudes about sport. On the other hand, scholars have been unable to determine who the Phaecians were.

I will yield to a temptation that has appealed to others and suggest that these strangers were Cretans and that the after dinner games which so impressed the Greek hero were illustrations of the charm and sensuality of those people whose mute monuments and art works suggest those qualities in life and sport.

The people who supplanted the Minoans as the effective political rulers of the Mediterranean had their administrative center in the Peloponnesus, that large, much indented peninsula connected to mainland Greece by the Isthmus of Corinth. The ruins of their capital, Mycenae, can be inspected about 100 kilometers east of Olympia. The Mycenean empire endured from about 1600 B.C. to about 1200 B.C. Like our knowledge of the Cretans, we glean some of our knowledge of the Myceneans from their monuments and their art. But in the *Odyssey* and the *Iliad* we also have many enchanting, orally transmitted legends about them. The literary and archaeological evidence suggests that these people, often called Achaeans in ancient times, were almost polar opposites in character from the Cretans whom they conquered and whose forms of art they adopted.

The Myceneans were a restless and pushy lot. The light sensuality of Cretan art, when absorbed by the Achaeans appears to have taken on aggressive power.

Their cities were placed near protected fresh water supplies and were surrounded by solid walls made up of fitted colossal stones. As in Egypt, royal tombs seem to have received an extraordinary amount of attention as public works and as repositories for precious objects. Some of the tombs of the Mycenean hero-kings have preserved quantities of decorated gold cups, jewelry, and other personal adornments. The decorative themes are, however, different from those in the Egyptian tombs. Almost uniformly the scenes are of action or violence. Lions run down fleeing antelope and drag them to the earth. Wild bulls charge menacingly rather than, as in Cretan art, cavortingly. Armored warriors slug one another. The depictions of persons are of men exclusively and they are invariably battling or hunting.

A military foundation of this first heroic age of Greece was the horse-drawn chariot which appears frequently in Mycenean art. And many of the depictions of what we will call sport were intended to assure the viewers of the readiness of the Mycenean ruling class to employ the instruments of their hegemony. Thus we can be reasonably sure there were chariot races and contests in spear throwing and in both the force and the accuracy of the bow-powered arrow.

Before going on to offer more conjectures (and conjectures they must remain) about the sport of the first Greek civilization it is prudent to mention the role of the hero in the Mycenean legends. Now Mycenean literature, like that of the Cretans, was not recorded in writing—this practical invention was employed only for preserving information too tedious to memorize. But memorized and recited Mycenean poetry was apparently obsessed with the lusts, accidents, campaigns, and travels of their restless rulers. So gripping were these stories that they lived on, finally being written down (after artistic mutations and embellishments) by the classical Greeks centuries later. Thus it was in Mycenae that Agamemnon, Orestes, and Electra lived and stories about them provided bards of the Mediterranean dark ages and, subsequently, Sophocles, Corneille, and Eugene O'Neill with the subject matter of tragedy. Thus it was from Mycenae that Achilles set out on the exhausting campaign against Priam's city to avenge the abduction of Helen. And it was on his long voyage back from Troy that the wily Odysseus, a Mycenean hero, had those unforgettable adventures.

The aspirations of the Mycenean upper classes seem to have been dominated by a quality which the later Greeks called *agón*, which was a general internalized compulsion to seek personal supremacy—that supremacy to be marked by the recognition of victory in public competition. The competition would occur in areas of life agreed to be worthwhile by the society at large. Since it will be necessary to use the word *agón* and the adjective from it, "agonistic," in later portions of the book, we shall state that *agón* was a personal element valued by the ancient Greeks and one which applied to more areas than those we now encompass in our "sport."

As was mentioned earlier, their monuments—architectural, literary, or artistic—suggest that for recreation the Myceneans mostly hunted or practiced for war. But their energy and earnestness also led them to pursue with all their power certain practices (we might call them games or recreations) which in most cultures are earnestly pursued only by children or entertainers. Mycenean men participated in short or long foot races, wrestling matches, weightlifting and other ostensibly useless activities with an intensity usually saved for those expenditures of energy that deal with getting and spending or life and death. A victory in controlled combat or the measured putting of a large stone could, if these were socially sanctioned and ceremoniously staged, be seen as an indication of favor from the Gods.

May we not therefore assume that, as with our depictions of the Mesopotamian princes and the Egyptian kings of the eighteenth dynasty, traditions, poetic and political, required that Mycenean rulers and aristocrats be viewed as athletic heroes? Moreover, we have quite a bit of evidence from later ages to show that in mainland Greece, the outcomes of athletic competitions were given symbolic significance that was intensified and abstracted and was different from the propaganda of the Asian emperors and from the ornament of the Cretans. Long before the time of the classical Greeks of the sixth to fourth centuries B.C., certain established sporting events were not specifically devised only for royalty or for entertainers. They were publicly performed according to standards that were acknowledged over a wide area and were accessible to a relatively broad range of the social classes. We will return to these matters.

To summarize and to elaborate some points made earlier: we have evidence from many sources to show that spectator sports are prehistoric and are more than a possession of city cultures. The ethnologists have shown that the ball games of the American plains tribes, the wrestling matches of Amazonians and the Papuans, and the high jumping of the African Bantu all attracted bands of connoisseurs and mobs of cheerers. Some sporting scenes in Egyptian frescoes include onlookers. A Minoan artist suggested sports fans by means of massed little arcs to indicate the bobbing heads of a sea of spectators. A carved relief from bronze age Yugoslavia shows some kibitzers who may have been critics of boxing style. We ought to assume that athletic contests, particularly if the competitors are exceptional, will attract the curious and enthusiastic. These performances were not much different from performances of dance or the theater which also provided pleasure and socially affirmative functions. However, it was not until pre-classical Greece that we see sport becoming so formalized and taking on rich symbolic meanings that were broadly integrated into social and religious usage. Among the pre-classical Greeks, athletic excellence as confirmed by a victory in a formal, public contest was viewed as a worthy, perhaps even a blessed, attribute of the outstanding person, the hero.

Several scholars have independently concluded that the athletic festivals which were common in pre-classical Mediterranean civilization and which captured the imagination of dozens of later generations have some remote origins in the funeral ceremonies of great men. Athletic contests might have been offered at funerals to give pleasures after death analogous to the pleasures enjoyed during life. Perhaps some people feared that he who was powerful when living might continue to exercise power malevolently against those who permitted him to die. Sacrifices, festivals, and games were necessary to appease the spirits of restless heroes. In Mycenean times the funeral of a hero was sometimes concluded with an actual combat to the death by professional fighters over his grave. The purpose of this fight was to punish in a fashion difficult for us to comprehend the presumed murderer of the hero. There is a lot of additional evidence to suggest that the earliest formal Greek sports meets were integrated into certain hero and death-cults.

In any case, careful excavations at ancient Olympia, where (later) the most prestigious athletic festivals of antiquity took place, show that the site was used for cult observances for at least a thousand years before the first named athletic victor in 776 B.C. At Olympia the interred sacrifices for a large funeral of Mycenean times included all the aristocrat's sporting and fighting equipment, not excepting the horses for a chariot. The Greeks of classical times knew that the territory of Olympia was sacred and had long been sacred. The explanations for Olympia's holiness tended to blur and alter as Greek religion and society themselves changed. For many centuries, as great athletes performed at Olympia and elsewhere in Greece, they performed not as mere muscular humans, but were elements in a sacred web that integrated their times with the ancient inspirational myths.

Though there were in the time of Homer a sporting public and something at least comparable to a modern sporting meet, there were still lacking certain distinctive athletic elements that were to characterize the athletic festivals of the greatest era of human originality ever experienced. We must wait until the next chapter before we can discuss sport and education, the athletic ideal in art, and the development of the sports star and specialist.

[3]

GREECE

In one section of the *Iliad* Achilles organizes some athletic games as a tribute to his dead friend Patroclus. In the course of the festival Odysseus, a favorite of the goddess Athena, wrestles with a younger man.

The two men leaned toward each other in the arena, and with oaken hands gripped one another's elbows. Think of timbers fitted at a steep angle for a roof a master builder makes to break the winds! The bones in each man's back creaked at the strain put on him by their corded thews, and sweat ran down in rills. Around their ribs and shoulders welts were raised by the holds they took, all scarlet where blood gathered. Without pause they strove to win the tripod. (From *The Iliad*, Book *XXIII*, translated by Robert Fitzgerald [New York: Doubleday, 1974] 557–58.)

The match goes on and on. The spectators become bored. There are two indecisive falls. Despite their efforts and the wrestlers' prayers to Zeus for help to end the agony, Achilles himself sees there will be no issue and calls the fight a draw. They will divide the prizes of a large metal tripod valued at twelve oxen and a slave woman valued at four oxen—presumably each will get eight oxen.

The foot race has as its prize, a great silver bowl. Odysseus enters this event as well. His opponents are two young noblemen. After Achilles points out the goal and starts them, Aias shoots to the front. Noble Odysseus comes up fast and approaches Aias so closely that his breath can be felt on the younger man's neck. Odysseus almost treads on Aias' feet, but he just cannot pass. The spectators are delighted and cheer them both on. Desperate for a victory Odysseus prays to Athena. "Hear me, goddess: Come bless me with speed!"

Simultaneously, as Odysseus feels a lightness in his feet, Aias trips and slithers in the manure of some recently sacrificed cattle. Odysseus wins and carries off the bowl. The enraged youth, while clearing filth from his mouth and nostrils, approaches the judges and protests: "Damn the luck: she did it for me, that goddess always beside him, like a coddling mother." The crowd laughs at him. Despite what appears to the youth (and to a modern audience, as well) to be a legitimate objection, the boost given by the goddess to her favorite was apparently part of the Greek notion of what was considered fair. We will return to this.

There are other sporting events in this curious (to us, at least) funeral celebration. The chariot race reads almost like a modern newspaper story. And Homer's epics contain many sports events. Some of Homer's battle descriptions resemble stories of team matches.

A general consensus is that these poems were first written down in about 700 B.C. and that they record an oral tradition based on much older events. Used with care, we can determine from them a great deal about the so-called Greek middle ages (ca. 1200–800 B.C.) and something about the legends passed to the poets of this age by the Myceneans who preceded them. In any case, it is indisputable that the great poet who preceded the golden age of Greece by several centuries expected an audience which welcomed suspenseful tales of athletics. Since the Homeric epics served partly as catechisms for heroic behavior in later ages, the attitude toward athletic competitions is significant. The poems contain several narratives of foot races, two of the long jump, many contests in tossing the spear, and some tales of discus throwing in which the hurled ingot was itself the prize. There are many descriptions of wrestling and boxing. As one might expect in stories about warriors, there are competitions in marksmanship with the bow and arrow. There are also scattered references to ball throwing, rowing, and competitive dancing.

Homer makes it clear that contests for athletes were adjuncts for many sorts of gatherings. The descriptions of the contests also reveal a near obsession with winning. The stratagems employed to win offend our sense of "fair play" as, for example, in the case of the goddess who blithely trips the superior runner, Aias, who we feel deserved the trophy taken by the wily Odysseus.

The quasi-sacred prestige of these epics among all the politically fragmented Greeks suggests that the sports Homer wrote about were more or less standardized over much of the Mediterranean world. On the other hand, the sports described are pursuits exclusively of the warrior-aristocrats who are the characters in the epics. For the sports of the non-noble classes in the Mycenean and pre-classical time (as for most preceding and succeeding ages), we have bases only for conjectures.

The later Greeks institutionalized only two sports that Homer did not mention. These are the pancration, a complicated form of wrestling to be discussed later, and the pentathlon which was a complexly scored combination of three field events, wrestling, and a foot race. Worth noting here is that Homer's competitors wore some sort of shorts. In the light of later Greek practice it is also curious that the hosts offered second and sometimes third prizes in games and contests.

For generations of Greek moralists, artists, educators and even athletes the epics became texts containing useful examples, parables and maxims that could guide their behavior. The tales of the Trojan War and the return voyages of Odysseus are filled with examples of egoism, false pride, unjust fate, undeserved suffering, and brutality which exemplified and reinforced the pessimism which later sentimentalizers of classical Greece have passed over, but which nonetheless clouded the Greeks' existence. The Homeric heroes were aggressive and boastful. The student of Greek history eventually comes to suspect that Greek heroes both before and long after Homer are indeed splendid to hear about, but might have been irritating or even menacing as sports companions.

In any case, it seems clear from a great deal of literary and archaeological material of the classical period that a distinction of Greek culture from Mycenean times onward was that it was a suitable, indeed a necessary, endeavor for a hero to pursue athletic distinction.

Homer's poems also provided the models for later epic poetry. Greek poets thereafter were expected to include sports events in their heroic narratives. The Roman poet Vergil (70–19 B.C.) in his *Aeneid* felt obliged to follow Homer in presenting a footrace in which the leader falls—only in the *Aeneid* Nisius slips in a pool of blood. It is noteworthy that in most of the later poems, as in Homer, the occasions for the most elaborate athletic meets are the assemblies of warriors and warrior-aristocrats on the occasion of a hero's funeral. Centuries later, when the formal Greek sports were mostly of antiquarian interest and even when they had fallen from use, sports analogies, sports rhetoric, and sports-writing hyperbole continued to be features of heroic literature. Even St. Paul repeatedly used conventional images and some analogies of classical sport in his writings. For St. Paul the life of the devoted Christian takes on some aspects of a continuous athletic contest.

Since this chapter was intended to concentrate on Greek sport in post-Homeric times, it will be necessary to provide some conventional narrative as background.

The decline of Mycenean hegemony in the eastern Mediterranean was rapid. Increasingly bold raids by unregenerate local tribes and by neighboring nomads made government difficult. Internal spiritual crises turned the Mycenean upper classes to foreign adventure, including piracy. One of these adventures was the Trojan War, which drew warriors away from government and used up much treasure. Finally, the citadels of Mycenae, Tiryns, and Athens (which for long was an important Mycenean city) could no longer be defended, and about 1200 B.C., bronze age civilization in Greece collapsed completely. Even the accomplishment of writing was forgotten. Tales of intrigue and high adventure lived on only in orally transmitted tradition.

Because of the repeated migrations and raids of scarcely civilized tribes from Northern Europe and Central Asia, the area about the Aegean Sea became chaotic. It was too risky for bands of people to make a decision for settled life. Some of these migrating people spoke languages that were ancestors of classical Greek.

During the two centuries or more of Greece's "dark ages" there remained a few centers of political order in the Mediterranean. The Phoenicians—whose cities were in what are now Palestine, Syria, and Cyprus—were traders who prospered and even established colonies. During the ninth century, more settled conditions in mainland Greece led the Phoenicians to export some ivory carving and fine textiles to the Peloponnesus and Athens. The most important accomplishment of the Phoenicians, however, was their uniquely spare system of speech notation. Some Greeks adopted this system in the ninth century. The first major literary works to be preserved in this script were Homer's poems.

For reasons that are complex and still unclear, about 900 B.C. the movement of barbarians slowed. Some of the peoples of the northeastern Mediterranean began the most richly creative period of political and intellectual experimentation the world has known. The basic political unit was the *polis*, a fortified independent city-state which lived off the wealth of its craftsmen and traders and from the surplus agricultural and extracted products of the surrounding countryside. The bewildering political variety of these hundreds of monarchies, oligarchies, timocracies, tyrannies, and democracies have been described in surveys of political history. A few of the city-states were successful in maintaining order and amassing great wealth.

The many *poleis* (plural of polis) shared a common language and common literature and therefore had enough of a basis to consider themselves all Greeks or, to use a Greek word, Hellenes. Certain ancient religious shrines—at Delphi, Delos, and Olympia—began to attract Greek visitors from afar and their regular festivals took on ever greater pan-Hellenic significance which tended to consolidate the politically disputatious little political units.

A few generations of assured security permitted some *poleis* to establish vineyards and orchards the surplus of which they traded. Some specialized in pottery manufacture or silver mining and the making of jewelry. About 750 B.C. the Lydian king of a *polis* in Asia Minor stamped some standardized, bean-shaped pieces of electrum (a mixture of silver and gold) thus indicating that he guaranteed their value. The adoption of coinage by other *poleis* in the next century greatly facilitated trade, and led to further economic specialization. Population increases too rapid to absorb caused the larger city-states to send out convoys of colonists. The Crimea, Southern Italy, Sicily, and much of North Africa became Greek. And along with specialized production, trade, and a money economy there flourished new classes of craftsmen, manufacturers, merchants, bankers, and ship owners who did not fit into the aristocratic slave-owning society assumed in Homer's poems.

The adjustments of one great city, Sparta, to general conditions of prosperity and social diversity are interesting not only for their wider importance, but also for Greek sport. The rulers of Sparta were descended from some invaders who subjected the peasants in a rich farming area to slavery. This was not untypical of the establishment of order in Greece in the eighth century B.C. But the Spartan warriors developed a political system in which their status was particularly exalted and that of the numerous serfs correspondingly debased. Yearly, for example, the Spartans could issue a declaration of war against the serfs so that any Spartan could slay an obstreperous serf without incurring blood guilt. Slavery enabled the aristocrats, who numbered less than one-tenth of the population, to devote themselves to civic duties—which in Sparta consisted largely of paramilitary training.

Historians, particularly those dazzled by the artistic creations of the Athenians, have maligned the Spartans too thoroughly. The Spartans were, after all, politically successful. By 546 B.C. Sparta was the strongest military power in all of Greece. And for more than a century before this time Sparta had been a leading center of the arts and philosophy offering hospitality to suitably impressed artists, poets, and philosophers from the whole Mediterranean. Spartans were known for the elaborateness of the masks and costumes worn in their processions and for the skill and endurance of their public dancers. A striking sight for visitors to Sparta was to see groups of sinewy boys, men, and elders, holding hands and doing line dances in her market place. All were naked. The Spartans were generally credited with abandoning the narrow trousers or shorts until then worn by athletes and for initiating the practice of covering the athletes' bodies only with olive oil as they practiced or competed. Anointing with oil may have had some sort of ritual significance. Subsequently, handsome Greek males were notorious for their eagerness to display their own tanned bodies and to offer detailed judgments on the good looks of others. Indeed the honor accorded to especially harmonious proportions became another and prestigious way of achieving public distinction.

Sparta's creativity and receptivity might have endured. However, the increasing wealth and political ambitions of other *poleis* threatened her security. A basis for her peculiar rigidity as well as her independence was the devising of a fundamental military innovation—the first one to rival the terrifying and expensive war chariot. This military invention was the disciplined, inspired hoplite or foot soldier, who with his fellows formed the phalanx. Besides their helmets, shields, and greaves (for protection of the shins) each soldier carried an eight foot pike and a short, double-edged sword. The phalanx normally consisted of rows of tightly packed hoplites eight deep. The massed troops drilled and advanced to the sound of a flute and drums. A phalanx was as effective as the amount of practice it engaged in and to the respect each man had for his companions. The phalanx became the military unit of most Greek city-states. The elaborate and time-consuming preparations for this military technique determined many of the forms of Greek society, but the effects were felt earliest and most severely in Sparta.

Essential for the success of the phalanx were each hoplite's subjection of his individual will, his numb determination and a mutual dependence—all of which are at odds with heroic ideal and with that extraordinary individualism which was the Greeks' blessing and their curse. The Spartans' dependence upon their phalanx led them to isolate males of the warrior class so that they could be more completely indoctrinated with patriotism and to maintain the fitness that phalanx training required. If born into a warrior's family, a boy was taken from his mother when age seven. He lived in a garrison until age 30 and was eligible for military call up until age 60.

The obsession with military preparedness explains several Spartan distinctions. They were noted for precision dancing of trance-like intensity, which was known to be training for the selfless, controlled, passion critical on the battlefield. The early inclusion of boys in an exclusively masculine social life provided an atmosphere fostering the pederasty for which the Spartans were especially famous. It is noteworthy also, however, that the Spartans were unusual in that their obsession with fitness led them to require that women as well train for athletics. Besides dancing and singing, the women were expected to run and do other exercises. The Spartans were unusual among the Greeks in that they sometimes had special athletic meets for girls and women.

Spartan athletes were examples for the rest of the Greek world. Between the 15th Olympic Games in 720 B.C. and the 50th in 576 B.C., Spartans provided 56 of the 71 known Olympic victors. In the prestigious one-stadium-length dash, of 36 known victors, 21 were Spartans. Olympia and its festivals were long employed by the Spartans as propaganda to demonstrate to her Greek rivals Sparta's artistic as well as her sports accomplishments. In the sixth century B.C. Spartan architects at Olympia erected a major new stone temple to Hera, the wife of Zeus, and decorated the site with statues of that goddess. The Spartans dedicated statues of athletes to commemorate their victories. For many generations, then, Olympia was to some extent an especially Spartan site, rather than one which belonged equally to all the Greeks.

Some of Sparta's distinctions were imitable. With increasingly productive agriculture, the consequent increase in land values and, necessarily, the very great cost of breeding and training war horses, even more *poleis* adopted the phalanx, but accompanied its introduction with a much broader social participation in the benefits of prosperity and high culture. Sparta had rivals in wealth and, potentially, military effectiveness. Booming Athens became a sea power. Frightened, unwilling to change their constitution, the Spartans became paranoid, withdrew from pan-Hellenic affairs, and became ever more dependent upon the yet more intense training of her military caste. Sparta was both feared and ridiculed by her Greek neighbors. By the end of the sixth Century Sparta also ceased participating in the Olympic Games.

The Olympic festival, which took place every four years, was the most important of the pan-Hellenic religious celebrations that gave the disparate Greeks occasional opportunities to pretend that they were one people. The enormous prestige of the Olympic Games, and their prestige long, long after the classical age, requires that we give some attention to their history and to the particular events that made up the classical athletic program.

Olympia is a pretty site in the western Peloponnesus. It is about 200 miles south and west of Athens. The classical Greeks most often attributed the establishment of regular formal games at Olympia to Hercules. Other local traditions had it that athletic contests first occurred there after the funeral of a local hero, Pelops. The German archaeological investigations during the later nineteenth century uncovered the foundations of Mycenean altars and gift offerings. It was obvious that the site had been sacred for many centuries before the Greeks used it.

We cannot be sure when the first sports competitions began at Olympia, but it seems likely that they occurred periodically before 776 B.C. when the name Coroebos of Elis was recorded as a victor in the dash of one stadium length. The surviving victor lists show that the very earliest winners (and presumably participants and spectators) in the first regular games were from Elis or other towns near Olympia. Later, Sparta, about 50 miles to the east, dominated the victor lists. By the time of Athenian hegemony in the fifth century, many victors were from the distant colonies in the Greek world, especially from what are now Sicily and southern Italy.

For centuries, the charming site at the base of a hill by the junction of two rivers was merely a level field with a few sacrificial altars at one end of it. Nearby was a measured-out, larger area called a hippodrome, which was the race course for horses—both mounted horses and chariot teams. A distinctive shrine was a cone-shaped altar composed mostly of the ashes from fires dedicated to Zeus. The holy precinct was under the protection of a nearby *polis*, Elis. This small city-state furnished the personnel who performed the regular daily, monthly, and yearly prayers, sacrifices, and dedications. Elis lived off the spending of pilgrims whose influx was heaviest during the splendid festivals which occurred every four years. Travelers regularly expressed their disgust at the Elian gougers of helpless tourists, but praised the conscientiousness of Elian officials and priests. An accepted principle of Greek politics was that Elis should remain independent as well as militarily insignificant.

The Greek compulsion to raise one's status among one's peers found many outlets at this bucolic site. As was mentioned earlier, the Spartans were the first to monumentalize their athletic successes. Other wealthy *poleis* added their own stone treasure houses to protect their donations to Zeus and Hera of gold plates and vases, statues of athletes, and other treasures. By the fifth century competitive gifts of architecture, victory statues, and valuables crowded the traditional sacred precinct. City-states that wished to use Olympia as a place to display their wealth (and symbols of power), twice forced the stadium to be moved westward in order to provide more space for gifts. The stadium and hippodrome were outside a wall enclosing a sacred area (called the *altis*) of temples, altars, and outdoor athletic sculpture.

The festival was well prepared. Every fourth year in the spring three heralds set out from Elis on routes that covered the entire Greek world. As they arrived at each *polis* or colony they proclaimed a sacred Olympic truce. Thereafter competitors and spectators traveling to or from Olympia were under the protection of Zeus. They dared not bear arms, nor could they be attacked by armed men. There were only a few violations of the truce during the many centuries of Olympia's fame.

Competitors with their trainers and provisions might arrive months before the festival actually began. Once at Olympia, the athletes were under the supervision of the Elian judges, who had to ascertain the athlete's eligibility. They had to be sure that every competitor was a citizen of pure Greek ancestry and had to decide if a youth might be too old to be included in the boys' events and should therefore compete as a man. Since Olympia attracted relatively few pilgrims except during the grand festival, the sites of the sporting events were overgrown and needed to be cleared of weeds and debris. The stadium had to be covered with a level layer of fresh sand. At Olympia the athletes did this work.

Great numbers of pilgrims soon made the green valley hectic. Delegations from distant cities vied with one another in the loudness of their cheering sections and the openness with which they displayed their valuable gifts. A city whose athletes were winners in previous festivals might ostentatiously add a victory statue to the hundreds that already crowded the sacred *altis*. Colonists from the Black Sea, Africa, or Sicily used the opportunity to gossip with tourists from their mother *poleis* in Ionia, Attica, or Lydia. Tyrants, kings, and the chief magistrates of other *poleis* used the guaranteed safety, the Olympia-inspired myth of Greek unity, and the pervading euphoria to conclude advantageous treaties. Wholesalers from the older manufacturing centers of Greece would sign contracts for the delivery of pottery, iron, and textiles and arrange for the long-term receipts of grain, ores, furs, and wood from the colonies.

There were hawkers of small votive statues for the independent visitor modestly to demonstrate his devotion to the presiding Gods at Olympia. More peddled snacks or souvenirs. There were performing jugglers, magicians, and soothsayers. Authors seeking pan-Hellenic recognition for their originality would read aloud from the porches of the temples. The disciples of rival philosophers met to argue. A great philosopher, Thales of Miletus, was one of the rare casualties at Olympia. At the 58th Olympics in 548 B.C., he perished there, from heat and thirst, at the age of 78.

The hosts of little Elis were in no position to provide comfort for the crowds. Wealthy visitors or delegations desiring to leave lasting impressions brought their trains of mules, servants who unpacked coffers of delicacies, and sprawling tents to be hung with embroidered tapestries. But when night came most people, athletes included, merely wrapped themselves in their cloaks, lay down, and stared at the moon and the constellations above the holiest spot in Greece.

As to the number of visitors at a major festival, such as the one at Olympia, we can be sure that there were many more than the capacity of the stadium, which held about 40,000 squatters and lollers. There were no seats. It would be idle to list here the many famous men who witnessed an Olympic festival. Everybody who was capable of doing so was supposed to go at least once. A Greek citizen's participation as a visitor there could be the high point of his life. Only late in Olympia's long history were athletes provided with baths and other plumbing, but there were never enough facilities for the crowded spectators. Days before the Olympic games began, the visitors lived in a stressful atmosphere that stank and was hot and dusty. Yet almost everyone on hand was in terrifically high spirits. Over all loomed the continuous hubble-bubble of energized, overjoyed Greeks trying to get some words in edgewise.

The formal festival occupied the five days of the second or third full moon (in alternation) after the summer solstice—that is, roughly from the twelfth through the sixteenth days of August or September. The first day was given over to oaths, sacrifices, and other rites. There was no organized attempt to gather all those present for anything like a general opening or closing ceremony. Various delegations and athletes offered gifts to the Gods they favored or who they prayed would favor them. Some of the prayers and sacrifices were offered before statues of legendary, victorious athletes who had been deified.

The most impressive object at Olympia was Phidias' colossal statue of the patron God in his temple, the largest on the site. This statue of the enthroned Zeus was called one of seven wonders of the ancient world and was probably the most admired art work in antiquity. Somewhat larger than a modern two-story house, this statue of Zeus was composed of framing supporting an exterior shell of ebony, gold, ivory, and precious stones. The ornamentation of the seated God's throne was particularly rich and was made up largely of athletic and battle scenes in gilded reliefs. When first seen from the great doors of its temple, the statue was illuminated by shafts of light at the pilgrims' backs and appeared to gleam with a power of its own. The impact of the statue on visitors was dazzling. Phidias' Zeus was surely garish when compared with the cool marble statues and architectural fragments in today's museums, but we must remember that in the times we are discussing, they too were brightly painted.

There were other impressive statues of Zeus. A Roman traveler, Pausanias, in his description of Olympia's monuments recorded:

But the image of Zeus of the Council Chamber is of all the images of Zeus the one most likely to strike terror into the hearts of sinners. He is surnamed Oath-God, and in each hand he holds a thunderbolt. Beside this image it is the custom for athletes, their fathers and brothers as well as their trainers to swear an oath upon slices of boar's flesh that in nothing will they sin against the Olympic Games.

The sports competitions began on the second day. In the morning the crowds assembled at the hippodrome, an elongated oval about 500 yards long east of the *altis* and south of the stadium. The most prestigious horse event was the race for the two wheeled chariot, a driver with reins and a whip, and a team of four. The race course was not around what we now feel is a proper race track, but about two columns, really rounding points, separated by about 400 yards. Since the number of entries was large there were elaborate procedures to insure a simultaneous start and an equal distance from the first rounding point to each team. The race was most often 12 laps (that is, 24 times the distance between the two columns) but finishers traveled farther than the figure of 9600 yards that simple multiplication gives us. The abrupt turns made cunning tactics of and control by the charioteer at least as important as mere speed. Smashups were common—indeed they were usual. Once in a race for 40 teams, only one chariot finished. Here, as in other sports events in classical times (and throughout the history of sporting events ritually or theatrically presented), the competitions were staged in as dramatic a manner as possible. We have eyewitness accounts of spectators abandoning themselves to frenzies of tension and advocacy. They shrieked, wept, embraced one another, insulted athletes in disfavor, and tossed flowers at those they adored.

At the end of the chariot race the owner of the victorious team bound a ribbon holding olive leaves about the head of the driver and the owner himself advanced to a gold and ivory table containing branches of olive leaves cut with a golden sickle by a noble Elian boy from a sacred tree near the temple of Zeus. A herald shouted the name of the victorious owner, that of his father, and the name of his city after which the chief judge placed a crown of leaves on his head. In chariot racing, the blessing and prestige of victory fell to the owners who necessarily were of great wealth. So symbolically indicative of riches and power was chariot racing that merely to *enter* a chariot in a major festival was to establish oneself as a figure worthy of deference in the Greek world.

Next came the horse race. The jockeys competed naked and rode bareback—the inventions of saddle and stirrups were still many centuries away. The spectacle of competing horses and riders did not stir the crowd as other events did. We do have some artistic representations of the small Greek horses being mounted by men. However racing jockeys and their horses have left few pictorial and fewer literary records. We are not even sure if the race was one lap of 400 yards or six laps or some distance between these figures.

Before the end of the victory ceremonies for the jockeys, many spectators began moving to the grassy banks of the stadium to watch the events of the pentathlon. These five events were the discus throw, the long jump, the spear throw, a sprint, and wrestling. In formal Greek meets the three field events were practiced only as components of this five-part event. The points system used to determine who won the pentathlon has been the lively subject of controversy among archaeologists and philologists. It seems certain that each competitor in the pentathlon did each field event five times and that tallies were kept. We have various and not consistent evidence indicating that it was not necessary for a decisive victor in the discus, spear throw, and jump to compete as a runner or to wrestle.

The graceful motions under full power of the big athletes who specialized in the field events often roused the massed spectators to raptures of admiration. The accomplished, honor-laden pentathlon athlete was the one most likely to be watched and sketched by artists. These artists were attempting (and succeeding) in their depictions of the moving male body to establish canons of human beauty.

During the evening of this second day, under the full moon, thousands of participants and spectators assembled to chant prayers and offer sacrifices. The usual sacrifices were dozens of black cattle at the altar honoring the distant mythical hero, Pelops, at whose funeral one legend had it that the Olympic Games first took place. There were processions of flower-bedecked revelers who sang songs as they danced in lines before going off to privately offered feasts or to their beds under the stars.

Most of the third day was taken up by formal observances in honor of the father of the Gods. A long procession wound about the sacred precinct and approached one of the oldest monuments at Olympia—the mound of ashes called "the altar of Zeus." There were Elian supervisors, priests, and servants leading the cattle to be sacrificed, and official delegations from certain *poleis* carrying gifts of gold and silver. Part of all the delegations were the athletes with their coaches and trainers. On a platform before the conical altar, observed by rapt thousands of spectators, officials with sacerdotal powers sacrificed 100 cattle, from which they cut off the thighs. These gifts were carried to the top of the cone and reduced in a fire to ashes so that the charred remains could build the altar of Zeus yet higher.

The only contests of this third day took place in the afternoon and were three races for runners. The "distance" event in the Olympic Games was first and consisted of 24 lengths (as at the hippodrome there was no curved track) about short turns in the stadium. The rounding points were separated by about 200 yards. The stadium itself was longer. The runners lined up at one end of the stadium and at the start went out to go around posts much as the chariots did. The success of a distance runner lay not only in his raw speed but also in his ability to defend himself in the course of the abrupt turns over a surface of loose sand. The long race offered the spectators the spectacle of the racers maneuvering for position, aggressive shoving, and many falls.

The dash of one stadium length was next. The victor in this event won, in addition to his olive wreath, quite extraordinary fame, indeed a certain kind of immortality. Coroebus of Elis, the first Olympic victor whose name was recorded, was the winner of the one-stadium dash in 776 B.C. In about 300 B.C. Greek historians began to use a pan-Hellenic time-recording scheme in place of the several regional and previously existing chronologies. Thereafter in the Greek world, time was ever more often reckoned in four-year periods called "Olympiads" (the festival itself was not an Olympiad). Each Olympiad took the name of the victorious sprinter at the Olympic Games that began the period.

The third and last race was the Greek's middle distance event of two stadium lengths. The line of runners dug their toes into the grooves of long marble blocks set into the ground. At the blast of a trumpet they made for the pole 200 yards distant, rounded it and rushed back to the line from where they started. Naturally the spectators were in a tumult.

Much of the rest of the day was devoted to a feast which, though the thousands of revelers were certainly joyous, had cultish overtones. It was believed that Zeus himself was present in an unseen form. The principal nourishment was the roasted carcasses of the slaughtered cattle that had been offered to Zeus that morning.

The fourth day of the competitions was devoted to what the Greeks called their "heavy" athletic events. Though we know quite a bit about how wrestling, boxing, and the *pancration* were trained for and practiced, we are not sure how many finalists performed at the great festivals before the spectators. It seems likely that knowledgeable Greeks would have preferred to see only the well-known and tested combatants, particularly in the *pancration*, which required more precise training and extraordinary grace and alertness. The victorious pancratist had more pan-Hellenic prestige than a boxer or a wrestler. Perhaps there were elimination rounds which might have been minor attractions for days before the formal bouts. It also seems likely that the best fighters would want to struggle where they could be most inclusively seen. But the sources available to us at present just do not permit firm conclusions.

A fourth heavy event was the race for foot soldiers, the basic element in the phalanx and the irreducible basis for Greek military power. The competitors were naked like the other athletes except that they wore a helmet and shin guards and carried a heavy shield. The race was two stadium lengths long.

The fifth and last day of the festival was mostly for rituals and processions, more ceremonies and banquets. Judges gave victors simple olive branches and circlets of flowers and tied long ribbons to their biceps and calves. Then the victors presented themselves at various altars, particularly that of the awesome Olympian Zeus, and thanked the Gods for their triumphs. Lines of naked youths, men, and elders holding hands danced to little bands of harpists, flutists, and drummers. There was another banquet on the flesh of more spit-turned oxen sacrificed during the day. Then the athletes and their cheering sections began packing for the long voyages by land and by sea to the distant and various parts of the widely dispersed Greek world that peacefully and joyously had been briefly (alas only briefly!) united at holy Olympia.

The most precious cargo that a delegation could take back with them to their *polis* was one or more victorious athletes. At Olympia itself, the official rewards for the victor were only symbolic.

The athletic victor anticipated more substantial honors afterward. His deeds had made him the subject matter for the finest poets. The victory odes of Pindar were chanted all over Greece before rapt audiences. In preparations for his pomp-filled return a special breach might be made in the city wall so that the victor alone could enter through it. The athlete's names and deeds were inscribed in the temples of the *polis* that sponsored him. A victor was given memorials in the form of conventionalized statues before the public temples. If an athlete was especially marvelous—if he was victorious in successive Olympic Games or in several other major athletic festivals of pan-Hellenic significance—statues might be made in the athlete's image. He also got more negotiable awards such as large jars of olive oil, cattle, and hard coin. The tyrant or town council might provide a pension to feed the famous athlete at municipal expense for the rest of his life.

Why so much a fuss for a mere athlete? Because to the Greeks an athletic victory was a harbinger of good fortune, an unequivocal indication of favor from the capricious gods. The Greeks had proof, in the *Iliad* and the *Odyssey*, that the Gods had singled out their favorites by giving them victory. As a symbol of his *polis* at a large meet, the athlete's victory was proof to a city's friends and to its enemies that rituals had been correctly performed, that pleas for intercession were being answered.

Athletic talent, potential or proved, was a precious commodity in the economic and political commerce of Greece. Established or promising athletes were therefore worth nurturing. The superior athlete, then, functioned in a quasi-sacred atmosphere, his performances ritualistically arranged and reverentially viewed. The awesome semi-divine status given the victor (significantly the classical Greeks abandoned the practice mentioned in Homer's poems of awarding second and other prizes) has never been equaled subsequently.

Many Greek city-states, and most especially the new *poleis* of southern Italy, which were rich but without an acknowledged cultural heritage, used whatever measures they could to procure winners. They recruited famous athletes and coaches from far away. The Greeks of Sicily and southern Italy were pushovers for trainers who claimed wonders for radical workouts and quack diets.

Some Greek fans built luxurious training facilities and provided baths and all-meat diets for their trainees. Sponsors prayed, sacrificed lavishly at the altars, offered huge cash bonuses, bribed judges, and gave themselves over to frenzied cheering for their darlings at the meets.

The description of five day festival lists the events as they were at about the time of the summit of Greek self confidence in the fifth century B.C. Much earlier, when the festivals at Olympia were still mostly of local interest, the religious ceremonies were uppermost, the sports events essentially the social adjuncts aristocrats expected when they got together in large numbers. The earliest contests may have been confined to races for sprinters, some chariot races, and boxing matches.

There were more events and festivals than were described in the paragraphs above. Age divisions for youths and grown men were added after Olympia became a destination of many pilgrims. Beginning with the Olympics of 396 B.C., the athletic events were preceded by competitions for trumpeters and heralds. Loudness alone was the criterion for judging supremacy. Later additions were events for the chariot pulled by a pair and races for mules. When the Olympic Games were already seven or eight centuries old, the Romans added some more events, but considering that the festivals lasted nearly 1000 years, the program was remarkably stable.

As the contests at Olympia gathered pan-Hellenic prestige in the archaic period (that is, before the fifth century) other regular religious festivals elsewhere added more athletic events, and eventually a formal program similar to that at Olympia. Three other festivals approached those at Olympia in prestige. At the Pythian Games in honor of Apollo at Delphi, the victors' garlands were of laurel. They occurred every four years in even years between the Olympics. At the Isthmian Games at Corinth to honor Poseidon, the symbolic awards were of pine branches. At the Nemean Games which, like those at Olympia, honored Zeus, the crowns of victors were of wild celery. The biennial Isthmian Games occurred in Olympic and Pythian years. The biennial games at Nemea took place in the years between. Thus there was at least one major Greek sports festival every year.

In bids for respectability and fame, as well as for the money that tourists spent, the priests of other holy sites and the boosters of certain *poleis* established other series of athletic contests. Each festival would be in honor of a particular god and each had distinctive victors' awards of wreaths, bronze tripods, ribbons or, as at Pellene, leather jackets.

Even sophisticated Athens established her own athletic festival as part of her self-appointed (and acknowledged) role as the "school of Hellas." Significantly also, the awards for victors at the Panthenean games were large painted black figure jars (amphorae) filled with the best olive oil. The containers and their contents were renowned Athenian exports of considerable market value.

As was the case with so much of high Greek culture, the participation in and enjoyment of festively staged sport was exclusively a privilege of males. We have observed that Spartan girls were required to train and had special competitions, but this was felt to be deserving of ridicule by the other Greeks. Inscriptions were found at Delphi and at Patrae on the Gulf of Corinth that may record women victors at some special games. The late Roman traveler Pausanias is the sole source for the claim that there were festivals for women athletes at Olympia. These documents, all dating from Roman times, are insufficient evidence that the classical Greeks had women's sports events.

Although some scholars think that unmarried women were allowed at some games as spectators, we have much more evidence that women were barred from sport festivals. The only woman allowed to be present at the Olympic Games was the white robed priestess of Demeter who occupied a solitary throne opposite the judges at the stadium. Rather exceptionally and oddly, we do have the names of some female competitors at Olympia, but these were *owners* of chariot teams who did not have to be present at the time of the race.

There were other recreational activities, such as swimming, several kinds of marksmanship, and ball play, which many Greeks also practiced and surely enjoyed, but which were not part of the formal program. The classical Greeks also had competitions in areas of endeavor which we do not consider sports. Some of these were many kinds of trumpeting, shouting (for heralds), dancing, and the playing of music. The Greek competitive sports that we accept as such were in three divisions, almost corresponding to those the Greeks recognized: track and field, combative sports, and events for horses. It is now time to distinguish these events from the contests of modern times.

Before discussing the individual track events, we might note again that the runners ran lengths rather than laps and they ran over loosely packed sand. The unit of measure was a *stade* or stadium length which varied from place to place, but was usually about 200 yards. The *stade* at a particular stadium was established by the distance between a grooved starting line and a line of marble slabs at the other end of the stadium. The runners wore no spikes nor indeed any other item of clothing.

A problem for the organizers in the race of one *stade* was to eliminate false starts. Ancient Greek sprinters were probably even more "psyched up" than modern ones. One solution was the *husplex,* an ingenious contraption which simultaneously released many leather straps against which the athletes strained while digging their toes into grooves of the marble starting line. They were simultaneously and quite literally unleashed. In most foot races the field of entrees was large—numbering 20 or even more. The release of the *husplex* and takeoff of the runners for the finish line was a spectacular sight that detonated the spectators.

For a race of two *stades* the racers dashed for the column in front of the finish line of the one *stade* race. They rounded it and headed back for the start. At the turn fouls and falls were common, for the desperate racers could crowd themselves into pileups around that pole. A cunning strategy might well have been to take a wide swing rather than a sharp one. Also it was distinctly advantageous for a leading sprinter to kick sand up into the eyes of his rivals. Though the shorter race was the more prestigious event, it can be seen that the race of two *stades* would have its own theatrical appeal.

The long-distance event for the Greek athletic meet was the race of from 12 to 24 stades (i.e., 6 to 12 laps or a maximum of less than three miles). Here the runners rounded one or the other of the two columns to begin each new length. This race, with its sharp turns, the need for deftness to extricate oneself from pileups, the premium on covertly tripping, shoving, or blinding one's opponents all made for a spectacular appeal quite apart from the pure speed of the contestants.

We have feeble evidence that at some festivals there were cross country foot races for men in armor over distances as long as three miles, but these races were exceptional. The Greek spectator did not like to have his darlings out of his sight and would very likely be offended by the sight of the exhausted, grimy finisher of distance races as we know them. How much lovelier was the ecstatic self-satisfaction of the finishing sprinter! The classical Greeks did, of course, have long-distance messengers who jogged the hilly tracks between the city-states, but these anonymous toilers were mere working men, not well-born youths to whom alone the ritualized athletic contests were open. The runner who brought the message from Marathon in 490 B.C. was a great patriot and a splendid distance runner but he was not an athlete. Significantly, the outstanding distance runners we know, so spare in the upper arms and haggard in the face, do not appear in classical art. As spectators, the ancients preferred the proportions, mass, and the high spirits of the young mesomorphs who were sprinters.

Naturally, we have no statistical norms or records for the running events, since there were no clocks, nor regular or even certified distances for the courses. In sporting events, at least, the Greeks were uninterested in quantified time or quantified distances. Superiority in Greek sport could be determined only by proximate combat. A Greek runner became recognized as supreme in his age by winning various and successive athletic meets. The more prestigious the meet (and presumably the tougher the competition), the greater the value placed on victory.

The Greek obsession with high performance had led to the devising of paraphernalia for improving marks in the field events. In the long jump, which was done from a standing start, the athlete carried in each hand weights of from four to eight pounds. The weights were usually of stone and were shaped to fit the hand gracefully. Appropriately swung, these could propel the jumper farther than he might go unaided. We have many surviving pictures of these weights.

Analogously, the spear throwing event was not a simple toss of a metal tipped shaft which was almost as long as the athlete was tall. In the stadium and on the battlefield the Greek athlete and soldier lengthened and made more accurate the throw with the help of a sling. This leather thong was looped over a finger of the throwing hand and wound about the spear to give it a stabilizing spin as well as additional force.

The reason for the shape of the Greek discus is suggested by the incident in the *Iliad* wherein the victorious competitor Polypoetes takes as his prize the very ingot of metal which he tossed farthest. Unwrought bronze and unwrought iron were cast into depressions in sand which produced the original flapjack shape. Though useless unless worked further, the valuable ingots were often on hand for demonstrations of power and gradually a technique (by no means unpleasant to watch!) arose for the hurling of the objects. Archeologists have found discuses weighing from between three to fifteen pounds. At a large meet the discus was standardized by having all competitors toss the same one. The smallest ones may have been for boys; the heaviest ones for training. It seems likely that an acceptable competition discus was not much different in weight or size than the modern one. Various surviving depictions of athletes in action suggest that the modern technique is similar to the ancient one in that much of the propelling force came from the centrifugal motion produced by the athlete's spin upward from a near squatting position.

In the three combative sports of Greek antiquity, there were no rounds or pauses. The opponents merely squared off and went at one another until the loser raised his arm to admit surrender. Lasting power and alertness were likely to be more decisive than the forceful onslaught of power. This was especially so among the best fighters, whose defensive technique was highly developed. Indeed, experts wrote books on the subject of endurance and defense. The presence of referees provided with switches and granted the power to impose fines also lessened the likelihood of ugliness in the fights at a big meet. The reluctance of fighters to attack (and thereby risk a crippling riposte) made all of the Greek combative sports, particularly when done by experts, more akin to dancing than to bloody slugfests. A wrestling match or a boxing match might last days and be boring. It appears that wrestling and boxing may have been accompanied by music for that reason.

In practice boxers used the punching bag, shadow boxed, and wore padded mitts with their sparring partners. In competition the boxers bound their hands and lower arms with long soft leather thongs. In Greek times these thongs were not intended to damage opponents, but rather to protect the wearer's hands. A treasured distinction of a great boxer was to have an unmarked face. A good face was proof of the ability to out-dance and out-feint lesser men who, after a bout that might last a whole day or more, collapsed from exhaustion. There were often boxing matches with a winner and a loser wherein no blow was struck.

The favorite participatory sport among the Greeks was wrestling. Indeed males of all classes were likely to consider wrestling with their friends a usual and natural recreation. In later Greek days each large *polis* had many special establishments where citizens could gather to wrestle casually or to kibbitz. Like all other athletes the grapplers were oiled, but the greasy quality was obliterated by the application of dust of various colors and textures which enforced grippability. Some powders were imputed with powers such as heat retention or dispersion or the casting of spells. We are not sure of the wrestling rules, and in any case they varied over time and place. But in general, wrestling was practiced with the combatants mostly upright. The object was to throw one's opponent so that his back touched the sandy ground. In serious competition a fall usually constituted a victory. Greek wrestling, incidentally, has little resemblance to the so-called Greco-Roman wrestling of the present, but was restricted by rules which varied according to whether the wrestling was for fun, for a trashy local trophy, or for a prestigious international championship.

The favorite sport for the more esthetically tuned spectators was the *pancration*, a kind of no-holds-barred wrestling. Even kicking (but, of course, not gouging) was allowed. Much of the action consisted of rolls and artful falls which were intended to break strangle holds or grips threatening broken limbs which produced the surrender of the lesser man. The *pancration* was more like modern judo than professional wrestling, in that it was methodical and perhaps even exquisite and elegant.

No rule books for this admired sport survive, though we know that among the Greeks this sport was difficult to master. The experts tended to be much admired for their grace and beauty.

The only animal which the Greek painters and sculptors treated with a respect rivaling that shown for the young male and female body was the horse. The ancient Greeks adored horses and were terrified of them. But such strong feelings had been general in most societies after the horse became an essential element for waging war and for defense against aggressors with horses. Even in times of peace the horse was a talisman of power, high caste, and good luck. Trained teams were especially splendid sights. From long before the time of the horse-using Hyksos (who we remember shattered Egyptian self-confidence) until the end of the nineteenth century, the sport horse has carried with it emphatic symbolic significance, perhaps even magic powers. Indeed the enduring aura of the horse may explain why horse racing continues to flourish in heavily industrialized countries, long after the animals have become useless militarily, for working the land, or for transportation.

Though many literary descriptions and artistic representations of riders, horses, and chariots have survived, we have no indication that distances in bareback or chariot races were fixed with any precision. The races for riders were usually about two miles. The distances for chariots were greater and could be as long as nine miles. Race results were not abstracted in terms of remarkable times or distances but were always given as victories by particular persons at particular places. We have no surviving examples of a Greek hippodrome or horse track. At Olympia there were elaborate starting gates which assured simultaneous starts. But the gates and indeed the whole course were washed away when the river Alpheos changed course. But there was not much to see there even in ancient times. Greek horse race tracks were merely cleared open fields.

We know from the many drawn and sculpted representations that the Greeks took advantage of their clear rivers and lovely coasts to swim and to dive. Indeed, one of the obligations of a father was to teach his children to swim for safety's sake. Some paintings (as in a recently discovered fresco from a tomb at Paestum) show that a swan dive from a high platform was worth recording as a lovely gesture. Most Greek swimmers apparently used the side stroke.

Surely some competitive, egotistical Greeks must have had informal races across rivers or to some island and back. But we have
no suggestion that social prestige was ever attached to the winners,
or that courses of standard length were ever established or that
swimming and diving were performed for spectators.

We also have some sculpted reliefs and vase paintings of Greek
athletes engaged in ball play. Some athletic historians have taken
the frailest of archeological and philological evidence to declare
that the noble Greeks, like us, played field hockey, tennis, and
football; but the very meagerness of the records and the desperation of these efforts prove the opposite point. The Greeks very
likely bowled skittles, played catch or monkey-in-the-middle, and
juggled, just as energetic, playful people in almost every other society have. But there were no team sports. The Greeks' conception
of an athletic contest did not include the cool-headedness, that
subjugation of the individual will, that strict constitutionalism of
rules, and the notion of fair play which have made modern team
games possible. We know from their political history that the
Greeks worked badly in committees. The Greek competitive
sportsman prayed that the gods would assist his total application
of spirit and muscle. The spectators and furthermore the society
around him expected the athlete to compete in a trance, a parox-
ism of effort. No room for team work here.

Despite evidence which suggests that high-performance Greek
athletics were confined to rather few sports, it seems that never
before, and possibly never since, have sporting competitions, with
their dramas, their metaphors, and their beauties been so deeply
integrated into the soul of a people. The Greek citizens wished to
convince themselves and all their rivals that they were the supreme athletic people. They and consequently all later generations
have viewed Hellenic athleticism as an inseparable element in that
unique amalgam of energy and ideas which produced a stunning
summit in cultural originality.

By the end of the sixth century B.C. every Greek city-state was
expected to have certain athletic facilities. The first gymnasiums
were merely level, partly shaded areas with nearby provisions for
resting and with a supply of running water. The word "gymnasium" itself means "exercise for which one strips." Prosperous

cities later built gymnasiums with colonnades, club rooms, lounges, small altars, and storage rooms for lotions, olive oil, and athletic powders. Still later there were bathtubs and showers in some places.

The gymnasiums and their pleasant surroundings were local resorts open to the whole male citizenry. Here boys and men smeared one another with the olive oil that was the essential uniform for workouts and competition. The wealthy men sprinkled each other with pulverized rare herbs and minerals; the regular patrons just used the fine sand that was the surface for all Greek athletic fields. After their workouts the athletes scraped themselves with the curved and cupped blade of a brass instrument called a *strigil* in order to remove the oil and dirt. Then they bathed: a plunge in a stream or a cold shower at a simple gymnasium; warm tubs or stream at the newer, bigger and richer ones.

Sometimes attached to the gymnasium, but more often existing alone, was another smaller facility. The *palaestra* was more specialized and might or might not be public. It was a sanded field surrounded by a colonnaded court. Most specifically, the *palaestra* was used for instruction and practice in wrestling, which healthy men entered into regularly and with great enthusiasm. The teacher there might also coach boxers and pancratists or train athletes in the three field events.

For centuries the gymnasiums and *palaestras* assumed central importance in the everyday lives of Greek males. Indeed, like the sporting events, the athletic facilities served to identify and reinforce Greekness. As was the case with athletic participation in every other age, we may assume that relatively few Greeks were performers who stripped to be watched by others. Most citizens gathered to watch others, to play board games, to catch up on the news, and to gossip. Above all to gossip. Socrates haunted these clubs. They were important meeting places for the mixing of generations, for debate, for the launching of plots, scandals, and new ideas and thus were important informal educational facilities. In the Hellenistic age they were the beginnings of some briefly successful and ultimately influential experiments as well.

In Athens in her best days there were three large gymnasiums;

the Academia, the Lyceum, and the Cynosarges. Plato and his companions were most often found in the Academia and the word endured to mean an institution of higher learning. Similarly, Aristotle preferred the Lyceum which has survived, linguistically at least, in the French *lycée*. A certain gymnasium might have a reputation as being a haunt for left wing political agitators or even for a group of loose young men who profited by the tacit homoeroticism that was a subtle, pervasive mood in much Greek social life.

The novelties and distinction of Greek art probably could not have come about apart from the erotic and emotional connection between performers and onlookers that existed in the gymnasium and the *palaestra*. The most comely or skillful wrestlers were very much on display. The keen admiration of them inspired some Greek poetry. Artists observed and sketched famous athletes and from their observations devised those ideal human types that, like other supreme Hellenic accomplishments in the arts, have stunned all later generations with their magnificence.

The earliest distinctively Greek depiction of the young male form was the *Kouros*, which was much like Egyptian and Mycenean standing statues of youths except that the Greek model was naked. But beginning in the seventh century the smiling Kouros began to show more muscle definition and his massive thighs and high rump became more indicative of ready strength. The athletic statues of the sixth century became more graceful and more specifically anatomical, though they remained essentially decorative and nearly symmetrical. By the early fifth century, brave sculptors were experimenting with the effects obtainable by sketching and then sculpting informally relaxed or even performing athletes. They sought to freeze for esthetic contemplation the exquisite moment of an ideal beauty in extreme stress. Evolution continued into the Hellenistic period when the most famous sculptors modeled from youths, dancing girls, old people, and even non-Greeks such as Negro musicians and other groups or individuals to produce statues that were sensual, sentimental, and dazzlingly refined in their finish and details. As long as Greek art remained in the hands of the Greeks, the object of the artist was not to portray particular persons, but to offer for display beauty or emotion itself. Significantly we have few ascertainable portraits of individual Greek athletes, but only ossified opinions of particular artists as to what was ideal—what an athlete ought to look like.

Large sized sculpture in marble or in bronze was the supreme Greek plastic art. But abstracted visions of ideal physical beauty also appeared as they evolved on the vase paintings, coins, carved jewels, metal work, and clay statuettes that the Greeks exported in great quantities and that were and remained concrete representations of Greekness all over the Mediterranean world.

This presentation of themselves by the Greeks in their poetry and in their visual arts has given us a far more detailed picture of their formal recreational activities than what we have for any other ancient people and has heavily influenced almost all subsequent opinions of Greek culture. Many later Philhellenes have tended to view the classical Greeks—every one of them, young and old, citizens as well as the more numerous slaves—as practicing sport from morning until night. The lovers of classical Greece wish to tell us that the *mood* of Greek culture was the same as that imparted to us from those cool, marble athletes on pedestals in our best museums.

But Greek sport was neither cooly prepared for nor passively observed. The passionate, indeed orgiastic, elements in Hellenic life also found plenty of expression in Greek sport, and in its theatrical presentation. Greek spectators used sporting meets as excuses for frenzied displays of adoration and hatred that amounted, as at some modern sport meets, to irrational (though temporary) transformation of character. The value attached to an athletic victory and the spiritualized eroticism attached to the athlete who could produce a yearned-for victory led to extravagances that run counter to Solon's apothegm "Nothing in excess."

That victors at Olympia, Delphi, or any of a number of other festivals took as immediate rewards blessings, ribbons, and crowns of symbolic vegetation should not obscure the fact that the spectators and the fans from the home town endowed these symbols with great, indeed burdensome, significance. Winners were certain indications to all observers of celestial favor. For the victorious athletes more substantial awards came later with their local exaltation and their gathering in of coin of the realm. The highly accomplished athletes who competed before crowds of berserks at the larger festivals were not (and this was especially true after about 600 B.C.) "amateurs." For an accomplished Greek athlete a contest offering merely sentimental awards was not worth traveling to.

The historian must emphasize that Greek culture was neither consistent nor stable over time, or wherever Greeks resided, but Greek history contained dynamic, dialectical elements that had their impact on Greek sport as well.

After the Peloponnesian wars, which curtailed the wealth, optimism, and stupendous originality of the Athenians, came the subjugation of the whole Greek world by Alexander the Great after 335 B.C. Greek self-confidence was permanently undermined, for thenceforth political independence or creativity (outside of intrigue or conspiracy) was impossible. Though evolution in the arts and sciences continued, and many Greek merchants became richer than ever, a certain cynicism, a languid virtuosity, a rather stubborn antiquarianism became rooted in high Hellenic culture.

Minor consequences of this pervasive adaption to circumstances were the adoption by the richer gymnasiums of warm baths. The ease of establishing social contacts made certain gymnasiums ever more the places for assignations or even first encounters. The insignificance of political ambition and the loss of political celebrations of local pride led to the placing of a heavier symbolic burden on sports victors. Pressure for outstanding sporting performance led to more thorough recruiting, more meticulously rational training. There became established categories of scouts, trainers, performance theorists, and promoters—all blood suckers who stood to profit along the way if their performers were isolated from society to be prepared by special diets, drugs, and single-minded grooming for supreme physical performance.

The Hellenistic sports industry was a response to ineradicable Greek desires for heroes in an age where there was no longer a sphere for heroes as there had been in the epics or in pre-Alexandrian politics. Professionals with their entourages went on circuits collecting wreaths, trophies, fame, and credits to be cashed in when they returned home. Fickle athletes (or those who managed them) were seduced from allegiance from one city to another.

One sprinter, Astylus of Croton, had won the races of one and of two stades in two successive Olympic Games, those of 488 and 484 B.C. This was an extraordinary accomplishment. Very likely because of substantial financial inducements from the tyrant of Syracuse, he entered the next Olympic Games (those of 480 B.C.) as a Syracusan. The people of Croton, enraged at his faithlessness, destroyed a statue honoring him and turned his house there into a prison.

Athletes who were especially large or handsome or whose list of victories were especially long were able to have statues erected that were not mere estheticized abstractions, but near portraits of the model himself. Even while the great athlete was still living, the loose and sometimes contradictory Greek panoply of gods was expanded to give sports heroes semi-divine status. The statues of certain deceased athletes, owing to their great strength and health while living, were endowed with curative powers.

Some Hellenistic social critics looked back on the golden age (indeed they tended to over-gild it somewhat) when there were more sports participators and when physical training for all youths was supposedly better integrated into general education. Excesses in sports and vulgarity on the part of the pliant athletes and their fans were believed to be conspicuous evidence that a certain organic unity—at once restraining and inspiring—had disappeared from the Greek soul.

In the sixth century it had been expected that victors at the festivals would become useful citizens once their sports careers were over. Later, however, the term "athlete" referred to a specialist performer. An early sports critic was the poet Euripides (fifth century B.C.) who wrote:

Although there are myriads of evils throughout Greece, there is nothing worse than the race of athletes. First of all, they neither learn how to live a good life, nor could they possibly do so. For how could a man who is a slave to his jaw and obedient to his belly acquire wealth to surpass that of his father? Nor, on the other hand, are such men capable of bearing poverty and assisting fortune; for because they have not formed good habits they find things hard for them when they come to face serious difficulties. In their prime they make a brilliant spectacle as they go about and are the pride of the state; but when bitter old age comes upon them, they are gone like coarse cloaks which have lost their nap. Yes, and I blame the Greek custom of assembling to watch these men and of honoring useless pleasures for the sake of a feast. For what good wrestler, what swift runner, or what man who has hurled a discus well, or planted a well delivered blow on another jaw, has ever defended the city of his fathers because of winning a victor's crown? Do men fight with the enemy holding discuses in their hands, or through the line of shields do they launch blows with their fists, and so drive the enemy out of the fatherland? No one indulges in this folly when he is close to the foeman's steel.

We ought then to crown with garlands the wise and the good, and whatever temperate and upright man best leads the state, and whoever by his counsels rids us of evil deeds, making an end to battles and strife; because such things are good for every state and for all the Greeks. (From the fragment . . . *Autolycus,* translated by W. S. Oldfather from Nauck's *Tragic Greece* Euripides fragment 282)

Though one of the earliest sports critics, Euripides is unusual because he does not recall for comparison some earlier, cleaner period in sport history when the excesses he attacks were presumably not present. It became almost universal for sports panegyrists and critics ever afterward to construct ideal versions of the past when clean, pure sport was integrated into all aspects of life and made it better. This imagined golden age of sport was thereafter assumed to have been just at the time of the zenith of Greek creativity, when inspired giants attained supremacy in every activity attempted.

As we know, the accomplishment of the most energetic Greeks in the classical period had an intimidating effect upon later ages. Sport was integrated into that society and subsequent lovers of Greece knew it. The consistently reverential view of classical Greek sport was reinforced by the paintings, sculpture, poetry, and educational theories that were the Hellenic exports and their immortal inheritance.

[4]

SPREAD OF
THE TASTE

A fault, indeed a tragic failing, of the classical Greeks, was their inability to arrive at a means of moderating inter-*poleis* ambitions. Deeper grounds for the political upheavals in the Eastern Mediterranean were overpopulation, and the economic power of new trading classes. In any case, Greek politics were in a continuous turmoil which began with the calamitous second Peloponnesian war (431–405 B.C.) and ended with the final Roman conquest almost 300 years later. The Peloponnesian wars had produced such a crop of atrocities of Greeks against Greeks that the tone of Mediterranean life was permanently lowered.

Despite devastation and uncertainty, the splendor of the creations of Greek genius continued to be apparent. Socrates taught philosophy to Alcibiades and Aristotle tutored Alexander the Great. Cultivated Hellenes in Attica, and indeed from as far away as Sicily and Egypt, continued to advance all the arts. But even the cleverest Hellenistic Greeks recognized that the originality, the arrogance, and the versatility of Periclean Athens (ca. 461–429 B.C.) had marked a zenith. Forever afterward that golden age and its heroes were to inspire and to be nostalgically reflected upon. With the ending of the *polis*, there came an end to heroic originality. A brief look at the career of the conqueror and Hellenizer Alexander the Great (356–323 B.C.) may illustrate the attractiveness of and the place of sport in that culture. The self-assigned mission of Alexander's father, Phillip of Macedon (382–336 B.C.), was to modernize that area of open fields and tough herders to the north of the Greek city-states. Modernization meant the forced, wholesale adaption of the techniques and elegant styles of classical Greece. Significantly, the wedding festival at which Phillip was murdered included prizes for athletes and for artists which were ceremoniously presented according to established Greek models.

Alexander himself, in order to lend prestige and splendor to festivals marking great events in his life, regularly staged athletic meets. His ceremonies at the ancient Egyptian city of Memphis included Greek games. There were sports competitions at Persepolis and Susa and at all his triumphant stopping places including the point of his farthest advance into India. He liked athletes as traveling company. One companion, Leonnatus, was so devoted a wrestler that he kept with him his own trainers and camels for carrying bags of special sand for his matches. The games and competitions among Alexander's soldiers, which were always those of formal Greek meets, were intended not only to declare the sophistication of a brilliant and frighteningly powerful provincial (for Alexander could never forget that he was born Macedonian and not Greek) but also to impress those whom he conquered with the worldliness and power of his entourage. The ceremonies for the funeral of his friend Hephaestion were said to have included competitions for 3000 athletes and artists. All the cities that Alexander founded included provisions for gymnasiums and wrestling schools.

Alexander's conquests in Africa and Asia vastly increased the area and population exposed to Greek culture. For centuries thereafter Greek language and Greek culture were espoused by every provincial who wished to succeed. And the complex of Greek high culture included the practice of a small number of narrowly defined sports and the inclusion of formal athletic competitions in public festivals.

In the Hellenistic age many Greek intellectuals became teachers, collectors, and contemplatives. The cynicism and pessimism that had always been elements in the Greek character were expressed in history writing, theology, and drama. Scholars established libraries and museums to preserve literature and antiques. The continuous demand in Asia and all around the Mediterranean for Greek luxury articles led to the establishment of factories to produce characteristic textiles, furniture, jewelry, and pottery in styles that had been fresh long before. The virtuosity, ornamentation, and highly finished surfaces that characterized Hellenistic sculpture were apparent in all these exported products. Under the political order imposed by the Romans there was more trade than ever before in the Mediterranean. Greek became a *lingua franca* and the Greek cities became cosmopolitan melting pots. The Greeks became more tolerant of others.

The specialization and more purposeful professionalization in later Greek sport was surely attributable to the high value that had always been placed upon an athletic victory. As early as the fifth century B.C. the gentleman-amateur-sportsman, who was the usual Homeric sports hero, almost completely dropped out of public competition. An exceptional class of competition remained the chariot race, which required great wealth even to be able to contend. The unscrupulous Athenean aristocrat, Alcibiades, in the Olympic Games of 416 B.C. entered seven teams, which won first, second, and fourth places, thus rehabilitating (disastrously for Athens, as it turned out) his soiled public reputation. As the generations went on, the victor lists from the great sports festivals were composed ever more of the names of carefully recruited and trained professionals from the provinces, particularly from Sicily and Southern Italy. At the major festivals the reverent and esthetically tuned spectators of earlier days were now overshadowed by cruder enthusiasts who cheered the massive brutes who trained for boxing and the *pancratium*. Much of the attraction was homoerotic as before, but it was now more voyeuristic, sadistic, and theatrical. The great ecumene that embraced Hellenic culture was now the sphere for a new kind of public entertainer who traveled with his coaches, masseurs, and cooks to those cities where the ovations and prize money were most generous.

The higher standards of performance and a more elaborate standard of festive trappings did not, of course, decrease the popular appeal of the sports. Indeed, gifts of architecture, art, and treasure heaped up at Olympia, Delphi, Corinth, and at the grounds set aside for sport at hundreds of other less ancient Greek or Hellenized cities.

Other institutions which institutionalized Greek sport were the gymnasiums and the *palaestra* or wrestling schools. This provides the occasion for a curious story. We know that there were many incentives for Asians to adapt Greek culture. Among these people were the ancient Israelites. Now physical recreation "for the sake of the game" and apart from military training was repugnant to the monotheistic, proud, and purposeful Hebrews (as it would be later to the Calvinists and other sects with a stern moral code). Furthermore, the close identification of sport with Hellenism caused religious and traditional Jews to condemn sport as threatening to the integrity of their own ancient culture.

It is significant that in 174 B.C. the Hellenizing high priest, Jason, had constructed a gymnasium in Jerusalem. Its intended members and participants would naturally have to participate nude. According to the book of Maccabees (I:1,15) some Jewish athletes eager to assimilate actually suffered cosmetic operations to conceal the fact that they had been circumcised. The gymnasium was just one facet of a policy intended to win over Judea's propertied bourgeosie (another tendered privilege was freedom from the poll tax) to Greek citizenship.

Religious Jews had to oppose Greek athletic festivals since they were inseparable from observances for idolatrous cults. Our evidence that the orthodox leaders were not entirely successful in resisting Hellenistic sport comes mostly from surviving polemics against the Jews who succumbed. All the same, there were Jewish sporting clubs. Jewish athletes from Tyre were allowed to participate in the 152nd Olympic Games, but they were instructed to see that the gifts they brought home should be devoted to some nonidolatrous purpose.

The first Jewish ruler to promote cosmopolitan sport was King Herod (born ca. 73 B.C., King 37–4 B.C.). Herod wished to demonstrate compliance with his Roman overlords and therefore urged the Jews to accommodate to the prevailing notions of sophistication. It is a testimony to Herod's political skill that he was able delicately and for so long to forward Hellenization without provoking the riots that would have brought down his fragile political structure. Parts of Herod's policy were gifts to Roman officials. Others were the stadiums, hippodromes, gymnasiums, and *palaestras* he ordered built in Tiberias, Jericho, and other cities.

Besides the athletic architecture he installed in or near the cities he administered, Herod contributed conspicuously to the Olympic Games. He also established an athletic festival intended to occur every five years after the inauguration of his new port at Caesarea. By offering large awards and by breaking with tradition and awarding second and third prizes, Herod attracted famous athletic stars to perform before the Jews. It is worth noting that Herod could not go so far as to build a Greek temple, erect statues of athletes, or offer sacrifices; that would have led to riots in Jerusalem. Therefore, his shows were rather austere in comparison with the religious paraphernalia that usually accompanied a festival elsewhere in the Roman-ruled, Hellenized world.

The point regarding the attractiveness of Greek culture (including Greek sports) can be made again by examining some aspects of the Etruscans' adaption of it. The origins of the Etruscans were unknown to the ancients and, despite the quantities of Etruscan artifacts which we have recovered, remain mysterious today. They spoke a language different from any other known and their meager literature remains untranslated. During the seventh through the fifth centuries these inhabitants of central Italy were a barrier to Greek colonial expansion northward from colonies such as Croton or Paestum. Compared with the immense durability of Egyptian, Greek, and Roman culture, the period of glory for the Etruscans was brief, for in the fourth and third centuries they were overwhelmed by the rough and ready Romans.

The Etruscans excite us because of their delight in lovely objects. There are, however, few motifs or objects (aside from jewelry) in their arts and crafts that were *sui generis*. The Etruscan artists were clearly inspired by the Greeks, who were their commercial and political rivals. In fact, most of the best surviving Greek pottery has been recovered from Etruscan tombs. Some Greek artists probably worked for the Etruscans. The already derivative Etruscan art styles in turn inspired less sophisticated people in northern Italy and in what are now Yugoslavia, France, and Spain.

Quite possibly the Etruscans imported their sport from the Greek towns in southern Italy, which were notorious for their promotion and adoration of outstanding athletes. Robust and happy scenes on gemstones, carvings, tomb paintings, terra-cotta statuary, relief sculpture, and vase paintings suggest that the Etruscans took on most of the Greek athletic program. Etruscan pictures show graceful, muscularly rumped athletes jumping with weights, hurling the javelin or the discus and boxing with their fists wrapped in soft thongs. There are also scenes of horse and chariot racing.

The Etruscans did not take Greek sport whole. It may be that mistakes in some Etruscan pictures of familiar Greek events are due to their enthusiastic adoption of Greek art and partial ignorance of what the Greeks were depicting. However, some pictures of Etruscan athletes show them wearing shorts, whereas the Greeks always competed nude.

It is worth observing here again that the sports in the classical Greek program which received regular artistic and literary attention were few by our own standards or by the standards of almost any other culture. The Etruscans on the other hand have left us many pictures of female athletes and more pictures of jugglers and gymnasts as well as some swimmers and divers. There is also a surviving picture of a type of pole vaulting for which we have no Greek or Roman mentions whatever. Like the Greeks, the Etruscans used the *palaestra* as a center for collecting active athletes, artists, and onlookers. The depictions of kibitzers in Etruscan sporting art confirm the claims of early Roman chroniclers that the Etruscans loved to watch sports events. Scenes of athletic audiences are extremely rare in Greek art. Curiously, in some pictures of Etruscan audiences, spectators allow themselves to be distracted by erotic byplay from the horse races or dances in military hardware.

Though the sports meets of the classical Greeks were widespread and frequent, the standards of theatrical presentation were spare by Etruscan (and quite possibly by Egyptian and Cretan) standards. The Etruscans were also horse lovers and one of their spectacles was a certain elaborate performance of groups on horses. The riders were costumed and the horses decorated. One is reminded of the choreographed routines of the Spanish riding schools of the eighteenth century.

Along with the dancers, jugglers, masked clowns, and byplay there were more sinister elements in Etruscan festivals. The performers were probably of much lower social status than the people who watched them. Were they possibly slaves or prisoners? We do not know. Early Roman observers claimed that the Etruscans had the first public gladiatorial shows and staged battles among wild beasts. The object in these contests was to display bloodshed, mayhem, and finally death.

Whether or not the Etruscans invented certain kinds of publicly and ceremonially sanctioned sadism, the Romans took some of these spectacles over when they conquered the Etruscans in the fourth century. Despite their exceptional military skills and organizing ability, the Romans of this, the Republican, period were without much that we could call high culture of their own. The job of dominating Italy, which they took over from the Etruscans, was made possible by their ruggedness and practicality. Their steady accretions of wealthy territory, the establishment of a governing class, and their exposure to more sophisticated peoples left them susceptible to civilized pleasures. The already venerable and widely propagated complex of Greek high culture could not be resisted. Despite the racial pride and austere self-restraint of the republican Romans, they succumbed, though not entirely, to Greek philosophers, artists, and taste makers. A persistent theme in social criticism throughout all Roman history was that the Roman virtues of self-discipline and submission to authority were damaged by the appeal of Greek hedonism. The simultaneous attraction and repulsion that characterized the Roman's feelings about Greek high culture characterized their views of traditional Greek sports as well.

If we claim that sport is an activity pursued playfully for its own sake, we have little evidence that the early Romans were sportsmen. Their most significant innovations were military. One was the legion. The early Roman legion was an improvement upon the Greek phalanx. The unit was much larger, numbering 4000 to

6000 men and thus demanding more individual discipline, specialization, and submission to commands from above. The conscripted, sturdy citizen-soldier (to be idealized by later Roman social critics) had to practice spear throwing, fighting with the short sword, and synchronized marching. Their splendid infantrymen enabled the republican Romans to expand their geographical control rather cheaply, because of the relative lack of costly corps of cavalry and war chariots. The legion was a stunning success and was the basis of the longest period of peace that civilized Europe has ever known. The technique of the legion did not remain fixed but evolved strategically and changed along with political and social changes over almost 1000 years.

For centuries Roman social critics, dismayed at the decadence they saw amidst them, attributed Rome's decline to foreign, principally Greek, luxuries and seductions. Greek sport was one of these infections. Many later Roman authors regularly scolded their sophisticated countrymen who ran, wrestled, and watched sport as the Greeks had. They idealized their tough ancestors who had worked hard, practiced with swords and spears, marched in full armor in company with their neighbors, and bathed in cold rivers.

The first Greek athletes of whom we have records in Rome were brought over by an impresario in 186 B.C. They were certainly professional entertainers. In any case we know that the Greeks shocked the Romans by stripping for their performances. Public nudity, which the Greeks considered esthetic and healthy, was later called by Cicero "the beginning of evil doing." The frequent alarm expressed by social critics about the costs of oil and prizes for athletes and the critics' sneering at the idlers who gathered at the gymnasium and *palaestra* are themselves indications that some, perhaps many, Romans had adopted the styles of Greek sport and were enjoying them. When Cicero says it is "disgraceful" for Roman citizens to travel to Olympia for the Games when there are crises at home, this shows too that people he knew had indeed gone there.

Examples of the Roman attitudes toward Greek culture, particularly regarding Greek athletes, indicate the steady appeal of Greece long after the Greeks were politically insignificant. Many wealthy Romans were aroused to enthusiasm by the nuances of the best

Greek works of art. Some yearned to possess as their very own examples of the supreme Hellenic art—sculpture. After the Roman conquest, purchase and plunder resulted in the large-scale transfer of Greek art works to Roman villas and public buildings. By the end of the second century B.C. there were already collections of Greek art in Rome and the supply of originals was running out. Greek entrepreneurs sketched and measured the precious originals and brought over skilled immigrants to Italy to make copies. The sculpture factories flourished for several centuries. The justly famous bronze original of Myron's *Discobolus* has been lost. The three fragmented marble statues of an athlete whirling out of a crouch to hurl the discus that can be seen in the museums of Rome are all copies. Of the many athletic statues of Phidias, the only originals that remain are the mutilated and corroded Parthenon friezes at present in the British museum. Lysippus' *Apoxyomenus*, a statue of a tall athlete cleaning himself with a strigil, though striking, exists only in indifferent copies. The over-muscled so-called *Farnese Hercules,* now in the National Museum in Naples, is a Roman work, but was probably inspired by an original of Lysippus. Our few originals of Greek athletic sculpture are pathetic remnants of thousands of bronze and marble statues that once enriched the sites of the great sports festivals. The *Charioteer of Delphi,* the bronze jockey from Artemesium, the large bronze *Zeus Hurling a Thunderbolt* (Poseidon Hurling a Trident?), all relatively recently recovered and now in Athens, compel our admiration. The recently discovered warriors of Brindisi are also magnificent. But none of these works were considered worthy of an artist's signature at the time of their production, none of them were distinguished enough to be copied, and none rated description by the Roman esthetes.

If Greeks came to Rome as teachers, performers, and craftsmen, the Romans, in turn, went to Greece as tourists, pilgrims, and benefactors. We should recall that the domestic living standards of the classical Greeks, even of most wealthy people, were so simple as to be rudimentary. Few cities before the fifth century could assemble the wealth to erect marble or even sandstone temples. The extraordinary building program of Pericles in Athens was made possible only by his extraction of tribute from other Greek cities.

It was not until after the Persian wars that the *altis* at Olympia began to be crowded with architecture and sculpture, thus forcing the shifting of the stadium to the east in the middle of the fourth century B.C. The years of lavish civic decoration for the Greek cities came late, at a time when the Greeks were politically ineffective. And many of the ornaments were the gifts of Roman Hellenomanes.

Herodes Atticus (ca. 101–177 A.D.), a Roman born in Greece, was the richest private person in all of classical antiquity. He was educated in Athens as a sophist and had a reputation as a rhetorician and as an orator. The Emperor Hadrian (r. 117–138), who also adored Greece, showed him great favor. Herodes Atticus also contributed to the education of Marcus Aurelius (r. 161–180), another admirer of Greece. Herodes Atticus restored old buildings or built new ones in cities all over the eastern Mediterranean. He gave a theater to Corinth and paid for the stadium at Delphi and the baths at Thermopylae. He was wealthy enough to consider financing the cutting of a canal across the Isthmus of Corinth. Owing to archaeological work done in Athens and Olympia, we have considerable knowledge of Herodes Atticus' gifts to these sites, which were already ancient and hallowed in his time. The Odeon in Athens, a Roman-style theater seating 5000, was partially hallowed out of the rock at the base of the Acropolis and is a monument to the millionaire's wife, who died in 161 A.D.

A much larger project was his gift of a stadium to Athens. The site was a long, narrow, natural depression near the left of the Ilissus River and beneath the Ardettus hill. Long before, in about 330 B.C., the orator and financier Lycurgus had ordered some excavating and filling, and thus turned a valley there into a huge stadium conveniently near the Acropolis. The place was thereafter the site of the Panathenean games. As was the usual case with the classical and Hellenistic Greeks, the stadium was still a rather utilitarian affair consisting of a flat, oblong surface with grassy banks for the spectators to loll or squat on.

It was one of the delights of the Romans to turn rude creations into architectural extravaganzas. At immense expense Herodes Atticus had the slopes at Athens precisely shaped and provided seating in Pentelic marble for more than 50,000 spectators. With characteristic generosity he also provided the new stadium with permanent gates, passageways, and colonnades. He also saw to it that the stadium had a great number of traditional statues, reliefs and other decorations in marble and gilt bronze, all signs of imperial Roman respect and generosity.

That the stadium at Olympia retained its rustic form during the centuries of Roman hegemony is probably testimony to the steadfast conservatisism of the local Elians, who continued to administer the Olympic festivals. Young Herodes Atticus had visited Olympia as a spectator at the Games and had even read his poetry and debated philosophy in the *altis* there. We can almost imagine a scene in which he pleaded in vain with a committee of Elian elders for the opportunity to tart up the grassy, weed-ridden, and buggy stadium. The Elians did permit Herodes Atticus to end at last the shortage of drinking water which for centuries had been a complaint of the pilgrims to Olympia. He ordered the building of an aqueduct. He was allowed to erect a building called the Nymphaeum where one branch of the aqueduct disgorged at the north wall of the Altis. It was a semicircular marble structure, domed, but open on one side. There were basins, columns, allegorical reliefs, and festoons in stone and gilt. The Nymphaeum held statues of the Roman imperial family as well as of Herodes Atticus and his wife. The architecture was showy and did not harmonize with the older structures on the site.

Some of the earlier Roman emperors had indulged in sport. As an old man, Tiberius (r. 14–37 A.D.) avoided public appearances, but as a youth he once won the four-horse chariot race at Olympia. A passionate fan of the Olympic Games was the Hellenomane Nero. It suited Nero's convenience that a unique, out-of-schedule, staging of the "Olympic Games" be held to fit in with his tour of Greece in 67 A.D. Nero himself entered in freshly established competitions for actors, heralds, and the playing of the lyre. And he himself drove in two- and four-horse chariot races. Another especially instituted event, the progress of which must have so ostentatious as to confound the eyesight of the spectators, was a race in which the emperor drove a ten-horse chariot. One must question whether it was even possible to get ten horses simultaneously to round the posts at the end of the hippodrome. To the surprise of no one, the young emperor was uniformly victorious, as musician or tragedian or athlete. A later generation of Olympic officials ordered Nero's name removed from the victor's lists and annulled the Games ordered by their bribed predecessors.

Nero's enthusiasm for Greek athletics found outlets in Rome itself. He provided olive oil and special skin powders for his athletic hangers-on. He attached a gymnasium to his public baths. In 69 A.D. the emperor initiated the "Neronia," a completely Greek-style athletic festival in which he urged Romans to compete. The historian and critic Tacitus (55–117 A.D.) later condemned such careless tampering with Roman tradition. In a period of moral uncertainty young men were, he claimed,

corrupted by these outlandish importations into becoming devotees of the gymnasium, of luxury and of unnatural vice. The next stage would be that they would be compelled to strip naked, put on boxing gloves and practice that form of exercise instead of war and arms.

Nero was not the first or the last to attempt to establish regular sporting festivals intended to monumentalize emperors and their deeds. After his decisive victory against Antony and Cleopatra at the battle of Actium in 27 A.D. Emperor Augustus initiated "Actian Games" at newly founded Nicopolis Actia in northwest Greece. For a time in the Mediterranean the Roman festival rivaled the importance of the Nemean and Isthmian Games, though not those at Olympia. Augustus also established an "Actia" in Rome itself and attempted to replace the centuries-old policy of reckoning time in four-year periods called "Olympiads." Augustus preferred "Actiads." Later Emperor Domitian (86 A.D.) initiated a festival called the "Capitolia" wherein the victors received crowns of oak, the symbol of Jupiter Capitolinus. In addition to these imperial indulgences, wealthy provincial Romans sometimes set up endowments for periodic sports meets which featured Greek events.

Surviving Roman architecture, inscriptions, and literature all suggest that throughout the Imperial period many Romans either indulged in or favored Greek sport. Some of this enthusiasm, like that of Emperor Marcus Aurelius, was probably a stylistic aspect of ruling-class philo-Hellenism. Latin literature contains metaphors referring to the tensions of foot races and wrestling and boxing matches. Vergil was obliged to include sports competitions in the *Aeneid* just as Homer had. But we must conclude that sport as the Greeks had known it never acquired authenticity in Rome. Greek athletic meets were favored by rich sentimentalists or by politicians or entrepreneurs eager to offer entertainment that was fashionable and popular. Professional Greek athletes most often competed as time-filling performers in larger festivals dominated by chariots, maddened wild beasts, and by gladiators with whom Greek athletes were most often compared.

In discussing Roman public festivals we come to some strange aspects of their culture. This requires some special attention to chariot racing, gladiators, and the baths. These three peculiar areas of fascination are inseparable from a discussion of Roman social policy, theater, and architecture. We must expose some strange aspects of Roman character such as their boredom, love of luxury, and cruelty. And with our treatment of these topics we approach the decline and end of Roman greatness.

Chariot racing as a technique and as elaborate theater was already well established in the eastern Mediterranean when the Romans took it up. They may have learned to train the team of four horses pulling a light cart and driver, which they called a *quadriga,* from the Etruscans. Though the Greeks had frequent local races besides the regular chariot competitions in the dozens of regular festivals, it is noteworthy that we have no surviving examples of a Hellenic race course or hippodrome. With characteristic rusticity the Greeks merely employed an open field and installed starting gates and rounding posts. This would not do for the Romans. In the centers of their cities they built hippodromes with spectator stands of wood or masonry, barriers to protect the onlookers and a long *spina* down the center of the course to separate coming and going teams. There were also plenty of decorative statues, banners, and obelisks plundered from Egypt. In present-day Rome one can still see all of the vast *circus maximus,* which was first laid out by Etruscan kings. It held a quarter of a million onlookers and is the most capacious sport facility ever to have existed. The *piazza Navona* in Rome is the site of another hippodrome and retains its ancient shape to the present day.

Hippodromes, like theaters, forums, colosseums, temples, and baths, were considered normal accouterments for a Roman city. In the capital itself, the popularity of chariot racing led to professional associations of drivers. Rival stables attracted fanatical and antagonistic allegiances. The colors of the blouses worn by drivers had taken on symbolic though ephemeral meanings by the first century A.D. We read in the records about the fans of the Reds, the Whites, the Golds, and the Purples. But two rivals were most persistent: the Blues and the Greens. The complex, passionate, and protean symbolism and enthusiasm attached to these colors led to portentous and occasionally ominous interpretations of race results by the enormous numbers of spectators. Rival politicians, mutually damning religious sects, feuding clans, or antagonistic classes, might attach their loyalty to one color or shift to another. This odd, but nevertheless real, rivalry led to bribery and riots that regularly disrupted urban life. Sometimes famous drivers or whole stables would abandon their traditional color to adopt that of their erstwhile enemies. To describe what "Blue" and "Green" signified in terms of ideological or political or social issues at one time might be inverted one or two generations later. These intense two-party allegiances became aspects of Roman public life that reached far beyond the race courses and outlasted Rome itself.

It may be generous to consider the preparation of the gladiators and their demonstrations within the embrace of sport. A frequent assumption by the historians (and sometimes of the Romans themselves) is that the Romans adopted gladitorial shows from the "cruel" Etruscans. However, it is worth noting here that human sacrifice has been ritualized by many sophisticated societies including that of the pre-Classical Greeks rhapsodized by Homer. In the Peloponnesian Wars Greeks often slaughtered Greek captives. Alexander the Great took few prisoners. Hellenistic boxers and pancratists whom the Romans encountered were usually brutalized professionals. What may be unique about the Roman gladiatorial contests is their extravagant realization and almost unquestioned acceptance.

In 264 B.C. the sons of one Brutus Pea presented three simultaneous gladiatorial contests upon the occasion of their father's funeral. We are thus reminded of the funeral games of Patroclus and of a prehistoric Mediterranean custom of fighting ritual battles at the funerals of great warriors. By 216 B.C. we have a record of ten battles fought on one occasion; in 174 B.C. in Rome there was a display of 74 gladiators lasting three days. Greater things were to come.

Even in later Republican days there were special schools to train the gladiators. The recruits were usually psychopaths, desperate slaves, or condemned prisoners offered the option of this trade or torture and death. There was a certain sadistic and erotic fascination on the part of many Romans with the performers. Despite the fact that the gladiators were despised—they ranked in social status with male prostitutes—magical qualities were attached to their appearance in dreams and to the weapons that had inflicted mortal wounds in the contests. An application of the warm blood of a slaughtered gladiator was sometimes thought to cure epilepsy.

The largest and oldest gladiatorial school was at Capua, which had earlier been an Etruscan city, in southern Italy. It was from Capua in 73 B.C. that the brigand Spartacus, who had formerly been a Roman soldier, led the outbreak of gladiators who attracted a sufficiently large number of social dissidents to threaten the very existence of republican Rome. The rebellion lasted two years. It required ten legions to put down and was celebrated with characteristic Roman vitality by the crucifixion of 6000 captured rebels whose displayed corpses lined the Appian way from Capua to Rome.

With as many as 5000 resident trainees, the gladiatorial school at Capua was the oldest, largest, and most prestigious. However, where Roman culture went, the institution went. All this required schools to contain and train performers and amphitheaters to display them effectively. Roman moralists were hard-pressed to justify these displays. Some claimed that distinctive military techniques—those which made legions more maneuverable, lighter and more flexible armor, and the short sword for slashing—originated among the gladiators. Some Romans recommended attendance at the contests as a means of accustoming effete youths to the sight of carnage: They would be more practically prepared for the horrors of war.

That expressions against the displays were rare is just more testimony to their enormous popularity. In the imperial period the frequency and grandeur of the gladiatorial contests and their sponsorship by the reigning emperors increased the honor of the imperial office. A long inscription of Augustus from about 10 A.D. states that in the course of his life this political genius had offered dozens of extraordinary displays which required 10,000 gladiators. Later, a birthday of Vitellius (15–69 A.D.) was celebrated by gladiatorial combats in all 265 districts of the Empire. Trajan in 107 A.D. offered a continuous entertainment for four months in which he equaled Augustus' figure of 10,000 men and added some 10,000 animals. The performances became ever more elaborate. The fighters were announced with fanfares and battled to the accompaniment of flutes, drums, and choruses. Munificent hosts offered sprays of perfume and awnings as shields against the sun.

The climax of the spectacle, of course, was to witness the killing of a human being. Rather than being matched with an equal, experienced gladiators naturally preferred being confronted with a desperate untrained creature, human or otherwise, whom they might use as a toy just as a cat does a maimed mouse. Laggards might be goaded into action by whips or by functionaries thrusting hot irons. Officials dressed as Charon, the ferryman of the underworld, administered the *coup de grace* with daggers. When the victims were at last dead, African boys raked sand over the pools of blood. The corpses were dragged off by more officials dressed as Mercury, who was the guide of souls to hell.

Sometimes the crowd by putting their thumbs up or waving handkerchiefs indicated their desire that the vanquished be spared death. This uncommon, generous act probably shows that skill was a scarce commodity that they wished to see demonstrated again. A fine battle (later to be rehashed by fans) would have equally matched warriors going at each other as they were urged on by their screaming trainers. A trained gladiator was a valuable property. Though the lives of the losers were sometimes spared, it was widely considered a measure of a host's munificence, if he had the fallen gladiators, even the best ones, publicly killed.

Candidates for the gladiatorial schools were difficult to obtain and they required long, expensive training. These outlays as well as the treasure expended for lions, elephants, and other wild beasts captured, transported, and maintained in fighting trim must have played some role in bankrupting the Empire. Nevertheless, the shows were integrated into Roman domestic policy and resisted eradication even when most upper class Romans were Christian. In about 400 A.D. St. Augustine recorded his horror at his friend's enchantment at an arena. Shortly afterward the gladiators were indeed abolished, but the shows with animals continued and were not officially ended until 681 A.D.

A generous definition of sport might include the Roman baths. Long before the days of Roman greatness, steam huts and soaking pools were known in Persia. Some of the soldiers of Alexander the Great liked them and, upon returning to Greece, arranged that warm baths sometimes be attached to gymnasiums. But the Greeks tended to view warm baths as an effeminate indulgence and (as has always subsequently been the case) bath attendants as rogues. The tough republican Romans had outdoor swimming pools and small private baths. The change from a technique for private cleanliness to public pleasure came slowly. Plumbing technology, the versatility of brick and mortar construction, and the taste for luxury eventually made possible establishments with rooms of hot dry air, steam chambers, and warm and cold plunges.

It was not until later imperial days that the provision of grandiose baths, like the gladiatorial shows, became politically necessary to purchase public support, not only in the capital city but also in the provinces. Where the Romans went, the baths went too. The first great public *thermae* in Rome were built by Agrippa in 21 B.C. The expenditure of Nero (ca. 65 A.D.) and the spendthrift Commodus (189 A.D.) show that in matters concerning the baths as well as the circuses Roman rulers felt compelled to compete with and surpass their predecessors. The grand remains of the baths of Caracella (ca. 217 A.D.) and Diocletian (ca. 302 A.D.) are splendid even today, but the ruins only hint at their immensity. Earlier, they covered whole acres. These complexes were veneered in precious marbles. They contained gardens, gymnasiums, courts for ball games, libraries, great halls for theatrical performances, and little nooks for mutual mischief. The prominence of pleasure palaces and the aqueducts to furnish them in Pompeii, Trier, Byzantium, or any large Roman town boggles the historian's imagination. Large areas of Germany were deforested in order to provide wood for heating the water for the baths. This strange indulgence seems to have been fully integrated into late Roman culture.

Selfish hedonism and sensual license in the baths and the fact that some arenas were sites of Christian martyrdoms may have been the basis of the supposed anti-athleticism of the early Christian fathers. However, some philosophically liberal panegyrists of sport oppose too sharply the contrast between the posited universality and benefits of antique sport and supposedly nonexistent Christian sport. Some modern enthusiasts for physical education claim that sport declined because Christianity is hostile to the body. Though the institutionalized forms of Greco-Roman sport, including the classical athletic program, the circuses, and the baths, almost vanished from Christian Europe we can attribute these losses more to the Christian disgust with pagan festivals than to the Christian attitude toward the body.

The Christians opposed and eventually abolished the public sacrifice of gladiators (who, after all, had souls) and then beasts. Christian theologians did not oppose fitness and cleanliness. The closing of the baths was due more to the breakdown of civic order that fostered the maintenance of the aqueducts. Many of the baths' halls were pragmatically converted to use as churches. Chariot racing continued where settled conditions permitted, and indeed was characterized by new excesses in Constantinople, which became the capital of the Eastern half of the Roman Empire in 330 A.D.

Returning to the Romans, we may survey the literature on sport which they preserved or originated. The very absence of a Latin literature on hunting suggests that they were unusual in rejecting this pastime which has been a distinguishing indulgence of the ruling class in almost any settled society. Some excavated large mosaics in Germany and Sicily show Roman aristocrats hunting enthusiastically. However, these art works may have been inspired by much older models. Though they cherished and indeed fixed the athletic ideal in the visual arts, the Romans scarcely bothered to translate or preserve the Greek training manuals and rule books that were known in the Hellenistic world. Nor did the Romans produce anything like the Pindaric odes to victorious athletes. The appearance of athletic contests in Latin epic literature is probably due to the prestigious momentum of Homeric forms. We do not even have much Latin literature opposing sport. There is, however, a great deal of Latin social criticism against the idleness and frenzies of sport spectators. Juvenal and Petronius wrote polemics against sports spectatorship.

To close this survey of sport in classical times, we return to the most prestigious sports festival in the centuries of Rome's waning glory. We have already seen that wealthy and sophisticated Romans went as pilgrims to Olympia and made gifts of architecture and art. Indeed, the rather austere and very old temples of Hera and Zeus contrasted with the luxurious hotels, dormitories for athletes, gymnasiums, and especially the baths that the Romans added to the site.

During the century before the reign of Augustus, there were no victory statues erected at Olympia, though the site was used and maintained. During the second century A.D. the traveler Pausanias described the architecture and treasures and retold the myths about the origins of the festival—at the time almost 1000 years old. Though the ancient religious ceremonies were cynically observed and the competitions were now spectacles having no connection with the vital spiritual concerns of the Greeks or the Romans, the charm and prestige of the site kept the festivals going. One is reminded of the popularity in the twentieth century of the performances of the Passion Play at Oberammergau.

Nero made some raids on the statue collections to decorate his palace in Rome, but the attempts of various Roman schemers to remove Phidias' colossal and precious statue of the Olympic Zeus came to nothing. The Olympic Games became part of Roman cultural politics. They took over the responsibility for keeping the site attractive and its managers politically neutral.

The well-armed and envious barbarians who threatened the outer reaches of the Roman Empire in the third century A.D. were less sentimental. Political disorder in Rome itself made it possible for a horde called Herulians to sail in 500 ships from the Black Sea for the Mediterranean. They occupied Byzantium, Corinth, and Argos and sacked Athens in 267. Olympia was threatened and the Elians decided that the stone from outlying buildings should be used to build a fortifying wall and towers to protect the central area with the oldest temples. The Herulians never appeared and the Olympic Games were resumed. However, we have only fragmentary lists of the victors after this time. The last Olympic victor whose name we know was an Armenian prince, Varaztad, who won the boxing competitions in 385 A.D. In 394 A.D. the Byzantine Emperor Theodosius the Great forbade the further reckoning of time in Olympiads and banned the observance of all pagan festivals, which would make the Games of 393 A.D. the last. He also took the gold, ivory, and ebony statue of Zeus to Constantinople, where it perished in a fire in 476 A.D.

Subsequent, additional bannings of the Olympic Games indicate that some sort of athletic meets may have continued there, very likely as manifestations of local nostalgia. But barbarian invaders repeatedly plundered Olympia in the fourth century. There was pressure from Constantinople to obliterate the lingering prestige of paganism by commanding the Christianized Greeks to destroy the remaining pagan holy sites. Earthquakes in the sixth century toppled the columns of the Temple of Zeus. Later the river Alpheas changed its course to wash away all of the hippodrome and to cover the rest of Olympia with layer upon layer of clay. Scholars in the middle ages could read some classical literature about the ancient Olympic Games, but their site was a mystery.

[5]

SPORT IN PRE-INDUSTRIAL
HIGH CULTURE

The cultures discussed in this chapter flourished apart from the chronological narrative scheme employed in the remainder of the book. Though well-integrated into the non-Western societies to be surveyed, the sports discussed, like those of the Egyptians, were particular adaptions to or reflections of certain economic and political realities. When the realities changed, the sports changed.

For one non-Western high culture, that of pre-Meiji Japan, there are a lot of visual and literary sources. Also, many of the venerable Japanese recreational forms have been maintained by antiquarian patrons and performers as Japan has rapidly modernized. What may appear below to be a disproportionate amount of attention given to classical Japanese sport is based not simply on the relative certainty with which one can describe it. Certain characteristics of pre-modern Japanese sport indicate the existence in Japan of structures in society that long underlay the extraordinary success with which the Japanese adapted to the social requirements of industrial production. But we must return to our narrative.

It seems that the complex culture along the Indus River during the fourth to third millennium B.C. had little enduring influence on the immensely various, resilient cultures that later developed on the Indian subcontinent. Archaeologists have found seals at Mohenjo-Daro and Harappa with scenes of bull fighting and acrobatics that tempt one to see parallels with the sports of the sophisticated Cretans who, like the people of the Indus, also had unwalled cities and whose political structures collapsed suddenly. The Aryan conquerors who in roughly 2300 B.C. destroyed India's first civilization brought with them the chariot and horse racing which, as in Greece, may have been popular spectator sports afterward. Indeed, in the Vedas, the great epic and instructional poems of these people, chariot racing is described in terms not much different from those of the West. The determination of winners (as in Greece) was attributed not to the skill and power of the victors alone, but largely to astutely applied magic, sacrifice, and prayers. Unfortunately for us seekers of certainty, the Aryans and many subsequent rulers of parts or all of India rarely built or sculpted in stone. If they had, we would have much more evidence. By employing the citations or allusions in the Vedic literature, we can deduce that at least some inhabitants of ancient India competed with the lance, mace, and dagger. Furthermore, the early inhabitants of the Indian subcontinent practiced hand-wrestling, boxing, swimming, diving, dancing, and dozens of activities we specify as sport. The epics that give us evidence for this existed for many centuries in orally transmitted forms before they were first recorded about 500 B.C. Generations of Indian bards before this time lacked the western obsession with chronological precision and we cannot know what parts or aspects of the epic literature are historical at all.

Little is accomplished by being exegetical with the sparse and equivocal archaeological and literary evidence for specific playful, physical educational, or paramilitary activities of ancient India. There are certain peculiarities of Indian culture that deserve attention, however. The caste system isolated and preserved a great variety of traditional mores and therefore a great variety of leisure and recreational activities. Novelties in games or competitions have been and still are accepted in India only by narrow sectors of the population. It is remarkable, for example, how readily the Indian princely class adopted polo and the blood sports of the British raj in the nineteenth century. And, we might note how, vice versa, the British rulers became passionate big game hunters just as the princes had long been expected to be. Wealthy Indians also became and have remained infected with the English enthusiasm for thoroughbred race horses. The levels of indigenous society that furnished high-level bureaucrats took to cricket. The Sikhs, members of a Hindu sect who regularly gravitated toward careers as policemen and soldiers, became supremely expert players of field hockey.

More in harmony with the passive other-worldliness of the Indian masses are physical activities that are private and demand extreme self-discipline. Some peculiar Indian physical activities are intended to help the individual to subjugate the external aspects of existence to the spiritual and timeless. Some yoga exercises such as the lotus position or standing on the head may appear to westerners as if intended to be showy, but the object of these and more spectacular exercises is to transcend the body by conquering its everyday limitations. Similarly, certain ancient Indian breathing exercises have as their purpose to deprive the brain temporarily of oxygen and so to induce visions of a universe apart from and superior to the ordinary world of the flesh. However fetchingly sensual classical Indian dance may appear to the western observer, its practitioners are not celebrants of sweaty physical effort, but communicators in refined symbolic language of traditional myths. It might be observed here that many esthetes of our own time analagously misobserve sun-illuminated medieval European stained glass windows. Most traditional Indian dances, like the windows at Chartres, are intended to be more vividly instructive by obliterating with beauty the spectators' mundane critical intelligence.

Many of the observations about sport in India also hold for the sports of ancient China. Lacking evidence to the contrary we may assume that sport was various among those classes having occasional or irregular leisure. Unlike the bards of India, Chinese historians were civil servants who had a strong chronological sense. They were directed to write official histories to prove the legitimacy of the regime that provided them with their rather pleasant jobs. As a result, written Chinese history, of which we possess a great deal, was concerned almost exclusively with the classes that made political and administrative decisions. Ancient Chinese art deals somewhat with military subjects, but more typically is concerned with exquisite landscapes and the details of a comfortable life, thus reflecting the scope and refinement of the civil-academic class from whom weapons and real power were barred. In Chinese art and literature there are only accidental, occasional references to folk dances and the keen interest of the peasants and villagers in wrestling and juggling. Here again, the unusual obscures the everyday.

In a description that is so brief as to be possibly disrespectful of a culture of great age and enormous cultural creativity, we might look at persistent themes and then some exceptional elements in Chinese sport. The millennia of stability in the class structure of China encouraged and preserved many individually distinguishable recreations or games that may have had similarities with practices elsewhere or even within China, but which developed delicate differences in order to designate and to preserve social distinctions.

A never-ending and dominant concern of China's rulers was (and remains) the task of maintaining the vast, relatively open frontiers of the enormous empire. A military threat or an invasion would rouse the generals to adapt and improve on the effective techniques of her less refined enemies from the cold North and the windy West. The military horse figured large in Chinese recreations, poetry, and art. As was the case all over Asia, seeking out and slaying the tiger (so potent a symbol of murderous anarchy) maintained the fitness of participating horses and riders. The conquered beast or other big game when displayed as a trophy was forceful propaganda to the common (that is, non-horse owning, non-arms bearing) people that the usually idle and isolated military class was protecting them from the chaos that the great beasts signified.

The fascinating question as to what people invented the horse blanket, the stirrup, and the bit is one that need not concern us much here. Like most innovations in horse management, they probably first appeared on the steppes of northern Persia. In any case, the employment of these tools spread throughout Eurasia between 400 A.D. and 900 A.D. Everywhere these techniques for better control of the animals led to public demonstrations of the new control. The controllers of horses were in control of everything.

The first polo mallets were probably much like the clubs used when running down game from a mount. After the invention of polo (very likely in the third century A.D. when we have our earliest records) it spread wherever fine horses were emblematic of political power. The game was played with varying degrees of costumed delicacy or impromptu roughness. Strikers, balls, forms of targets, and numbers of participants varied. The Chinese game usually was played between small opposing teams of riders who attempted to impel with their mallets a wooden ball through a net-backed hole in some boards supported by goal posts. Sometimes polo was less of a strategic game between teams and more a kind of target practice. Since sport horses require a grand and dependable source of wealth for their breeding, training, and maintenance, the numbers of people who indulged themselves with their use was small except on the great steppes of Mongolia where pasture lands were so readily at hand.

On the other hand the distinctive paramilitary exercise (with far less potential for playful invention, let it be noted) of the ranks in China was archery. Competitive archery has been so common in many societies as to be beneath notice. The composite bow, like the military horse, was a technical advance of critical, almost magical significance. Its importance in war led to its symbolic significance in peace. In China, archery practice was not confined to the free men who were soldiers, but was also recreationally and ceremoniously pursued by some levels of society above them. But the higher classes could not practice the same archery that the common soldiers or hunters did. Over time various kinds of subtly distinguished archery developed. Certain types of bows, arrows, or targets acquired allegorical or ritual meanings and so dignified the users of them. The rough peasants might shoot at squawking ducks or squealing piglets offered as prizes at a local festival. A mandarin might demand a park-like, isolated area for bending his polished bow and induce in himself a ritual trance before releasing the string impelling his straight arrow to the target. He and his companions might compete in the obscure complexity of the poems they wrote about the pleasureable act. For the higher aristocrats there were restrictive contests wherein elegantly costumed contestants shot arrows three times—once forward, once to the rear and once from the side of a galloping horse. As in Egypt there were contests to shoot heavy arrows through pieces of fabric or copper.

Other publicly performed recreations were class specific and class exclusive. A centralized regime with the objects to defend boundaries and to maintain internal stability cannot symbolically reward social disruption by allowing ambitious members of the lower orders to compete in contests of physical skill with their betters. During an early dynasty high ranking ministers used in their bows thongs taken from leopards. This accomplishment would not be compared with the performances of the emperor, who alone used the tendons of a tiger. The bow strings of lower officers came from bears.

The observations regarding class-specific paramilitary competitions and their socially stabilizing importance can be extended to the combative sports in China. Unlike the Greek wrestling, which could be and was indulged in naked by all citizens with a wide range of earnestness and skill, there were many kinds of Chinese wrestling and boxing. Wrestling at village festivals could be lusty and rugged and with rules that were specific for certain regions. But for the coifed and costumed gentleman wrestler, his recreations, like his public life in general, required the mastery of a subtle and exclusive code of behavior. His sports were fastidious with many prohibitions to prevent alike embarrassments to losers and hubris to winners. Indeed, traditional oriental wrestling may have attracted strong fighters desiring to win, but it was very much like dance. We might note here that formal wrestling among the classical Greeks and the performances of world-class figure skating were and are performed to music which heightens the esthetic pleasure of the spectators.

The boundaries that we moderns use to separate "sport" from other areas of human endeavor have been indistinct or not worth noticing in other cultures. The Chinese martial exercises which could be engaged in competitively were at once workouts for fit-

ness, paramilitary gymanastics, preparations for spiritual composure, and of course dance. One form of martial exercise which has
evolved to become democratic and international is T'ai-Chi. But
the popularization has developed in a democratic and international
age. The traditional Chinese had many kinds of (again, class-specific) fitness dances. Some were like acrobatics, and others, when
apparatus was employed, allowed all sorts of dazzling endeavors
which we might sum up as "circus tricks." Then, as now (and
perhaps everywhere and always), circus entertainers performed
from the backs of horses and trained all sorts of animals. They
worked with balanced tables, spanned ropes, spun hoops, and
tossed balls, clubs, and knives. As always the most skilled feats of
a Chinese acrobat are believable (if then!) only in the seeing.

The Chinese kept good historical records. We have, for example, surviving pictures and rule books for a game comparable to
modern golf. It was played for hundreds of years after it was first
mentioned in the sixth century A.D. A 32-chapter manual for "Wan-
Chin" specified dimensions, materials, and conditions for the links,
balls, and clubs, the numbers of players, fouls, as well as the rules
for determining a winner and for punishing losers. It was assumed
that only a gentleman would play the game and the rules warned
against double putting and changing the position of the ball dis-
honestly. The "Wan-Chin" rules tell us that the good or "witty"
player depended not only upon his adeptness with the club, but
the sharpness with which he observed his opponents for the ner-
vousness that made aggressive attacks more effective. Some statesmen became so infatuated with this "golf" game that they neglected their public duties.

There were many Chinese ball or (perhaps more inclusively)
projectile games. As among the North American Indians or the
ancient Egyptians, the balls could be small and hard or could be
straw filled or air-filled bladders. The Chinese invented a projectile consisting of a light copper cone with feathers stuck in its rim.
In other words, it resembled a badminton cock. The object (as in
many descriptions of pre-modern ball games in other societies) was
not to win a contest, but merely to keep the ball in the air or
moving. There were no point systems or defined teams. There
were varying numbers of players who employed various parts of

their bodies to contact the projectile. In northern China there was one kind of "football" that disallowed the use of arms and which served the very practical and necessary purpose of keeping the players' feet warm. Most ancient ball games had few rules in our sense. They were more like our games of "catch" or what American youths do when fooling around with the frisbee.

Though certain Chinese games do suggest the codified team games played for mass audiences in the twentieth century, we cannot push the parallels far. Chinese society was rigid—almost the only possibility for upward movement was within the mandarin-dominated civil service. The ball games, like archery and various martial exercises, were class specific and were performed (if there were audiences at all) before small groups of knowledgeable esthetes. The socially open (for active player and passive spectator alike) mass sports of modern basketball and football are substantially and allegorically different.

The claim might be put forward that the Chinese throughout their long history practiced more sports than any other people. In any case we have indications, some detailed, some fragmentary, of an enormous variety of activities we might call sport. But, as in the case of the North American Indians and the Egyptians, it is probably the fortuitousness of the evidence that gives this impression. For other societies with less a sense of chronological order, less careful observers, and a less respectful climate, the many games, competitions, and ceremonies that absorbed participants and observers and enriched their cultures have all vanished without a trace.

If the recreations of traditional China offer mostly technically interesting parallels with modern sport, in traditional, pre-Meiji (that is, before 1868) Japan, the parallels in society and in sport are more provocative and suggestive. Japanese high culture was an adaptation of the much older cultures of China and Korea. It was much like the uncultured republican Romans' adaptation of the complex of Hellenistic high culture. During the Nara period (646–794 A.D.) the Japanese adapted mainland philosophy, religion, art, architecture, educational curricula, and bureaucratic techniques. For one thousand years afterward, Japanese style—meaning the surface manifestations of Japanese culture—resembled that of China. All the time, however, Japanese geography, economics, and class antagonisms produced a dynamic, unsettled society much different in its essentials from that of relatively stable China.

The economic development of Japan in the period 1000 to 1500 suggests parallels with developments that were taking place in Europe at roughly the same time. There were similarities to European feudalism in that a political system evolved that was based upon the contractual rights to land of the people on it. The military hierarchy was held together (treacherously, as it regularly turned out) by oaths of loyalty. As in Europe, dialectical economic evolution gave rise to towns and to aggressive classes within the towns that did not fit into the traditional systems of creating wealth that were based on the exploitation of agricultural land and its laborers. Neuroticism and discontent among the warrior clans led to chronic internal violence. Continuous destabilizing elements were the sporadic contacts with Europeans which brought in, among other things, Christianity and firearms. Just as the obsessive religiosity of fifteenth-century European art and the sweet charm of chivalric poetry obscure from us the brutality and turbulence of the society that produced them, so do Buddhist and Zen scrolls, spare calligraphy, and the fragile tea ceremony obscure from us the unsettled conditions of pre-modern Japan. Even after the strict, self-imposed isolation of the Japanese about 1630, the ruling cliques (themselves in a continuous, competitive turmoil) were unable to combat the formation of a vigorous, irreverant manufacturing and trading class which developed money and banking, new forms of mass entertainment, and art—for example, Kabuki theater and the mass-produced wood-block print.

Those who have considered the speed and success with which the Japanese adapted Western techniques late in the last century have detected certain suggestive similarities with England in the seventeenth and eighteenth centuries. England was also geographically insular, and also characterized by continuous social violence. And England was the seed bed for the first appearance of that self-sustaining process of creating new wealth which we call the Industrial Revolution.

Aside from some enchanting surface products of high pre-Meiji culture such as the employment of space in two dimensional art, most of the products of that culture have remained exclusively Japanese. This holds true for Japanese sport. Japanese sport has received quite a bit of description, but very little analysis, from even Japanese historians and cannot receive here the attention it surely merits. Nevertheless, based on the small amount of historical literature available to western scholars, we might conclude that because of its variety and certain peculiarities, Japanese sport deserves a close look.

We cannot ascertain which recreations the Japanese travelers brought back from their embassies to the Tang (618–907) Empire in China. We may assume that there were much older Japanese sports which were resistant to modernization. We know that Japanese archers have always gripped their bows on the lower part, while elsewhere in Asia the grip is in the middle. But the Japanese adapted several kinds of Chinese archery competitions, for example shooting for accuracy while riding a horse.

Returning to the horse, its military importance was crucial for 2000 years in the vast open spaces of the Eurasian mainland, especially in China. But in striking parallels to the classical Greeks and the pre-industrial English, among whom the light military horse was rarely agriculturally useful or militarily essential, the Japanese endowed the fast, maneuverable horse with near magical attributes. The Japanese feudal class alone had the land, wealth, or legal right to own horses. They took over Chinese polo, which they played for a long time with only slight variations. Some forms of Japanese polo used a system wherein the balls were scooped rather than struck. In certain festivals warriors also tilted at targets and had horse races along short straightaways.

In the early centuries of Japanese history the landowning and soldiering classes (which in later times were socially separate and distinct) also devised competitive demonstrations for sport horses comparable to western jumping contests. Elegant performances for an elegant public.

Incidentally, modern dressage competitions for horses and riders are usually offered by the very rich for the observation of the very rich. Though modernized by objective point systems, dressage is actually a kind of dance performed within rigidly formalized conventions. Dressage (along with the required routines of competition figure skating) is the modern sport which is most like many traditional aristocratic Japanese sports. In Japanese paintings the horse often appears bathed in an aura of magic that recalls the classical vase pictures and the sculpture of Greek horses as well as the nineteenth-century paintings and sporting prints of English thoroughbreds.

The Japanese apparently did not play the Chinese court ball games in which there were winning and losing teams. But in the tenth century (possibly earlier) the Japanese elegant classes did adopt a Chinese ball game which they characteristically refined. The four corners of a six- or seven-meter square *kemari* field are still marked by willow (southeast), cherry (northeast), pine (northwest) and maple (southwest) trees cut back to be just four meters high. There are eight players, two to a corner. Each kicks a leather-wrapped ball three times and passes the ball to the next player, who then gives his three kicks, and so on. The object is to keep the ball from falling to the ground. This game (but is it a "game" in the modern sense of the word?) became ritualized. Certain families appointed themselves custodians of *kemari* and devised subtleties which only they were allowed to teach others. Among the precious, idle rich who performed in dark, flowery silk costumes, *kemari* became as circumscribed and as exquisite as the composing and writing of 17-syllable poems. Exceptional performances merited immortalization by the chroniclers. A Japanese scholar has found a statement dating from the year 1208 saying, "Kicking has been done 980 times and then 2000 odd times. The ball was as if hung from the sky without any fall to the ground." This may be our earliest numerical sports record, though the statement implies that there were earlier remarkable performances that had hereby been surpassed.

As is often the case in Japanese and in other societies, a game devised for the pleasure of one class can wander to others. The *kemari* masters could not prevent varieties of the game from being enjoyed by samurais, monks, women, and even children. The game faded from popularity only to be revived several times by athletic antiquarians. In our times the priests in some temple courtyards play the game in a sort of esthetic trance.

In Japanese sports groups of enthusiasts showed persistent tendencies to adopt, preserve, specify, estheticize, and refine. This was especially the case with sports that may have had paramilitary origins. I must quote a Japanese expert:

The military arts performed in the second phase of the feudal age (roughly 1573–1867) ran into as many as 60 kinds, of which horsemanship, archery, spearmanship, swordmanship, gunnery and Jujitsu were the mainstay. The archery was branched into more than 50 schools, horsemanship into more than 60, spearmanship into more than 140, swordmanship into more than 150 and Jujitsu into more than 170 (Sasajima, p. 197).

The rules for the correct performance of each of these skills were usually not written, but were passed from one master to another as secrets. A new sport might arise when a great master decided to distinguish his school by varying the feathers on an arrow, the distance of the target from the shooters or the prayers internally offered by a solitary archer before releasing the bow string. Archery could take on particularly complex forms. One contest of marksmanship (or was it horsemanship or a team game or dance?) had three teams of twelve mounted archers each of whom shot at dogs. The blunted arrows had holes in them to produce a desired whistling sound. The rules for *Inouimono* specify the diameters of certain inner and outer boundaries, the precise nature of the surrounding bamboo palisades, and the nature of the sand surfaces. On the scene were functionaries to release the dogs and referees to score the hits. The preparatory arrangements necessary to produce an *Inouimono* performance seem so complex as to try our imaginations, but apparently the performances were not infrequent. It was publicly performed for the last time in 1870 before a visiting American, President Ulysses S. Grant. Shortly thereafter, *Inouimono* was abolished out of consideration for the dogs.

Another form of archery was *Toshi-ya*, a combination of rapid, distance, and accuracy shooting. Championships took place in a particular temple in Kyoto which had a long gallery before it. The object was to shoot as many arrows as possible in 24 hours through a distant 4.54 meter-wide open space between the eaves of the main temple and a gallery. On April 16, 1686 Daihachiro Wasa, a

court retainer of the Kisha clan, made 8132 good shots out of
13,053 tries, thus establishing a record so stunning that it discouraged further attempts. And so, *Toshi-ya* languished and perished
as a sport. But other high-performance archery sports with quan-
tifiable records were devised for men of various classes as well as
for boys.

There is more evidence that the Japanese occasionally quantified
exceptional performances of skill or strength and immortalized
these acts in writing or other monuments. From the late seventeenth century and well into the twentieth century, certain peasants and stevedores gave sideshow performances of their great
strength. Competitions with standardized rice bags, sake barrels,
or big rocks might be held before authorities at certain shrines and
the victor's names inscribed on plaques. As early as 1836 "men of
strength in Edo (Tokio)" were ranked according to their performances with standard weights.

The evidence that some pre-Westernized Japanese adapted ceremonial sports for demonstrations of skill or power verifiable by
numerical specifications suggests the appearance of something we
might call "nascent sports records." It also suggests that there
may have been certain structural similarities between Japanese society and the society of pre-modern England, which provided the
seedbed for sport as we now know it. Some special characteristics
in Japanese sport also suggest that certain prerequisites for modernization were present in Japan long before her striking modernization at the end of the nineteenth century.

The psychological shocks endured by the Japanese after the
coming of Commodore Perry's squadron to Tokyo in 1853 led
rather rapidly to the ending of Japan's isolation. One of the few
traditional sports to survive into the present on a broad, popular
(as opposed to an antiquarian) basis was Sumo. This specialized
kind of wrestling had been performed on an organized basis for
centuries. Sumo selected out practitioners who tended to be fast
moving though grandly corpulent. The occupation has remained
in certain family lines. Sumo fathers encourage their sons to marry
the daughters of other Sumo fathers in the hope of producing a
championship grandchild. Indeed, the devising and preserving of
the distinctive Sumo type suggests parallels with the Japanese ac-

complishments by patient, selective breeding of enormous chry-
santhemums, dwarf trees, long tailed roosters, and the bizarre mu-
tants of carp which we call "goldfish."

In the seventeenth century Sumo was performed before paying
spectators from several classes as a means to raise funds for the
construction or reconstruction of shrines or temples. Sumo made
a rather graceful transition to a professional sport with ancillary
academies, promoters, and lucrative gates. It became the favorite
spectator sport in the vigorous town culture of the later eighteenth
century. Though popularized, Sumo was not vulgarized. The
modern sport retains the ceremony and refinements (the wrestler
must not hurt his opponent) of ancient Sumo.

Judo, it should be noted, is the only Japanese sport that has
become internationally practiced. In 1882 a Japanese professor,
Jirogo Kano, was alarmed at the rapid replacement of the traditional martial arts by European military exercises. Taking elements from an ancient and potentially lethal combative sport, Jujitsu, Kano codified a new and milder form of self-defense that he
called "Judo" which, roughly translated, means "gentle way."

Jirogo Kano wanted his new sport to accomplish a great deal.
Judo was to maintain the essence of the aristocratic martial arts
which were intended to fortify composure, self-confidence, and
patience as well as to promote health and suppleness. But Judo
was exceptional in the Japanese sports context (and indeed in any
sports context except that of modern times) in that it was open to
all the classes. The rankings would be based on results or performances verifiable by judges without prejudices and solely on the
basis of accomplishment. The modern notions of equality of opportunity and of progress were implicit from the start, as can be
seen in the range from white (beginner) belt to black belt ranks,
with classes in competition, certification regulations for teachers,
and even provisions for women.

It is true that in its ceremony and the recommended trance-like
concentration Judo sentimentally recalls certain ancient traditions
of the Orient. But the deliberate contriving of Judo for modern
times is more aptly compared with the purposeful invention by an
American of basketball for comparable reasons at about the same
time. The philosophical underpinning and organization of Judo is

strongly reminiscent of the schemes of German and Swedish ideologues who systematized gymnastics. It is significant that Professor Kano was a traditionalist and a patriot who was roused to action by anger at what he perceived to be Japan's decline—
particularly her military inferiority. Later he urged Japan's adoption of Western sports and became the first Japanese representative on the International Olympic Committee. His career suggests
striking parallels to that of Baron Pierre de Coubertin (1863–1937)
and others who promoted the international standardization of sports
competitions.

If we knew more with precision, we could devote more attention to the sports of Islam. The amazing conquests of the Muslims
in the century following the prophet Muhammad's death in 632
A.D. were to a great extent due to their rapid adaption of massed,
mounted warriors armed with the composite bow. Polo, which we
have already mentioned several times, probably has no date of invention, but is rather a predictable corollary of the need to keep
horses and riders fighting fit.

The various team games played from ridden horses and other
displays of practiced horsemanship that were spread all over the
steppes of central Asia had a common and special basis. The great
Asian plains were unusual (as were the great plains of the North
American West and those of Argentina in the late nineteenth century) in that horses were bred in the wild and were cheap. The
animals were hardy and disposable and so were likely to be employed in risky (especially for the animals) maneuvers by a rather
broad spectrum of the social classes. Elsewhere and almost always
horses have been too precious to be regarded as playthings except
by the very rich.

And so, the center of attention of the horse sports in Muslim
Asia was more likely to be on the keen and enduring rider rather
than, as it was in the west, on the exceptionally bred and trained
beast and its indulgent owner. Horse sports were common beyond
the already vast areas of Muslim control. The rules of the games
(mallets could take a wide variety of forms) and accompanying
ceremonies and costumes were sufficiently specific so that particular games were only locally playable, but polo or comparable

competitive displays of strenuous horsemanship were (and in many places still are) common from Hungary to Manchuria and from Arabia to the Caucasus.

There may have been more Muslim sports than we now know about. The dependence of the sports historian on visual evidence is weakened by the Muslim religion, which has prohibited the use of images. But there still exist ancient polo fields in Isfahan and Shiraz and in other great cities of central Asia. The willingness of some Persians and the Moguls to circumvent the prohibition against images has left us carpets with hunting scenes and ravishingly lovely miniature paintings of games on horseback.

The Muslims, in addition to preserving a great deal of the pagan literature, science, and philosophy that was lost to the Europeans, also preserved the Roman institution of the baths. Though their baths were not of Roman grandeur, the followers of Muhammad were using public baths for purposes of cleanliness, social contacts, and sensual diversion when even wealthy Europeans employed only perfume to combat the human tendency to stink.

Travelers' accounts, some pictorial representations, and surviving folk practices all testify to the keen interest of the Muslims as practitioners and as spectators in strenuous dancing, weight lifting, body building, and gymnastics. We just do not have enough information to fit these activities into the particular and social forms of the Muslim world. We can, however, note that the Muslims deny sports and their pleasures to women.

The analytical historian lacks not for pictorial representation of what looks like the sports of the pre-Columbian Amerindians. However, the apparently rudimentary purposes to which the early Mexicans and Peruvians applied their written languages and the lack of empathy on the part of the European travelers who described their cultures before they were destroyed are hindrances to our own understanding. Perhaps yet more of a barrier to such understanding is the gulf between those high cultures and the ones that have formed us. We stand awed before depictions of intricate astrological speculation, the monuments raised by especially vicious forms of slavery for festively staged human sacrifice. Indeed the sculptures, pottery paintings, and manuscript drawings of what we assume are athletes show them burdened with heavy, fantastic costumes and curiously lacking in joy.

We have some surviving clay figures of vigorous and powerful Mexican wrestlers. Their equipment or costumes suggest the estheticized sport of the Japanese combat schools. We also have many representations of swimmers and of runners who also are plumed, girdled, and loaded down with ceremonial paraphernalia. We know there were Mexican board games that suggest the Eurasian precursors of checkers and backgammon. My claim that juggling and acrobatics may be universal is supported by some frescoes and by the descriptions of some post-conquest travelers to Central and South America.

The most striking and evocative evidences of Mexican sport are the numerous ballcourts and the portrayals of the athletes in the games (if they were indeed that) that were played in them. Several dozen courts have been found in the Yucatan and there were surely many more in central Mexico. The games or ceremonies apparently varied from site to site. The grounds might not be level and the shapes were not necessarily rectangular. The visual evidence has tempted some moderns to see parallels with the court games of our own times. Players with different functions wore costumes of distinctively different configurations and colors. Rings high on the walls of some ball courts remind us of American basketball. The helmets and padded costumes worn by some excavated clay figurines recall the equipment of American football players. In one respect, some players were indeed modern; they used large and small balls that were made of rubber—an invention that altered the Europeans' ball games only late in the nineteenth century. But the games are surely more like the games of the North American Indians of more recent times (indeed, were perhaps ancestors of them) and took place in sacred and not in easy-going circumstances. Other aspects of the court contests suggest the public cruelty of Rome. The scenes of the costumed losers recall the festive executions of gladiators. (We cannot be sure they were losers. In the light of the prestige accorded to some victims slated for ritual execution and cannibalism, perhaps they were winners.)

The broad geographical spread of these ball courts and their inclusion in temple complexes show that they were a public manifestation of sacred life. And Mexican religious life was obsessed (by our standards) with astrology. Some performers represented the sun, the moon, or other celestial forms. If parts of the contests were left to skill or chance, the process and results were interpreted oracularly and provided the priests with hints as to which deities should be satisfied in order to guarantee the orderly progress of the seasons, to secure good harvests, and forestall the ineradicable terror of social chaos.

As in other cultures, we should not jump to conclusions on the basis of an abundance of a particular kind of evidence. We must not assume that the rather gruesome reminders of what looks like sport in pre-conquest Amerindian culture can lead to responsible guesses as to what the masses of people in these civilizations did with their free time. All we have are some accidentally surviving remnants of official architecture and decoration. Most of it is grim.

If the Mexicans of the present are anything like the Mexicans of the past, they suggest a different kind of social and religious life. Their free-wheeling and joyous Catholicism, their ravishing, infinitely inventive music, their expectations and reveling in fiestas, and their openness to strangers all suggest that beneath the ceremonialized obsessions of the ancient priestly classes there lay a voluptuous tradition of playful inventiveness in quite another spirit. This happy tradition has not left traces that the historian can work with.

[6]

EUROPE, 500–1750

Attempts to reunite the parts of the Christianized Roman Empire all failed. Stability and literate culture survived only in the East. Emperor Justinian (r. 527–565) residing in Byzantium established political order over Eastern Europe. For long the center of power in Eurasia was the splendid city (later Constantinople, now Istanbul) between the Black Sea and the Eastern Mediterranean. It was not conquered by the Turks until 1453.

The Christian Empire survived so long in the face of Muslim and European threats because of its effective taxation and administration systems and a large army that was alert to innovations in military technology. The official language was Greek and the Eastern Empire governed most of the lands of classical Greece. The great city at the Bosphorus was in many ways comparable to the older capital at Rome whose imperial task it inherited. Both Rome and Byzantium were huge, having populations of close to a million. Both contained a variety of cosmopolitan adventurers and fickle masses of unemployed free people. In Byzantium—even more than in Rome—power centered in the emperor. Alterations in power were the result of court and military intrigue. In both cities public festivals were part of state policy. If Christian dogma in

Byzantium tempered the more lascivious and ghoulish aspects of Roman spectacles, the passions aroused in the hippodromes in the cities of the Eastern Empire probably exceeded in intensity those in Rome.

Chariot racing in the Eastern Empire was technically similar to what it had been among the Greeks a thousand years before. There were events for chariots pulled by especially bred two- or four-horse teams and driven by professionals. The usual distance was seven laps of a roughly 900 meter course. Each lap was essentially two straightaways marked, as all ancient race courses were, by rounding posts. There were hippodromes in all the large towns, but in the capital the setting was especially elaborate. Remotely controlled rows of fountains kept a visual record of the elapsed circuits. The program could last a whole day. The opening ceremonies included blessings by orthodox priests. The emperor himself gave the signal for the first race by dropping a handkerchief. In the intervals between the races there were exhibitions of African beasts, parades of musicians, and decorated floats. There might be interludes with mimes from India, Arabian clowns and acrobats, and huge Scandinavian dancers dressed in animal skins. One impresario had a procession of dogs dressed in the conventionalized costumes of all the peoples known in the world. One dog was known for its ability to find hidden objects; another could select from the enormous crowd that person who was the most avaricious or the most generous. One might admire a gigantic crocodile on a chain or a mule with two heads.

The stables, the drivers, and their training schedules were constant and controversial topics of conversation that were socially sanctioned and that permitted social intercourse across the lines of an extremely complex and rigidly regulated class system. Here it might be noted that in Byzantium philosophical discussion and political activity were scarcely possible for all but a few people. Intellectual life was the concern only of the Orthodox hierarchy whose interest was in stability and self-preservation. In a society where there was considerable wealth, energy, and idleness, horse races are remarkable for the attention and importance placed on them.

The practice in later imperial Rome of identifying rival stables by the color of the jackets worn by the drivers continued in Byzantium. In the hippodromes, certain sections of the stands were occupied by rival mobs of partisans who excited the drivers and who excited themselves with massed, synchronized cheers resembling battle cries. As in Rome, the attachment of theological disputants, craft interests, ambitious families, army corps, or economic interest groups varied over the long run. For centuries the leading colors were blue and green. The passionate rivalries they inspired suggested more fundamental antagonisms. But the anti-Semitic party might in one generation be partisans of a stable whose drivers wore green and then cheer blue in the next. If the ruling dynasty were Blues, a powerful, rival family would be Greens. A rebellious son would as a matter of course become the fan of a color opposed by his father.

In the first centuries of Byzantine supremacy, debates over the true nature of Christ's divinity were so widely attended as to be menacing to political stability. It goes almost without saying that these trivial (in our eyes) debates masked fundamental economic and social conflicts. In the sixth century, for example, the Blues were likely to be orthodox trinitarians, while the Greens were dissident monophysites who held that God had one composite nature. But the party allegiances are more accidental than fundamentally significant.

A climax of this particular rivalry came one day after a period of general unrest. On January 11, 512 fighting broke out in the hippodrome in Constantinople. Subsequently there were riots which spread far beyond the city and lasted for days. Destruction was vast and estimates of the numbers of those killed in the disorders ranged from 30,000 upwards. This was a setback for the most passionately observed official sport in ancient times, but chariot racing went on for centuries more in Eastern Europe and so did the rivalries of the Blues and Greens.

The animals upon which all this attention was focused were a bother and were very expensive to maintain. Nevertheless the sport horse throughout Eurasia was an essential talisman of sophistication and power. These small and delicate horses (ponies by today's standards) could be employed for long and rapid cavalry maneuvers only if the rider was himself small and lightly armored, and rode bareback. The late invention (roughly 1000 A.D.) of the harness, which did not press against the horse's windpipe, delayed the effective employment of the creatures as draft animals.

The aura of splendor as well as the utility of the horse was intensified by several technical developments which probably originated among some people of the Asian steppes, but which were soon adopted by the Byzantines. These were the horse cloth and saddle as well as stirrups, spurs, and bridle bits, which gave the rider much more precise control over the beasts. The use of metal shoes expanded the kinds of terrain and the distances over which a horse could be taken. These technical advances added to the weight carried by the animals and therefore, if taken altogether, would have been only of potential significance had there not appeared the "great" horse.

The first big horses (perhaps it was only one) occurred as genetic accidents somewhere in North Africa or Persia about 300. They were subsequently bred back and their offspring were adopted by the generals of Byzantium who fitted these horses with the new technology for control and who covered the horse and rider with armor. The cataphract, a protected cavalryman equipped with bow and lance, became the bulwark against the more numerous, but lighter cavalry of Europe's enemies.

The technique migrated. In Western Europe the armored, mounted knight became the military and thus the political basis for the imposition of control after the disorder following the disintegration of the Roman army and bureaucracy. Feudalism, which was based upon the submission of a farming population to mounted warriors in return for protection, proceeded unevenly, but was solidly established in northwestern Europe by about 1100. Military men, who alone were allowed to own horses, bear arms, and travel, provided protection against marauders who had regularly thwarted the efforts of peasant communities to plan for the future. Where there were armed knights, lands were fertilized, crops rotated, herds built up, forests and swamps cleared, trading centers established. Thus was established the basis of Europe's prosperity and glory.

In much of Europe the local knight lived in conditions that were but little better (except for his horse) than some of the peasants he taxed or otherwise exploited. Indeed, the poor nobleman was likely to be perpetually squeezed for tribute and military service by his overlord and this lord in turn by remote and still more powerful great noblemen. But the more basic division in feudal European society was between the horse owning, arms bearing aristocrats and the fixed agriculturalists whose labor supported them.

The usual histories dwell on those rare occasions when large members of the military caste went off to battle the pagans or to battle assemblies of other knights who were loyal to a rival great lord. Though a warrior was expected to be in a state of readiness for confrontations with his enemies or the enemies of his king, prudent knights carefully avoided battle, since a contest could result in the knight's death or, almost as bad, the loss of his horse and equipment. So, in order to make clear their menacing power to the fixed population and to maintain or advance their prestige among their peers, members of the aristocracy, perhaps more subconsciously than otherwise, developed distinctive and distinguishing paramilitary sports: the hunt, the joust, the tournament, and the duel.

It should be noted that whereas feudalism took root in a primitive, rural economy with local jurisdiction, the resulting stability encouraged an inventive and expanding population on fertile land. New techniques in agriculture and manufacture and the flourishing of new trades gave rise to occupations and groups of people who were not adequately encompassed by the political theory of feudalism. Europe's intrinsic wealth in minerals, soil, and people and its social dynamism formed a richly various kind of new high culture. At any time after 900 or so, European culture was much different than what it had been a half century earlier or what it would be a half century later. New means of creating wealth, new classes, new ideological viewpoints and new arts were absorbed, if not always harmoniously, into the old political forms. Political unity was never achieved over any large area for long and so stultifying political and social conformity was never imposed or even expected by medieval Europeans. The hereditary aristocracy could continue to extract and enjoy wealth created by the efficient peasants on good land in a climate that permitted useful labor almost the year around. Less oppressively and less efficiently, the crafts-man, trading, and managing classes were also taxed to support the feudal system. The preservation of learning and the advancement of philosophy were due to the monastery schools and universities. However, the aristocrats remained the patrons and inspirers of courtly poetry, formal music, and the prestigious arts. The feudal caste maintained its political hegemony over Europe long after the dissipation of the gloom and disorder that was basis of its assump-tion of power. Mounted knights were themselves outdated by the evolving use of disciplined infantrymen armed with pikes or long-bows. Firearms made the cataphract a clumsy anachronism. Though feudalism was supposedly abolished in England in 1662 it was not done away with legally until 1789 in France and 1861 in Russia. Europe's aristocracy dominated international politics until 1914. The fleet, glistening sports horse, the magic beast that had legitimized power in Egypt and in Greece and which identified and circumscribed power as Western culture matured has even in our days not lost its effect as a talisman of the rich and mighty.

Throughout the medieval and early modern periods, ever more powerful supra-local authorities sought always to preserve the mil-itary men and supplies they could draw on by forbidding and pun-ishing local wars. Constricted opportunities for military adven-tures led to the proliferation and elaboration of the knightly recreations.

The heavily taxed, sullen, but defenseless peasants probably saw the members of the aristocracy most often (or in any case, most vividly) when they were hunting. In medieval Europe (as earlier in Egypt and China) the hunt became elaborated into a semi-for-mal public performance covering an enormous area. The running down of a stag or a fox might be the climax of an organized hunt, but the social institution was an official gathering of like minded people who indulged in the conspicuous comparison of costly horses, dogs, arms and costumes—all of which validated status within the hunting class. The exquisitely fashioned rifles with in-lays of gold and nacre that one views in our present museums were not made merely for shooting, but were utensils for demonstrating the taste, ready wealth, and therefore relative rank of their posses-sors. The hunt could be and was justified as an institution for keeping the hunter and his mounts in fighting trim. But we can well imagine that the aroused hunter, shouting with pleasure as he raced in glittering costume across the peasants' fields on his snorting mount, was a terrifying sight that demonstrated to those less fortunately placed that the object of the hunter might as easily be a dissident human as a frightened fox.

Leisured Europeans hunted with horses, dogs, hawks, and falcons. The medieval sportsman probably hunted with companions who spoke his local vernacular. Some cosmopolitan hunters, however, commissioned Latin literature on the hunt. Much of this writing was of a veterinary sort dealing with the breeding and maintenance of sporting horses and dogs. A sort of climax was reached with *The Art of Hunting With Birds* (*De arte venandi cum avibus*), the product of 30 years of part-time work by one of the most accomplished persons ever to leave his mark on our records. This man was the Holy Roman Emperor Frederick II (born 1194, r. 1220–1250). His great book on falconry has not come down to us in its original form, but one copy, the "Mazarin" manuscript, has 589 pages. Frederick II wrote of his fellow falconers: "Of those who follow this art there are some who practice it neither to satisfy appetite nor for the sake of gain nor even for the joy of the eye, but only for the sake of having the best birds of prey which shall bring them surpassing fame and honor, and take delight in this, to have good birds."

Significantly, we have almost no literary records of fishing. Angling was either a degrading trade or, if pursued leisurely for pleasure, was done silently and was believed to be worthy only of classes who did not write and were not written about. Izaak Walton's *Compleat Angler* (1653) was the first book by a literary artist to treat sport fishing as something that was possible to do elegantly.

Similarly, though we have many medieval pictorial representations of swimming and though we must assume that outdoor swimming was pursued as a means of survival as well as a pleasure, we have little to show that swimming was taught, perfected, or competitively pursued until late in the Renaissance. With the foundations of a tradition of theoretical literature on ideal forms of education we have some praises of swimming as a conditioner of the body and some attempts to arrive at ideal forms of swimming. The early literature on swimming seems to have developed apart from swimming pools or even many swimmers. Swimming theory was a development comparable to the analytical speculation that was simultaneously concerned with ideal systems of gymnastics. It was a long-lived intellectual trend, the harvest of which would come only in the modern period of Europe's history.

In many places in Europe the ancient baths survived and some medieval towns built new ones. But the baths were intended primarily for cleanliness and cures. Loose and lascivious people went to certain baths for contacts and if pleasures were to be obtained there they were concupiscent and not athletic.

Johan Huizinga, the medieval historian and the important philosopher of play, has claimed that the real sport of the medieval aristocracy was war. However, even Huizinga would have to acknowledge that wars were infrequent. Few people spent any significant part of their lives in real war. Even in protracted wars the severe sufferers were likely to be those whose lands lay in the paths of plundering armies. It might be more accurate to say that the sport of the military class was ceremonialized *preparations* for war—which was what the tournaments were.

A practical justification for tournaments was that they kept horses and riders in fighting trim. But jousting also allowed rivals to settle disputes in ways that lessened the risk to the disputants of the loss of horse and equipment which were the foundations of high social status. These festivals were taking place in France soon after the establishment of feudal order in the eleventh century. Their origin was practice combats between two knights. The combatants fought within the lists which were barriers enclosing a field. A tournament, properly speaking, was an encounter between two groups of knights, but the term could be applied to a large festival as a whole which might last several days. The heavily padded, ribboned, and plumed warriors rode at one another along a barrier, parallel with the spectator stands, that prevented the horses from colliding. Each rider held before him a lance and carried a sword. The object was to unhorse one's opponent with the long tilting spear.

The formal tournaments became laden with ceremony that consumed ever more time, energy, and money and was ever more lavishly staged. Indeed the preparation for them dominated the lives and consumed the treasure of many aristocrats. They were usually held at the invitation of a great noble who provided the lists and the spectator pavilions for personages. There might be a "queen of beauty" and her court selected specifically for the occasion. Trumpets (an instrument whose employment was forbidden to persons not of noble birth) announced the jousts and there were lots of musicians to provide for the intervening dancing and banquets. Like the knights and their families, the officials and spectators competed within *their* circles in the gorgeousness (and therefore expense) of their costumes. Jousting led to a steady demand for costumes that were protective and functional as well as new and splendid. The tournaments supported a whole industry of designers, craftsmen, and purveyors. The costumes of textiles have perished, but many of the costumes of metal have survived and are common museum accoutrements that remind us of the intricacy and fantasy of medieval fine workmanship.

The great tournaments were subjects for exquisite paintings, tapestries, chroniclers and poets. Chivalric love stories, another preoccupation of the military caste, could have their climaxes in jousts where supplicants for favors from a fair lady and thus their amorous fates were determined by the results at the lists. As in the Homeric contests, the outcome of a ritual battle (and not only at the tournaments) was often seen as the judgment of God. Strange quasi-Christian rituals were added to preparations and unfoldings of a tournament, even though Christian theologians condemned the tournaments as pagan, vain, and murderous.

But as early as 1184 Frederick Barbarossa staged an imperial festival in Mainz at which there were claimed to be 40,000 knights. The most ornate of all tournaments took place in June of 1520 when King Henry VIII of England met King Francis I of France at a large open space in northern France. The kings of the time could never joust against one another because of the fear that political status would suffer from the oracular importance attached to a defeat. In any case, "The Field of the Cloth of Gold" lasted almost three weeks. Henry stayed in a temporary "castle" provided only for the occasion. There were 2800 tents for less distinguished participants. Gold fabrics and ornaments were given, received, and displayed by knights and ladies who jostled with mountebanks and vendors of all kinds. On the occasion, conspicuous expenditure was more important (and more memorable) than the many ritual combats which were theatrical (though still risky) evocations of an age and a class whose days were numbered. This grand international festival was anachronistic, outrageously expensive for all concerned, glorious, and silly. But it made a great impression on the age and was less damaging to social order than an equivalently expensive war would have been.

The great tournaments could be splendid and enormous because the class preoccupied with them was rich and cosmopolitan. The rules or standards of behavior of the aristocratic class were similar over vast reaches of Europe. This was most exceptional. The accepted conditions of games and contests have throughout mankind's existence almost always been narrowly regional. Therefore the tournaments of medieval Europe may be compared to the Olympic Games of Antiquity and the football (soccer) matches of the late nineteenth century as exceptional, ceremonialized festivals that identified and reinforced supra-local loyalties or principles.

A less publicly practiced form of combat for the European aristocracy—the only class, we recall, that was allowed to bear deadly weapons—was the duel. This means of settling a quarrel or of deciding a point of honor had no counterparts in classical cultures. The institution may have been an inheritance from prehistoric Europe. The Roman historian Tacitus, in his *Germania*, says that the prehistoric Germans might pit the captive of a hostile tribe against a tribal champion and then view the outcome as an omen for a considered war. Deeply ingrained in pre-Christian European morality was the notion that the Gods favored the brave and strong. Later the wager of battle probably evolved into a form of trial in which it was assumed that the Christian God intervened by giving victory to the more just of two disputants. The judicial duel was permissible throughout European feudal society from Sicily to Sweden and entered customary law. The dueling code became a unique and ineradicable element in European aristocratic culture. The duel between two men fought outside the courts to settle otherwise irreconcilable differences was thought by the class to whom they belonged to be thrilling and correct.

France, whose kings and nobles set so many fashions, became

and remained the land where duels were most frequent. A partial explanation is that the aristocracy there was more numerous, more likely to be impecunious, and less socially mobile than elsewhere in Europe. The duel was quasi-institutionalized in the French fencing schools. Catholic officials opposed the duels because of Christian dogma. Kings opposed them because they were damaging to the officer class and affronts to their authority. But official attempts to stifle the bloodshed were effective only sporadically. Punishment for the victor sometimes meant the confiscation of his lands by the Church. One memorialist (Fontenay-Marevil) recorded that between 1601 and 1609 some 2000 men of noble birth perished in duels. In 1632 in an attempt to make shameful the fashionable vice, two men who killed each other were stripped and hung by their heels for public display on a gallows. But the duels revived again and again in France. Even after the abolition of feudalism, they became frequent in the nineteenth century between bourgeois politicians and the journalists who had attacked their reputations. They used pistols.

In England the duels were less common with the exception of the period during the Restoration (after 1660) when there was an aristocratic reaction of gallantry and loose living against Puritan rigidities. The duel was a frequent theme in Restoration literature and afterward. In the nineteenth century Robert Browning and William Thackeray took duels as literary themes. As in France duels could not be confined to aristocrats and took place among the bourgeoisie too. Until recent times Englishmen have had reputations for being especially pugnacious. The duel in England might have been a much more lethal social institution had it not been for the relatively strong monarchy and a more effective legal system. In addition, as we shall see in the next chapter, some surrogates for duels were sought and found.

Until the first World War duels were authorized by the Prussian army code in grave cases of personal differences. There existed a "board of honor" which attempted to solve the difficulties between two officers, one of whom had challenged the other, before allowing the resort to deadly weapons. But an officer who was not prepared to accept a challenge and fight if the judgment of his regiment demanded it had to leave the German army.

The long history of dueling fraternities in German universities is another testimony to the persistence of formal combat in the European consciousness. It is true that the *Mensuren* or formal duels have been delethalized by padding and restrictions as to the sort of blows that might be struck. They now bear little resemblance to the duel *à outrance*. Point values are awarded on the basis of cuts (*Schmisse*) made. But the student duels still take place in Germany despite generations of opposition at almost every level of authority.

European literature and the pictorial arts were for centuries the possession of the small leisured class and of their religious and bureaucratic servitors. That we have relatively little concrete information about the sports of the trading, craftsman, and peasant classes should not lead us to conclude that they did not play or compete. In almost every society he or she who is strongest, fastest, and most precise or most adept is admired. Recognition of physical superiority in a particular social group can be obtained by superior performance in recognized athletic tasks. The athletic type may be universally admired. As David Hume (1711–1776) noted:

It is certain, that a considerable part of the beauty of men as well as of other animals, consists in such a conformation of members as we find by experience to be attended with strength and agility, and to capacitate the creature for any action or exercise. Broad shoulders, a lank belly, firm joints, taper legs; all these are beautiful in our species, because they are signs of force and vigour, which being advantages we naturally sympathize with, they convey to the beholder a share of the satisfaction they produce in the possessor.

Dance, for example, in all levels of European society has been practiced and has often contained competitive elements that allow the demonstration of universally envied control, agility, and power. Religious or political holidays were the occasions for gatherings of people anticipating spectacles of competitive physical ability. Local or traveling jugglers and acrobats have long been integrated into European cultural life. The ancient tradition of competitive singing in medieval German cities is well known. Richard Wagner's opera *Die Meistersinger* deals with just such a contest. What we now view as strictly sporting events, such as wrestling, ball games, and marksmanship, could be formally staged at holiday festivals. By this we mean that they had some rules and some judges. But the rules were unwritten and so were only of local validity.

Though we may claim that a person of whatever class who had any leisure time to practice was an active sportsman if he performed in public, we must make some important distinctions. Aristocratic sport was cosmopolitan. Aside from messagers, peddlers, and sailors, aristocrats were the only people who traveled. The rules for dueling and the joust were similar in Poland and in Spain. On the other hand, all nonaristocratic sport was local, usually of great age, and of interest only to the folk in the neighborhood. The groups of craftsmen or shopkeepers who assembled for parties that included target archery in the Low Countries or Germany were not interested in competing with similarly placed burghers in a town fifteen miles away. The regional, free-for-all ball games of northern France were not played in the Rhineland, which had games that were generically similar. The wrestlers of one Swiss valley could compete only with their near neighbors. The fame of an exceptional Scottish log tosser extended no further than the range of the dialect he and his spectators spoke. The elaborate horse races and mock battles of various communes in medieval Italian towns were performed only within those towns, not between them.

Most of the Italian cities had yearly festivals which were affirmations of local pride. In many respects the sports displayed were at least outwardly comparable. The horse races of Sienna are still performed in the town's square and are much photographed by tourists. But a large portion of the town's citizenry prepares for and participates in these races because the momentum of their lives demands it. The race is for them and not for the cameras. An interesting example of an annual festival which began in the eleventh century and was still performed in the early nineteenth century was the "Giuoco del Ponte" (Game of the Bridge) of Pisa. Pisa is divided by the river Arno. A team theoretically consisted of everybody on his side of the river, and the actual players were chosen from among them. The players on each side were further divided into six or more companies which contained thirty to sixty "soldiers." Each group had distinctive, colorful uniforms and large silk banners with inspiring devices and slogans distinguishing particular districts of the city. Preparatory costume-making, banquets, drills, and processions—mostly local, some city-wide—occupied the months before the actual "ponte," which took place on January 17. The site of the mock battle was a bridge over the Arno. The warriors were padded. Their armament and protection was a light, long shield strapped to one arm. The object was for one team to reach the other side. The time allowed for the game in the seventeenth century was about 45 minutes; earlier it had been longer.

The teams clashed and the whole town cheered them on. Swimming combat continued in the Arno when combatants were knocked off the bridge. When time was called judges determined who had captured hostile territory and thus which side of the city won. Then the victors abandoned themselves to delight and unrestrained mutual admiration. The losers also feasted joyously and began planning for next year.

In Northern Europe the civic festivals of the non-mobile, non-peasant classes were comparable, but were more likely to focus on various contests in marksmanship. The archery contests had origins in attempts by regional authorities to establish popular militias made up of practiced bowmen. In England, and in Flanders, particularly, it was assumed that the best defense a central authority could have against a mounted army was a large corps of practiced yeomen and marksmen. But the archery contests took on a momentum of their own and from the late fourteenth century spread throughout the German speaking countries as *Schüzenfeste* (shooting festivals). And, like the civic ball games and horse races of Italy, there were occasions for gathering together, dressing up, side shows, speechifying, and especially overeating and drunkenness with one's own kind. Victors and prizes were more the occasions for festivals than the objects of it.

The crossbow, a later development and a more expensive instrument, tended to identify people with higher status than those who used the more traditional bow. But a wide range of classes overlapped in this festival. Some in Flemish towns were widely advertised in advance and drew great throngs of people from a large area. The festivals were durable. Belgian and German immigrants to America in the early nineteenth century brought their archery festivals with them and they survive rather feebly in the northern middle west. The "turkey shoots" of the American rural South may have a connection with marksmanship contests of late Medieval Britain.

There were many comparable civic festivals which the local citizenry anticipated with excitement and which were locally specific. These cyclical occasions provided for what may be near universal desires to "dress up" for some partly tamed aggression and some participatory drama without a known conclusion. The European civic contests may be loosely compared to the athletic festivals of the classical Greeks and the circuses of the Romans and the Byzantines. However, in the towns of medieval and early modern Europe the civic festivals tended to institutionalize only local loyalties by a settled population. The "ponte" of Pisa was, necessarily, only playable (fightable?), there.

Comparable to the urban mock battles are the peasant ball games which were probably even more common, but for which we have only scraps of evidence. So natural were these competitive meetings that only exceptionally were they noted—usually by an effort of some authority, civil or ecclesiastical, to regulate them. Sometimes the ball games are mentioned because they did *not* take place owing to a plague, famine, or peasant revolt. We know, for example, that on Christmas day or Mardi Gras the peasants of neighboring villages in Normandy and Brittany regularly met for confrontations in open areas to kick, throw, or smuggle inflated animal skins to the "enemy's" goal. The goal was some point, line, area, or hole agreed upon in advance that was separated from the friend's goal by distances as great as a mile or more. Teams might number dozens or hundreds. Indeed, victory sometimes came to the team capable of mustering overwhelming numbers. Sometimes the "ball" (often a pig's inflated bladder) was advanced by clubs, and sometimes the object could only be kicked. Rules tended to be fixed in tradition, but were not important anyway. The anticipated fun was in the rough and tumble melée itself.

In medieval and early modern times wrestling, viewed in general and not in its hundreds of variants, was probably practiced throughout Europe at all levels of society. The youthful Tudor King Henry VIII was a powerful and famous wrestler. The noblemen who wrestled well enjoyed wide fame for strength and agility. However, aristocratic wrestling was probably quasi-private and overlayed with ceremonial trappings just as the martial and equestrian sports were. We cannot be sure that the literate bourgeoisie wrestled much. They were, however, the intended market for some literature on wrestling.

There are many manuscript illustrations of wrestlers. Some of the first illustrated printed books—for example, Fabian von Auerwald's *Ringerkunst* (1539)—were on wrestling technique. Albrecht Dürer made more than 100 drawings of holds that were in vogue in South Germany in his time. Wrestling, besides its controlled homoerotic elements for the participators, provides voyeuristic stimulation (as well as challenges to his virtuosity) for the artist as well.

Yet, despite wrestling's universality, it has, paradoxically, been narrowly local. The breadth and variety concerning the position of the wrestlers at the start of a match, prescribed clothing, permissible holds, the definition of a fall, and time permitted all favored the development of mutually exclusive refinements. The holds could be very restricted. In some parts of Eastern Europe, the fighters clash only with their right arms and attempt to upset their opponent's stance. The slightest movement of a foot may signify a defeat. Most Germans barred all tripping and holds below the hips. In the Swiss and Tyrolese valleys there were until recently many varieties of wrestling called *Swingen* (swinging). Here the opponents wear special breeches to which the holds are confined. There was a similar kind of wrestling in Iceland. Even when wrestling rules were being codified in England in the later nineteenth century there were still "Cumberland and Westmoreland," "Cornwall and Devon," and "Lancastershire" styles in England alone. This was long after England had been transformed and relatively homogenized by the enclosure movement, the Industrial Revolution, and its railroad network. Earlier the rules were more rooted in local customs and therefore were more particularized, various, and, it follows, mutually exclusive.

Peasant ball games and wrestling were distinguished by simplicity of equipment, the ease of gathering contestants and spectators, and the local specificity of regulations. The planning for sports festivals and the heightened, happy emotions of spectators during a meet tended to strengthen community solidarity and exclusiveness. The nontransferability of athletic skills kept the reputations of strong men local. The brawling player-spectators at the ball games opposed players who had nearly identical local and social interests. There was almost no possibility that competition in sporting events (as with other formal social undertakings such as dining or courtship) might take place between members of different classes. Publicly viewed sporting events, therefore, worked to preserve and to celebrate the existing social and cultural distinctions.

The historians of politics and of ideas look to Italy in the fifteenth and sixteenth centuries. There, urban life and international trade had never really ceased after the fall of Rome. Society never became entirely local. If one wishes to use the term "dawn of a new era" to describe the beginning of modern European history, the dawn probably first broke in Italy. However, we must not overstress the abruptness of the Italian novelties. We can use the term "Renaissance" to apply to a period of history between medieval and early modern times. Historians now believe that the Renaissance, even in Italy, marked no sharp break from previously existing modes of life and thought. There was no Renaissance in science or philosophy in Italy and throughout Europe the age remained deeply Christian. However, the visual arts and literature, particularly, were transformed by a keener, more profound interest in the Greek and Roman classics.

The enthusiasm of literate Italians for the classics also provided a foundation for some new attitudes toward individual destiny, government, and education. All these notions accentuated a notorious tendency for Italian political life to be suddenly altered by violence. Communal revolts were common in the cloth manufacturing towns of the north. Local government was subject to seizure by military adventurers or demagogues. It is worth noting here that the great attention given by the early Medicis to tournaments and festivals in Florence was part of their general policy of giving an attractive luster to what was, in traditional political theory, their illegitimate enjoyment of power.

An attempt has been made (and, until now, more or less maintained) in this book to keep separate the often related areas of sport and physical education. And indeed this separation can be maintained for almost all of the societies or movements studied so far. Sport as recreation has customarily grown or altered within particular social classes over long periods of time. Traditional popular sports justify and reinforce the existing position of the class that practices or observes them. However, with the rise to prominence and influence of a group of publicists in the Renaissance, both in Italy and elsewhere in Europe, we enter a new period in sport history. Recreation, games, competitions, and exercise became subjects for pondering, analysis, and debate. The basis was laid by which some sports would be lifted out of their benign evolution and neglect to become civilized and to serve ideological purposes. European intellectuals began to subject sports (like everything else) to examination and to consider them for use.

The first important ideologues of physical education were Renaissance humanists. They were the propagators of a fresh notion of the whole man in which man's body was to be elevated to the rank that his spirit held in traditional Christian theology. The humanists passionately cherished classical antiquity as they understood it. Their utopian object was to approach in their own time a richness of existence equal to the richness of life as it presumably was in Periclean Athens. The new men who would inhabit the world they envisaged would be created by new means of education. Their authorities were classical educational theorists such as Philostratus and Lucian, but most especially Plato according to his recommendations in various books of The Republic.

That enthusiasm for classical art and literature affected the visual arts is attested to by the ravishing productions of Renaissance craftsmen and artists who reestablished the athletic nude as the subject for their supreme endeavors. Regarding the many-sided individualism that found extreme expression during the Italian Renaissance, Jacob Burckhardt (1818–1897), the great scholar of that epoch, and admirer of Renaissance individuals, asked his readers to

consider for a moment the figure of one of these giants—Leon Battista Alberti (b. 1404? d. 1472). His biography . . . speaks of him but little as an artist, and makes no mention at all of his great significance in the history of architecture. . . .

In all by which praise is won, Leon Battista was from childhood the first. Of his various gymnastic feats and exercises we read with astonishment how, in the cathedral [at Florence] he threw a coin in the air till it was heard to ring against the distant roof; how the wildest horses trembled under him. In three things he desired to appear faultless to others; in walking, in riding, and in speaking.

This famous encomium goes on to describe the accomplishments of Alberti (best known as an architect) as a composer of music, as a scientist, an inventor, a theologian, a prophet, and a stylist and wit in several languages. Furthermore

the deepest spring of his nature [was] the sympathetic intensity with which he entered into the whole life around him. At the sight of noble trees and waving corn fields he shed tears; handsome and dignified old men he honored as a "delight of nature", and could never look at them enough. Perfectly-formed animals won his good will as being especially favored by nature; and, more than once, the sight of a beautiful landscape cured him. . . . It need not be added that an iron will pervaded and sustained his whole personality; like all great men of the Renaissance he said, "Men can do all things if they will."

As well as we are able to determine, Alberti and many others after him actually lived as claimed. They were vigorous all-rounders. Some Renaissance intellectuals pondered the means that would allow large numbers of comparable individuals to be created or educated. A few humanists succeeded in applying their convictions as to the proper regime for producing, by means of education, well-rounded supermen.

One of the first to go rather far was Vittorino da Feltre (1378–1466) who established a school for the Gonzaga princes in Mantua in 1423. Wealthy children from other parts of Italy were also admitted. Besides drills in Latin and Greek and lots of history reading, which were all traditionally considered desirable, da Feltre required swimming and running as conditioning exercises. There were also excursions into the surrounding countryside to encourage fitness.

A major contribution of da Feltre and other teachers after him was not merely the adding of deliberate preparation and respect for the body, but the conviction that the integrated training of mind and body should be more than the paramilitary or martial conditioning. Before the educational debates and experiments of the early modern intellectuals, there was scarcely any education in literacy for the children of noblemen. Reading and writing were tools for the labor of monks and servitors. The physical education of noblemen was traditionally limited to riding and fencing, which were essentially preparation for elegant display and threatened violence.

We must make a distinction here between the many projects for education (some of which included physical education and a few of which were briefly in effect) and the sort of education that actually became established in Europe in early modern times. A humanistic education based on classical languages and authors and which came to be expected for the upper bourgeois classes in later centuries was, in fact, not hygienically superior to the more narrowly theological and practical education in the medieval monasteries and universities. The small, exclusive schools for children of the nobility, with their emphasis on manners, dancing, fencing, and ignorance, continued to function long after the class that they patronized was in decline.

Though rather small numbers of any classes actually received much formal education until the nineteenth century and the education that did take place was stultifying, the theorizing was continuous and, as we shall see in a later chapter, had some effect. It was expected that an ambitious philosopher would devise educational schemes that were the logical products of his analyses of the potentialities that lay within human nature and social life. Castiglione's *Courtier* and Niccolo Machiavelli's *The Prince* have to be seen partly in this light. In many of these books there were provisions, some of them specific, for physical education.

The list of northern philosophers who proposed specific regimes for young bodies (as well as young minds) is long and distinguished. Here we can include Martin Luther (1483–1546) who favored certain recreational exercises, especially fencing and wrestling. The Swiss reformer Ulrich Zwingli (1484–1531) proposed specific diets, clothing, and exercise to encourage strength and agility. In the novel of François Rabelais (1490–1553) the young hero, Gargantua, is provided with ideal tutors who, besides lecturing on academic topics, teach the youth how to ride in full armor, vault on horseback, leap from one horse to another, and use the battleaxe, pike, sword, dagger, bow, and crossbow. He must practice weight lifting, wrestling, running, broad and high jumping, swimming, and rowing. The pupil must also correctly climb ropes, masts, trees, and walls. Michel de Montaigne (1533–1592) devoted an essay to the necessity of strength and health in the body for the proper care of the soul. The Englishman Thomas Elyot (1490–1546) proposed an ideal education for young gentlemen in his popular treatise, *The Boke Called the Governour* (1531). Elyot specified regular physical exercise including such activities as heaving the heavy stone and the bar which were folk and not aristocratic exercises. John Milton (1608–1674) in *Tractate on Education* (1644) proposed a Spartan type of physical regime for gentlemen's sons so that they would be "perfect commanders in the service of their country."

Some further points must be made about the literature of educational reform which became popular when the Renaissance humanists employed the printing press and which flourishes still. Fundamental to all this literature is a denial of the orthodox view of man's nature as fixed and essentially evil. All were convinced that latent good might and indeed must be advanced by a proper scheme of education. The existence and continuous enrichment of this theoretical tradition indicates that the nature versus nurture debate is a very old one and that ever more European intellectuals sided with nurture. Man (or at least European man) was, in established theory, ever less condemned by his sinful nature and fixed by the social position of his parents. Experience or, more properly, education could prepare individuals and agglomerations of them (that is, society) for better things. The intellectuals of that and subsequent ages have assumed that the proper spirit was most likely to flourish in a healthy body which, like a noble spirit, was not necessarily a gift of God, but something that could, and imperatively should, be systematically acquired. From the standpoint of medieval Christian theology, and in fact when viewed from most of the systems of thought the world has known, these are radical and arrogant assumptions.

However, we must stress that the educational theorists of the fifteenth through eighteenth centuries had little reason to assume that their projects would take a concrete form. Their essays were speculations, not practical outlines. They were a philosophical-literary form elaborating speculation about human nature. They were a form of social criticism which veered ever farther away from fatalistic Christianity and were also rebellions against established order—whatever it might be. The child was seen as pliable and, conceivably, even good. What paradise might result if children were given educations that fostered health and goodness? As it was, until the nineteenth century, all over Europe the nobles were supervised by subservient tutors and whiled away the hours in little academies. The children of the moneyed classes attended classical gymnasiums or the decrepit universities. All other education was informal.

The observations on the purely literary nature of educational theory as social criticism hold for the products of two especially important philosophers. John Locke (1632–1704) was already well known for his seminal *Essay Concerning Human Understanding* (1690) when he published *Some Thoughts on Education* in 1693. As a theorist of human nature and the formation of character, Locke was probably the most influential philosopher of the "enlightenment" or the "age of reason" in the eighteenth century. His specific proposals for bringing up children correctly were not, in essence, much different from those of many of his predecessors. Locke, like others, urged plenty of exercise, loose clothing, and the banning of sweets from the diet. He recommended irregular meals to train the child to endure hunger. He also proposed shoes with thin soles and purposely made to leak so that the pupil could be toughened to the discomfort of cold, wet feet. It was more Locke's general view that character could and should be formed—rather than his specific urgings—that gained prominence due to his splendid reputation as a philosopher.

Yet more influential was Jean Jacques Rousseau's (1712–1788) time bomb, the educational romance *Emile* (1762). In *Emile,* as in his other writing, Rousseau's social criticism was not offered in veiled or sedate forms. His passionate conviction as to the essential nobility of all men and the corrupting influence of traditional society as well as his effectiveness as a literary stylist and propagandist made him the most influential and destabilizing philosopher of modern times. Rousseau posited a natural man, untainted by the pessimism of Christian (or any) dogma and utterly free from class preconceptions. Rousseau's writing was intoxicating to read. His passionately stated as well as specific proposals for radical political change in *The Social Contract* (1762) had an immense impact on certain political programs of the French Revolution and on radical political reformers thereafter.

In Rousseau's novel the hero, Emile, is an innocent orphan who receives an ideal education in the country from his wise tutor (who is a mouthpiece for the author). The tutor enthusiastically and with conviction prescribes detailed physical exercises but little different than those recommended by generations of reformers who preceded him but adds the anti-aristocratic proviso that Emile must learn a trade "not so much for the trade itself, as for overcoming the prejudices that despise it." *Emile* also contains some rhapsodic praise of nature. Rousseau had a genius for encapsulating his views in memorable language. Some lines of *Emile* deserve quoting here:

The body must be vigorous in order to obey the soul.
A good servant must be robust.
The weaker the body, the more it commands. . . .
If you would cultivate the intelligence of your pupil, cultivate the power which it is to govern. . . .
Give . . . his body continual exercise.

Rousseau's educational ideas, like his ideas about natural law and political justice, had immense consequences, not so much in his own time and not especially in France where he was viewed as an amusing wild man and a curious dilettante who wrote very well. His ideas on physical education had the most impact in German translation and from Germany had an impact that is still dynamically with us. We shall return to this in a later chapter.

In the meantime, European sport in accordance with new social conditions continued to evolve without assistance or much notice from intellectuals. Peasants who were restricted in their movements continued to find escape from the dreariness of daily life in competitive dancing, foot races, wrestling, weight throwing, and the brawling ball games that had been adjuncts of local festivals for centuries. In many parts of Europe concentrations of free, wealthier peasants were rather common after the fifteenth century. Many could bear some arms and own horses. After jousting died out among the nobility in the sixteenth century, there were periodic rustic tournaments in many places, some of which have survived until recently in Eastern and Southern Europe. The costumed participants rode their work animals to tilt at targets rather than at each other.

The immense impact of King Louis XIV (1638–1715; r. 1643–1715) on his times extended far beyond his principal political tasks of taming France's military-aristocratic class and using France's armies to extend France's borders. When young, the "Sun King" was an accomplished gymnast and dancer. He had splendid legs which he displayed in tight hose at every opportunity. He also hunted frequently and enthusiastically. An unshakable object of the King's long reign was to deflect the aggressive ambition of his restless nobility by convincing them to devote themselves to elegant display, intrigue, and service to his, the King's, person. He was successful. The modes established at the palace of Versailles became European modes. High-heeled shoes, brocaded suits, and powdered wigs, by being established as *de riguer*, discouraged rough and ready strenuous sports. Duels were often fought ceremoniously as before, but without sweat, with pistols. The perfumed, artificial modes of the seventeenth and eighteenth centuries made it also a century of personal filth. It was a low point in the history of swimming, the bath, and personal hygiene. This was the elegant, stylized society in which Jean Jacques Rousseau moved as sort of an amusing freak and which he lashed out against in (among his other writings) *Emile* (1762).

Altered forms of society elsewhere gave rise to new forms of sport. In the rich towns of northern Europe, the new classes which prospered had new recreations. For a while tennis was a rage. The various kinds of European "real tennis" were probably refined descendents of various ball-and-bat games which may be as old as society itself. But they were different. The European games of the eighteenth century were more like our various handball and racket ball games than our present "lawn tennis," which developed very quickly in Victorian England. We possess some stringed court rackets of the fourteenth century and know that there were established forehand and backhand strokes. Teams played more often than singles or doubles. Tennis was at first assumed to be a "royal" game and was played in the moats of castles. Several French kings tried to ban their game as a pastime for priests and the lower orders, but they could not prevent the spread of the taste. The tennis game that became fashionable in the large towns of northern France was played indoors in an enclosed court. The game was called *courte paume* in Paris, though the name, "tennis," is most likely derived from the French command, *tenez!* ("take it!").

In the year 1596 there were 250 courts in Paris alone. Some 7000 people were supposed to be living off the game, including manufacturers of rackets and balls, teachers, custodians of the courts, and professional performers and hustlers. By the early seventeenth century, the game had traveled far from Paris and was played all over northern Europe by urban citizens prosperous enough to pay the steep rental fees for the courts. Then, like so many pastimes adopted by the same affluent classes in society who have puffed up and then abandoned modes in dress, the arts, and ideas, tennis became *démodé*. The courts, which in some cities had been more numerous than churches, were demolished or turned to other purposes. The game survived among a few English enthusiasts who for generations played it on the closely cropped lawns of their country estates.

In no large section of Europe was the aristocracy less influential or the ease of social movement greater in the sixteenth and seventeenth centuries than in the towns of the Low Countries which are now Holland and Belgium. An especially hard winter that caused the Dutch waterways to freeze over brought out great numbers of citizens on their ice skates. The lively panoramas of rich men, poor men, and those in between associating (if not fraternizing) in motion or fallen on the ice were occasions for seventeenth century Dutch artists to immortalize in delightful canvases. The tendency for the ubiquitous team ball games to take on new forms in new social and technical conditions produced some games in Holland that might be forerunners of modern ice hockey.

The game of golf (*kolf*, a club, in Dutch) may have a common ancestor in some games of ice hockey. At some point some Hollanders began knocking a ball for accuracy at a pole or a hole in the ice. Pleasure in the sport was too keen to be suppressed as one waited for hard winters. Anyway, hard winters became less frequent all over Europe in the later eighteenth century. The game could be played in parks. Those eager for distinction and achievement began driving the hard balls over expanses of country. But the game of golf may have existed in simple forms in many places much earlier.

Long before the prosperity of the Dutch and Flemish towns, a driving game was known in Scotland where in 1457, 1471, and 1491 the Scottish parliament passed statutes to restrict its popularity which was supposedly interfering with the practice of much more essential paramilitary archery. Some monarchs took up golf and in the seventeenth century believed it to be especially royal and Scottish. For generations after the union of Scotland and England (1707) an enthusiasm for golf was symbolic of irredentist patriotism. Golf became a fashionable pursuit of wealthy Englishmen and then Americans only after 1880.

For a long period of European history, then, we can conclude here that new recreations and games were harmonious adaptations of new classes to their leisure time and ambitions, and the techniques at their disposal. The traditional and new sports appeared sometimes in their arts and were mentioned in their letters and diaries, but the integrated naturalness of the sports in evolving society caused the sports to be unworthy of careful description and analysis. Chroniclers are attracted to the unusual. Physical education was a lively philosophical and literary topic, but had little effect on actual lives. The impact of these ideas came only in the nineteenth century.

Indeed, sport as we know it has only tenuous connections with the casual, fashionable, and narrowly class-specific and class-stabilizing recreations of the pre-modern Europeans. Modern sport has rather particular origins in particular places and in social and ideological conditions which are the subjects of the next few chapters.

[7]

ENGLAND:
LAND OF SPORT

The changes in English sport in the seventeenth, eighteenth, and early nineteenth centuries deserve detailed examination, because it seems that recreations having some characteristics of modern sport first appeared and found wide popular support there. Sport as we know it appeared in peculiar social conditions and took forms in accordance with the desires for pleasure or display of certain social classes. These modern sports, or more interestingly (and less precisely for the historian) these attitudes toward sport, later evolved more rapidly in America and subsequently conquered the world.

One might, like the anthropologist, suggest the deeply human and the basically social bases of competitions and games or like the chronicler describe similarities in our sports and the sports of people who have preceded us. That is, we can suggest, on the one hand, foundations and, on the other hand, superficial parallels. But historical origins lie somewhere in between and that is why we must look at what was distinctive about English society.

We know that almost all the field events of a track meet were invented by English university students. They invented the running broad jump, the triple jump, the hurdles, and steeplechase

races. They also established the standard track distances. Englishmen set the distances for swimmers, for rowing competitions, and
for horse races of all kinds. By selective breeding Englishmen established the modern race horse and most recognized varieties of
sporting dogs. They built the first sporting yachts, racing sculls,
and row boats for trained crews. They also devised the first football goal posts, boxing gloves, stopwatches, and most other sporting equipment for which they set the earliest standard dimensions,
weights, materials, and so on. Englishmen "invented" (that is,
they first wrote down the fixed rules for games which had been
variously played earlier) of almost all the team games now played
from football (both Rugby and soccer) to polo. So rapid, and more
particularly thorough, have been the advances of these standardized sports and games that it is easy to forget that most of the
events, games, and equipment of modern sport are not much more
than a hundred years old. Some other field events are of Scottish
origins. Until fifty or sixty years ago it was widely assumed that
only English-speaking people could enjoy and achieve distinction
in sports which are now played and observed everywhere.

There are other English innovations that are less concrete and
more difficult to identify than hurdle races, wickets, and single
sculls. Perhaps more indicative of changes in ideas or culture were
such things as handicaps to increase the excitement at a finish line,
odds (as in betting), the concepts of the sporting "amateur,"
sporting "fairness," and the notion of a sports record. Yet more
profound and yet more difficult to dramatize or specify in modern
sport are some conceptual bases, latent within sport itself. These
are conceptions about the correctness of submitting individual wills
to a common purpose and the profits to be gained from long-range
planning—in other words, teamwork and training. All of these
new elements in public life developed amid general approbation
and ostensibly apart from economic and political activity in England at the time, and were thus scarcely noticed by social critics
or, later, historians. It cannot be a coincidence that other fundamental changes with vast consequences also developed and took
on momentum in England in the late eighteenth and nineteenth
centuries. I refer to the Industrial Revolution which was disruptive and therefore well noticed.

This book cannot re-examine the origins of the Industrial Revolution—the work has been splendidly done by whole corps of fine historians. However, it must be noted here that, if economic transformations have social and ideological bases that precede, accompany, or follow them, English sport, because of its subsequent impact, deserves some thoughtful consideration. The value in prestige or price placed upon the results of a horse race or other well-publicized sporting contest is of more than anecdotal interest. The same might be said of gentlemen who ran for public applause, the de-brutalizing of boxing, and the creation of written rules for team games. All of these novelties indicate changes in society and may, in turn, point the way for other changes.

An old and indeed still common explanation for the distinction of English sport is that Englishmen have always been more sporting. This has to be put aside. All societies with some leisure and a festive tradition have had various theatrically offered competitions and games. If one examines the Europeans by class rather than by their location, for many centuries, recreations and games were remarkably similar for similarly placed people from Sweden to Italy, England included. Village football on saint's days was widely indulged in among European peasants. Isolated areas everywhere regularly had festive performances of locally specific wrestling. Until the later Middle Ages, the aristocrats were the only persons allowed to play with weapons. The first fencing manuals were Italian. Later they were in French and German, but all circulated widely.

There are, however, some special English conditions. The Anglo-Saxons were isolated and had a defensible seacoast. The Norman invasion of 1066 was sudden and effective. The imposition of feudalism and central authority was complete. England has since then had unfortified towns, a relatively open interregional transportation system, and aristocratic, professional, and commercial classes that felt themselves to be more English than local. Some social historians over stress the extent of movement of individuals from one class to another in pre-industrial England. Nevertheless social mobility, upward and downward, was more frequent than on the continent. One consequence of this mobility was a corresponding social insecurity. Here primogeniture (the inheritance of property and title, undivided, by the oldest son) played a role among the nobility. Younger sons received aristocratic educations before being reduced to bourgeois status. Also the cozy comradeship and isolated rusticity of the upper-class schools and universities were open to moneyed pupils of the commercial classes. Continental schools were narrowly constricting and exclusive.

More so than on the continent commercially earned riches and political wizardry could and did attract royal favor and subsequently the land and title that meant official elevation to the aristocracy. Despite some continuous enrichment from below, primogeniture and competition among them made the English aristocrats far less numerous than their counterparts in France or Germany. Unlike the situation on the Continent, aristocratic position in England was apt to be more substantially based on great wealth, influence at court, and measurable accomplishment than merely on aristocratic ancestors. Wealthy, landed Englishmen were apt to be avaricious and cruel.

Lovers of England (particularly those not living there) have for centuries praised the relative flexibility of English society, which certainly contributed to proto-democratic evolution. England's political disruptions have been far less severe than those of France or Germany. Anglophiles have passed over the greater economic violence. Examples are the enclosure movement, which dispossessed peasants of land, and the disruptive industrialization and urbanization of the early nineteenth century. The genial patron of artists, the witty courtier, the inventive entrepreneur of industry, the colonial planter, and the sturdy yeoman are all English types. But so are such types as the third son of a great house forced into a degrading marriage and the church or trade, the royal favorite ruined by a whim, the slave trader, the lower class misfit killing himself or herself with cheap gin. English society—like that of Greece in the fifth century and that of the northern Italian towns in the Renaissance—was uncertain and dangerous and (perhaps, therefore) susceptible to fundamental cultural innovations. The harshness of English society may be reflected in the harshness of English legal punishments for minor infractions, the poor laws and—arriving at some points bearing on our subject—certain specifically English entertainments.

Continental travelers in the seventeenth and eighteenth centuries were astonished by the unapologetic passion with which Englishmen from the king to the most ordinary laborer, from the prince to the pickpocket relished such spectacles as bear baiting, dog fighting and cock fighting. Despite the horror these entertainments regularly inspired in moralists, they were suppressed only slowly by the steady pressure of evangelistic Christians in the nineteenth century.

England was also distinguished by its relative wealth. The small class of great landowners was not the only class that was better off than its continental counterpart. English laborers in the countryside and in town, despite their chronic economic insecurity, were more likely than continentals to be regular eaters of meat, wearers of woolen clothing and leather shoes, readers of books, spectators at the theater, and participators in sports entertainments. It may be possible to make the case that the relative robustness of the Englishman opened possibilities for a more lusty exploitation of leisure and a freer experimentation with the existing European forms of spectacle and play. We know that many Englishmen experimented with new means of harnessing resources and creating wealth. Some were remarkably successful. Modern sport and the Industrial Revolution have common origins in the dynamism of English culture. And sport can be distinguished first.

English horse racing was distinctive and deserves some careful attention because of the developments it fostered. A later development was the replacement in England of the duel by regularized, tamed boxing. The uniquely English codification of the rules of cricket and especially football will also receive attention.

I have already discussed the persistent aura of power that has surrounded the sport horse since beginnings of high civilization. In England, as elsewhere, the large horse of chivalry was a basic determinant of much of the structure of the early medieval economy and, consequently, medieval politics. The thoroughness of the imposition of the feudal system by the Normans made more effective a pervasive yearning to improve the breed. Succeeding ruling dynasties in England enforced laws requiring their subjects to protect English stock. William the Conqueror himself had a fine

Spanish horse and his barons collected stock for their estates. Subsequent generations imported larger and swifter stallions and mares. Continental exporters knew that English nobles would pay the highest prices for exceptional animals. The Crusaders brought back with them faster and more manageable Arabians. Edward III forbade the export of proven stallions. Richard III tried to limit the prices that English dealers could charge for them. Henry VII and Henry VIII continued to import horses from Turkey and Spain and to forbid the sale to foreigners of fine stock. National laws required the destruction of inferior horses, mares, and colts in order to protect English blood lines.

Over the centuries English sport horses did indeed improve— so much so that they eventually constituted almost a new breed. Even before the Tudors there had evolved in England a new variety of animal alongside the powerful mount of feudal warfare. These sleek and slender animals were not robust enough to carry a knight and armor, but they were fast and obedient and a ravishing experience to ride on a hunt. Pairs or groups of these gorgeous beasts might be matched in an informal race set up as a means to determine which of several horses was indisputably superior. The employment of carriages for long-distance travel also favored the manageable, fast horse.

But a historian's recourse to practical explanations is not adequate to explain the enchantment of the classical Greeks, the Byzantines, and of pre-modern Englishmen for the sport horse. In late medieval Europe, the mount for a cataphract and the smaller cavalry horses alike were diminished strategically by the innovations of bowmen, pikemen, and then marksmen with crossbows or arquebuses. Highly bred horses became increasingly impractical for work and for war and remained expensive to breed, train and keep. However, the possession and demonstrative use of superior sport horses remained an essential symbol of wealth and political power in England. Splendid horses publicly and festively distinguished splendid Englishmen from inferior ones—even wealthy ones—elsewhere.

It merits restatement here that the most prized, and indisputably verifiable quality of a fine horse is its speed. We can assume that for millennia and nearly everywhere horses have been raced to give evidence to prospective buyers. Races of fast horses established the prestige of their owners before the eyes of rivals and the general public. Horse races were common adjuncts of civil festivals in medieval towns—as they still are in Sienna.

In England, some refined methods of comparing sport horses appeared in the late sixteenth century. Pairs of mounted hunters followed dogs which, in turn, trailed the scent of a dead cat towed for many miles. The horse that arrived first at the end of a predetermined distance or which led for a measured distance of (for example) 240 yards was declared winner. The events might be announced in advance for public delectation. Owners and spectators who felt insightful could bet on the results. In the course of the seventeenth century, the variety of races proliferated. There was a steady tendency to arrange races so that they could be better observed by more people and so evolved (independently of classical hippodromes—all of which had disappeared) a race course for many horses. They were ridden by jockeys (from "Jack," a name applied to a small person or to persons of common origins). The ovals had broad curves rather than the turning posts of ancient race courses. Promoters might advertise some dog races as part of a program. Large numbers of people paid their admission, and many intensified their concern over the outcomes by wagers. Prizes were offered by patrons or by festival entrepreneurs. All this, but perhaps most of all the fame accruing to the owners of winners, stimulated rivalry and emulation by wealthy losers. By the late eighteenth century there were permanent courses, regular meetings, and a class of bookies. There were trainers, jockeys, a quasi-scientific training literature, and an agricultural industry devoted to improving the breed.

The essential instrument for this kind of costly indulgence and ritualized entertainment was (and remains) the thoroughbred horse. These animals are splendid to observe in action, but what they gave the English—or perhaps reinforced or most vividly demonstrated to them—was a new abstract value: something exquisite and worthy of a noble quest. It was a dynamic abstraction of pure time and pure space to produce visible fleetness—speed. Like the inspiring abstractions, beauty and power, speed must be at least partly concretized to be experienced or, more especially, remembered. Speed was eventually monumentalized in sports records.

Wrestlers. From a tomb painting in Thebes, about 1450 B.C.

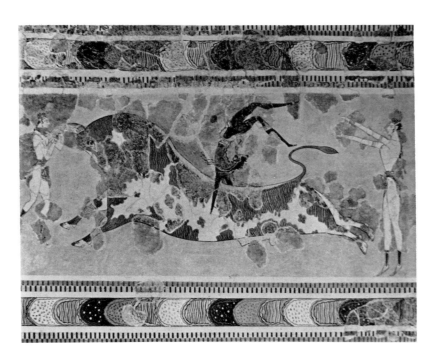

Cretan acrobats with a bull. From a wall painting in Knossos.
About 1500 B.C.

Athletes and one non-athlete (second from left). Vase painting from
fifth-century B.C. Athens. (The British Museum.)

Wrestlers and a referee: Painting on a vase from
fifth-century B.C. Athens.

Chariot race with spectators. Painting on a vase fragment.
Sixth century B.C. Athens.

Head of a chariot driver. Fifth century B.C. Delphi.

Engraving on a discus of a long jumper. Fifth century B.C. Greece.

Statuette in bronze of a chariot horse. Greek, fifth century B.C.

Diver. Wall painting from Paestum in southern Italy.
Fourth century B.C.

Acrobats. From a mosaic in Sicily. Third century A.D.
(Bildarchiv Schweiz. Turn- und Sportmuseum gestattet.)

Wrestlers. From a Japanese print, about 1840.

Wrestlers. From a Japanese print by Hokusai (1760–1849).

Kemari players. Japan. Twentieth century.
(Bildarchiv Schweiz. Turn- und Sportmuseum gestattet.)

Ballplayer. Mayan culture. About 600 A.D.

Fencers. Drawing by Albrecht Durer (1471–1528).

Fencers practicing. Engraving from an Italian manual of about 1680.

Player of a game on ice. Romein de Hooghe (1645–1708).

The pedestrian Captain Robert Barclay. Engraving of 1809.

Boxers with spectators. Aquatint by Robert J. Cruikshank (1789–1856).

Turners at a festival in Switzerland. Etching about 1865.
(Bildarchiv Schweiz. Turn- und Sportmuseum gestattet.)

Wrestlers. By Gustave Courbet (1819–1877).

Boxer. "Salutat" by Thomas Eakins (1844–1910).

Athlete. Bronze statuette by Franz von Stuck (1863–1928).

Athlete. Bronze statuette of a "Young Cyclist."
Aristide Maillol (1861–1944).

Shot-putter. Bronze statuette. R. Tait McKenzie (1867–1938).

Cyclists. Oil painting. Lyonel Feininger (1871–1956).

Gymnast. Still from Leni Riefenstahl's *Olympia*.

The idea of a sports record is something new under the sun. And as a notion accepted outside of Anglo-Saxon society it is very new indeed. This talisman of modern sport probably has its origins in several pre-existing conditions that have been singled out by many historians, attempting to determine which special factors in the English experience led to the "take-off" phase of industrialization there. The sports record presupposes a keen appreciation of measurable accomplishment and, necessarily, precise measurements of time and space—thus alluding to more novelties which were first and most vividly apparent in England. That large numbers of Englishmen quantified time and especially time in the future may suggest that here was another fulfilled precondition for disciplined industrial production. The determined quest for certain forms of sporting supremacy and the methodical preparations for them did not appear suddenly. But their appearance was evidence of portentous attitudes regarding present work and present time as quantities of investment employable to produce greater products in the future.

Another essential precondition and basis of high-performance modern sport—and it must be mentioned almost as an aside here—is the notion of the essential identity of humans across the traditional castes and over the generations. "Democracy" or "equality of opportunity" or even the French *carrière ouverte aux talents* cannot be used here. And naturally the notion that noble and serf might be equal are contrary to those assumptions that regulated European society—and indeed any society at any time—until the modern age.

To return to horses: a celebrated and early accomplishment of speedy horsemanship was that of Thomas Wolsey (1475–1530) who in 1508 carried Henry VIII's proposal of marriage for the hand of Margaret of Savoy to the Emperor Maximillian. Wolsey used relay horses to travel from Richmond to London, where he took a barge to Dover. He sailed to Calais where more relay horses awaited to carry him to Flanders. His determination and luck held for the return, and Wolsey completed the round trip in three and a half days. The accomplishment was at first doubted, then acknowledged, and finally admired; and it brought some early preferments to that magnificent and greedy statesman and ecclesiastic.

The chronicles or memoirs of the sixteenth and early seven-

teenth centuries contain ever more frequent descriptions of remarkable journeys—most often inspired by urgent royal messages.
One remarkable case was the carrying by Robert Carey, the seventh son of a great lord, of the news of the death of Queen Elizabeth I to Edinburgh in 1603. Our sources do not tell us how many
horses Carey employed, but he is supposed to have required only
60 hours including breaks for sleep to cover the 400 miles. That
accomplishment may have been the speediest transit of the distance before the days of the railroads. There was a growing tendency for horsemen to claim and achieve fame for traversing shorter
distances for more trivial stated purposes. Here we might mention
a celebrated ride in 1612 of Henry, Prince of Wales, from Richmond to Bever in Nottinghamshire (a distance of a little more than
100 miles) in two days in order to be with his father, James I.

In the later seventeenth century we come across claims that a
certain rider went 100 miles in one day—the purpose merely being
the accomplishment (and the fame that came with it) itself. Certain noblemen began to make wagers with others that they could
ride a certain distance a certain number of times in less than a
certain number of days—for example the stretch London–York to
be traversed five times in less than six days. Then later we hear of
shorter distances ridden on a single horse. For example, an exceptional black mare was ridden to a point nine miles distant and
returned in 55 minutes.

Care in breeding produced speedier horses and in the early eighteenth century horses with well-known ancestries were claimed to
be capable of traversing 20 miles in an hour. By this time the four-
mile-long race around an oval course had been developed for the
theatrical display of these handsome animals under full speed. We
hear of colonels who wagered that a certain horse could (or could
not) run four miles in eight minutes. It was widely believed that
the miracle horse of the eighteenth century, "Flying Childers,"
(born 1715) was in 1721 capable of briefly reaching that magic
velocity of a mile a minute. It is no longer believed to be possible
(and indeed all of the claims above are suspect for the same reason) because of the imprecision of the clocks and the suspiciously
laid out and calibrated courses. Shortly afterward, in response to
a need, a fairly dependable stopwatch was invented. In 1731 dur-

ing a "race against time" (itself an extraordinarily arrogant and even poetic conception), on which 1000 guineas had been wagered, Lord Cavendish was required to carry three different stopwatches. He rode to a point 21 miles distant. All the watches registered less than the critical time of one hour and five minutes—the least favorable only 16 seconds less. So Cavendish won the large wager.

The thoroughbred horses—both those that rode in a race with many proximate competitors and those that rode against the abstract opponents, time and distance, were subjected to long-term preparations which we can call "training." Expensive horses had to be meticulously, almost scientifically, nourished, conditioned, and exercised. It is probably incorrect to explain the origins (as is sometimes done) of the English madness for betting as an extension of the medieval idea of the trial by God—a European means of determining justice. Success in early modern English sport was not the result of prayers but of the rational applications of time, energy, intelligence, and financing. And so racing results were seen at the time.

Formal footraces before large numbers of spectators were an English invention (or reinvention, if we consider classical sport). The popular acceptance of heroes of running was partly prepared for by a widespread enthusiasm among many classes of Englishmen for theatrically presented speed by ridden horses. The first formal English foot races we can read about were arranged between certain servants called "footmen." In the sixteenth century a footman's job was to run in front of and beside heavy coaches, leading the horse teams away from exceptional hazards in the wretched roads and supporting the carriages when they tilted dangerously. Not unlike the eccentric noblemen who kept about them Bantu, Sioux, giants, or dwarfs, some Englishmen sought out the fleetest footmen, whose prowess was verifiable in proximate contests.

The first footmen distinguished themselves by very long runs. As early as Queen Elizabeth I's time we hear of the feat of Langham, an Irish footman, who ran a total of 148 miles in 42 hours including time for sleep. Langham fetched some medicine for Lady Berkeley and for this he received a new suit of clothes. Later there were cases of wealthy men matching their footmen as they might match their horses, in races of ten or more miles. But humans who acquired notoriety for their swiftness were not always servants. An impecunious knight might seek to raise himself in the eyes of a great lord by walking a great distance to pay him homage. The same Robert Carey who as a horseman carried the news of Elizabeth's death to Edinburgh had earlier walked to visit Lord Essex in Portugal. The journey took 12 days and Carey was rewarded with 2000 pounds, a sum that permitted him to live nicely at court for some time afterward. As is evident from many entries in Samuel Pepys Diary, King Charles II himself sometimes practiced fast walking for pleasure.

Though receiving less general aristocratic patronage and less spectator enthusiasm, races of humans against one another or against time evolved in differentiation and precision. Very early there was a distinction between running and heel-and-toe walking. For example, in 1670 a certain Digby lost by one half minute a bet of £50 that he could walk (he might not run a step) five miles on the Newmarket race track in less than an hour. Digby performed barefoot, clad only in a loincloth. The King, the court, and a large crowd were on hand for the spectacle. Some time later a man chose to run as nature made him around St. James's Park at the peak of the promenade time. Though some ladies shielded their eyes, most of the onlookers cheered. The athlete calmly reclothed himself near Whitehall at the end of his tour. Our source for this incident comes from the memoirs of a German traveler, Baron von Pollnitz, who characteristically neglected to give us any details about the time or the distance or whether the wager was won or lost. These omissions suggest that at the time, the value placed on all these last named factors was exclusively English. It seems likely, however, that the wager was over a certain time or a certain course and not over the audacity to appear before society naked. Runners who were serious, then as now, tried to carry as little weight as possible, and it was not unheard of or unexpected for a professional runnner to wear the ultimately simple costume of classical antiquity.

As has always been the case popular competitions were staged for better viewing and keener mass enjoyment. In the course of the eighteenth century, a racing meet at Newmarket, Ascot, Epsom, Doncaster, or at many other places in England became far more than the main event, which was a proximate run of between six and ten renowned horses for four miles around an oval track. A derby was a festival requiring preparation. It was the occasion for a vast assembly which, though containing representatives from the fashionable world (indeed fashion in clothing or carriages was first displayed at such occasions), also mixed representatives of disparate classes. The eighteenth-century program included handicap races which, it is worth noting, are indicative of a particular precondition of modern sports—the desire of the organizers to make a contest's outcome excitingly uncertain by trying to assure equal conditions for all competitors. On hand were also hawkers of snacks and souvenirs, jugglers, organ grinders, beggars, pickpockets, touts, tipsters, and established bookies.

The parimutuel industry appeared in response to an opportunity. Betting is not new, of course. Homer described the anxiety of bettors at a chariot race. Betting was integrated into the religious rites and ancillary sporting contests of the American Indians of the central plains. The Egyptians made small wagers in board games and the Romans informally risked small sums on the toss of dice or at gladiatorial contests. But betting as it developed in pre-industrial English society is something without comparable forerunners. English wagering may be evidence of a view of the world which prepared the ground for other English innovations that have received great attention from social historians. English sport betting is far removed from the notion of pure chance (as in a lottery, for example) or from trust in fate (as in the medieval trials by God). He might also pray, but the early English horse bettor and his descendents believed that their appraisals of the entered horses or the conditions of a runner (often himself) were more knowledgeable and objective and *therefore* superior to that of his counterwagering opponents. The wagering of the modern Anglo-Saxon was essentially different than that of the Greek sprinter or American Indian ball player who, though he may have diligently trained for his contest, saw victory as the affirmation of religious rituals being correctly performed.

In medieval England (as elsewhere in Christian Europe) certain

judicial decisions were turned over to God, who presumably determined the outcome of the combat of irreconcilable opponents.
That God was the sole judge, and not the prowess of the litigants,
is proved by the fact that hired champions might be allowed in
battle. But God was out of the picture in the enlightened English
sporting contests of the eighteenth century.

Rational betting might be compared with some early examples
of speculative fever—for example, the tulip craze in seventeenth-
century Holland or the speculations surrounding John Law's monetary schemes in Paris. Many of the speculators were people whose
theology (while paradoxically determinist) favored individualism
and a rational analysis of time, energy, and money. These people
sought accomplishment and its expected verification: success. English betting, however, was not theological. The English wagerer
was more like a capitalist speculator. The wagering individual felt
that he would profit from his superior gauging of an artificial,
staged situation (a horse race, a foot race, a boxing match, a football game, etc.) which was designed to go either way.

By the beginning of the seventeenth century in England, there
were instances of single bets of £1000—much more than the price
of a superior stallion—on the outcome of a horse race. A total of
£6000 was supposed to have been bet in 1618 on a race before
King James I between an Irishman and an English footman. By
the end of the seventeenth century further complications (or really
equalizations) were added to horse racing by elementary handicap-
ping. Horses had to be of similar ages and had to carry similar
weights. Winners might share the total amount wagered—thus
foreshadowing the parimutuel concept. By the end of the seventeenth century there were odds of 2–1 or 5–1 in certain races.

By the beginning of the eighteenth century, there were wagers
on the outcome of sensational, unusual, and therefore more risky
tasks. In 1709 a 64-year-old German won a wager of £100 that he
could walk 300 miles in Hyde Park within six days. A source of a
slightly later time tells us that,

In 1729 a Poulterer of Leadenhall Market betted 50 pounds he would
walk 200 times around the area of Upper Moorfields in 27 hours and
accordingly proceeded at the rate of five miles an hour on the amusing

pursuit to the infinite improvement of his business and the great edification of hundreds of spectators.

A little girl, just 18 months old, was claimed by her backers in London to be able to walk the length of the Mall (about a half mile) in 30 minutes. After the bets were laid, the toddler accomplished the task before the admiration of thousands in just 23 minutes.

It had long been a custom in the English countryside to have occasional "smock races" for women. The winner would win a smock or loose dress of a thin fabric in which she was expected to pose after she was awarded it. In London in 1725 great numbers turned out for a four-mile race between two young women for a two-guinea prize. Part of the large crowd may have been attracted by the promoters' intention to have them run nude, but this plan was overruled and they ran in loose blouses and drawers. There was another race between four pregnant women. There were spectators and bettors on hand for wheelbarrow races, throwing contests, and hopping and jumping competitions. Curiously, in these races, like those of the classical Greeks, there were usually only first prizes and none for subsequent places.

On a wager of 20 guineas, Lord Dunblain in 1683 was challenged to traverse 60 yards in 20 leaps—"which he accomplished in St. James Park, about the middle of Pall Mall, on the Pond side with great ease to the admiration of all the Spectators" according to a newspaper of the time. There were contests or races against time for dwarves, men with wooden legs, and other cripples. There were also prodigious feats of eating or drinking accomplished for a prize or to win a bet.

The passion for spectacularly staged contests urged on by sadistic onlookers or wagerers did not go unnoticed by the moralists and social critics. English authorities had always attempted to regulate English sports. In the thirteenth and fourteenth centuries there were repeated royal attempts to outlaw sporting games of village against village and peasant contests in running, leaping, and tossing the bar or stone. Military strategists believed these idle pursuits interfered with the more useful one of archery practice or contests against targets. It would be centuries before sporting contests would be praised as part of education and as practices forming good character. It was obvious to many that spectator sports aroused the mindless pleasure of idlers. The Puritans attacked sporting entertainments as the work of the devil. English social critics, moralists, and theologians in the eighteenth century were especially horrified by wagering, which brought ruin to some members of all the classes and which supported a dubious class of dopesters, loansharks, and bookies. It has always been common for a proud people to attribute their vices to poisoning from lax neighbors. But Englishmen could blame no one but themselves for wagering. This way (to employ some rhetoric used by critics of the vice) "of getting rich with little pain or ruining themselves with little pleasure" appeared spontaneously out of English social conditions.

There is a point to be made here. The English commercial, investing classes were contemporaneously betting on *their* superior gauging of probabilities when they insured the passage of ocean ships, financed crops in distant lands, bought and sold futures, and warehoused commodities in expectation of a rise in price. The first capitalists were therefore bettors. Seen more positively we can suggest that a propensity for weighing hazards, a talent for abstracting likelihoods on distant events, and for betting on the basis of superior information were all sure signs of a novel and creative mental outlook that later characterized the entrepreneurs of the industrial age. Probability theory and rational analyses were applied to far more than sporting amusements. Their vigorous application to the market place and to industrial production had immense consequences for the future.

Modern boxing also developed out of particular English conditions. Boxing as it came to be formalized in England with its etiquette, written rules, taming and gentler gloves, rounds, referees, and point systems had no connection with boxing as it existed in classical antiquity and had only tenuous connections with the boxing of any other age. Modern prizefighting as it evolved in England in the eighteenth century can be more correctly seen as a constructive response to the European vice of dueling.

The duel had endured in Europe as a relic of the chivalric contests which distinguished the elegant (armsbearing) classes from the lower orders. In England, as elsewhere in Europe, dueling inspired fine craftsmanship and satisfied the honor of superior swordsmen and marksmen. However, the duels also brought about far too many personal tragedies, insulted Christian morality and common sense, and challenged established power. The duels may have satisfied dark needs in certain souls. Only in England were substitutes found.

There are several partial explanations for this. Here again, one must mention the relative effectiveness of the central government. Many continental states declared death or the dispossession of property as the penalty for participation in a duel, but English laws were more likely to stick. The smaller numbers and better education of the English nobility also worked against the duel. A French victor in a duel might be considered a hero (one recalls the tone of Rostand's *Cyrano de Bergerac*); an English winner (for example, Lord Byron over Mr. Chaworth in 1765) was more likely to be condemned as a brute among his peers.

The attitudes of Puritans were not remarkably different from several groups of continental Protestants, but the Puritans governed England for long periods in the seventeenth century and continued long afterward to set standards for moral earnestness in the upper levels of society. Certain social historians (for example, Dennis Brailsford in his *Sport and Society*, 1969) have made it clear that, while the Puritans were unable to eliminate or, at the time, even seriously reduce the English popular taste for dancing, blood sports, or betting, in the long run the moral earnestness of the Puritans created an atmosphere in which some recreational activities were encouraged as good and some were consistently condemned as the work of the devil. So there was steady pressure against the atrocities of the pit sports and murderous human combat. The so-called common sense of the eighteenth century Englishman, at least as it was manifested in recreational and physical education, was partially due to energies deflected away from the gruesome and orgiastic.

Another social base of opposition to dueling was among the increasingly influential calculating, trading and manufacturing classes who opposed it, not necessarily for its absurdity, but for its exclusiveness. The intelligent thing for offended noblemen to do would be to wrestle, but given their need to remain noble they could not, since wrestling was lower-class, dirty, and unceremonious.

Various simple kinds of boxing did exist among the lower orders in England. There were few rules. At the end of the seventeenth century, we begin to find mention of "prizefighters" who bloodied themselves before spectators—the one to remain standing taking the prize. The fighters were usually butchers or assorted ruffians and were probably viewed as disposable—much like pet dogs or gamecocks. In the seventeenth century, by a process whose precise steps cannot be traced, buffing or boxing became differentiated and some matches were more than mere pit battles. To lengthen the contests and to hold the critical attention of a paying audience that very likely was also a theater audience, matches were divided into acts called "rounds." The "bruisers" as they might be called, performed in the open air in a roped-off stage called a "ring." Rounds were at first not of a specific length, but ended when a fighter fell or was knocked to the ground. A referee declared the winner when his opponent could not meet the call for the next round.

Larger numbers of critical, paying and, of course, betting spectators analyzed the skills of the contestants. Prizes grew larger. Sensible boxers toughened their hands by pickling them in an alum solution. They ran distances and in place to improve their endurance. They wore padded mitts in practice with sparring mates. There were plenty of low tricks known to the skilled and unscrupulous, but no prizefighter could kick, hit below the belt, or hit a man when he was down because the referee (himself an invention of great significance and consequence in the history of modern sport) might declare a forefeit. By the beginning of the eighteenth century, there existed a new theatrical entertainment with recognized rules and a tradition. Boxing permitted the indulgence of participators and voyeurs in a rigidly staged demonstration of violence that was gruesome and tense, though rarely deadly. Long before we read the names of celebrated runners in the newspapers, we know of celebrated prizefighters.

The most celebrated of these was James Figg, who died in 1734. Significantly, we know nothing of Figg's origins. He merely appeared in London as an outstanding swordsman, cudgeller, and boxer. He earned enough to add an amphitheater to his house in Marylebone Fields. Mostly he promoted and staged pugilistic or sword fights between men, and occasionally, women. He also staged bear baitings, tiger baitings, and once advertised a bull fight that never came off. Figg himself was a big, handsome man, who in his career of some 300 fights (we are not sure how many of these battles were boxing matches), was beaten just once—and that was when he was sick and by a man whom Figg had defeated before and would again. Figg also gave costly lessons in the "manly" or "noble art of self defense."

James Figg was a national celebrity. He was fictionalized in literature and was a frequent subject for prints which sold in large editions. Collectors of fistiana prize his admissions tickets, some of which were engraved by William Hogarth (1697–1764). More important, Figg was sought out as a teacher of swordsmanship to well-born young men. Later this fast-moving impresario offered the same clientele boxing lessons. But the boxing Figg taught was of a special kind. Boxing for the elegant classes integrated codes of gentlemanly behavior. Upper-class boxing was made relatively clean by the expected maintenance of an upright posture and by the addition of well-padded boxing gloves. Figg could not meet the demand for lessons. Soon other fencing masters were offering boxing lessons to elegant young men.

At about the same time in England, and in England alone, the wearing of a sword (long viewed by the middle classes as a silly arrogance) fell out of fashion to be replaced by the less exasperating (if only slightly more democratic) walking stick. After about 1750 the wearing of a sword became an anachronism, a provocation. Foreigners who flaunted a sword in the streets of London were apt to be set upon by annoyed natives and suffer the sword to be broken.

The shedding of the menacing sword could be, of course, an incitement to taunts by the notoriously disrespectful English lower orders. We hear, beginning about 1730, of noblemen who lay wig aside to descend from their horses or carriages in order to have a punch-out with an insulting passer-by. Such *lèse majesté* was almost inconceivable on the Continent. More English gentlemen practiced boxing with or had informal matches with their social equals. Naturally, they wore heavily padded mitts. Later the more confidently skilled and proud might appear in a public ring to defend their honor or to claim a prize against a member of their own or (rarely, but increasingly often) a different class. The fights were governed by an atmosphere of "fairness" and by the referee enforcing rules that were not class specific. Publicly viewed and journalistically recorded sport, then, was unideologically moving toward democratic notions. In the middle of the eighteenth century, a Frenchman who had traveled in England noted: "Each nation has its customs. In France one sings to amuse oneself. Here they pass the time slugging one another [*on fait le coup de poing*]."

Later in the century, along with the appearance of the "gentleman" boxer we begin to hear of the "gentleman" walker or runner. Certain distances or times became recognized as standard. One route was from the university city Oxford to London (roughly 40 miles). Competitors might strive for a best distance for one hour. Then a tendency developed for distances to be no longer traversed by walking, but by all-out running against a stopwatch, which by the end of the eighteenth century was calibrated in fifths of a second. Sometimes there were bets or prizes, but gentlemen "pedestrians" usually performed for the fame or for the self-satisfaction alone.

The outstanding pedestrian of his age was Robert Barclay Allardice (1779–1854), a Scottish nobleman better known as "Captain Barclay." Remarkably large, handsome, and intelligent, Barclay was devoted to scientific agriculture and wrote articles on the subject. He could lift a half a ton. He could also remain cheerful for days on end while on the go. In 1801 he walked 110 miles in 19 hours and 27 minutes in a muddy park. In 1802 he walked 64 miles in 10 hours.

One morning at 5:00 in 1808 the great pedestrian began walking and traversed 30 miles while grouse shooting.

He dined at 5, walked 60 miles to his house at Ury in 11 hours, and there after attending to business walked 16 miles to Lawrence Kirk, danced at a ball, returned to Ury at 7 A.M., and spent the next day partridge shooting, having traveled 130 miles and been without sleep for three days.

Barclay's most broadly observed feat was to walk one mile in each of 1000 successive hours, which he did at Haymarket from June 1 to July 12 in 1809. He averaged 14 minutes 54 seconds per mile in the first week; 21:04 in the last week and lost 32 pounds along the way. Though little prestige was attached to sprints in his time, he is supposed to have run the quarter mile in 56 seconds. A much more usual or standard competitive event was to attempt to traverse the maximum distance in a timed hour.

After the well-observed appearance in English life of figures like the boxer James Figg and aristocratic pedestrians such as Captain Barclay, there appeared in the English public scene a series of men who steadily increased the distance for the hour run. With them, we have the reappearance in popular culture of an attractive figure who had been absent since classical times: the sports hero. Famous runners or walkers had their performances described in the newspapers, charged fees for their appearance before the broad public, and were presented to royalty.

We know that as English society became transformed by industrialization, the qualities of rationalization, standardization, calculation, and measurement became ever more integrated into English life and culture. These same attributes came ever more to characterize English popular pastimes as well. English sport developed so spontaneously and harmoniously with the times that it was scarcely noticed as remarkable by the social critics then or by social historians afterward. Sport, like manufacturing and trade, became ever more directed to attaining efficiency and its emphatic evidence, statistically provable and stateable accomplishments. Like concurrent movements in law and government, which led to codifications, constitutions, and rationalization, sport became codified, and civilized by written rules which were enforced by supervising officials (the equivalent of judges and jurors). English sport then, supported, reinforced, and reflected fundamental assumptions that were necessary to maintain a public consensus when the folk and local culture were uprooted. They underlay the social discipline needed for subjection to industrial work.

One might have expected that constitutions (rules), rigid borders (boundaries for cricket fields), hierarchies (captains for football teams), and absoluteness (the precisely measured mile run) might all work against the broad acceptance of new games and athletic activities. Play and recreation are supposed to be the opposite of all the stern attributes named above. But the new sports were in harmony with England as it entered the industrial age. Though it is indeed the case that millions of industrial workers were kept by the six-day week and 12-hour day from any recreation whatever, great numbers of craftsmen, traders, supervisors, entrepreneurs, students, and dilettantes embraced the new nonlocal restrictive sports. They sought earnings, fame, and pleasure as participators; amusement as spectators. Sport not only eased, but actually promoted, the mental adaption of the whole population to the demands of the modern world.

Athletes and fans, sports entrepreneurs, and administrators, in the nineteenth century did more than merely regularize and delocalize the old recreations of the upper and lower classes. They also propagated accomplishment-oriented new sports. As was mentioned above, the walkers became separated from the distance runners who later, in turn, were separated from the sprinters. Distances for foot racers (as later for rowers and, later still, swimmers) became quantified, transferable abstractions. Distances were no longer local—say, from Oxford to London, from a village pump to a tall hedge visibly distant, or from two docks on the upper Thames, but were removed from locale or terrain and set at 20 miles or a mile or 100 yards. The stones or logs that strong men competitively tossed in folk festivals in Ireland or Scotland varied in weight from five to fifty pounds. In Dublin, in 1857, a group of sports officials (their names have all been forgotten) dechauvinized the putting of the shot when they fixed its weight at sixteen pounds. The program of field events expanded with high and low hurdles, standing and running broad jumps. Perhaps more important than the formulation of these individual sports was the fact that the modern sports program as a whole was (and remains) open ended. As with laboratory experimentation (with which certain comparisons are obvious), once competitive conditions were made universally applicable, outstanding accomplishments in time, weight, or distance were precisely verifiable anywhere. Wagers and records could be established for a great variety of new high-performance activities. These new categories of competition were without tradition and therefore classless. The social mobility of boxers and runners plus the widespread addiction to gaming led to the proliferation of equalizing weight classes in boxing and wrestling.

The speed with which the lower orders were eager to compete in activities which had traditionally been class specific also led to that curiously anachronistic reaction, the establishment and enforcement of amateur regulations. In 1866 the Amateur Athletic Club adopted the rule of the Henley Regatta Committee that excluded from amateur competition not only professional watermen, but anyone "who is a mechanic, artisan or labourer, or engaged in menial activity."

Amateurism

By about the beginning of the nineteenth century, some qualities of English sports made them very much different from the old recreations from which some of them had evolved. England was the home of the mass-produced sporting print, tip sheets which were evolving into the sporting press, and the first practical athletic training literature since classical Greece. Englishmen were naturally the first manufacturers of standardized sculls, footballs, and, later, team uniforms.   *equipment*

One of the more remarkable distinctions that continental travelers observed when they visited England in the early nineteenth century was that many of the new sports had become integrated into the social life of the English college preparatory (called "public") schools. On the continent the local academies and bourgeois lycées were small, cheap, and narrowly class specific. English schools were open to all boys whose parents could afford the high cost. These schools were usually located in the country on spacious grounds. Discipline and performance standards were strict in the classroom, but on the outside, the boys aged from ten to eighteen were left to form their government. The younger "fags" were ruthlessly dominated and used by the older boys. The system wrecked some lives, but it also encouraged the development of strong leaders. The atmosphere in these schools was violent, but delightful and challenging for many. So were the athletic sports and the games.

The boys in the preparatory schools came from families of the nobles, the gentry, and wealthy entrepreneurs—the same classes that were leading and being led by the changes in the production of English wealth.

The evolution of public school recreations in the nineteenth century resembled in some ways the evolution of recreation outside the schools. There was a steady tendency to make games less spontaneous and less physically hazardous. In the schools officials standardized competitive conditions and made some traditional country games more subject to laws and hierarchical control. Thus (though this was not the object in the beginning) the application of rationalization and standardization made the sports less local and more transferable. So in the public schools a civilizing process regarding recreation was underway that was comparable to what had begun earlier (and was still underway) in foot racing and boxing.

Standardized rowing events, cross-country foot races, and football were slowly integrated into the noninstructional part of life at public schools and, later, universities in the middle decades of the nineteenth century. Intercollegiate committees reconciled differences in local practices and made possible contests between their respective teams. Later, traveling European Anglophiles favoring educational reform in their own countries carried these standardized games to where they had no past at all, but where, in some places, social, cultural, or ideological conditions provided a welcoming atmosphere.

We have earlier noted that many educational theorists, most influentially John Locke and Jean Jacques Rousseau, had favored a "balanced" education—that is, one in which the pupils' bodies as well as their minds were prepared for life as adults of the ruling class. The attainments of wealth and power by the English entrepreneurial classes in the nineteenth century colored the impressions that envious foreign observers of English education took back to their home lands. As we shall see, many foreigners (as well as some Englishmen) saw in the nonlocal, civilized, democratic competitions and games the potential for constructively altering national character elsewhere. English football became one of the more successful exports of the later nineteenth century.

Various games between opposing groups which have as their object the propelling of a ball (or stuffed sack or inflated bladder)

with feet or hands have been ceremoniously or delightedly practiced by people as various as the Aztecs, the Maoris, the Eskimos,
the Japanese, and the ancient Romans. Football (to use here a
term that must remain for a while rather widely inclusive) was
widely indulged in all over medieval Europe usually on feast days
in winter (it kept the players warm) and most usually among the
peasants of contiguous villages. We have more archival documentation testifying to village football's popularity in England because
central authorities and the moralists so continuously, vigorously,
and futilely opposed it. The games may also have been offensive
to outsiders because of their roughness and the extreme pleasure
they provided for the participants. A most usual rule was that the
ball might not be handled, only kicked; therefore "football." There
were few rules and they were never written. Old men and women
and children were not excluded. Spectators might join in and people could change sides. Injuries and deaths were most frequent
when the teams (which could easily number a hundred to a side)
were rival villages with ancient enmities—which were perpetuated
by injuries during the football games. In such contests the intervening distance—which could be more than two miles—provided
the area over which a stuffed pig's bladder was pulled to and fro.
There were no referees or time outs. The game could last a whole
day. The melée was more important than a victory. With darkness
contestants and spectators abandoned themselves to riotous drinking.

In the early nineteenth century, there developed at a few of the
rusticly located English preparatory schools some varieties of
"football" wherein the teams were of equal numbers and the prescribed areas and goals were smaller. There were variations to suit
the pupils (who were not rude farmers), the numbers willing to
play, and the various kinds of terrain. The game was slowly
tamed—for example, when the game was played on a flagged,
walled course, quite sensibly there developed a kind of no-hands,
no tackling, dribbling game.

The football game played at Rugby School evolved in some distinctive ways in the late 1830s and early 1840s. At the time Rugby
School, located southeast of Birmingham in central England, was
already two centuries old. The Rugby boys allowed certain players

under certain specified conditions to carry the ball. In order to forestall on-the-field wrangling over the conditions allowing and restricting ball handling, rules were first sketched, continuously altered, and then published in 1846 as *The Laws of Football Played at Rugby School*. Rugby boys took the constitutionally established game with them to Oxford and Cambridge. Football began to conquer England. By 1863 there were 20 Rugby clubs in London alone.

In the meantime other varieties of football, for example, the dribbling game as it was played at Eton, Harrow, Westminster, and Charterhouse, also acquired ever more precise, restrictive, written rules. A desire for larger leagues led to constitutional compromises by committees of club officials. Sets of rules became homogenized. The public school class of Englishmen gradually was won over to the Rugby variety of the game, which allowed carrying the ball and tackling. A more restrictive variety of football, allowing no use of the hands, was enthusiastically taken on by working class players and spectators.

For football, 1863 was a decisive year. At that time attempts on the part of some committees to harmonize the two leading sets of rules failed conclusively. Rugby Union and Association Football were launched on the way to separate evolutions. Socially well-placed Englishmen and Anglophiles took their game with them as they traveled. The ball-handling variety of the game subsequently evolved anew in the American colleges. The worldwide spread of Association Football (called in the United States "soccer" and elsewhere simply "football") was later, but was far more universal. Football is now played at various levels of skill almost everywhere.

Rugby tended to have its popular strength among the professional classes. Association Football was more appealing to working class spectators. The various football games met (and continue to meet) astonishing success both as active and as spectator sports. Indeed the bitterest disputes in the early decades of football were not over the rules but over what was to be done with the money earned by paid admissions to games. The uniform almost uncritical enthusiasm that greeted collegiate football in America and Association Football almost everywhere else might force the historian to ask the question as to why such socially harmonious forms of entertainment were not devised and propagated earlier. The answers lie partly in the simultaneous development of such things as railroads, which permitted teams and spectators to travel, and cheap newspapers, which told the newly literate of coming and newly finished festivals. But, more profoundly, modern football can only be played, theatrically presented, and joyously observed in societies that have been at least partly deracinated, partly tamed, and partly regularized for modern industrial, market production. For modern life demands rigid sectioning and observance of time, treasures and rewards verifiable accomplishment, and demands the sublimation of aggression. Thus the nascent industrial classes of the twentieth century have become passionate consumers of a dynamically evolving new kind of theater which sanctifies and reinforces both our social restrictions and our material accomplishments.

[8]

INDUCED SPORT

Jean-Jacques Rousseau's didactic novel *Emile* (first published in 1762) was a time bomb. In it Rousseau attractively presented proposals for a "natural" (as he saw it) education. These proposals inspired influential followers. Thus Rousseau provides a connection between the long tradition in Western culture of *discussing* physical education and the designing of schemes that were actually put into effect. The first "balanced" educational programs (that is, those not solely concerned with mental education) were launched by Germans.

The distinction I have tried to keep between separate physical education and sport is difficult to maintain after the end of the eighteenth century in Central Europe and, later, in many other places. Because of their adaption of consciously devised physical exercises as a means of furthering mankind's progress—a great goal of the Enlightenment philosophers—new forms of sport were invented. Those synthetic sports, or more exactly, the intellectual and political atmosphere in which these sports were propagated, had consequences for the future.

In the eighteenth century it was far from uncommon to assume that society could be reformed in accordance with intelligent, hu-

mane planning. One holder of this view was Johann Bernhard Basedow. Born in 1723, the son of a hairdresser, Basedow managed to
study theology and philosophy in Leipzig and later became a
teacher for short periods in several schools for aristocratic children. He was sometimes very effective in inspiring the young. A
reading of Rousseau's *Emile* inspired him to write specific proposals for educational reform. His most successful publication was his
Elementarwerk (1774) in four volumes which outlined in detail how
one could develop the intelligence of pupils by bringing them in
contact with real life. The money and fame received from this
great seedwork permitted him to found a small school in Dessau.
He named his school the *Philanthropinum* (friends of man) because
it expressed his views. The school was open to pupils from all
classes. Alas, Basedow could not hold many of his pupils for very
long and irritated his colleagues. He apparently could not succeed
in an employment requiring patience and regularity and resigned
from his directorship in 1776. Other teachers, all calling themselves "Philanthropists," continued Basedow's practical work elsewhere, but the school in Dessau closed in 1793, three years after
his death.

However difficult Basedow was as a colleague, his *Elementarwerk*
attracted great admiration, being translated almost at once into
French. While it was open, the little school at Dessau was a place
of pilgrimage for educational radicals. The extreme political fragmentation as well as the cultural dynamism of Germany at the end
of the eighteenth century were conducive to local experiments in
education. Several new schools in Germany and Switzerland were
inspired by Basedow's writings and were run by teachers who had
earlier been trained at the first "modern" school at Dessau.

The most influential of these schools was the one sponsored by
the Duke of Saxe-Gotha in Schnepfenthal and opened in 1785.
The leader at the school for fifty years was Johann Friedrich Guts
Muths (1778–1839). Guts Muths was an appealing person. He was
stable, methodological, and well educated and well read in philosophy, the arts, and the sciences. He was also skilled in woodwork-
ing and drawing and gymnastics. He was therefore remarkably
well suited to apply to the field of education the grandiose, encyclopedic, achievement-oriented conceptions that were dominant in

other areas of intellectual life in the Enlightenment. His general intention, and the program at his school, was to occupy the children, who of course lived there, with ceaseless, organized activity. Visitors commented on the pupils' frugal diet, airy quarters, and cleanliness, and their hikes, garden work, riding, swimming, and running of laps around a track. Everything was organized. Significantly, Basedow had earlier written that play should be regulated for "reasonable purposes." Traditional children's games, which encouraged spontaneity, fantasy, and useless fun, were to be suppressed. Guts Muths and other Philanthropists invented so-called games with elaborate rankings of the "players" in which the children were required to respond quickly to their superiors. The games could be seen as models, perhaps mirror images, of the order, sobriety, and constructiveness that were the bases of the success of the bourgeois class from which almost all the pupils and teachers came.

One of the near-sacred texts of the Philanthropist educational philosophers and educational technicians was the autobiography of Benjamin Franklin. This American *philosophe*, we recall, revealed the secret of his amazing versatility and accomplishments to be his mechanical and rational direction of all his energies so as to maximize profit and the other conventional measures of success. Accordingly, the German children had their lives organized according to a "reasonable" encyclopedic conception. Guts Muths designed tables in which a pupil's weekly performances in swimming, jumping, and running were recorded—the expectation being that they would steadily improve. Long runs around a track were recorded with stopwatches with divisions of one-fifth of a second. Performances for distances as long as a mile were recorded to decimal places. The teachers praised those who could hop great distances or who could stand on one foot for a half an hour. Winners in the performance rankings were given prizes and could read their names in the school paper. The losers, particularly chronic losers, felt wretched.

Open, lumpy meadows, ponds, trees, self-made balls and bats, hoops, dolls—the ageless, wasteful, minimal equipment necessary to support spontaneous play were all, one could believe, tools to be banished to the distant past. Aided by an optimistic view of man's perfectability, a scientific view of the universe, and their own free and inventive minds, the Philanthropists could do better. It must be mentioned that the Philanthropists' schemes for physical education were not the only concerns of their lives as reforming intellectuals. Basedow was a theologian and most of his writing was on theology. His *Elementarwerk* was an encyclopedic plan for education which, like the many eighteenth-century encyclopedias with which it can be compared, had supplementary engravings to assist teachers and pupils. The prescriptions for physical exercises were remarkable because they were so specific and novel. Most often the Central European ideologists of physical education shared the political preoccupations of their bourgeois professors and colleagues. They were historians and passionate folklorists who suffered because of the perceived, centuries-long failures of the Germans (later the Czechs and others) to be unified politically. Without being Communists, they were revolutionaries who were disgusted by law codes based on birth and social position. We shall return to the ideological connections of sport and equality later.

The German physical educationalists prescribed regular "exercises" (not play). The exercises were performed as commanded at certain times at certain places in prescribed ways. It is due partly to the philosophical impulses of the German reformers (and most especially to Guts Muths) that so much of modern sport is characterized by tools, special training, and statistics. This rationalized containing of sport to place, time, performance, and apparatus is most obvious at present in gymnastics with the horses, bars, rings, and mats. A sports field in Berlin or Jena in 1815 could be a forest of poles, ropes, weights, and bars for swinging, stretching, hopping, jumping, and climbing—in all of which the pupils (later students and adults) were expected to give their utmost to approach or surpass statistical norms. As German gymnastics found increasing international practitioners, many pieces of equipment were abandoned. On the other hand, in the course of the nineteenth century (and this too must be attributed to the cultural favoring of rationalization, measurement, and purposefulness) other competitions and games, some of them antedating culture itself, were codified, democratized, and equipped. We leap ahead of the story here, but I must suggest that the high hurdles, the pole vault, the Marathon race, and written rules for ball games—all of which were invented in Western Europe—are the creations of technicians and intellectuals and are evidence of something new and characteristic of modern life.

I would be shirking my duty if I did not show some similarities in the transformation of sport taking place in Central Europe and those in the Anglo-Saxon (that is, British and American) world. In both areas there was a new concern with measurement, norms, and high performance. The new sports were assumed to be open for the participation or observation of all. Indeed the notion of a sports record, first invented in England and later accepted in Central Europe, can be seen as a celebration of and reward for (among many things) equality of opportunity—and equality of opportunity was a centerpiece of the Liberals' political program.

But the differences in Anglo-Saxon and continental sport are rather fundamental. The nineteenth-century sports of Central Europe from Scandinavia to Switzerland were much more consciously devised. They were also determinedly uplifting, healthy, and intentionally ideological—which ever more came to mean patriotic. Continental sport had almost nothing to do with capitalistic money in the form of prizes, wagering, or admissions charges. Despite their political liberalism, the Philanthropists were almost always sycophants dependent upon state or princely support to put their inspired schemes into effect. The little boarding schools all lost money. European physical education and gymnastics in the early nineteenth century was one culmination, and a visible one, of a grand philosophical tradition dating from the Renaissance. It was supported by all the giants of the Enlightenment.

The techniques and events of Anglo-Saxon sport did infiltrate Europe later in the century. Sport all over the world was far more earnestly regarded after the Olympic Games of 1936. However, it is still the case that sport on the European continent is much more in earnest than it is west of the English channel.

Returning to the descendants of Basedow, we should note that they were all, like the literary titan Johann Wolfgang von Goethe, good European cosmopolitans. If they had notions of political reform, they believed it would come about through the inculcation of philosophy through the proper preparation of children of pre-university age. The latent inspirational capabilities of the systematic new exercises for modern man were first appreciated and then dramatically employed by Friedrich Ludwig Jahn, a major figure in ideology, politics, and sport. Jahn was born in 1778 the son of a north German preacher. Until he was elderly he was distinguished by unusual good looks, great energy, and grace in movement. He was a natural athlete, but his yearnings to distinguish himself as an intellectual were hindered by his impatience and disregard for authority. Though he attended many schools and was considered a university student into his thirties, Jahn never completed the requirements for any formal degree. He did more than his share of brawling and precociously wrote some essays on the need to invigorate the German language. He probably suffered more keenly in spirit than most other young Germans under the occupation of Napoleon's troops which began in 1806. Jahn's patriotism was at first not unusual. Like other publicists urging the freeing and unifying of all Germans, Jahn wrote rhapsodically of the patriot's view of Germany's past and of the desired future. He and others projected a great age when his people would no longer have to endure the tyrannies of petty princes, absentee bishops, and foreign looters, but would democratically and all together develop their genius. Nor was Jahn unusual as a German patriot when he denounced cosmopolitanism and foreigners in general and Jews in particular.

In 1809 Jahn got a job as a teacher in a school, the Grey Cloister (*Graue Kloster*), and began ten years of furious activity. His own vitality and his eagerness to perform exercises along with his pupils seem to have inspired them to work hard and joyously at gymnastics. Jahn widened his sphere to another school in 1811 and also opened an exercise field, apart from a school, that was open summer and winter and open as well to older students. In his employment of equipment, his encouragement of high performance, and his integrating exercise into a higher community ideal, Jahn's program was dependent upon the thorough work of Guts Muths. However, Jahn encouraged more invention in routines and favored especially the horizontal bar and distance running. He wished to open the benefits of exercise to all and preached companionable physical activity to university students with whom he developed fitness exercises and new games that were almost like military maneuvers. In keeping with his primary role as a political agitator and German patriot (his *Deutsches Volkstum* was published in 1810) Jahn would not describe his physical activity with any foreign word. He chose *turnen*, which was purely German, and—from this came *Turner* (a Jahn-inspired gymnast), *Turntage* (a sports meet for Turners), and other words with *turn*- as a root. Simultaneously Jahn was writing patriotic literature, serving as a spy against the French, and launching a movement, his *Turnbewegung*, to establish exercise fields *(Turnplätze)* all over Germany. Henceforth, I will use "turning" as though it were an English word. Jahn inspired his disciples to teach their pupils to regard themselves as a guild for the emancipation of the fatherland. Jahn himself led a battalion in the rebellions that freed his people from French troops in 1813.

Honored as a hero of the German liberation, Jahn returned to Berlin in 1815 as a state teacher of physical education. In the meantime, his ideas about turning had continued to evolve. In his own mind—and he was eager to communicate his views to others—his system was freed from the cosmopolitan, rationalistic motives of the Philanthropists. He envisioned a state supported *Turnbewegung*. His turners would improve their physical health the better to work for their fellow Germans. The whole German people *(Deutsches Volkstum)* would revel in the joys of struggle and growing strength. A paradisiacal democracy would be the natural result. Significantly, all turners, regardless of social position, addressed one another with the affectionate *"Du"* rather than the formal *"Sie,"* and this remains true today in German sports circles. Jahn's *Turnplätze* were intended to serve as assembly places for the public life of the entire population. The radical philosophy of his patriotic sport as well as the techniques of his sport appeared in his *Deutsche Turnkunst* (German gymnastics) in 1816.

After 1815, the restored conservative rulers in Europe and especially in Germany were opposed to the dynamic notions of Jahn, his inspired disciples, and any other excitable political radicals. After the calamities brought about by the French Revolution, they wanted stability above all. Enforced by the Austrian Prince Metternich, there was a system of secret police, censorship, and informers to suppress agitators. As would be the case many times in the decades ahead, idealistic youths, barred from creative activities they could pursue together, became enthusiastic sportsmen. Prussian authorities were easily convinced that Jahn's sport was threatening to public order. Jahn, now called "Turnvater Jahn," became more convinced of his mission of patriotic defiance. He became a leader and a hero to societies of frustrated, radical students who held torchlight parades, bonfires on the tops of hills, and even festively burned some books they thought were opposed to their free institutions. The stabbing and murder of August von Kotzebue (born 1761, a playwright and sometime spy of the Russian government) by a German enthusiast for liberty on March 23, 1819 was the excuse for authorities to attack the centers as threatening upheaval. Student political organizations were banned. Jahn had earlier been forbidden access to the largest *Turnplatz* in Berlin. On the evening of July 13–14, 1819, police pulled him from the bedside of his sick child and took him to the prison at Spandau. Though released less than a year later, "Turnvater" Jahn's spirit was broken and he was little more than a monument until his death in 1852.

In the meantime several comprehensive systems of physical and intellectual education launched by Philanthropists continued to flourish. Guts Muths continued to devote himself to his little school in Schnepfenthal until his death in 1839. Though the political status of the Philanthropists and that of the patriotically inspired turners were very different, the Philanthropists did accomplish something of much greater significance than the methodology of their social apparatus and training routines. By the 1820s there was permanently injected into Germany's public and intellectual life a deep concern for purposeful physical education. At the time political fragmentation, rigid social divisions, and governmental penury and neglect prevented all but a few of these projects from being put into effect. The most economical school system to operate is one of rigidly disciplined large classes which are fed knowledge requiring only memorization to absorb. A so-called "balanced" (that is, integrating planned physical activity) education required vastly more space, equipment, and personnel. The sport ideologists and educators were almost always praised and rarely financed—matters we shall return to when discussing modern developments in Great Britain and America as well.

German intellectuals and esthetes were also the first to focus their scholarship on ancient Greek sport. And later in the century German archeologists, solidly supported by the wealthy Prussian royal house, were the first to do systematic excavations at ancient Olympia. Germans became and remained attached to Olympia and indeed to all aspects of Greek sport (see chapter 10).

Archaeology and swooning over the bonds between Greece and Germany remained preoccupations of a numerically small, though well-placed elite. Throughout the nineteenth century, the aforementioned German earnestness about physical education became integrated into many aspects of German life. There were too many positive or at least useful aspects of Jahn's combination of ideology and communally practiced activity for the turners' movement to die. Along with the student political clubs and other revolutionary organizations, the Prussian government suppressed the *Turnplätze*. But they remained open in Sachsen-Weimar, Oldenburg, Braunschweig and in other parts of Germany and gradually even the more authoritarian governments permitted their revival. There followed a period of irregular growth. By the 1850s and 1860s there were regional organizations establishing contacts between local clubs, turners' newsletters and regional meets for competition and conviviality.

The various local turners' clubs increasingly drew their membership from levels of society which were being created by Germany's especially rapid industrialization and urbanization. Typically the members were skilled workers, functionaries, and small businessmen—people with careers that were rather abruptly fashioned out of a society only recently shaken from poverty and generations of regional isolation. The clubs prospered. As is still the case in much of Central Europe, the sports clubs acquired financing from membership fees and some governmental subsidies. The cozy clubs had meeting rooms, bars, and organized outings and other festivals. There were ever more planned physical activities and excursions for women and children. It was only much later that Central European gymnasts developed the foundations for the routines and training systems for the exquisite performances one sees now in international competitions. Then (and until very recently) the prestige of a sportsman could depend less on the enthusiasm and effectiveness with which he trained and more on the energy he devoted to organizational and promotional work for the club. Those clubs were most admired which had the most participants. The high points of a late-nineteenth-century *Turntag* or sports meet were the deliriously exciting performances in unison on broad green fields of thousands of men, women, children, and even elderly people.

By the 1870s and 1880s the turners' movement had evolved far from its origins in the German enlightenment and conspiratorical nationalism. The previous failure of the revolutions of 1848 and the triumph of "blood and iron" (to employ Otto von Bismarck's phrase) in manipulating German national unification had politically defused the turners and other democrats and liberals. German unity had been achieved not from below and not at all idealistically, but by the exercise of diplomatic wizardry and the Prussian army. Subsequently, the political program of the turners became uncritically loyal to the imperial state and narrowly and passionately chauvinistic. In the German *Kaiserzeit* the turners' enthusiasm now stabilized the system rather than threatened it.

The citizens of this new state felt the presence of the state more than citizens in other lands did. Both local and the imperial governments regularly encouraged physical recreation to further the health and the feeling of community (*Zusammengehörigkeitsgefühl*) which well-equipped, well-organized, and safe ideological sport could promote. However, toward the end of the century there were some ominous discoveries about the usefulness of sports clubs. Certain manufacturers established internal sports clubs for their workers and found that they were welcomed as a benefit and as a focus for intra-company loyalty. Systematic physical training was introduced in all the military services. The Marxist Social Democratic Party of Germany—the largest socialist party in the world and the most threatening opponent of the autocratic regime—organized its own sports clubs and deflected the loyalties of their sportsmen from the employer and the state and toward class solidarity. The ideology of the socialists' sports clubs was one that was Marxist, socialist, and potentially disruptive. By the early decades of the twentieth century it was apparent to some observers that sports clubs and sports rallies could be used to support a variety of political ideologies.

German sport before 1914 did have the characteristics described above, but was yet more various than I have suggested. There were devoted *Turnvereine* among the German enclaves in Czechoslovakia, Poland, the United States, and Argentina. The language used in these clubs was German and the ceremonies were designed to intensify loyalty to the homeland. The clubs sent delegations to the now enormous international meets which were thrilling patriotic reunions. The larger *Turntage* attracted vast assemblies of people who were *participants* and not mere spectators. The many national, in some cases international, turners' newspapers (*Turnzeitungen*) provided bonds between separated members and were forums for disputes within the movement.

These disputes, though ostensibly over small matters such as sorts of equipment, the encouragement of virtuosity, or the requirements for admission to a club, were often presented in ideological terms. The editors of the turners' newspapers, the professors of physical education, and other sports bureaucrats were proud, excitable, and very conservative. Perhaps in Germany before World War I both dogmatism and passion were necessary for the maintenance of any orthodoxy. No other European nation went through such a rapid industrialization, urbanization, increase in population, and consequent shift in the class makeup of society. Some historians have described the industrialization of Germany as "violent."

German intellectuals and German sportsmen were subject to a variety of ideological and cosmopolitan currents which they embraced or resisted and which gave a peculiar overheated tone to debates over turning, gymnastics, physical education, and sport. One debate that rocked the turners' movement came about when a physical educationalist who had access to important ministers in Berlin became exposed to and converted to Swedish gymnastics. As we shall see, the Scandinavians minimized the use of apparatus in their own kinds of philosophized sport. Some powerful people proposed some reforms in the way that certain routines were carried out. There was a broadly based uproar. The turners seemed unable to conceive of sport not transpiring at particular times in prescribed ways at particular places—all of which had established justifications. That innovating physical educationalist who might propose calisthenics or informal free exercises (roughly comparable to the Royal Canadian Air Force routines or "aerobics") could be attacked as an unpatriotic libertine, a philosophical heathen.

All Germans could not stay isolated from the great cosmopolitan movement of Anglo-Saxon sport. English businessmen and students took football with them to Hamburg and the university towns. Upper class travelers, who were almost *ipso facto* not chauvinistic, returned from England in the 1880s and 1890s after exposure to some English sports and soon there were small groups of dilettantish football players, boxers, and rowers. Displays of these sports attracted more members of the leisured classes, the very people who had first embraced these sports in England earlier. "Sport" entered the German language and its manifestations could be seen. The word "sport" and all that it meant was threatening to the turners.

The established German turners long resisted the spread of the two most natural sports, wrestling and running. Those who wrestled were considered vulgar exhibitionists. As Jahn's influence waned, they scorned running, the most basic of all conditioning methods and the most elementary of all competitive sports. They demeaned "human speed" as a pursuit more suited to animals bred for it. Distance running was believed to be damaging to young lungs. Competitive endurance running was introduced to the Germans in the 1890s in an underhanded way, as long-distance military pack marching. The 200 meter dash was first admitted in a *Turnfest* in 1889 and then as a part of a combined (that is, an ancestor of the Decathlon and Pentathlon) event. "Sport" for a long time in Germany was identified with other seductive and non-German cultural currents of the age. Nevertheless, Anglo-Saxon sport, with its stress on opposing competitors, individualism, hierarchies, heroes, and records, continued to make inroads in German cultural life.

We must go back again in time. The grace with which Jahn's movement, which was well observed by foreign travelers, became integrated with the two other progressive movements of the age, education and nationalism, indicates that similar programs might have found similar responses elsewhere. Indeed, other restless patriots had been inspired by Rousseau's proposals for a "natural" or "balanced" education and the didactic publications and experiments of the Philanthropists. To the devisers and ideologists of each system, theirs seemed quite special and uniquely correct, but, in fact, they were remarkably similar. Their widespread appeal suggests that the systems of gymnastics were particularly suited to an industrializing, culturally uprooted, frustrated, and patriotic population.

A contemporary of "Turnvater" Jahn was Pehr Henrick Ling (1776–1839) who came to be called "the father of Swedish gymnastics." The similarities between Ling's career and Jahn's (and furthermore those of other leaders in physical education) are instructive.

Ling's ancestors were peasants who had recently risen to the clergyman-teacher class. He was the youngest of six children. His father died when he was four, his mother when he was thirteen. His childhood and early youth were filled with disappointment. Only his remarkable mental gifts, energy, and originality kept him from desperation. He attended the universities of Lund and Stockholm and along the way learned several European languages. He gravitated to Copenhagen in 1799 and there was introduced to the circles of professors and poets who had, in turn, been inspired by the Romantic poets, particularly Schiller and Goethe. Ling learned of the ancient epics of Norse mythology, the Eddas and Sagas, which had been preserved in Iceland, and embraced these old stories to reinforce his democratic patriotism. During his five years in Copenhagen, he translated some Romantic lyric poetry into Swedish, wrote a three-act play in Danish, and made many sketches for his later literary works. He must have been aware of Guts Muths' *Gymnastics for the Young*, which was translated into Danish and published in 1799. He certainly read *The Encyclopedia of Bodily Exercises* published by Gerhard Vieth, another influential Philanthropist at the same time. He was also a pupil at a French fencing school.

In the fall of 1804, Ling took a job as a substitute for an aged fencing master at the University of Lund in Sweden. The man died and Ling began the campaign to establish gymnastics, until then unknown, in Sweden. He imported apparatus from Germany, but simplified the exercises. During the eight years Ling held his position in Lund, he gave lectures and short courses all over Sweden in fencing, gymnastics, and swimming. By the time he was appointed fencing master at the Royal Military Academy near Stockholm, he was renowned.

It is important to observe here that Ling's fame in his lifetime and later (like the fame of all the heroic physical educationalists of the nineteenth century) was due only partly to his work as a gym teacher. Or better stated, Ling's mission as a molder of his nation's bodies was intimately integrated into his self-imposed mission as a poet, a moralist, and a patriotic publicist. Sweden had suffered desperately throughout the Napoleonic wars. She lost her last possessions south of the Baltic to Prussia and then suffered the loss of Finland to Russia in 1808. There was continuous disorder in the royal succession which was settled only by the assumption of the monarchy by Jean Bernadotte, a former General of Napoleon, in 1818. He reigned as Charles XIV. (He had been elected "crown prince" in 1810.) Ling, besides his public lectures and essays on the Norse myths, wrote many other critical and literary works. His collected writings fill three large volumes. Only a small proportion deal with gymnastics.

Besides being an energetic writer, Ling seems to have been an inspiring teacher and a most realistic political intriguer. It is in this last category that he differs from Jahn and others. Ling very early was noticed by and attached himself to the Swedish royal family. A durable accomplishment was the establishment of the Royal Central Institute of Gymnastics (*Kongl. Gymnastika Central-Institut*) which he founded in 1813 and has flourished since then. The Central Institute acquired and retained a decisive influence not only on educational programs in the schools, but in the national policy for advancing the physical condition of the entire Swedish population. An important part of Ling's contribution is a system sometimes called medical gymnastics. It is worth noting again that from the beginning of his fame, Ling was inspired by patriotic and paramilitary motives. His own introduction to physical training was through fencing, which he mastered. The Bernadotte King required officers in the Swedish army to complete Ling's course and later Ling's methods were integrated into all military training in Sweden. When it was learned that French and Prussian soldiers were being drilled in the use of the bayonet, Ling in 1836 published a manual on bayonet fencing.

Throughout the nineteenth century, Ling's work and the work of his successors at the Central Institute continued to be integrated into Swedish life, whether it was military preparedness, universal education, or rehabilitation of the injured and sick. Throughout this period the Swedish approaches to gymnastics appeared to their advocates and to their counterparts in other countries to be distinctly different from the systems developing in Germany or Denmark or elsewhere. From the vantage point of the late twentieth century it seems that all the systems had their ideological origins in the salient intellectual movements of the nineteenth century: rationalism, romanticism, nationalism, democracy, and a certain educational messianism. Nevertheless, details of the exercises and the order in which they were to be pursued were devotedly attacked or defended. One is reminded of the learning brought to bear in the Middle Ages on what now seem tiny details of Christian ritual.

The members of a school board in the late nineteenth century in, say, Pennsylvania, Toronto, or Tokyo might meet with propagandists of proven systems to consider which system of physical education they should introduce into their ambitious primary school system. Board members could be astonished at the heat, philosophical subtleties, scientific findings, and mutual denigration of various advocates. To the beginning observer, the systems seemed roughly comparable. There were, however, certain distinct characteristics of the work of Ling and his followers. A most obvious difference was a relative lack of dependence by the Swedes on apparatus. A partial explanation of the simplicity of Swedish gymnastics is that the Swedes, who were very poor and isolated until the middle of the twentieth century, *had* to get by with skilled teachers and little equipment. Ling's followers would argue that the Swedish way was so meticulously thought out with regard for the *natural* needs of human biology that apparatus was useful only as an accessory. Another difference was the relative lack of differentiated levels of performance for participators at various levels of strength and agility. Swedish gymnastics suppressed competition and emphasized the duty of each member of a "class" to promote or support those who were less naturally gifted. Because Swedish gymnastics was so determinedly oriented toward the health of the masses, it steadily resisted evolution into a sport allowing quantified judgments of relative skill or theatrical, individual presentations. It required the determined work of a lot of statistically minded and performance oriented athletes, officials, and technicians, as well as cooperating athletes, but German turning in the course of the twentieth century became an Olympic sport.

Other peoples in Europe also developed their superficially distinctive, nationalistic, and broadly based gymnastics traditions. The Danish system has steadily functioned as a rallying element for the nation. There were more modest, or at least less influential, systems of gymnastics in Switzerland, the Netherlands, and in some parts of the vast and various Russian and Austro-Hungarian empires.

One of the areas where Jahn's *Turnen* had provided a focus for German pride was in Bohemia, an area that is a large component of present-day Czechoslovakia, where the German speakers were outnumbered four-to-one by Czechs. The Czechs, in turn, were a minority within the Austro-Hungarian Empire, which was ruled by German speakers in German-speaking Vienna. Dr. Miroslav Tyrš and Dr. Henry Fugner, the founders of Czech gymnastics in early 1860s, methodically distinguished their system from that of the well-entrenched turners. They stressed a lack of equipment, a broad social appeal and discipline—for example regarding punctuality and attendance on the "Sokols." "Sokol" comes from the Czech word for "falcon." A Sokol wore a red shirt and a red cap with a feather in it. The Sokol movement very early recruited women who wore a neat, free-flowing uniform. The Czech language was concurrently being formalized as a literary language. This process was part of the national awakening which Tyrš and Fugner passionately favored. Czech terms and commands were synthesized for Sokol activities.

After 1870 or so, the Czechs were especially vigorous economically and culturally. The Sokol organization embraced an ever wider social spectrum and was a forcing house for Czech national pride. Tyrš had from the beginning envisaged the Sokols as fulfilling a Darwinian function and they assumed a self-confident, quasi-military stance. Furthermore, the Sokol movement was encouraged by Czech (but not Austrian) authorities.

By the time of the outbreak of war in 1914, the Czechs had created the most highly industrialized part of the Austro-Hungarian Empire. The Sokols were the basis for much of the inspirational and organizational activities behind the revolution of 1918 against Austrian rule. The movement remained an integral part of Czechoslovakian cultural vigor and pride. Since the Sokol movement supported *established* authority in the 1920s and 1930s, it became ever more broadly based. The ideology and membership of the Sokols transcended the squabbling political parties. The annual meetings in Prague drew hundreds of thousands of participants (not merely spectators). However, stadium capacities and the administrative techniques of the time determined that 17,000 was about the maximum number of athletes that could participate in one synchronized demonstration.

After the Nazis succeeded in wrecking the Czech state in 1938–1939, German imperial policy required that the Sokols be expeditiously suppressed. Systematic Czech physical training programs revived after 1948 but, as elsewhere in the Soviet bloc, the sports stressed were those internationally certified as Olympic. An essential element of the Sokol movement, purposeful irredentism, was ruthlessly extinguished.

The appearance of consciously Jewish gymnastics provides us with yet another and final opportunity to examine the intimate connections of ideology and politics with a certain variety of modern sport. Jewish sport and physical education, in particular its ideology, were to have considerable impact on Jewish history in the twentieth century. A closer examination provides not only an interesting story but the establishment of a narrative thread that will reappear subsequently.

The very first Jewish sports organization was founded in January 1895 in Constantinople. The founding members of the *Israelitische Turnverein* were German-speaking physicians, engineers, and other professionals who had earlier been members of German turning clubs but who were humiliated by the anti-Semitism that was a growing element in German patriotism and that quite naturally became an important element in the patriotic movement of the turners. The Jews wished to do their exercises uninsulted. A club of Jewish turners was also established for similar reasons in Bulgaria in 1897.

A more substantial beginning of Jewish sport might be dated from the founding in Berlin in 1898 of the club, "Bar Kochba" and the beginning in 1900 of the publication of the *Jüdische Turnzeitung* (Jewish Turning Magazine). But we must go back a little bit in history, for the Jewish sports movement, like everything dealing with sport east of the Rhine, had much to do with ideology and the internal evolution of the various national states.

It is well known that Zionism, the striving movement of Jews for their own national state, gathered much of its impetus from the anti-Semitism which, although a latent issue for much of the nineteenth century, first began to be demagogically employed against Jews in the 1890s. A decisively influential leader of Zionism was the Viennese journalist, Theodor Herzl (1860–1904), who called the first Zionist Congress in Basel in 1897. Herzl believed that Jews would never be accorded dignity or safety until they, like other nations, had their own modern territorial state. That the prospective inhabitants of this state should also be allowed their own mutually supporting, paramilitary gymnastics movement seemed self-evident to another early ideologist of Zionism, the neurologist and celebrated social critic Max Nordau (pseud. for Max Südfeld, 1849–1923). In a speech at the first Zionist Congress in Basel, Nordau, in a style that was characteristically vigorous, stated: "We must devote ourselves to the task of re-creating muscular Judaism (*Muskeljudentum*)."

In an article for the Jewish Turning Magazine in 1900, Nordau elaborated:

For a long time, far too long a time, we have practiced mortification of the flesh. It would have been far better, if we had cared for our bodies rather than neglected and abused them. We should now fasten upon some of our most ancient traditions. Then we might all again be deep-chested, straight-limbed, keen-sighted men.

There are no people in the world for whom gymnastics (*Turnen*) could have so splendid a result as for us. Gymnastics is destined to fortify us in the body and spirit. It will give us self-assurance.

Subsequently, the interaction of anti-Semitism and Jewish self-consciousness, which have always been mutually reinforcing, grew apace. Quite significantly, new Jewish sports clubs frequently took the name of "Bar Kochba," after the leader of the heroic resistors of the Romans in the great revolts in Israel in 130–35 A.D. Other clubs called themselves "Maccabi" after the hero Juda Maccabeus who led the patriots that defeated Syrian invaders in 168 B.C.

Almost needless to say, the proponents of "muscular Jewishness" met opposition. The liberal Jewish assimilationists who had come so far since the Jews were freed in the eighteenth century were revolted by those blatant declarations of Jewish specialness which they felt exacerbated the anti-Semitism they also feared. The assimilationists believed that anti-Semitism was a sickness that would pass, particularly if all Jews behaved just like Gentiles. And orthodox Jews were aghast at these modern European heresies: the semi-nakedness, the vulgar rhetoric, and traitorous meddling in worldly politics.

Still, the movement for Jewish sport spread. At the sixth world Zionist meeting in Basel in 1903, 35 turners' clubs gave the delegates demonstrations of their skills. A tournament of exclusively Jewish gymnasts in Berlin in 1905 attracted sportsmen from all over Europe. Vienna attracted 3000 members from 16 European clubs in 1907. In the meantime, the movement to establish a Jewish national "home" in Palestine was underway. By 1908, there were sports clubs in Jaffa and in Jerusalem.

All the while, the strength of the various European integral nationalisms and of their poisonous offspring, anti-Semitism, continued to grow. Jewish reaction, particularly among the well educated bourgeoisie, was now fortified by an organized, well-thought-out program, Zionism, of which sport was a part. A world Maccabi Union was formed in 1912, and under the auspices of this organization groups of gymnasts toured Palestine in 1913 and 1914. There was movement underway (later realized) among the Jewish gymnasts to replace the German commands of "Turnvater" Jahn with Hebrew terms. So sport also provided an opportunity for the revival of the ancient language that was eventually to become the daily speech of modern Israel.

Jewish sport would have great local and international consequences in the later twentieth century. Ideological, consciously created sport on the Central European model became and remained intimately integrated in the nascent and then realized Jewish national state.

It is time to offer a summary of a narrative covering a broad time span, a great geographical area, and a lot of ideological and political threads. All of these issues provided foundations for sport in much of the world in the twentieth century.

In Europe several purposefully devised and nationally specific schemes of physical training had provided channels for the general broadening and intensification of political life in the nineteenth century. These schemes were devised by ideological dilettantes and propagated by patriotic rebels against established authority and then, as they became mass movements, were transformed into loyal, stabilizing elements in the new, more or less democratic states.

That the schemes of the turners, the Sokols, the Maccabis and other gymnastics movements improved the health and morale of their members goes almost without saying. But by the beginning of the twentieth century, it was clear that these movements could be employed to further a variety of political objectives. The evolution of ideologically oriented, mass sport evolved throughout the twentieth century and most originally in Germany. In late Wilhelmenian and Weimar (1919–1933) Germany there were rival organizations of sportsmen in the left and the right political parties.

As the twentieth century went on, the older, more secure democracies of the United States, Great Britain, Canada, and France paid little attention to these movements. Countries with entrenched social elites and single-party political systems, such as those in Spain or Latin America, either did not have the critical mass of middle class men to establish such movements or did not allow them to begin. However, community physical training for purposes of strengthening political solidarity became an inseparable part of the totalitarian regimes of Fascist Italy, Nationalist Socialist Germany and, later and much more elaborately, the Soviet Union and its client states.

[9]

AMERICAN SPORT
TO THE 1920s

The factors that set the shape and destiny of American sport are comparable to those for other aspects of American culture. Europeans sufficient in number to alter the nature of the land first came in the later seventeenth century. The enormous expanses of territory and the scattered aboriginies inspired continuous fear and contempt. As soon as the colonists knew that they had the foundations for a secure economic existence, it was necessary for them to offer evidence of their separation from nature and barbarism.

Only exceptionally were the transplanted Ennglishmen descended from secure, landed gentry. However, as soon as their wealth permitted, the ambitious immigrants imitated the distinguishing styles of the gentry in the homeland. Colonial churches, civic buildings, and fine houses were adapted from English architecture books. The best pieces of American furniture were graceful simplifications (a natural consequence of the readily available fine woods and expensive skilled labor) of the designs published by English cabinet makers. Harvard and subsequent American colleges were rustic imitations of Oxford and Cambridge.

And so it was with American sport. Unlike the restrictive conditions everywhere else in the world with regard to horse raising, good grazing land was cheap or readily acquired by clearing. So horses were cheap too. The American sport horses of the seventeenth century were small, hairy beasts descended from the earliest utilitarian imports. There were races on the English model with wagers, spectators, and a measured course almost as soon as there were established settlements. English stallions of proven lines were imported in the early eighteenth century. By 1776 there were 27 stud farms in Virginia alone. As would always be the case with American-based English sports, horse racing was less formal and even less class specific than in the homeland. Almost any white man could own a horse and find somebody to stake his horse against. Well into the nineteenth century horse races of various levels of formality were usual adjuncts of reunions, picnics, and fairs.

Colonial Americans with the wealth and ease that allowed elegant pretension also aped the English in their observations of etiquette and ceremony surrounding the hunt. Well into the nineteenth century Americans imported expensive saddle horses and trotters, pedigreed dogs, racing boats, and other special equipment. American gentlemen imported English books on sport and magazines devoted to the hunt. They set the proper tone for those who could afford these public demonstrations of sophistication.

We know less about the lower classes. Among the urban working class and in the frontier settlements Americans probably were somewhat more unruly than Englishmen were. All of the English blood sports were popular and had a continuous history. Dog fighting and cock fighting on eighteenth-century models still take place surreptitiously but with an enthusiastic following in the American rural south. Some street fighters cultivated a long fingernail for the purpose of deftly gouging the eyes of an opponent. As we know, all Americans could bear arms and many did. Rough and ready duels were a regular hazard. The American Western film has mythologized these aspects of frontier life.

Some colonists might look on and bet as indigenous players did at the Indian ball games. The whites, like their European forebearers, used the rivers and lakes only for bathing. If they learned to swim at all it was the dog paddle to save themselves in an emergency. They were astonished that some Indians frolicked in the water. Some Indians were observed racing across the water employing an alternate, over-the-head arm stroke.

At regional social gatherings plantation owners might wager on their Negro jockeys, oarsmen, or boxers, but if there were indigenous sports among the imported Africans, they have left no traces. American sport for a long time was English sport transmitted and adapted.

The great exception, of course, was baseball. It is probably descended from an ancient, variously played, English folk game called "rounders," which had the distinctive bases. The game evolved separately in the early nineteenth century in New England as "baseball." One distinguishing and very important quality of baseball was that (however much the game did, indeed, resemble games played in many places for millennia) it was *believed* to be historically and exclusively American. Some of its distinctions were constitutionalized in a set of written rules in 1845. Authoritative rules were necessary if teams from different localities were to be able to have a contest with reasonable assurances as to what the game played was a contest of.

English football had received its first set of codified rules three years before, but baseball spread much more rapidly and uniformly than English football or cricket did. If constitutionally certified, restrictive, civilized games are particularly suitable for an uprooted population undergoing rapid social change, baseball fortuitously appeared among a population eager for it. The history of baseball is a long success story. The game quickly became somewhat more than a pastime for dilettantes from neighboring towns. It evolved into a fresh form of popular theater acquiring much of its distinction through the efforts of energetic country entrepreneurs. There were leagues, players' organizations, newsletters, and delegates to rules-change meetings before the game was twenty years old.

Other American games would acquire acceptable rules and subsequently be organized and commercialized. However, none but the first would occupy so warm and secure a place in the American soul. Baseball made and kept heroes. Baseball had legendary good times and legendary bad times. Myths (for example, the claim that baseball was invented by a certain Abner Doubleday in Cooperstown, New York in 1839) were more treasured than baseball's facts. The "summer game" is played everywhere on fields of green grass—or an artificial surface resembling it. It remains stately and ceremonious. It is the game of patriots and sentimentalists. In no other sport are the notorious American yearnings for clean heroes and verifiable achievements made more manifest by acknowledged statistical records. Besides bubblegum cards, the first "halls of fame," Broadway musicals, and dozens of popular songs, baseball is the only American sport to have inspired solid histories as well as native literature of epic splendor.

In addition to the recognition of baseball as the national game, several other enduring characteristics of American sport were well-established rather soon. Underlying and basic for all American sport (as well as for so many other distinctive aspects of American culture) was the widespread presence of relatively unfettered, healthy, well-paid, literate males. One would have to go to Australia to find a comparable geographical, economic, and social situation. And indeed, the (later) evolution of Australian sport offers striking parallels.

Everywhere in the modern world moralists have attempted to promote or suppress particular games and competitions. Christian puritans have always seen the universe as their province and necessarily attempted to regulate popular entertainments in America. In the 1860s ministers and good Christian women were annoyed and publicized their chagrin that professional baseball players might earn more than a Christian minister. The same groups who founded the Society for the Prevention of Cruelty to Animals and campaigned for prohibition and votes for women sought to outlaw all public games and contests on the Sabbath. Certainly part of their disapproval was based on the mindless and immoral pleasure with which most Americans assisted in the spread of their new trans-regional, highly structured games and recreations. Many people, not only Christian moralists, have always assumed that God placed men and women on earth for more serious pursuits.

The moralists accomplished some things. Though never entirely eliminated, bull-baiting, dog fighting, and cock fighting were legislated out of legal existence. Collegiate sport, particularly football, has steadily acquired restrictive rules and protective equipment that has made it less lethal. Until about 1920, professional baseball games could not legally be played on Sundays. European spectators at the "Olympic Games" of 1900 in Paris were amazed to learn that several Yankee athletes refused to compete in events scheduled long before to take place on Sunday.

But what is far more remarkable than the restrictions on American sport is the extent to which sport had from the very beginning been benignly regarded by Americans of authority. American politicians, bureaucrats, social critics, academics, and intellectuals have either happily participated in or aloofly ignored these dynamic developments in American popular entertainments. American physical education, participator sports, and commercially theatricalized games and competitions are areas that have been regarded as (a) unworthy of serious consideration, (b) vulgar, (c) perfectly harmless, (d) sacred, or some combination of the above by almost all Americans of influence or analytical or critical bent.

American sport has evolved steadily as a result of continuous small decisions, few of which were worth noting at the time. The changes have been determined by entrepreneurs and chance operating in particular milieus offering opportunity for innovation. The first baseball park builders, founders of sports magazines, editors of sports pages, promoters of prizefights, manufacturers of sporting goods and developers of country clubs operated in a fertile atmosphere. Besides the growing population with the characteristics mentioned earlier, the country's banking system was flexibly capable of supplying venture capital. The vigorous working population and the capital available were combined with a dynamic technology that not only permitted the distinctive development of America's vast geographical extent and potential riches, but also the development of new forms of entertainment. It is worth noting that some of the first distinctive American contests were steamboat races in the 1830s. These races at first thrilled the passengers on hand, added to the prestige of winning captains and their crews, and fostered local legends. But with the spread of the telegraph in the 1850s, the races acquired much larger followings. Soon there were more appealing contests to be excited about.

The railroad not only facilitated the spread of sport in the nineteenth century, but may explain it. As soon as possible the best race horses were moved by rail to seize purses for their owners as well as to move breeding stock around. The moving of baseball teams in the 1840s and 1850s by railroad from one city to another forced the creation of mutually agreeable, trans-regional, readily available, written rules. Baseball had to be organized and harmonized into uniformity. Players and spectators alike had to know the precise conditions of play before they arrived for the spectacle. As the railway network extended (there were over 30,000 miles of track before 1860) so did the extent of written, adjudicable rules of competition. The suppression of local variations extended subsequently to collegiate rowing, prizefighting, and other sports. The development of national forms of sport was further advanced by the first American lithographic prints of yachting races, notorious pugilists, baseball players, and gleaming thoroughbreds.

American sporting loyalties tended to remain local. One rooted for his home baseball team. Particular American sports—both for participators and spectators—tended to remain class specific. But with the ever greater efficiency and economy of the national communications and transportation systems, regional variations and techniques of the sports themselves steadily withered away.

By removing so many men from their localities, the Civil War accelerated the trend toward national sports. Baseball with its predictable rules was played in the military bases and prisoner camps in the North and South. Even before 1865 one could see some particular and persistent characteristics of American sport: the ready adaption by entrepreneurs of new technological techniques, the impulse to organize extra-regionally, the enchantment of Americans with statistically stateable, verifiable sports accomplishments. Some of these developments were particularly American and elsewhere in the world they were long dormant or of little interest.

During the decades following the Civil War certain aspects of American sport became entrenched. The evolution of American sport was, of course, a reflection of more basic changes in society: the growth of great cities connected by communication and transportation networks, the ready experimentation with new technology, and new organizations for industrial production. The benign government was another factor. The same forces that made the young nation a populous industrial power made American sport.

After the war, railroads allowed ever greater ranges for the movement of baseball teams and fans. Teams from Detroit, Milwaukee, Dubuque, and Chicago competed in a baseball tournament in 1866 in Rockford, Illinois. In 1869 the Cincinnati Red Stockings made a transcontinental tour. The establishment of "Leagues" under profit-oriented managerial control in the 1870s provided models for other American sports that later professionalized. The profits in sport for the railroads, however, came not from the movement of the "nines" but from the movement of thousands of fans. Later in the century, it was customary for the financiers of the electric street railways, the "interurbans," to provide ball parks and grandstands at the ends of their lines into a city's far suburbs. Players and fans paid fares and the surrounding land, purchased in anticipation, rose in value. The athletic facility was a sign of civilization and attracted permanent residents.

The nearly universal availability of the telegraph was made more effective in the 1880s by the adaption of techniques to send several messages simultaneously over the same wire. Pool rooms and saloons all over America installed receiving sets to keep their customers up-to-date regarding nationally important baseball scores and track and fight results. The heavyweight boxer John L. Sullivan (1858–1918) reached his great notoriety more suddenly and more broadly than any athlete before him because descriptions of his bouts went all over the continent via the electric wire in his championship decade (1882–1892). The particular reputation of the great brawler was, of course, the creation of himself and some surrounding publicists, but the extent of the reputation was a creation of the telegraph. Western Union paid 50 operators to send out 208,000 words of description following John L.'s fight with Jake Kilrain in New Orleans in 1889. When Jim Corbett beat Sullivan in 1892, 300 saloons and billiard halls in New York alone were supposed to have received the news.

The establishment of mass journalism is explainable partly by the waiting for words by the literate populace and the exploitation of techniques for high-speed typesetting and printing. Much of the news came from the wire services and the news that increased circulation most was sport news. The new American sports boosted the sports pages and the sports pages dramatized and made yet more appealing the pseudo events of mass sport theater. The sports pages regularly produced heroes for a society that seemed unable to produce many heroes in other areas of public life.

That sports events are not very substantial events, that athletes are almost intrinsically boring, and that not many noticeable changes of any significance take place in American sport has been known for a long time. In sports reporting, as in almost all aspects of American sport, intelligent reporters and critical editors stayed away. From the very beginning, the overwhelming mass of sports journalism has been slovenly, childish, and venal. The intelligent and skilled writers (and there were many) who started in sports journalism usually fled to forms of journalism allowing greater individualism when the opportunity occurred. Typically sports writers were poorly paid and were often tools of the promoters. They got passes to events and the company of sweaty masculine men. A sports businessman of the 1890s is purported to have said, "Sports writers—you can buy them with a steak."

Except for the pretentiously wealthy who raced big yachts or who enthusiastically embraced British lawn tennis and modern golf in the 1890s, few Americans were any longer curious about British sport. The discretionary income of the American public fertilized specifically American sports literature and magazines. An Irish immigrant, Richard Kyle Fox, founded the enormously profitable *Police Gazette* in 1874 and fed its eager readers a diet of crime stories, girlie pictures, and gossip (much of it made up) of prizefighters and star baseball players. The *Police Gazette* was a fixture in barber shops, pool halls, and anywhere else where men with an hour or two of leisure would gather for chat. The *Gazette* is supposed to have printed 400,000 copies of its issue on the Paddy Ryan–Joe Gross fight in 1880.

There was money in sport. An illustrative success story of the "gilded age" is that of Albert Spalding (1850–1915). Spalding appeared first before the public as a 17-year-old pitcher for the Rockford, Illinois baseball team. Later he was a pitcher and captain of the championship Boston team. Then he was a manager and owner. He began selling baseball equipment in 1876 and manufacturing it shortly afterward. He also branched out into making equipment for various other sports by acquiring smaller firms. He managed to get the Spalding "Official League" ball adopted by the professional baseball league and various college conferences. He had a line of balls ranging in price from five cents to $1.50.

The *Dictionary of American Biography* describes Spalding as "a big fellow physically, and a genius for organizing and directing." In addition to owning teams, he wrote a guide and a history of baseball. He arranged for international tours of baseball teams. Baseball eventually established itself in a small way in Cuba and Japan. In the 1890s he was a true captain of industry. Spalding could set prices of many categories of sporting goods and promote their consumption in his various magazines. Albert Spalding was the director of the American section on sports at the Paris Universal Exposition of 1900 and for his work received a rosette of the French Legion of Honor.

Sporting goods manufacturers and various marketing operations by the turn of the century could present to the American consumer the standardized equipment and mass-produced widgets that provided amusement or sustained fads in America (later the world) thereafter. Americans already mass produced cheap, reliable pocket watches. The step to stop watches was simple. American vulcanized rubber dramatically altered the game of tennis. The rubber-wound ball made necessary the expansion and the consequent rustic estheticization of golf courses. Pneumatic tires transformed sulky racing and then bicycling. Ball bearings were applied to roller skates in the 1880s, which led to a boom in the construction of roller rinks. Every town had to have one. Necessarily there were competitions on roller skates in elegance, speed, and endurance.

The large-scale production in the 1890s of the practical and exhilarating "safety" bicycle with equal sized wheels and rear-wheel chain drive led to the displacement of roller skating as a recreational sport. Bicycles were excitingly more complex technically and much more expensive. And then the bicycle was supplanted in the enthusiasm of those who loved speed by the vastly more technically enchanting and more expensive automobile. Alert American industrialists and promoters satisfied all of these demands.

The monopolists of the sports industries were like the tycoons in other industries. Albert Spalding bought a Michigan lumber mill to assure supplies of wood for his baseball bats. Albert Pope purchased a steel mill to supply frame tubing for his bicycles. It is worth noting here that Orville and Wilbur Wright, the brothers who produced the first successful flight of a motorized airplane in 1903, were bicycle makers. In his industrial embrace, Henry Ford, whose first fame came as a maker of race cars, eventually surpassed them all.

There were some other seedbeds of American sport. Even before the Civil War the United States had 250 colleges. In 1880 England, with a population of 23 million, was getting along with four universities, while Ohio, with a population of three million, had 37 institutions of higher learning. By 1904 about 250,000 young Americans were enrolled in universities and colleges. The numbers in Germany and in France were approximately 20,000 each. A visit to one of the American campuses gave a false impression. They were pretty, well-kept places and the healthy students carried books. But the American college typically offered an easy and irrelevant curriculum. By the late nineteenth century the American college had evolved into a peculiar institution which performed the socially tranquillizing function of keeping the boisterous children of the prosperous classes out of the way for a few years. In order to keep themselves busy the students developed what historians of American higher education have called "the extra curriculum."

Debating societies, fraternities and sororities, and literary clubs were all part of the "extra curriculum" even before the Civil War. So was sport. The first intercollegiate sports event was a boat race between Harvard and Yale on Lake Winnepesaukee in 1852. Various American colleges developed their own varieties of English Rugby football in the 1860s and 1870s. The "Princeton rules" of 1867 specified 25 men to a team. Around 1880 there began the evolution of the distinct American collegiate game, emphasizing tactics and strategy. Presidents, professors, and puritanical educational reformers watched horrified and powerless as college sport evolved rapidly in the 1880s and 1890s. A lot of ingenuity and youthful energy went into the development and proliferation of

American collegiate sports. Football attracted the most attention.

Despite the roughness and frequent injuries that occasionally were fatal, the game could not be suppressed. Hard play produced victories—so much desired by students, alumni, and journalists of the local newspapers. The "sports craze" of the 1890s on American campuses affected baseball, rowing, and track and field, but it was collegiate football that produced the most appealing heroes, the notoriety, the gate receipts, the alumni support, and the big state appropriations.

By the turn of the century, sports within American academia had matured and had acquired their relentless dynamism. There were college colors, college yells and college mascots. Harvard had fewer than 5000 students in 1903, but in that year opened a reinforced concrete stadium seating 57,000. The first international track meet took place at Manhattan Field in New York on September 21, 1895, between the London Athletic Club and the New York Athletic Club. Americans won all eleven events. Princeton and Harvard athletes dominated the first "revived Olympic Games" in Athens in 1896. American collegiate track-and-field athletes and swimmers were the usual victors in the Olympic Games until 1936.

The partially parasitic, partially symbiotic integration of certain high-performance games and competitions in American academic life is one example of the organic integration of various new sports into American life generally. As was the case with sport in other areas of American society and culture, the rapid and harmonious profusion and elaboration of collegiate sport was made easier by the impotence of political and moral authorities.

A commission summoned by President Theodore Roosevelt in 1905 and various efforts in concert by university presidents succeeded only in slowly modifying the rules of collegiate football so that the usual injuries were mild and the deaths much less frequent.

Indeed, among the masses of Americans, sport came to be considered a civic obligation, a moral good, something of quasi-sacred significance. Patriots were especially eager that corruption be prevented or disguised in baseball, "the national game." The Young Men's Christian Association (YMCA) led the way in proposing organized training and team games as methods for absorbing the idle time of poor city boys and instilling in them the habits of good hygiene, self-discipline and respect for officials. Basketball was specifically "invented" by a YMCA official in 1892 for skillful play year-round on the YMCA indoor playing areas.

Urban settlement houses and eventually churches also promoted the standard American sports because they presumably developed leadership and built character. The moralists may have been unable to suppress pool halls, gambling at the dog and horse races or mayhem on the football fields, but they could encourage the conquering of sloth by regular athletic training, the suppression of the ego in team play and the posing of the hygienic and dependable athletic hero.

If the new sports of the young democracy were all the while class-specific and possibly class-defining, no one objected because almost no one noticed. An ambitious person could place himself in society by practicing certain sports just as he wore certain clothes and frequented certain clubs. Many of the numerous very rich at the turn of the century had so much money that they were in danger of running out of things to spend money on. Where once the English gentry were to be imitated, now they were to be surpassed. The "gilded age" was one of enormous teak and mahogany racing yachts, splendid seaside "cottages" where Irish servants maintained tennis courts and country clubs with vast landscapes of golf courses. A correct diversion for the very rich was, as it remains, the establishment of a thoroughbred breeding farm. The purses in the more visible jockeyed or trotting races grew ever larger.

A college degree became a credential necessary to insulate middle-class youths from the necessity to do work that might be soiling. Graduates remained loyal and collegiate sports attracted audiences far beyond the campus population. College games made diverting newspaper reading. Until about 1900 the conservative urban dailies resisted the yellow press's exploitation of sports news. But it became undeniable that sports journalism built and held circulation in all classes. Sports news gradually took up more space in the papers. Editors dedicated to some ideal of quality might try to get and keep sports journalists who had a sense of irony and wrote good prose. But, as always, sports readers seek a sentimental sense of community, not new information or good writing.

The new specifically American sports were still not established

among the working classes, most of whom were still rurally isolated, hobbled by the 60-hour week, or close to their European
origins. But the process of homogenization went on relentlessly.
Ever more working people were seduced by the promoted spectacles of prizefighting, "professional" (that is fake) wrestling, and
bicycling. Baseball was universal. "Sandlot" teams performed in
the provinces. A variety of the game called "softball" and employing a smaller diamond and a larger ball encouraged more play by
amateurs and women.

By the turn of the century American sport had evolved into a
pattern or system that was unique. Sports spectatorship and (far
less) sports participation, sports business, and sports myths were
smoothly integrated into American life. The process had been swift,
but it had been natural and had gone much farther than the evolution of sport anywhere else in the world.

By 1900 the United States was no longer an isolated outpost of
civilization. There were over 75 million inhabitants. Americans
were already innovators in the industrial production of items ranging from false teeth and sewing machines to skyscrapers and bat-
tleships. American riches also financed the establishment of a rich
and at least partly distinctive high culture. At the great international universal expositions or world fairs, American stained glass,
art pottery, sculpture, and paintings won gold medals. Many travelers from abroad felt that the young nation was much more creative, vigorous, and politically moral than the purportedly stag-
nant countries of Europe. America, like Greece in the fifth century
B.C., Northern Italy in the fifteenth century, and England in the
early nineteenth century, was attractive, seductive, and imitable.
As always, admirers saw what they wanted to see. And a lot of
them observed American sport.

Innovation in American sport was slowing by 1914. There were
few new sports or even wanderings of certain games and spectator
activities from one class to another. An exception was the almost
sudden desertion after about 1905 of the audience for bicycle racing who shifted their attention to automobiles. However, this particular recognition of the metaphorical as well as actual vigor of
the internal combustion engine was but one aspect of a sudden
and portentous development in American culture.

As always the very rich demonstrated their power to outsiders and to each other by conspicuously expensive sports. More people were rich, there were more yacht races and country clubs. The integration of sport in the working classes was aided by better and cheaper transportation and communication, greater disposable incomes, shorter working hours, and the assimilation of second generation children.

This last point merits some stress. To become an American thoroughly meant not only the mastering of the language and certain little graces of everyday life. One had also to accept the myths, the spectatorship, and (to employ a word of the great American sports writer Robert Lipsyte) the "manchat" of the sports news as provided by the newspapers and accepted without question by one's companions in the neighborhood or on the job. In the 1920s, the created heroes of the gridiron, the diamond, or the ring had millions of fans concerned with their accomplishments.

There was a growing reverence for ultimate, verifiable accomplishments and those who accomplished them. This may be related to a concomitant weakening of the attraction of the talismans and heroes of religion, the state, and of other semi-sacred institutions. In sport there was a peculiar obsession with precise statistics. As we have seen, there were varified records for a type of arrow shooting in pre-Meiji Japan and for certain kinds of horse races in late-eighteenth-century England. In the course of the nineteenth century, with the wide acceptance of precisely defined competitions and the precise measurement of time and space, sports records became widely acknowledged monuments (though temporary ones; that was part of the enchantment) of modern life.

Track-and-field records date from the Oxford–Cambridge meet on March 5, 1864 at Christ Church Ground at Oxford. Supreme performances were noted and acknowledged in many British sports thereafter. Americans took over these sports, but intensified their concern with the essence of high performance in them. The enormous geographical extent of America still prevented ready contact among the dispersed universe of eager competitors. But precisely specified contests and precisely regulated competitions within them could allow the creation of supra-regional heroes by impartially and technologically confirming the bases of their new fame. Competitors did not have to be on the spot to compete. In fact, they did not compete with each other. The point to be made is that the foundations of sporting fame were entirely new and were uniquely suited to the ideals of a new society. The new society was equalitarian, literate, accomplishment oriented, optimistic, materialistic, relatively traditionless, and geographically dispersed. The athletic hero was a spontaneous, natural creation rising from the circumstances and ideals of a new age.

Baseball, the American sport of nostalgia and sentiment, became and has remained the sport of many statistics and records. Players have their batting averages. Pitchers have their win-lose and earned run averages. Sluggers have their home runs. All of these can be divided into statistics for a season, a series, or a lifetime. But there are literally hundreds of records for such things as stolen bases, no-hit games, in a certain season or leadership in three-base hits in consecutive seasons. The possibilities of devising new records are almost infinite. The ability to concoct new records is an amusing device used in one of the splendid baseball novels, Robert Coover's *Universal Baseball Association, Inc.,* . . . (1968). Heroic players in retirement list their records in the backs of their (ghostwritten) autobiographies.

As early as 1886, Montague Shearman, an Englishman, an enthusiast for the new sports, and one of sport's first careful historians, observed that among the Americans, the pursuit of the record was becoming an "obsession." American sports may have had English origins, but they had taken on a lot of particular American traits.

A sort of holy grail of American sport during the gilded age was the "mile a minute" which was believed to be attainable on a bicycle. A carefully technical article in *Scientific American* of July 15, 1899 tells how Charlie Murphy finally accomplished this. Some sponsors laid down a smooth wood platform between the tracks of a 2.25 mile straight run of the Long Island Railroad. They bolted a wind screen to the back of a fast locomotive. Charlie's racer had a very large chain wheel and a small rear sprocket. As the locomotive reached the necessary velocity, he kept his front tire within a foot of a guard bar just in front of the screen. Five trustworthy men held precision stop watches as the locomotive held its speed.

The mile was clocked at 57⁴/₅ seconds. For years afterward Charlie Murphy rode his bicycle on rollers on the stage before respectful vaudeville audiences.

The fascination of sports fans with verifiable high performance was not solely an American taste but is an integral element in modern sport that Americans were the first to fix on so enthusiastically. As the world modernized, it took on modern sport and fascination with its fetish, the record. Some of the first international sports heroes were American bicycle racers, including Charlie Murphy. That some Harvard and Princeton athletes won so many events at the Olympic Games in 1896 is due partly to the accident that few Englishmen took the invitations seriously or bothered to appear. But American athletes continued for half a century to be the outstanding performers at all international competitions ranging from pugilism to long-distance airplane flying. That so many Americans were so distinguished is not so much confirmation of the superiority (long since waning) of American flesh and will but rather a clear indication of the fact that much of the world has embraced modern sport subsequently.

As always, the patriots in America and the admirers from abroad saw in American culture what they wanted to see. One could exaggerate the extent to which American sport was the creation of a democratic consensus, the celebration of merit, or even the promoter of good health. There have always been undercurrents of uneasiness and criticism of modern sports. The cadres of persons who considered themselves the reservoirs of morality who were likely to favor temperance and universal suffrage continued to see sports as incitements to drunkenness, occasions for wagering, the spilling of blood, and the profanation of the Sabbath. Sport distracted men from the earnestness of life and the obligation to further moral progress. But these objections remained undercurrents.

Sport remained, in fact, a preserve of male participators and spectators. The hobbled acquiescent housewife and the depraved vamp were persistent female ideals. English and continental travelers were astonished at how sickly American females in the city looked. The first American women bicyclists encountered ridicule because they wore a kind of trousers. Well into the twentieth century American female athletes were expected to excel only in certain "graceful" sports. The relative decline of American distinction in international sport competitions is partly explained by the fact that other nations have been much more thorough in their preparation and support of promising female athletes.

Since the federal government, all local governments, and indeed the popular consensus provided little room for tampering with either sport or the traditional attitudes regarding the rights of Negro people, American sports as they evolved tended to reinforce the isolation of the Negroes from participation in American life. For about a half century after 1880 the situation of blacks in sport, as in other aspects of public life, actually got worse. They were effectively barred from being professional bicycle racers, jockeys or even prizefighters. Jack Johnson was briefly an exception. Until the 1920s only a few very secure eastern colleges and then a few large state universities in the Midwest and California allowed some exceptionally adept and polite Negroes to play football or to be on track teams. The Negroes at their racially exclusive colleges competed in the American sports among themselves and before black spectators. There was a black professional baseball league, but the reputations of accomplished players remained local and race-specific.

By the early twentieth century the enormous continent was bound together by splendid transportation and communications networks. Certain sports heroes had millions of fans from coast to coast. College football and the other Ivy League sports were gracefully established at the University of California and at Stanford University. Newspapers everywhere took ever more of their sports news from the wire services. But despite the various modern elements and the wide appeal that characterized modern sport as it evolved, like American religion, American politics, and American work, sport also worked to reinforce social distinctions and certainly licensed some social injustices. As always and as everywhere else, relatively few participated. Despite various and continuous proposals to do so, physical education was never integrated into American primary, secondary, or community education. Some of the middle and lower classes might observe and gamble on the horse racing of the rich, but many more were inspired by the pastoral myths, patriotism, and stately order of baseball. American sport was not yet pervasively a mass movement. Until after World War I large groups were still not participators in mass culture. They were farmers having no access to rapid transportation, urban life, or daily newspapers. They might be immigrants or industrial workers restrained by the long work week. Or they were women for whom convention prescribed very narrow corridors of behavior.

In some ways, this chapter's concentration on American sport over a long period in a book that claims to be a universal history has been misleading. By 1914 trans-regional, constitutionally regulated, accomplishment oriented, statistically verifiable, civilized Anglo-Saxon sport had taken root in many other places besides the United States. Transported English sport found especially enthusiastic practitioners and spectators in Australia, where the further independent evolution was rapid and richly creative. There were football clubs in Hamburg, St. Petersburg, and Johannesburg in 1914. In England itself sport was homogenized and extended by the dense transportation network, the market oriented press, democratic ideals, and greater wealth and leisure. Cricket, which a century before had been narrowly aristocratic, drew spectators from a wide spectrum of the social classes. But after the war England was no longer the place from which innovations in sport came.

[10]

THE MODERN
OLYMPIC GAMES

The prestige of the classical Greeks was never entirely eclipsed. The Byzantines preserved much of Greek classical literature. Throughout the Middle Ages the Greek-inspired monuments of ancient Rome could be seen, indeed admired, in many places in Europe. In the late medieval period, certain intellectuals were especially attracted to the philosophical works of Plato and his followers.

The prestige of the classical authors and other ancient heroes was especially great during the fifteenth and sixteenth and seventeenth centuries in a period of literary and artistic enthusiasm which historians conveniently call the Renaissance. Italian princes and the humanists around them collected and republished most of the classical texts that we now possess. Italian architects, painters, and sculptors were inspired by classical models to establish standards of visual beatuty that have been challenged only in recent decades. Traditionally in Europe a person's education was judged on the basis of how well he had mastered the old literature in Latin and Greek and how sincerely he expressed his admiration for the titans who had created it.

The climate, economic bases, and class structure of early modern European society were, to be sure, all different than those of the Greeks and the Romans. We have already observed that European sports had no continuity with the games and contests of the Greeks and Romans. They were, instead, natural adaptions that sprang anew out of local peasant culture and from the need of the noble classes to demonstrate their ascendency. However, among the well-educated, along with an interest in the classics of literature, a curiosity about Greek sport and the sport festivals never died entirely.

Though earthquakes had toppled its monuments and silt from shifting rivers had covered them, Olympia and its games were remembered. Shakespeare alluded to the "Olympian" Games in *Henry VI* and in *Troilus and Cressida*. So did John Milton in *Paradise Lost*. Voltaire, a charmed spectator at an athletic festival in England in 1727, wrote in a letter that he felt that he had been "transported to the Olympic Games." In the eighteenth century musicians composed pieces containing "Olympic Games" in their titles. Many English and French authors mentioned the Games, always with respect, in their works.

It was the Germans who in the end became most sentimentally attached to the site of Olympia and the great festivals that had taken place there. A most energetic and devoted scholar of Greek art was Johann Joachim Winckelmann (1717–1768). Winckelmann's etchings, descriptions and praise of Greek monuments inspired generations of European artists and writers—most of them Germans. A German, Johann Heinrich Krause, (1802–1882) was the first scholar who systematically and critically assembled all the known materials about Greek sport. One of his books, published in 1838, was about the festival at Olympia which, in the meantime, had been rediscovered.

In August 1776, Richard Chandler, an English traveler used a description of Greek monuments written by Pausanias in the second century A.D. to guide him to a desolate place in the Peloponnesus where all he could see were some walls and parts of some huge Doric column drums. A French military expedition sent in 1829 to help the Greeks in their wars of independence against the Turks included a group of reverent scholars. They hired some local laborers to excavate the area around the temple of Zeus.

It was, however, Germans who began the systematic and eventually complete excavations at Olympia in 1875. Archaeologists and sports scholars such as Ernst Curtius (1814–1896), Friedrich Adler (1827–1908) and Carl Diem (1882–1962) proposed and directed the excavations and cataloging of artifacts. The financing of the work was provided by governments resident in Berlin (later Bonn). Olympia and its festivals became in modern times particularly German. However, the Germans never became so sentimental as to attempt to *revive* the Olympic Games.

Early in the seventeenth century a certain Captain Robert Dover established on his estate in the Cotswolds an annual two-day feast and sports meet. Dover and his friends were well-educated and so he nostalgically named his festival the "Olympick Games." Some of Dover's friends were poets who in 1636 published some witty verses dedicated to the host. The verses were stuffed with allusions to the sports festival of antiquity. The Cotswold Olympics consisted of such folk contests as pitching the bar, throwing the hammer, jumping and wrestling, and included dancing to the shepherd's pipe. The events changed, but the festivals were revived from time to time well into the nineteenth century. Other local sports festivals in England were also dignified with the appellation "Olympic Games."

While the ancient site in the Peloponnesus was still a forlorn spot, the newly independent Greeks also staged modern "Olympic Games" in their small, but growing capital at Athens. Evangelios Zappas (1800–1865), a wealthy grain dealer, in 1858 offered King Otto of Greece an endowment for "the restoration of the Olympic Games to be celebrated every four years following the precepts of the ancient Greeks, our ancestors." Accordingly a festival took place in Athens on a Sunday in 1859. The spectacle included a sprint called the *diaulos,* a longer race called the *dolichos,* the tossing of a discus, a long jump, and the throwing of a spear at the head of a steer. Clearly it was all an attempt to lend legitimacy to a central myth of the modern Greek nation: that this state is the legitimate heir of the most richly inventive and influential culture the world has ever known. But the Athenians had no athletic tradition whatever. For the populace, the whole affair was just a diverting folk festival.

The periodicity of four years could not be maintained, but there were "Olympic Games" again in Athens in 1870, 1875, and 1888. Though the judges wore frock coats, they were called *"Hellanodi–cai"* after ancient usage. For the Games of 1875 the Athenians tidied up the site of the stadium of Herodes Atticus, once a splendid construction of white marble, but by then a grassy ravine.

It was only natural that modern, high-performance sport would eventually be included among the great cultural manifestations of the later nineteenth century. But the inclusion came rather late. The first world's fair, London's Crystal Palace Exhibition of 1851, was one of the happiest events of the epoch. Later world's fairs—particularly those in Paris in 1855, 1867, 1878, and 1889, and those in Philadelphia in 1876 and in Chicago in 1893, tended to be ever larger, more idealistically educational, and more inclusive. Indeed the world's fairs of the later nineteenth century can be compared with the simultaneous assembling, editing, and publishing of the several, many-volumed national encyclopedias as well as the stocking of the splendid national research libraries and the devising of the universal systems of classification (of which the Dewey Decimal system was one) to keep comprehensible and accessible the expansion of knowledge.

The Paris Universal Exposition of 1878 was the first to include international congresses for such diverse specialists as dentists, historians and statisticians. This kind of altruistic internationalism led to further internationalism of all sorts in the nineteenth century. The Universal Postal Union had already been established in 1875. There was convention to standardize patent laws in 1893 and one to standardize copyright in 1887. The Paris Exposition of 1889, for which the Eiffel Tower was built, included a vast range of instructional exhibits and international meetings of scholars, scientists, and academic specialists. It attracted 40 million admissions—more than the population of France at the time.

The French then prepared for an Exhibition in 1900 that would attract 100 million visitors and planned attractions for every person of prominence in the world. There would be, among others, congresses for bibliographers, coin collectors, photographers, hypnotists, and beekeepers. Shortly after the organization began in 1892, the bureaucrats in charge accepted proposals for a congress on physical education that would include some exhibitions of sports and games.

In view of the advancing freedom of movement of so many Europeans and the idealistic cosmopolitanism of the time it may seem odd that internationalism came so late to sport. Partial explanations, or at least clarifications, are at hand. Sport in fact remained remarkably chauvinistic until well into the twentieth century. One can indeed show that early in the nineteenth century some fit and talented pugilists and distance runners worked a betting circuit that included Britain and North America. Famed Scottish strong men performed at "Caledonian Games" in eastern Canada and the United States in the middle of the century. A track meet took place between the London Athletic Club and the New York Athletic Club (the Americans won all eleven events) at Manhattan Field on September 21, 1895. Anglo-Saxon sport was spreading geographically and among more people. Football of the tamed and regulated sort that had evolved in England in the 1850s and 1860s was being played in South Africa and in Australia in the 1890s. However, these new supra-local sports and games were noticed by only a few of the intellectually and politically alert people in advanced industrial states such as Germany and the Scandinavian countries.

Rationally contrived forms of exercise or gymnastics and projects for universal physical education were established in many places in Europe. But devised modern sport (for example that of the turners or the Sokols) as well as organic, high-performance, spectator sport (for example that of the British and American collegians or the bicycle racers of the 1890s) remained outside of the vision of most of the bureaucrats who ran the modern states and who had stakes in the great world's fairs.

I have already claimed that performance-oriented, disciplined, democratic, theatrically presented sport suits well the spiritual and mythic needs of a rapidly industrializing society. Modern sport might well have become international sooner had there been large meets that might or might not have been called "Olympic Games." But that the summit demonstrations of modern sport now take the regular form that they do can be largely attributed to the vision and tenacity of Baron Pierre de Coubertin (1863-1937).

Pierre de Coubertin was born of aristocratic parents whose own ancestors had served the rulers of France for centuries. Pierre conceivably inherited and/or absorbed the notion that it was correct for him to devote his life to the task of advancing French political and cultural primacy. But the French Third Republic of the 1890s could not claim cultural, economic, or military primacy. The Germans had forced France to suffer a humiliation in the war of 1870-1871. France stagnated as other modern nations boomed.

Coubertin's education was Catholic, classical and, he later concluded, much too disciplined, authoritarian, and cramped. He later dallied in the salons of Paris. He rode the family horses, learned to scull and to box. He made friends with some left-wing Catholics and (rather bravely considering his origins) called himself a Republican. Like all the intellectuals of that time and place he brooded over schemes to reinvigorate France. Armed with letters of introduction and generous letters of credit he traveled in England and in North America.

Coubertin was envious that the English had gained great wealth, acquired a vast empire, and evolved politically without social convulsions. Like another French Anglophile before him, Hippolyte Taine (see his *Notes sur Angleterre*, 1872), Coubertin was especially impressed by the unique English upper-class preparatory schools. Projects for sweeping educational reform were discussed everywhere. It was widely conceded in France that foundations for Germany's dynamism were her expensive, far-reaching systems of primary, technical, and scholarly education. Coubertin concluded that, if Germany's successes were due to her citizens' educations, the comparable triumphs of the English and Americans must be attributable to their educational customs.

Like most travelers at any time anywhere, Coubertin saw what he wanted to see. He determined that the distinguishing characteristic of Anglo-Saxon education was that it was "balanced"— that is, the English and Americans educated the body as well as the mind. Their schools were in park-like settings, the students participated long and with pleasure in character-building, body-building events of their own devising.

At Princeton University in 1893, Coubertin befriended Professor William Milligan Sloane (1850–1928) who thereafter encouraged the Frenchman to enforce the strictest principles of amateurism. Sloan and the men of his class favored what he called "clean sport."

As early as 1889 Coubertin had begun to apply his energy and treasure to the task of organizing sport (such as existed) in France. He favored the sport of the English and American wealthy classes and wanted it, somehow, to be integrated into French education. Coubertin's great insight (and possibly a cynical one) was that while sports training and sports performance of the Anglo-Saxon variety could appeal to only a few performers, the appetite for festivity is nearly universal. Accordingly, his organizational meetings for sports bureaucrats and educators were laced with banquets, oratory, and musical interludes. His cross-country meets, rowing races, or football exhibitions were ended by fireworks displays or torchlit processions. Significantly, Coubertin had little contact with athletes. He was most sedulous in his wooing of those politicians or bureaucrats who might enforce a more "balanced" education for all Frenchmen.

Some famous politicians and litterateurs graced a meeting of his *Union des sociétés françaises des sports athlétiques* late in November 1892. There was a bicycle race before the inaugural breakfast and a fencing match before the opening of a new clubhouse. In his final speech at the closing ceremonies Baron Pierre de Coubertin proposed that "on a basis conforming to modern life, we reestablish a great and magnificent institution, the Olympic Games."

His plans for Olympic Games were vague and long remained so. He believed he could introduce a series of sporting competitions into the great exposition planned for Paris in 1900. He organized a preparatory "Congress" of physical educationalists for June of 1894. Representatives from twelve countries appeared. Professor Sloane from Princeton was on hand. At the opening ceremony, the delegates heard a soprano supported by harp and a chorus sing a newly discovered "Hymn to Apollo," which the French school at Athens had deciphered from some ancient marble tablets. A Captain Viktor Balck was prepared to offer Stockholm as the site for a modern international sports festival. The Hungarian delegate to the Congress had authorization to propose that the first Olympic Games of modern tims take place in Budapest.

Coubertin was, by this time, discouraged with the narrow vision of the bureaucrats organizing the Paris exposition. The delegate from Greece was Demitrios Bikelas (1835–1908), a historian and a poet who had access to the Greek royal family. When Bikelas proposed that Greece, the home of the ancient Olympic Games, be the home of modern games to take place four years before the Exposition in 1900, Coubertin and Sloane accepted. The rest of the delegates voted in favor of Olympic Games in 1896.

Preparations began at once. Athens was, at the time, a dusty city of some 100,000 souls far out on Europe's periphery. The constitutional monarchy was bankrupt. The Prime Minister told Bikelas that there would be no "Olympic Games" in Athens for the simple reason that there was no money in the public fisc to pay for them. Bikelas sent for Coubertin, who came to Athens and convinced King George and his brothers to take command. Appeals to wealthy Greeks overseas brought in large sums including one enormous contribution to restore in white marble from Pentelicus the marble stadium of Herodes Atticus. Sales of special "Olympic Games" postage stamps were successful; so were advance payments for the rather expensive tickets to the events.

Coubertin insisted that the Olympic Games should be "on a basis conforming to modern life." There would be gymnastics, some bicycle races, fencing, and contests in marksmanship. All of these sorts of contests were more or less known and trained for in Europe—to some small extent even in Athens. But Coubertin also insisted that the focus of attention in the stadium, which could hold as many as 90,000 people, be typically American and English track-and-field competitions. At the insistence of a friend, the classicist Professor Michel Bréal (1832–1915), Coubertin added to the program a so-called "Marathon race," which would begin at the site of the renowned battle and proceed westward for some 40 kilometers over the roads to Athens and to the finish line at the stadium.

Astonished at being well-financed, the organizers in Athens accepted Coubertin's conceptions of festive presentation. There would be opening and closing ceremonies. Winners of events would be declared by the raising of their numbers and their national banners to the top of prominent flagpoles. As Coubertin demanded, there would be no medals of gold (which stank of lucre) but only silver and bronze medals to distinguish first and second places respectively. There would be ancillary parades, concerts, and opera performances. The organizers considered and then rejected Coubertin's suggestions redolent with classicism for competitions in art and in music. They also disappointed Coubertin by rejecting Coubertin's planned events for horses and riders of the sort that did not exist in Greece. The yachting events were eventually cancelled due to cold and windy weather which lasted all during the Games from April 5 through 15 (March 24 through April 3 on the old Greek calendar), 1896.

The local population was enthusiastic. Small gymnastic societies took on new members who were coached in routines that had been perfected in Northern Europe. On the fields near some villages there were impromptu contests in heaving the shot or tossing the javelin (for distance according to modern usage). The Greeks had earlier revived the classical discus throw and this was on the program. Some massively muscled sailors in the Royal Navy were given leaves to practice for the event. Soldiers and some shepherds plodded the hilly road from Marathon to Athens accompanied by cycling trainers with stopwatches.

It turned out that the overwhelming majority of competitors who appeared for all the events were Greek. Sloane had been able to recruit some Princeton juniors on the track team. They were joined by five Harvard track-and-field athletes, and two marksmen and a swimmer from Boston. Six self-proclaimed Englishmen entered various events, but one was an Australian, another was a South African, two were tourists passing through, and two bicyclists were servants at the British Embassy. These last mentioned caused a terrific hubbub because, since they were working men, they could not be considered "amateurs" in the English sense. In the end they competed. There was a Swiss, a Dane, a Swede, and an Austrian. The only Italian who appeared had walked from Milan as part of his training, but could produce no amateur credentials when he arrived and so was not allowed to compete. There were a half-dozen cocky Hungarians.

The only large group of Europeans were some turners from Berlin who were indirectly invited by the Greek Royal Family. Many turners had a well-thought out opposition to Anglo-Saxon sport and indeed to foreign sports of any kind. The issue of German participation in the international sports festival in 1896 was part of a long, intensely debated struggle in which the German cosmopolitans steadily made gains. The Germans who did show up in Athens were defensive and stiff in their manners and did not endear themselves to their fellow competitors, Coubertin, or the Greeks.

The athletic results of the Games might have been foreseen. The Germans won almost all the gymnastic events. One of them, a Herr Hoffmann (whom one observer called "the best athlete there"), actually won in wrestling and in rope climbing as well. A Hungarian, Alfred Hoyos, won a couple of swimming events. The track-and-field events which Coubertin succeeded in giving central prominence were dominated by the Americans. The college boys also won the hearts of the Athenians with their geniality and their barbaric college cheers ("It is the cry of the wild Indians!" some Greeks murmured). Though their performances were inferior to the best of what they had done at home, they had to win their events because only they (and a couple Englishmen who took some second places) had actually trained for competition.

The great exception was Spiridon Loues, the winner of the first Marathon race ever. Astonishingly, a large and international group showed up for the start on the morning of April 10, 1896. Most fell by the way quickly, however, and Loues was thereby elevated to a status that recalled the respect given to Greece's heroes of antiquity. Greeks were second and third in that same race and the majority of the few finishers. Locals also won some marksmanship and fencing competitions and a certain bicycle "Marathon" race as well.

These victories and the happy progression of the festivities all occurred, it should be emphasized, when the local economic and political prospects were especially dismal. After the athletes and tourists went home the national finances deteriorated further and then in February 1897 some politicians engaged the nation in a disastrous war with Turkey. Small wonder then that the happy "Olympic Games" came to be recalled in yet happier terms. Even before the Games of 1896 were over, some prominent citizens and the Royal Family were determined that the modern Olympics should remain in their original place. However, in the face of Coubertin's opposition, the government was able to arrange only a sort of rump "Olympic Games" in 1906 in Athens.

It would be some time before an international sports festival would take place in anything like the circumstances that Pierre de Coubertin had viewed as proper. The French organizers of the Paris Exposition of 1900 did indeed provide time and space for a congress of physical educationalists and a suitably encyclopedic drawn-out display of recreational pastimes, sports, and games. Coubertin for a while attempted to stage some "Olympic Games" outside the embrace of the enormous exposition and then gave up. He attended few of the hundreds of sports exhibitions that took place in and around Paris from the end of May to the end of October. He did succeed in getting official recognition that the contests in (among other things) golf, rugby football, croquet, and even the Basque game of pelote were all part of the modern Olympic Games. Some of the many victorious American athletes in Paris first learned that they had participated in Olympic Games when the engraved certificates of awards presented to them declared this fact. Michel Theato, the Frenchman who won the Marathon race which went through the center of Paris, learned that he was an official "Olympic victor" twelve years later.

The attempts of Professor Sloane and Baron de Coubertin to have independent Olympic Games in New York came to nothing. The Games of 1904 were absorbed in the organization for the world's fair of that year in St. Louis. There were fewer competitors than at Paris and those who appeared in St. Louis were overwhelmingly Americans. There were exhibitions of basketball, baseball, lacrosse and motorboating. There were also so-called "Anthropological Days" in the course of which American Sioux, Filipinos, Ainus, and Patagonians gave demonstrations of their indigenous contests. Despite the carnival atmosphere there was a sort of core Olympic program confined to two weeks in September and consisting mostly of the track-and-field events that were regular parts of American college meets.

It was with some satisfaction that Coubertin looked forward to the Olympic Games that some Englishmen requested for London in 1908. But this festival was subsumed into an ambitious Franco-British exhibition that was itself an aspect of the rapprochement of the two traditional enemies in the face of German power and diplomatic irresponsibility. The sponsorship, however, allowed grandiose financing that provided for a new stadium at Shepherd's Bush capable of holding 100,000 spectators and having a proper 100 meter swimming pool in the center of it. British officials were experienced at handling large events such as the Henley regatta, various derbies, football cup matches and national track and field championships. So Coubertin assented to having all the judges British. There would be for the first time a parade of athletes and gold medals for victors. Another innovation was the inclusion of women, who gave demonstrations of tennis and who also participated as halves of the ice skating pairs.

British and American athletes dominated the publicity which was, for the first time, world-wide and considerable. The winning performances were generally outstanding. However, the whole show was overshadowed by the bitter antagonism between the Americans, many of whom were of recent Irish extraction, and the British amateurs who were of the socially elevated classes.

What muddles! The British judges obviously cheated in some cases and were accused of cheating in many more. Some officials bodily assisted Dorando Pietri, a Marathoner who was collapsing near the end of the finish line, so he could beat out an American, Johnny Hayes, who was coming up fast. Some judges and some English journalists objected to the frictionless, thin, and clinging American swimming suits. Though the majority of the competitors were English, Americans had been much more dogged in their devotion to training and once again dominated the track-and-field events. There were also competitors from many parts of the British Empire and from many countries in northern Europe. More

squabbles marring the Games were those among the various Scandinavian and the German gymnasts who could not devise a mutually agreeable system for judging supremacy in their events.

The general mood of the completed Olympic Games in London
in 1908 was one of patriotic acrimony rather than of enhanced
international harmony. The way was paved, however, for the first
international athletic festival that would incorporate the lessons
learned in London and that would also benefit the hosts and the
guests.

The Swedes prepared for the fifth Olympics of the modern era
well. The substantial profits from a special national lottery provided the essential substance for any large festival. Some 500
Swedes divided into 26 committees that worked four years full
time to organize. Spectators in London had filled the hastily built,
ugly stadium only on the last days of those Games. The stadium
in Stockholm held only 30,000 and from the outside looked like a
handsome medieval fortress. Since only a few Swedes were ac-
quainted with the modern track-and-field program, national preparations included the recruitment and training of athletes. Six
months before the Games were to open, fifty athletes were taken
to a special camp run by an American trainer of Swedish origin.
This was, of course, a violation of the amateur rules, but then, as
later, when this technique was employed, the officials of the International Olympic Committee looked the other way.

The Stockholm Games of 1912 had 3889 competitors from 28
countries compared with London's 2035 competitors from 22
countries. Of course, a large number of those "competitors" were
Scandinavian gymnasts who took part in synchronized displays.
Still, the excellence of the facilities and the general harmony of
the procedures went far to establish the wholesomeness of the
Games. By this time the American invention of "sports pages" in
the daily newspapers had been adapted as a circulation boosting
device all over Europe and indeed almost anywhere where there
was widespread literacy. The sports dramas that took place in
Stockholm were international news.

To be sure there were incidents. The German victors in the 400
meter relay race were disqualified after a judge determined that

the third runner had overstepped the permissible line before passing the baton. A photograph, published that evening in the Swedish newspapers, showed the judge to be wrong; but standards of
even international sport were not yet so exquisitely precise as to
accept scientific proof as evidence. The victor in the modern pentathlon and the decathlon, who was probably one of the greatest
athletes of all time, was Jim Thorpe, an American Indian. In January of the next year, Thorpe's medals were taken away and his
name struck from the record books because it was discovered that
he was not an amateur. He had previously played baseball for $60
a week.

As president of the International Olympic Committee, Pierre de
Coubertin was forced to adjudicate some delicate diplomatic disputes. Finland, which was part of the Russian Empire, wished to
enter its own team. St. Petersburg was opposed. The imperial officials in Vienna opposed the marching in the opening ceremonies
of separate Czech and Hungarian teams. Coubertin wanted all the
teams to march separately with separate flags, claiming that there
was a sports geography that was different from political geography.

In the end, because their tradition of separate Olympic participation dated from 1896, the Hungarians had their own team and
their own flag. The Czechs marched and competed as Austrians.
The Finnish solution was most complex. They could have a separate team that would march beside the Russians, but would not
be required to carry the Russian flag. However, in the case of a
Finnish victory, the Russian flag would be raised during the victory ceremony. As it turned out the Russian flag was raised nine
times—in every case for a Finnish victory.

Whether there was or was not a sporting geography, benefits
from the relatively harmonious Olympic Games accrued to more
than the medal winners. Like the Greeks sixteen years earlier, the
Swedes employed the festival to demonstrate to their visitors and
to the world's newspaper reading public their prominence on the
world scene. And again, as the Greek royal house did, the Swedish
royal family installed themselves with some flair in the festivities
in order to claim or to demonstrate their importance in a consti-

tutional government. After Gustave V told Jim Thorpe that Thorpe was the most wonderful athlete in the world, the American replied, "Thanks, King."

After 1912, opposition to the modern Olympic Games and the program that they contained was insignificant. The world's fairs, which had previously been focused on didactic internationalism, were no longer taking place on a regular basis. Coubertin himself had changed. His schemes to strengthen French youth found no echo in the ministries in Paris. His rhetoric favoring high-performance sports and he himself were greeted the world over. He had become sufficiently cosmopolitan to accept the proposal that the sixth modern Games take place in the capital of Imperial Germany. Coubertin may have given the 1916 Games to Berlin because he hoped that the Emperor's well-known delight in sport spectacle would distract him from political ambitions that many Europeans feared would, if not deflected, lead to war.

The new stadium in Berlin was dedicated in 1913. Carl Diem, the young head of the German organizing committee, had urged the government to do everything possible to discover and develop athletic talent for the prestigious track-and-field events. Alvin Kraentzlein, the American victor in the 60 meter hurdles, the 110 meter hurdles, the 200 meter hurdles (actually he was one of the very first athletes to use the foot-forward, *grand jeté* technique), and the long jump at the Games of 1900, was already coaching German track athletes. The "Olympic Games" postage stamps were designed by a noted painter and sculptor of athletes, Franz von Stuck.

Since his generals had assured William II that the battles would be brief, preparations for the Berlin Olympics continued after the great war started in August 1914. The French, English, and Russian generals had also assured their leaders that the war would be brief. Coubertin too tried for a while to pretend that the war would be brief and would not shift the site. Though the 1916 Games never took place they still are considered the sixth in the series. Coubertin who had been ignored in France moved his family and the International Olympic Committee to neutral Switzerland.

Little will be lost by considering the next three Olympic Games more or less as a unit. They all took place in northern Europe, according to a format that had been foreseen by Coubertin long before. The fact that the Belgians had suffered badly at the hands of the Germans who wrecked the Games of 1916 led to the giving of the seventh modern Olympics (1920) to Antwerp. The facilities and festivities were, of necessity, somewhat austere, but numerical and international participation was even greater than at Stockholm. The Games of 1924 took place in Paris. The facilities were good, the participation numerous and international. All the same, attendance at the many events scattered about Paris was only occasionally heavy. High-performance sport based upon English and American events had been accepted in several industrial countries, but still did not appeal to the masses of Frenchmen. The Games of 1928 in Amsterdam were well planned, well participated in and well observed. In all of the international sports festivals of the 1920s there were, of course, "incidents," those *contretemps*, injustices, or errors in anticipatory planning that provided, for a while, salable journalistic copy. However, the meetings were only of local political significance.

In the 1920s high-performance cosmopolitan sport continued to evolve and to be acknowledged as valid—perhaps as attractive— by ever more people. In all of the industrial nations, traditional rituals and local loyalties steadily weakened and the dramaturgy and distractions of sport made steady headway among the masses. Almost all large daily newspapers had allocated sports pages whose filling up was the task of ambitious sports reporters. Later in the 1920s a new kind of sports journalist appeared—the sports broadcaster who had a certain amount of radio time to make attractive and to fill up. This was the period when many American universities were building football stadiums holding many times their total enrollments, when pugilistic heavyweight championships produced million-dollar gates, when the first riots broke out at South American soccer games. The wire services (which after 1926 could also almost instantaneously send pictures of overseas broken finish tapes, knockouts, or winning goals) made sport theater in Madison Square Garden an enchantment for radio listeners or sports-page readers in Warsaw or Montevideo as well as New York.

The Olympic Games in the 1920s were international news. Because the continental Europeans had no historically legitimized or organic sports festivals such as those based on big league baseball (as in America) or association football (as in Britain), the Olympic Games loomed rather larger in European consciousness than they did in North America or (on the other hand) in the somewhat isolated USSR or backward parts of Asia, South America, or Africa.

Like the great world's fairs of the last half of the nineteenth century the Olympic Games of the twentieth century became steadily more ecumenical. There was a tendency for the organizers of each Olympic festival to view their predecessors as competitors whose statistical marks for numbers of national or individual competitors, expense, as well as for sporting records all had to be surpassed. The open-ended games became steadily more inclusive. The major example is the establishment of regular "Winter Olympics." International competitions in skiing, though confined to Scandinavia, had taken place in the late nineteenth century. There were "Nordic Games" in 1910, 1914, and 1917; and then again in 1922 and 1926. By the early 1920s the annual Holmenkollen Week of winter sports near Oslo was organized and festively presented much like the Olympic Games. Coubertin had admitted figure skating to the London Games in 1908; speed skating and ice hockey to the Antwerp Games of 1920. An "International Winter Sports Week" at Chamonix in 1924 was in 1926 retrospectively recognized as the "First Winter Olympic Games." Of the winter sports that were internationally recognized in 1928, the Netherlands could offer facilities for only those that might take place on flat land, so the rather full program of the second winter games were in St. Mortiz in 1928. However, the Winter Games took place in the same nation as the summer games in 1932 and again in 1936.

The Winter Olympics provided tribunes for the establishment of dozens of heroes of the modern era. None of these equaled the fame of Sonja Henie the solo figure skater. Competing at Chamonix in 1924 before her twelfth birthday she was eighth and last. She was fifth in the world's championship in 1925 and runner up in 1926. But she was never beaten again. Her father and she worked meticulously and with total devotion not only on her skating technique, but also on her costumes and the minute details of her public appearances, including her incessant smile. She trained for supremacy with a tenacity that few athletes were to approach until much later. After winning her third Olympic gold medal in 1936, she moved to Hollywood.

Olympic track-and-field competitions for women began in 1928, though they had competed earlier in gymnastics, swimming, and in other sports traditionally considered more suitable for them. As the Olympic program grew, women participated in more strenuous sports. Most nations readily accepted the idea that high-performance sport was correct for female competitors. However, in the lands where these sports originated, and especially in the United States, physical educators and sports functionaries often assumed that the aggressiverness required to achieve distinction in international competition was defeminizing.

In the 1930s and after World War II, women were often Olympic heroes and, if they garnered medals for the national team, were great national heroes. However, the later a nation took on cosmopolitan sport and the less firmly modern sport was established the more likely it would be that they would produce women capable fo medal-winning performances.

The equalitarianism, selection by merit, and individualism of international sports ideology eventually assured that, despite the countervailing aristocratic bias inherent in the idea of amateurism, black people would compete in the Olympic Games. William De Hart Hubbard, an American, won the broad jump in Paris in 1924. The relative ease of transport permitted more than just a few American Negroes to compete in the Los Angeles Games of 1932. However, until the 1960s, when some Africans broke records in distance events, it was assumed that blacks would do best to concentrate on sprints and the long jump.

For the first 40 years of the modern Olympic Games, American white track stars and swimmers consistently dominated the Summer Olympics. The large, well-nourished population, the established traditions for preparation in many sports, and the widely, uncritically accepted notions about the wisdom of investing present time for future results (that is, training) accounted for such domination. But by the late 1920s Olympic victors might come from anywhere. Many illustrations can be used here: In the 1920s the Finns' rigidly disciplined and severe attitudes regarding training brought about fundamental changes in preparations for long-distance running. Paavo Nurmi, the Finn who dominated the distance events in the Olympics of 1920, 1924, and 1928, submitted to special diets, ran extraordinary distances as part of his long-term preparations, and while training and competing carried a stopwatch which he meticulously observed and obeyed in order better to apportion his remarkable staying power. The French continued to be supreme in Olympic cycling. Hungarians (particularly Jews) and Italians regularly won gold medals in fencing. Aristocratic Hollanders and Swedes regularly gave outstanding performances in the equestrian events. The winner of the Marathon in 1932 was Carlos Zabala, an Argentinian. The winner of the 100 meter dash for women in 1932 was Stanislawa Walasiewiczowna from Poland. Teams from India or Pakistan won gold medals in field hockey from 1928 until 1968. Uruguay won in soccer in 1924 and 1928. Officially no one is supposed to rank the national teams by means of point systems or by the number of medals. All the same, everyone knew that in 1928, when the Germans for the first time after the war were allowed to compete in the Games, they finished second to the Americans. In the 1932 Games in Los Angeles, the Japanese were second.

Participation became broader, facilities improved, measuring devices were made automatic and more exquisitely discriminating. Records in high performance sports were regularly set in an atmosphere of wonderment and jubilation that was only slightly clouded because one knew that sports records were ephemeral things that progress (a key word of our epoch) required to be surpassed. Internationally accepted and honored sports records were vivid, though abstract, symbols sanctifying industrial society's accomplishment principle and, since they were ever being superseded, provided irrefutable evidence of the relentlessness of progress.

The Olympic Games as a form of international theater "progressed" too. In his later years, (he died in Geneva in 1937) Pierre de Coubertin greeted the tendency for accomplishment-oriented sport to approach the characteristics of "ritual," "cult," or "religion" (he employed all of these words in these contexts). The Summer Olympics which took place in southern California in 1932 provide an opportunity to observe the progress of international sport into a dynamic movement of considerable significance.

Boosters in Southern California had been trying to persuade Coubertin and the International Olympic Committee to give the Games to Los Angeles since 1920 and were promised them for 1932 as early as 1923. The grandiose preparations were already well underway (they included a new stadium seating 104,000) when the American stock market crashed late in 1929. The world's money wells dried up and the industrial world entered its worst economic crisis. Would the organizers be able to pay for the show? Would the organizing committees of foreign nations have the money to send their teams that far?

The Southern Californians offered enticements. They were prepared to feed, house, and otherwise care for every competitor for $2 a day, and for their intended guests they built a new "Olympic Village" of some simple two-room cottages on a barren hilltop on the western outskirts of Los Angeles. There were lots of tours for the athletes and free, regular transportation to the competition sites. The studios in nearby Hollywood donated films for the athletes to view at night. As it turned out bonhomie was established early. Thereafter any city that wished to be a host for the Olympic Games had to provide an Olympic Village.

No strangers to synthetic festivities, the Los Angelinos added a few touches to an already heavy, but gracefully carried burden of Olympic symbols and rituals. Ever since 1896, the once rudimentary award ceremonies had become steadily more lavish. Coubertin consented to first place medals of gold after 1904. There was a "parade of nations" first at the opening ceremonies of the Stockholm Games of 1912. Coubertin himself designed an "Olympic" flag of five interlocking rings that was first flown in 1920. In Antwerp in 1920 one athlete, Victor Boin, a Belgian fencer, stood in front of the assembled athletes and, for all of them, recited an "Olympic Oath." At Los Angeles the pace of accumulating traditions was speeded up. At the opening ceremonies there were thousands of band musicians, salvos from cannon, and ecumenical assemblages of national flags. The Californians revived a touch used in Athens when they released hundreds of white pigeons. They added an appealing (if entirely original—for there were no historical antecedents) "Olympic flame," a torch that was to burn in a big brazier over the peristyle of the stadium until the Games ended.

There were, of course, "incidents." Paavo Nurmi, upon arriving in Los Angeles, learned that he was no longer an amateur since he had shortly before enjoyed a lavish "expense account" for a certain "exhibition tour." Another Finn, Lauri Lehtinen, twice fouled an American, Ralph Hill, as Hill tried to pass near the finish of the 5000 meter run. Still, Lehtinen was declared the winner before an outraged crowd. Ralph Metcalf shared the general impression that he had been the winner of the 100 meter dash and, like the crowd, was astonished to learn that a photo-electric timer proved that Eddie Tolan was the victor and was (as the winner of this event was called) "the fastest man in the world."

In general, the Los Angeles Games (as well as the Lake Placid Winter Games that preceded them) were harmonious. Much of the good feeling left by the California Games of 1932 can be attributed to the open-handed eagerness of the population of the state to please. In general, the athletes were consistently polite in the face of the officals' decisions, thus contributing to the pervasive good feelings. For example, at his victory ceremony Lehtinen pulled Hill up on the winner's pedestal and pinned a little Finnish flag to Hill's sweater. Politest of all were the Japanese, who had been instructed to congratulate the winners of each event they competed in. And the Japanese judges (after the muddles of the 1908 Games the judges were always from several different nations) and coaches regularly shook the hand of a judge who shared the nationality of the winning athlete or team. The practice became contagious and in southern California, where fears of "the yellow peril" were pervasive and sometimes vicious, the crowds became partisans of Nippon. With some 143 athletes on hand, the Japanese were the second largest team and their male swimmers set many records.

In fact, almost all the statistical norms for supreme performances in all sports were sharply altered in Los Angeles in 1932. This was so not only in the track-and-field events (only the records for the long jump and the hammer throw were unsurpassed). Records tumbled in the large rowing program, in cycling and in most sports that women competed in. Many of the Olympic records set in Los Angeles would stand until the 1960s.

One could, and many did, attribute the peak performances to superb facilities, a milieu of good feeling, and a beneficial climate. What the Los Angeles Olympics actually indicated was the dawn of a new era in athletic training. Thereafter, ambitious athletes took on a much heavier burden of self-discipline. Conditioning became specialized, scientific, and methodically directed at the establishment of new records. This subsequently led to an almost monstrous value being placed on sports championships and a terrific burden on those young people who were directed to achieving them.

The Olympic Games of 1932 were well reported and widely broadcast and were thus a world festival. However, few observed the Olympics in Los Angeles as keenly as the large German team and, most especially, the sports officials that accompanied them. Just before the Summer Games of 1932 began, the officials of the International Olympic Committee had decided that Germany, rather than Spain, would have both the Winter and Summer Games four years later.

The leader of the German delegation was Dr. Carl Diem (1882–1962), Germany's most prolific sports historian and Germany's leading sports educator and sports functionary. The German team at Amsterdam had harvested many medals, but the team in 1932 brought back few. This was especially disheartening, because the Germans could have used some good news. In 1932 Germany was suffering from the depression more than any other European nation. The country was enduring ever greater political disruption.

Nevertheless, Carl Diem in Los Angeles amassed "sketches, models, addresses, flags, programs, tickets, etc. that had been carefully collected for us" (as he wrote later). He took notes as he chatted with the designers of the elevators and the telephone systems. He photographed workshops and garages and took metric measurements of the cottages at the Olympic Village. He recorded for his files the statements of the chefs there as to the dietary preferences of the participating nationalities.

The Germans would do better. Carl Diem was one of the Germans who was preparing for extraordinary exertions to offer the world the most splendid sports festival yet.

[11]

AMERICAN SPORT
IN RECENT TIMES

Sports participation, sports theater, and the integration of sport into American culture continued along lines that had been established earlier. Just as innovations in American technology and styles of consumption tended to inspire changes in the behavior of people far beyond American borders, American sport had some foreign imitators too. As was observed earlier, the forms of American sport were largely taken from English innovations of the early industrial age. Americans elaborated English sport into something very American. Sport history may have its own periodization. The two decades after 1920 may be viewed as the epoch in North America when sport assumed its mature (though still dynamic) capitalistic forms.

There were no convulsive changes in the underlying processes in society that affected American sport. The 1920s were more than ever before a fertile time for entrepreneurial innovation and for the rise to public notice of "stars." And the expanding (and therefore young and therefore relatively aggressive) male population was, more than ever, healthy, literate, socially and geographically mobile, moneyed, and leisured. The secularization of all aspects of life was accompanied by the deterioration of local loyalties and of religious affiliations. A sort of demystification affected all areas of culture save sport. As before, accomplishment-oriented consumer sport attracted few iconoclasts or even critics. There was a lavish elaboration of the recent tradition and almost everyone was pleased.

In journalism a general shifting away from earnestness proceeded while newsprint fell in price and improved high-speed presses rolled faster. Sports reporting increased circulation which attracted advertising which lowered the necessary sales price—thus forming a profitable circle that made editors forage for narrative writers to fill the ever grander allotment of columns for sports news. Sports writers and their writing remained, as always, aimed at an audience that wanted escape: attractive stories of struggles for success merited accomplishment and hope for a better future. There was little room for irony, skepticism, or even much literary shading. Inventive sports writers adapted the jargon of the playing fields and employed fresh metaphors to vary the streams of prose. In baseball, they wore out their Thesauruses to find fresh ways to describe the little sphere that was the object of all that scurrying about.

The appetite for sports escapism in the 1920s went through all strata of the population. The *New York Times* and the *Washington Post* succumbed. The quality newspapers attempted to hold the better writers and allowed some cynicism into their editorial policy toward sports writing. It is true that the sports pages provided the earliest opportunities for many American literary artists to appear fluently in print. It is also true that when free to leave, many of them did so and later recalled with distaste the narrow yea-saying that sports journalism demanded. The mature literature and social criticism of Ring Lardner, Paul Gallico, Leonard Schecter, and Robert Lipsyte are all striking in their bitter rejection of the myths that are regnant in (to employ the title of Lipsyte's 1975 book) "Sportsworld."

An examination of sports broadcasting also provides opportunities for looking at some changes in American culture. The technological bases of radio lay in scientific discoveries around the turn of the century. Broadcasting, much like sport, evolved rapidly due to the energetic distribution by capitalists of the technical wonders to a moneyed populace that welcomed the novelties. Radio, like sport, evolved apart from political or social policy. No intellectuals or esthetes were on hand. There was no regulation by authorities, save when demanded by manufacturers to allocate bands of the air waves. Like sport, radio grew organically out of the potentialities in American mass society.

Radio first demonstrated its commercial possibilities when Pittsburgh's station KDKA broadcast the Harding–Cox election returns on November 2, 1920. On April 11, 1921, KDKA offered a blow-by-blow description of the Johnny Ray–Johnny Dundee boxing match. During the rest of 1921, stations in Schenectady, Jersey City, and elsewhere broadcast descriptions of speedboat races and football games.

Tex Rickard, the most successful of the era's sport promoters, worked with John Ringling of the circus family, J. Andrew White, the editor of *Wireless Age,* and David Sarnoff, the general manager of Radio Corporation of America (RCA) to arrange for the broadcasting into movie theaters and assorted halls from Maine to Miami of the Jack Dempsey–Georges Carpentier fight of July 2, 1921. The consortium and the boxers attracted some 300,000 paying listeners. Station WJY, founded in order to broadcast the Dempsey fight, later transmitted verbal descriptions of the World Series of 1922.

All of these broadcasts, like those of the news or an opera, had as their object to promote sales of receiving sets, which were costly and had high profit margins. There were 60,000 sets sold in 1922 and this provided the basis for some regular programming. The rapid expansion of production was one sign of an ebullient age. By late 1928 there were more than ten million radios in the nation. When the first Rose Bowl college football game was broadcast on New Years Day in 1927 it made use of a "network" of stations across the country.

Entrepreneurial competition brought down the sales prices of radios and their profit margins. The saturation point was approaching before the decade ended. There was a demand for programs greater than could be financed by electrical equipment manufacturers. Other industrialized countries usually provided listener-

financed and state-subsidized didactic or otherwise socially beneficial radio programming. In America radio was subject only to
technical regulation. Radio time was offered to the free market.
By the late 1920s radio broadcasting (as was previously the case
with newspapers and was subsequently to be the case with television) depended upon advertising revenues. By 1930 national advertisers demanded evidence that their expensive messages were
being heard and formed a "Cooperative Analysis of Broadcasting"
which used telephone interviews to determine listener attendance
to programs. The ratings services refined their techniques and extended operations in the 1930s and 1940s. That most Americans had ready access to on-the-spot baseball descriptions and that
sports broadcasting occupied a lot of the air waves indicates that
commerce responded to the desire of the populace for that kind of
thing.

The ubiquitousness and vivid immediacy of sports journalism
and sports broadcasting were both symptoms and causes of the
growing delocalization, secularization and homogenization of
American life. The World Series, one of Joe Louis' defending
matches, or a bowl game were major national events that bonded
the classes and regions of the enormous nation. In the emotions
they aroused and the symbolic lessons they offered the sporting
events rivaled earthquakes, ominous diplomatic crises, and presi-
dential elections. Consumer sports of course were not always subject to the vagaries of fate. The corruptions of commercial sport
have always been disguised by a venal directing establishment and
protected by the public which prefers wholesome, uncomplicated
myths. During the long American Depression the headlines on the
newspages were a continuous record of man's failures; the sports
pages recorded his triumphs.

So pervasive was the acceptance of sports ritual and of sports
myths in the period between the wars that moralistic objections
could scarcely be heard. When, after more than a year of refusals
on the part of sports writers and various sports bureaucrats to believe that it was indeed so, some players of the Chicago White Sox
were found guilty of taking gamblers' bribes to throw the World
Series of 1919, there was widespread outrage at the profanation of
"the national game." A business man who committed a compara-

ble crime would have been more severely punished, but the guilty players were merely banned for life from further professional play. A newly formed national commission headed by a former federal judge with almost dictatorial powers guarded the game and its public from further scandals. Furthermore baseball was isolated from disruptions that might occur in the market place by its exemption from the anti-trust laws. Out of their narrow talents and certain dependable skills, and with the help of a market oriented consensus, promoters and media functionaries fashioned inspiring heroes out of rather ordinary entertainers like Babe Ruth, Lou Gehrig, Joe DiMaggio, and others.

Some of the sports stars of the day rose to prominence in the face of widespread popular assumptions. There were some female stars. But they were far from fitting any conception of the ideal American woman. Most often they and their accomplishments were depicted as freakish. One of the first was the all-rounder Mildred "Babe" Didrikson (later married name, Zaharias) (1914–1956). She was a natural athlete who seemed to do everything right. First prominent as a baseball and a basketball player, "Babe" entered the 1932 Olympics in Los Angeles and won gold medals in the 80-meter hurdles and the javelin throw. Because of an unorthodox "diving" technique, her record jump of 1.67 meters (5 feet 5¾ inches) was awarded only second place.

"Babe" was unapologetic about her love of competitive sport. She disavowed the conventional trappings of femininity. She boasted that as a child she had never played with dolls. She recalled that when she paraded into the stadium in Los Angeles in 1932 she had to dress up: "I believe that it was the first time I had worn stockings in my life, and as for the shoes, they were really hurting my feet." She trained hard and spoke of her pleasure in effort; her ecstasy at winning. All of this made her newsworthy and therefore a good puller of crowds for professional appearances. She later went on to play in exhibition baseball games and to win seventeen international titles as a golfer.

Another and possibly comparable journalistic focus of attention was six-foot-tall Helen Stephens who won the 100 meter dash and anchored the winning 400 meter relay at the 1936 Olympics in Berlin. Later billed as "the world's fastest woman," Helen Stephens toured with the "House of David" (the males wore long beards) exhibition baseball team. She also performed certain track-and-field events at state fairs. Spectators sometimes hooted at her as she tossed an iron ball from hand to hand. Angered, she would command the public address announcer to state her challenge to any male present to put the shot with her. Few did and they always lost.

The reigning queen of winter in the 1920s and 1930s was Sonja Henie, the petite Norwegian who always smiled in public and who had dominated singles figure skating between 1927 when she won her first world championship and 1936 when she won her third Olympic gold medal. This tough performer then migrated to Hollywood. As an actress she was wooden, but she skated like a dream before the cameras and later, smiling fully, in her own traveling "ice revues." As an entertainment entrepreneur she became rich in addition to being famous and even married three successive millionaires. Henie was not the first or the last star of sport to become a star of money.

So America did have some sport heroines. But it is sage to observe that all of these women made their reputations on the world scene first. Didrikson and Stephens were rarely treated respectfully in the press. Both were actually warm, wholesome, versatile, intelligent women. Henie alone created and maintained her persona as an awesome royal personage. The media apparatus established and exploited them as oddities rather than inspirations for masses of girls and women. Far more than was the case in other industrialized countries American physical educators continued to promote nonstrenuous programs for females. American tradition tended to glorify achievement in males and to ridicule it in females. Several times we have observed how modern sport concretizes the enlightenment principles of accomplishment (records), constitutionalism (rules), fairness, and democracy. As we have seen, sport in the United States celebrated these principles for men only.

Enlightened or progressive views of social morality in America also conflicted with American tradition regarding the separation of the races. Racial separation was the rule in social and cultural life generally and so was the rule in American sports participation and spectatorship. It is worth recalling just how exceptional two Negro stars were during the 1930s. Joe Louis (1914–1981), heavyweight champion prize fighter of the world 1937–1949, rose to prominence amidst the rotten, readily manipulated organizational apparatus of professional boxing. Jesse Owens (1913–1980), the great sprinter, achieved his fame in the kind of sport then most characterized by objective criteria and verifiable accomplishment. Nevertheless, parallels in their careers are striking and instructive. Both were relatively light skinned, handsome, socially self-effacing, and managerially manipulable, in short, "good niggers." Like many well-paid athletes, they did not prepare well for their futures. Both, but most particularly Louis, made fortunes for their promoters and lived out their post-sport lives as debt-ridden publicists.

Until well into the 1960s newspapers in the southern states would not publish photographs of Negro athletes. In fact, for a century after the ending of the Civil War, the tradition in the culture and constitutional safeguards of states' rights guaranteed that modern sport in the southern states would undergo separate evolution in Negro schools and colleges as well as the organizations for professional sports such as baseball.

The installation in 1946 of Jackie Robinson (1919–1972) as the first Negro professional baseball player in the previously all-white leagues was eased by the fact that Robinson was self-effacing, coldly self-contained, and a superb (and therefore potentially winning and therefore valuable) athlete. This innovation occurred just after the unprecedented racial mixing in the vast military buildup (*not* subject to states' rights) for the second world war. A laudable insistence on exemplary justice motivated those who saw this issue through. But so did the yearning for victory and profit of the owner of the Brooklyn Dodgers. The ongoing and still incomplete integration of American sport really came about as a consequence of the belated onslaught in the 1960s and 1970s of American conscience-ridden jurists, educators, and media leaders against the most obvious affront to liberal democratic ideals.

Racial integration among the professional middle classes and among workers on the job has gone far, though this same process has probably isolated yet further the black underclass. And integration has proceeded most smoothly in the American South. But again, this last factor is also attributable to the general prosperity and more wholehearted joining of the American ecumene on the part of the Old South. Everywhere racial integration in sport has gone very far. Black track-and-field stars have arisen because they have produced unambiguous results. Results make the difference. Black football and basketball players are necessary to make up viable teams that must compete against teams that have also hired talented blacks.

By the early 1980s superior black (like white) athletes determined by the media to be newsworthy could supplement their incomes by declaring their preference for certain brands of razor blades or automobiles. Some were managed by hard-bargaining agents who took 10 percent off the top. A few of them redecorated the movie-star palaces they purchased in Hollywood and a few even became movie actors themselves. The very pleasure that the best black athletes communicate by their success obscures millions of foreordained disappointments. Hundreds of thousands of less than supremely talented black children are inspired to waste their youths in dead-end sports programs in the American schools and colleges. The cynicism with which university football administrators dominate their charges and actually deny many black players (and many whites as well) educations has been a national scandal. For the percentage of black athletes (or even white athletes) who achieve substantial lifetime earnings in their profession is pathetically small. Sport heroes, and the mythic aura that surround them, have masked continued corruption in high-level sport and have been socially retarding. The power and money in American sport remains with the promoters and managers and financiers behind the scenes, where blacks are almost absent. Black children would be far better served if they were inspired by bank presidents, advertising executives, and surgeons.

It is wrong to suggest that the illusions surrounding black sports entertainers are unique to them. In America (as in all the capitalist countries) the career of an athlete, whether black or white, male or female, is temporally and economically perilous. The market demands for unambiguous results and correct behavior leads to the casting aside of those who are no longer capable of producing victory or salable personas. The youth whose determination produced superlatives in physical achievement is only exceptionally adequate in the open economy when his prowess is declining. It is significant that the area of professional American sport that offers to its practitioners the greatest safety and the longest careers is the one which is most frankly entertaining and where the results are dubious in the extreme. Careerists in "professional" wrestling, those grunters and groaners who perform (for high fees) before working class audiences are intelligent, physically fit, skilled performers. Until the early 1970s when professional baseball, football, basketball and hockey players unionized, professional wrestlers as a class also had higher lifetime earnings than any other athletes. The wrestlers protect each other, give good value when they perform, and when no longer capable of skilled exertion are well capable of administrative work in their circuits.

To return to our chronological outline: World War II disrupted millions of lives. However, the continuities, the major trends in American society were scarcely altered. Like the Civil War and World War I, the new war, with its mobilization and shifting of people, acclerated the de-ethnization and de-regionalization which had been steadily underway. All the armed forces required physical training programs of which traditional American sports were integral parts.

The atrocities of Hiroshima and Nagasaki would continue to haunt some American consciences, but the overwhelming productive power and the armies of America were widely attributed with having saved the grand corpus of Western civilization. In contrast to the behavior of American politicians after 1919, those in 1945 were determined to devote some energies to the reconstruction of a shaken world. American prestige has never been higher; all things American were never been more subject to admiration and imitation. As was the case with Greek culture in the fifth century B.C. and English culture in the nineteenth century, sport was acknowledged everywhere to be an integral part of the package of American culture.

The recovery of the American economy from the depression was thorough. In 1946 the Americans embarked on a quarter century of economic expansion so ebullient as almost to amount to a period in history. Cheap gasoline and official policies favoring cheap credit over very long terms favored home ownership and consequently led to the urbanization of huge areas of countryside. Since immigration had been severely curbed in the 1920s the last of the first-generation ethnics grew older and less conspicuous. Their newspapers and radio programs foundered in neglect. The abandonment of many of their neighborhoods to migrating southern blacks was another sign of increased movement and homogenization in American cultural life. Very likely the most effective leveler of American culture in the era of prosperity was television—a curiosity in 1950, but in almost every house a decade later.

Television is pervasive and powerful—so very pervasive in fact that we attempt to assess just how powerful it has been with great uncertainty. This is no place for repetitious statistics or claims about such matters as the manipulation of national consumer markets, the demeaning of literary education, or the formation of "global villages." Television and the financial and bureaucratic structures (all still dynamically evolving world wide, let it be noted) directing its programs are so all-enveloping as to deny us a lofty position from which to appraise the impact. Video programming has certainly enriched many lives that otherwise would have been more isolated and locally restricted. But, in America, at least, the financing of broadcasting by advertisers has established a cynical directing establishment and a consistently low level of ideological or esthetic standards.

As with the mass newspapers and with popular radio, sports broadcasts occupy large and prominent parts of television's fare. As with other media, the prominence and nature of televised sports in the United States is the result of alert functionaries *responding* to the desires (as determined by the statistically democratic and dependable ratings systems) of the consuming public.

In the United States sports programming is often seen in "prime time," which, of course, is the "highest and best use" of the airwaves. Since they have long been expensively sponsored, sporting events have from the beginning been the earliest beneficiaries of technical advances such as zoom lenses, stop-action tapes allowing instant replays, and split screens. Golf tournaments are the most costly production jobs, since they can require up to 20 camera crews. But then, of course, golf dependably appeals to a demographically specifiable, attentive audience that has lots of money to spend.

American sport has itself been altered by television broadcasting. A network functionary is on the field at professional football games to signal the officials when to call time out for commercials and when the game can resume. The home consumer of televised sports is removed from the community of theatrically aroused spectators on the spot. He is a critic, not a celebrant. The precision that technically exquisite television reveals has led to desires for more precision and more revelations of it. Television encourages ever more refinement of skills. A consequence of this has been to allow increasingly the substitution of skilled player "specialists" with specific roles, more coaches, increasing bureaucratization, and technical exactness everywhere. Examples are designated hitters in baseball and place kickers in football. Professional and intercollegiate football, which attract the largest television audiences for sport, have been especially subject to the trends cited above.

The dispersed community of sports viewers have statistically verifiable characteristics. Automobile makers, airlines, oil companies, and breweries are the sponsors who bid highest to reach the sports viewers who are educated, male, and who have large disposable incomes. In short, we can make the claim that the responses of free market forces determine that television sports programming is directed at an audience that consists of cadres that include the American elite. Whether the electronically transmitted sports that these people consume is mere entertainment or whether these dramas may themselves set much of the tone of American life is a subject that will be deferred.

To continue: as before the war, the integration of sport into American culture at all levels has proceeded smoothly. Sports heroes, sports paradigms, sport rhetoric, sports myths became difficult to separate from trends operating in the culture at large. Some extended illustrations may be instructive here.

Joseph William Namath, born and raised in a Pennsylvania steel town, was a distinguished quarterback at the University of Alabama before he let a law firm represent him in late 1964 in the bidding for his skills by professional football teams. On January 2, 1965, Namath signed with the New York Jets, then in the American Football League, for three years at $387,000 per year and a Lincoln convertible. Namath was at once newsworthy. With some amused grace he helped television cameramen and gossip columnists to chronicle his sports, business, and venereal careers. He remained for some time a supremely talented and touchdown-producing quarterback. Soon he was famous not simply for his acknowledged accomplishments, but because he was famous. Namath was one of the outstanding "hyped" personalities of his time. His earnings increased steadily and thus raised the bidding for the services of other exceptional players.

Namath referred to himself rather cunningly as "Number One" and his vendable newsworthiness caused him to be referred to by others as the "savior of the American Football League." He even had some physical disabilities which increased his public appeal. His knees gave out at last during the 1977–1978 season, but during the season before when he was ranked thirtieth among the League's 31 quarterbacks, he still earned $450,000.

Shortly before the 1979 baseball season, Pete Rose, a third baseman was induced by a three-year, $3,200,000 contract to move from the Cincinnati Reds to the Philadelphia Phillies. The sum was a cool business gamble on the part of the owners of his new team. Like most of the stars who are able to command such very large sums, Rose was attractive as a personality, newsworthy aside from his undeniable skills and, most importantly (but never explicitly acknowledged), Caucasian. The payback for the enormous sums promised Rose (and comparable sums promised others) was intended to come mostly from elevated advertising rates. The fees would be based on the higher television ratings that a successfully created star can produce. By 1981 the highest rate charged for a half minute commercial was approaching $100,000. It is worth observing that the emoluments tendered to sports stars were comparably dramatic (if less financially grand) for supremely skilled and otherwise newsworthy soccer players in capitalist West Germany and Brazil.

The sports pages and televised sports commentaries in America and elsewhere are laced with information only peripheral to competitions and contests as such. One reads regularly of salary news items such as those above. But there are also tales of replaced administrators, shifted franchises, banquets, awards, rises and falls, and lots of ceremonies. In short, these are the items that also mark shifts in power and the use of resources in other aspects of a rich, dynamic, bureaucratic culture.

The steady trend for sport to become ritually integrated and earnestly or even quasi-sacredly regarded in modern life is illustrated by the success of "Halls of Fame." The first and still the most famous is "The National Baseball Hall of Fame and Museum" in Cooperstown, New York. The myth (long since demolished by baseball's conscientious historians) that baseball was "invented" in Cooperstown inspired a town booster to open a tourist attraction there on June 12, 1939. A lot of old baseball players (including Babe Ruth) were on hand for the broadcast opening ceremonies. They (and subsequent heroes of the national game) offered as relics their lockers, uniforms, bats, balls, and gloves. Pilgrims were likely to sleep, eat and otherwise spend more than the admission fee in Cooperstown. In 1968 the Hall of Fame was greatly expanded with halls of marble pillars and a library of baseball. Recently, it added a Negro League photographic collection, among other things. The librarian has a file of statistics on the career of every major league player. There are many relics: for example, a torn shirt sleeve of 1938 belonging to Johnny Allen and Napoleon Lajoie's three thousandth hit ball. "Great" players are honored by individual photographs which are displayed in a special shrine.

The North American entrepreneurial spirit has been unconfined. One could not let so fine a financial and publicistic success go unimitated. Halls of Fame sprouted in many places in the United States and Canada in the 1960s. The Professional Football Hall of Fame opened in Canton, Ohio in 1963 and was later doubled in size to include a movie theater, expanded research library, two "enshrinement" areas, and a new and much larger gift shop. The International Hockey Hall of Fame and Museum in Kingston, Ontario opened in 1965. There is the expected display of old ice skates and some pucks commemorating "historic" goals. There are "memorials" to dead hockey greats and color shots of living ones. One can see an actual hockey stick from Russia and Det Clapper's sweater worn when he retired from the Boston Bruins in 1947. The San Diego Hall of Champions opened in 1961 and features more than 1400 pictures of area athletes who earned national recognition. In 1974 two historians, Guy Lewis and Gerald Redmond, published a then-curerent, 185-page directory of sports halls of fame and museums called *Sporting Heritage* (South Brunswick, N.J.: A.S. Barnes). "Shrines," "relics," "heroes," "monuments," and other sacred rhetoric is employed with much less irony or apology than one encounters in Christian theological circles at present.

A dependable theme arousing outrage in America (as well as elsewhere in the industrial world) is frequency of sports violence or rudeness. Popular riots of happiness have occurred in Pittsburgh or Columbus, Ohio on the occasion of an eagerly anticipated, but uncertain victory. Hundreds of incoherently loud, young, male drunks roam streets lined with retail shops. The mobs frighten people, some of their number may pass out. Some windows are smashed and cars overturned. The crowds are unable to obey bull-horned commands to disperse and some policemen may get bruised. On December 30, 1978, Woody Hayes, the head football coach of Ohio State University, rushed out on the field in the last minutes of a game between his team and that of Clemson University. Hayes punched Charlie Bauman who had intercepted an Ohio State pass and also hit another Clemson player on the scene. A national television audience saw Hayes' churning arms. Although in the course of that game several players were more severely injured than Bauman was, it was the Hayes–Bauman incident that received the attention of national television and newspaper editorials. Hugh Hindman, who had long before played under Hayes and was then the Ohio State Athletic Director, almost immediately fired Hayes.

The most discussed individual at the Wimbledon tennis tournament in the summer of 1981 was John McEnroe. McEnroe was less interesting for his talent (although he was the male singles champion) than he was for his remarkable behavior. He refused to attend a final banquet and was verbally abusive to some officials who were judging his games. His unruly temperament got far more

232 AMERICAN SPORT IN RECENT TIMES

attention than the fact of his victory over Bjorn Borg or indeed lots of major political news.

Another diversion in the summer of 1981 was the strike by major league baseball players. They wanted to earn much more. The number of people involved was small and so were the issues. But it was a shock, almost a blasphemy to the sports page reading public. Baseball players were not supposed to care that much about money.

The recital of mob disorder, of individual rudeness, or of self-interested disruption could go on. Perhaps the incidents are, as regularly claimed in the sports pages, increasingly frequent. But in the light of the enormous number of sporting events and the emotions aroused in millions, perhaps billions of players and spectators, the occasional prominent occurrences of disorder may illustrate something very different. These celebrated aberrations may instead illustrate the profundity of the integration of formal sport into American life. Otherwise stated, the very attention given to exceptional disorder is a socially sanctioned command to observe the assumed and sacred order that almost universally prevails underneath it all.

If accommodated by the formal structures of a game, hallowed by unwritten codes of spectator behavior, or sanctioned by long usage, some violence or victimization is acceptable, perhaps ineradicable in American sport. Professional hockey players understand that they could very well be crippled in the course of their performances that are called sometimes "play." The expense, authoritarianism, cool violence, and imperviousness to change of American intercollegiate football mocks and degrades the declared educational missions of most American universities. The talented youths and accomplishment-oriented coaches who are at the mercy of the economy of high-performance sports entertainment live and work in an atmosphere of character submission and earnestness that is much attenuated in all other areas of American culture. Furthermore, the whole sports society, but especially those parts of it (such as baseball and professional football) that influence the movement of large sums of money is served by a pious media establishment in television and the newspapers which steadily promote high-performance sport as not merely interesting but as something profound and semi-sacred as well. Sport becomes ever more earnest and has long since taken on elements of the sacred. It is worth dwelling on the fact that Presidents Gerald Ford, Richard Nixon, and Ronald Reagan played collegiate football. In a land where televised professional football appeals especially to upwardly mobile males, the most upwardly mobile of all was the nation's most zealous fan. One of Nixon's treasured friends was George Allen, then coach of the Washington Redskins. They were together on the phone a lot. Allen often philosophized, "Winning is everything. Every time you win, you're reborn, when you lose, you die a little." President Nixon hung around the Redskins and urged Allen to try specific plays of his invention. Nixon's public and private life was weirdly colored with, perhaps molded by, the sports page and locker room rhetoric of "team play," "playing the game," strategy, and, above all, winning. It is possible that some aspects of the recent disappointments that Americans have endured can be attributed to a tendency among those at the highest levels of American society to permit sports rhetoric, metaphors of winning and losing and game dramaturgy to supply patterns for dealing with issues that are in deadly earnest, that have a logic rooted in the real world, and are not games at all. We know now that the high-level strategy in the Indo-China adventure was planned and executed on the basis of parables drawn from professional baseball and football. One campaign for a step-up in bombings was called "Operation Linebacker" and Nixon's code name was "Quarterback." All the same, and almost eerily, Nixon was "the least active of American presidents since the crippled Franklin Roosevelt," and once he told his Sports Advisory Council: "I really hate exercise for exercise's sake. . . . There is a tendency with television for people to just sit there with their feet up, eating pretzels and drinking and that is their participation in sports. I don't think that is bad."* The case of Richard Nixon is instructive because he provides an extreme example illustrating the contrast between his cynicism regarding traditionally accepted reli-

*Some specifics of and the quotes in the above paragraph have been taken from Robert Lipsyte, *Sportsworld: An American Dreamland* (New York: Quadrangle, 1975), 11–19. Lipsyte was a sports editor for the *New York Times*. He claims that "sportspeak" has become the style of figures ranging from Charles de Gaulle to Elridge Cleaver.

gious or moral codes and his earnestness regarding the fragile traditions or dubious moral issues posed and acknowledged in modern sport.

The air time of professional football television broadcasts is the most costly to purchase because it reaches the presumable big spenders, who we may assume are the decision-making elite. The structures of theatrically presented and televised sport will continue to evolve. Sports rhetoric seems to be gaining currency in broader sections of the society. Games and contests, team play, heroes of accomplishment, and the drama of winning and losing provide vivid metaphors that are alternatives to (though not wholly excluding) the Judeo-Christian tradition and established loyalties to community, locality, and family. Modern sport surely contains within it elements of definite and powerful spiritual forces. Only a few critical voices are heard.

The disparateness and feebleness of the critics of American sport probably serve to point up the extent to which sport's economic structure, personnel, dramaturgy, and ideology all serve to legitimize the continuing integration of sport in culture. Prominent in the public eye are those critics who assert that the bosses of sport (whoever they are) have not been sufficiently aware of the liberals' imperatives to advance democratic opportunity and to assure that rewards are based on objective criteria. Constitutionally based guarantees against discrimination by race have been enforced to assure that talented black athletes have access to rewards that go along with certain positions in big-money sport. Black athletes now dominate basketball and are prominent in baseball and football. Their rarity as captains or coaches is at least partly attributable to the racism that exists among audiences and owners, as well as to the media managers who fear that racism.

Judicial pressures for racial integration have been most effective in the public school systems, where basketball, football, and baseball have long been major sports. Sports that traditionally develop skilled practitioners and knowledgeable observers outside the public educational systems—tennis, golf, rowing, distance running, and others—remain class specific and, reflecting fundamental attitudes in the society, racially exclusive. These American sports and others continue to evolve exclusively in the private sector and will remain impervious to public pressures.

American sport has not remained entirely uninfluenced by the ideological feminism that has become a warm issue in American culture. Moral pressure, lobbying, legislative acts, and judicial enforcement against established sexism in American sport have been effective only in the schools. This is thanks to the enactment of Title Nine, the usual appellation given to a section, "Prohibition of Sex Discrimination," in the Education Amendments of 1972. These amendments applied to several major federal legislative acts that were put into effect in the mid-1960s.

Most typically what the advocates of Title Nine want enforced is the equalization of expenditures of public revenues for each sex. The enforcers of Title Nine have succeeded in requiring the sexual integration of some grade school physical education classes, some newsworthy occasions of boys' baseball teams being required to accept girl players, and the establishment of some collegiate athletic scholarships for women. But the physical education departments and, more so, the sports administration bureaucracies in American education, from the grade schools to the great universities, have always been quasi-independent. High school coaches and university athletic directors delay, prevaricate, juggle figures, and otherwise resist the efforts of feminist ideologues to make their sports the cutting edges for an introduction of their vision of American society. And sport is included in the feminists' vision of the correct society.

It is true that popular feminism has brought along with it an increase in the physical confidence of millions of women. It took a very short time in the late 1970s for the female long distance runner to become a common sight in the American tree-shaded suburbs. The media hero makers have adopted as pets some talented female tennis players. A major event for readers of the sport pages was the victory of 29-year-old Billy Jean King over 55-year-old Bobby Riggs, the odds maker's favorite, on September 20, 1973 at the Houston Astrodome in a nationally televised match seen by an estimated 48 million.

Some critics of American sport are perturbed that the worldwide preeminence of Yankee athletes has steadily declined. The loss of supremacy is most evident in international meets, most particularly the Olympic Games. And the victors over talented Americans are often seen as symbolic representatives of the enemy, rival ideology of international Communism. Teams from the so-called "Comecon" nations, particularly those of the Soviet Union and of East Germany, customarily tally up the most points in their staged meets with Americans or Britons or anyone else. Most people know that these victories are attributable to long-established, state-directed, and popularly supported systems of recruitment and scientific training.

In a suggestive throwback to the significance given to a sporting victory in a formal contest in classical Greece, the American critics curiously accept the claim that statistically verifiable superiority in modern sport is evidence of superiority in areas of life or philosophy or fate that are not subject to the manipulation of a few physically talented individuals or to statistical verification or to any other sort of verification. Some of these critics align with the feminists to point up the vastly grander efforts the Communists devote to female recruitment and training. Periodically there are legislative proposals to force the squabbling and feeble amateur and collegiate national sports organizations to cooperate for the greater glory of the American flag. There are proposals in the American Congress for public sports academies on the totalitarian model. But the Olympic Games and indeed any international competitions matter far less to the American public than specifically American and local sport. It may gall millions of Americans that a Russian is certified to be the strongest man in the world and that a Romanian gymnast is acknowledged by an international panel of judges to be the world's most beautifully agile female. The triumphs of the supreme athletes of the Communist states are to a large extent (and acknowledged almost everywhere to be so) the products of ideology, state planning, and foreign policy. American sports would have to go through major convulsions before they would be subject to these factors.

Americans have continued to get the sport they want. American sports may preoccupy the American spirit, provide employment for a lot of American workers, and fill the otherwise idle hours of American people. But sport in America continues to evolve in the private sectors and is directed by free choice. Athletes, their managers, and their fans have remained impervious to conventional ideology.

[12]

THE OLYMPIC
GAMES, 1936-1980

The Olympics assumed grand importance with the Games of
1936 in Nazi Germany. The forty-year-old Olympic movement
carried with it new creative possibilities for educators, artists, and
politicians. Athletes of world championship caliber had increased
their symbolic importance while they narrowed the range of their
personal behavior in more normal walks of life.

In 1932 their ideology required that the National Socialists oppose the Olympic Games, which were commonly assumed to be
cosmopolitan, democratic, and racially inclusive. The ostensibly
pacifist, international festival scheduled for 1936 had been awarded
to the Weimar Republic the ruin of which the Nazis completed
when they seized power in January of 1933. Hitler had theorized
but little about sport before 1933. Sport according to the Nazis
was to be directed exclusively toward attaining fitness or, conceivably, training for such activities as the throwing of hand grenades.
Hitler's racial tenets also required that the Germans separate
themselves utterly from lesser peoples, particularly Negroes and
of course Jews. Ultimately, as we now know, Hitler rigidly held

his hatred of pacifism and of Jews to the catastrophic end of the most interesting political experiment of modern times. However, soon after their seizure of power in Germany, the Nazis made some practical compromises.

The modern Olympic Games harmonized well with some venerable German ideas and trends. The pseudo-classical, theatrical pretensions of the modern Olympics provided a dubious, though attractive link with many traditions in German literature and art. German scholars had led the way in the study of Greek sport. Ancient Olympia had itself become linked with the fortunes of the vigorous German states thanks to the state-subsidized work of German archaeologists there.

In the western suburbs of Berlin the facilities for the never-held 1916 Olympics still stood, awaiting the chance for Germany to offer an international festival to the world. And since the end of the war in 1919, many Germans had become more devoted to and more adept at cosmopolitan sport.

German physical education and public recreation had—as we have seen—taken form and evolved since the end of the eighteenth century in an atmosphere of informed debate. These debates had been nurtured by various, sometimes opposing, political ideas as to what was best for Germany. A late intrusion into Germany had been high-performance, individualistic, Anglo-Saxon, amateur sport. Games and competitions that were invented by Englishmen made steady headway among the more leisured and educated, cosmopolitan classes. On the other hand these imports were vigorously opposed by the patriotic, idealistic turners. Their defenders were forced to devise a propaganda, indeed an intellectual justification, for modern sport. Before sport as internationally practiced could be viewed as something earnest among the bureaucrats of German education, it had to establish claims that sport, like turning, was healthy, a stabilizing force in the state, and was somehow not foreign, but German too. So in Germany, modern sport acquired sophisticated justifications which it never had before.

That sport became integrated into German life was partly owing to a series of rugged experiences Germany went through that gravely weakened class solidarities, local loyalties, and the ordinary man's political judgment. Germans had endured, with only a

vague understanding of what caused them, the violent industrialization of 1870–1905, the apparently abrupt military collapse of
1918, the political revolutions of 1919–1920, the devastating currency inflation of 1922–1923, the depression of 1930–1933 and then
the radical political transformation after 1933. Times of great disruption offer opportunities for energetic men with ambitious projects.

Two of these men were Carl Diem (1882–1962) and Theodor
Lewald (1860–1949). Diem had been a middle-distance runner and
had founded his first sports club in Berlin when he was 17. Much
like Pierre de Coubertin (and like many other important bureaucrats of sport) Diem was an Anglophile and foresaw educational
and political usefulness in training, competition, and sports festivities. He led the German expedition to the (rump) Olympic Games
in Athens in 1906 and to the Olympic Games of 1908 and 1912.
He was the organizer of the aborted Games planned for Berlin in
1916. Diem was the usual expert of Weimar politicians in questions regarding physical education. In 1920 Diem established and
administered the world's first academically respectable college for
physical education teachers, *Die Deutsche Hochschule für Leibesübungen* in Berlin. He wrote voluminously about sport, taking always the position of advocating enthusiast.

Lewald was already 73 years old and had had a long career as a
bureaucrat when the Nazis came to power. Though a Christian,
Lewald came from a family of distinguished Berlin Jews. Though
himself not an athlete, he was a fan. His enthusiasm for sport had
eased his way among prominent politicians in the Imperial and
Weimar regimes. As early as 1900 he was the official expected to
arrange state financing for German cultural manifestations (including touring Olympic teams) abroad.

That the Germans had not been able to offer the world a sports
festival in Berlin in 1916 had been a great disappointment to Diem
and Lewald. The vengeful barring of German teams from the
Olympic Games of 1920 and 1924 was an insult only partly avenged
by the outstanding performance of many German athletes at the
Amsterdam Games of 1928. That the International Olympic Committee gave the 1936 Games to Germany was largely because of
Lewald's tireless appeals to the committee's members all through

the 1920s. Long before 1933 Carl Diem and Theodor Lewald were determined that the Berlin Olympics should be the most splendid sports festival the world had yet seen. The coming of the Nazis shook but did not destroy their conviction.

The Games projected for Berlin in 1936 had already energized many Germans. Certain National Socialists, notably Josef Goebbels and then Hitler himself, became convinced that an international festival in Berlin could be useful. For a few months in 1933, Diem and Lewald were in suspense and then were assured financing and a freedom to invent a festival that exceeded in grandeur anything they might have expected from a bourgeois-democratic regime. Significantly, the facilities from 1916 were pulled down and rapidly replaced by a complex of sports architecture grander than any American or Briton had imagined.

In the meantime the Nazis put into effect a radical plan for mobilizing national energies that could not help but alter German sport. Fitness was declared a patriotic obligation. Paramilitary exercise, competitive sport, and even patriotic discussions were demanded of the schools and sports clubs. The vigorous anti-Semitic campaigns affected sport as well. On April 1, 1933, when a boycott of Jewish businesses went into effect, the German boxing federation announced that it would no longer tolerate Jewish fighters or referees. On June 2, 1933, the new Nazi Minister of Education announced that Jews were to be excluded from youth, welfare, and gymnastics organizations and that all facilities would be closed to them. Some Jewish sports officials committed suicide. By 1935 Jews were denied access to public and private practice fields and could not compete with Aryan (that is, non-Jewish) athletes. Some well-known athletes emigrated. Naturally these remarkable events were noticed abroad. Some critics of the new Germany also claimed that the ideology of the National Socialists did not accord with the peaceful altruism of the never precisely presented "Olympic idea" and that, therefore, the Olympic Games of 1936, like those of 1916, 1920 and 1924, should be cleansed of German participation.

A boycott movement against the 1936 Olympic Games sprouted, grew, and then perished in the United States. Elsewhere there were only a few protests. Because of his great prestige abroad, the Nazis were forced to keep Theodor Lewald in place. Lewald, in turn, assured sports bureaucrats from abroad that reports of persecution against Jews were exaggerations and that, in any case, the Olympic Games of 1936 would, as required, be free of politics of any sort. As proof of the Nazis' good will, Lewald pointed to the presence on the German team of Helene Mayer, who, like Lewald, was half-Jewish. Blonde and very good looking, Mayer had won the women's fencing event in Amsterdam and was the world's foil champion in 1929 and 1931.

Everywhere sports leaders and heads of nations accepted German assurances. Coubertin's claims for the general beneficence of the Olympic Games were well established. Sports functionaries and political leaders in Italy, Japan, Great Britain, the United States, and elsewhere also wished to use the Olympic Games to demonstrate the vigor of their athletes and (thus, symbolically and by extension) the vigor of their political systems in the face of worldwide depression and disillusionment. Most exceptional were some morally offended and mostly socialist Europeans who were arranging some protesting "Peoples' Olympics" or "Workers' Games" for Barcelona in 1936. The Barcelona Olympics never took place because of the Spanish Civil War.

In Berlin it was apparent that the Olympics would be a splendid spectacle indeed. The Germans had determined that the fine presentation in Los Angeles would be overshadowed. For example, the "Olympic Village" for the male athletes in Berlin was set in a park-like area and consisted of permanent cozy cottages near restaurants, recreation halls, and jogging paths. Some boulevards in Berlin were renamed for the Games. The stadium was no mere bowl of spectator seats, but was a columned, grand conception that held 100,000 people.

An endeavor of the National Socialist program was to embrace all Germans in their public festivities which were designed to furnish pleasure while inspiring optimism, devotion, and hard work. Some aspects of the 1936 Games marked advances in the development of totalitarian ritual.

An attempt to draw the German rural population into the festival was an *Olympia-Zug,* a caravan of trucks and trailers that traveled some 10,000 kilometers while touring the countryside. The trailers contained tents which when erected held pictures of classical Greece, German athletes, sporting art, models of the new sport complexes in Garmisch, in Berlin, and short sound movies of German athletes in action. Also displayed were some more conventional Nazi propaganda photos of exemplary, smiling work battalions, and panoramas of ranks of zealots marching in the party rallies in Nuremberg. The red, white, and black flag of the Third Reich flapped over the displays and the swastika was everywhere evident.

Of far more than rural interest was the "Olympia Torch Run," a delightful and quite original (for there were neither ancient nor modern prototypes) fabrication. Clad in costumes inspired by figures on Attic vases, some Greek maidens ignited, with the help of a huge Zeiss lens, a flame at the temple of Hera in Olympia early in July 1936. Several thousand relay runners carried the flame through Greece, Bulgaria, Yugoslavia, Hungary, Austria, and Germany to Berlin and, as they did so, were focal points for delightful ceremonies participated in by millions of people. The last torch runner was a blond Berliner, clad in white. On either side were three dark runners clad in black. They speedily advanced in unison as a "V" to the stadium where the fair youth left them and climbed to a colossal brazier atop a tripod. There he lit the fire that dominated the site for the next two weeks.

Young, fragile, or entirely synthetic sports myths inspired many ceremonies in Germany in 1936. The winter Games at Garmisch added elaborate opening, closing, and award presentation ceremonies and new artistic effects at night with torches carried by skiers. At the winter and summer Games at night there were vast colonnades of brightness created by circles of upward-shining antiaircraft lights. There were displays of ancient and modern sporting art. The Olympic Games encompassed balls, receptions, ballets, and concerts, international boy scout encampments, and enormous demonstrations by massed gymnasts. Despite the technical imperfections of the equipment at hand, some Olympic sporting events of 1936 were broadcast to television receivers at various assemblies elsewhere in Berlin.

The 1936 Olympics were also the occasion for the realization of a new kind of art. Athletes had, of course, inspired the artists of classical antiquity. Indeed athletic art on vases, the statuary, or even sports victory poetry exported the classical Greek spirit. Since that time, recreational or agonistic activities by handsome people had been a characteristic of fine art. In the twentieth century many artists had employed the cool eroticism, the power, the immediate appeal, and the violence of boxing, football, and cycling in their works. Well into the 1930s, however, the esthetic potential in modern sport had been ignored by even artistically innovative cinematographers.

Leni Riefenstahl (1902–), an actress turned film director, had made some thinly plotted adventure films in the late 1920s. She opportunistically sided with the Nazis and made *Triumph of the Will*, a film of the party rally in Nuremberg in 1934. She gratefully accepted the assignment to record the optimistic pageantry of the Berlin Games for those who might wish to experience the festival in the world's movie houses. She had a staff of 80 cameramen and assistants, the best equipment, assured state subsidies, and the protection of Carl Diem and Theodor Lewald as well as that of Josef Goebbels and of Adolf Hitler himself.

The raw product of Leni Riefenstahl's efforts was some 400,000 meters (about 1.3 million feet) of exposed film that covered not only most of the sports events from many angles but also such events as the torch run from Olympia, the opening and closing ceremonies, and many antecedent accomplishments and accidents. She began a close association with that precious footage, eliminating, repeating, compressing, combining in order to compose and orchestrate the film that was to be an artistic distillation of modern sport.

Riefenstahl later recalled her work with these strips of film: "I suspended them . . . in order to look at them, compare them, so as to verify their harmony in the scale of frames and tones. Thus in the long run, as a composer composes, I made everything work together in the rhythm." The result was a two-part, six-hour film called *Olympia*, which was released late in the summer of 1938. There were four different soundtracks, in German, English, French, and Italian. The film performed its intended social function of bringing the Olympic Games to the masses only in Germany and Italy. Elsewhere public attitudes toward Germany delayed a recognition of its splendor until decades later.

Riefenstahl's film accepted and indeed hardened all the synthetic myths about the modern Olympic Games. She intertwined symbols of Greek antiquity with motifs of industrial society's sport theater. She ennobled good losers, supreme winners, and dwelled on fine musculature, particularly that of Jesse Owens. She was the first cinematographer to use slow motion filming and radical cutting to reveal the intensity of effort required for supreme athletic performance. Some of *Olympia*'s sections, most particularly the one dealing with platform diving, may be unsurpassed in esthetic intensity. In any case, the film was and remains a shock because of the success with which Riefenstahl preserved and communicated some of the esthetic potential within modern sports and their theatrical settings.

The originality and supremacy of *Olympia* has been tested since its release. Subsequent Olympic Games have been filmed, and rather successfully so, in Rome in 1960 and in Tokyo in 1964. Faster lenses, zoom lenses, color film, and a few new tricks have brought the cameraman and his audience closer to competing athletes, but the first, sudden, and successful filming of a great sports festival, that in Berlin of 1936, remains the best.

The benefits brought to the hosts of the National Socialists' Olympics in Garmisch and in Berlin were substantial. Despite apprehensions and misgivings, the Nazis, fearing foreign vengeance, did not hamper Jews or Negroes on other teams. In fact, the sports hero of the summer games was Jesse Owens, a supremely handsome and poised Negro from Ohio State University. Owens was the victor in the 100 meter dash when he equaled the Olympic record, in the 200 meter dash, as anchor in the 400 meter relay, and in the long jump where he set a new Olympic record. The audience in the stadium wholeheartedly cheered "Yes-sa Ov-ens!" (for so his name came out from German orthography) almost as much as they cheered Hitler.

Though not at all an athlete or even a sports fan, the biggest single winner in the Games of 1936 was the leader of the Third German Empire. Despite some early fears, Hitler's lieutenants, among them Carl Diem and Theodor Lewald, had demonstrated to the whole world that the new Germans were administratively capable, generous, respectable, and peace loving. Furthermore, any of the point systems that journalists devised (against the strictures of the Olympic idealists who claim that to struggle is more important than to win) showed that, for the first time in their 40-year history, the victors were not Americans, but Germans. Impressive also was the fact that all the point tabulations showed that Mussolini's fascist Italians were third and well ahead of the democratic French. And the Japanese, who were also the carriers of an aggressive patriotic ideology, were well ahead of the land that had invented sport, Great Britain.

By the mid-1930s Olympic sports events were broadcast or written about the world over and the results were widely interpreted as portentous symbols. The indications might be that totalitarianism and the submission of individual wills to the commands of the aggressive state were most likely to produce more concrete indications of success in the wars that many people feared were imminent. Conclusive evidence is lacking that the winners of the Games of 1936 were emboldened by these sports successes to reach for more substantial political victories. However, we do know that Hitler, particularly, was greatly emboldened by the generally acknowledged, domestically and internationally, triumph of this festival grounded on the pagan (though very new) rituals of modern sport.

And so, the modern Olympic Games achieved their mature form. They were financed by a national state in order to further the domestic and foreign policies of that state. The Italians and Japanese, among others, had demonstrated conclusively that Anglo-Saxon sport as it had evolved since the turn of the century was not culture specific, but that the modern sport program, like modern industry, lent itself everywhere to the rational use of human resources and long-term planning. "Olympic" theater and symbols were still in the process of accretion and solidification, but enough ritual had evolved to permit the festivals to be presented in accepted and seductive forms. The world was made aware of a new variety of machinery to manufacture heroes.

The Japanese swimmers, runners, and gymnasts who performed so well at the Summer Games of 1932 and 1936 might be viewed as symbols of a nation desperate for success. The westernization and industrialization of Japan had been turbulent and disruptive.

Indeed political determination amidst social disruption may be partial explanation of the ease with which many Japanese became fans for many sports that had no apparent historical bases in their culture.

The modernizers of Japan adopted massed physical education and high-performance sport much as they adopted the lapeled business suit and the assembly line as integral parts of the program necessary to catch up with and to participate fully in the modern world. The Japanese had joined the International Olympic Committee in 1912. Many Japanese who sought to make a mark in the world were eager to be hosts for the Olympic Games. Their campaign was successful. For 1940 the winter Games were scheduled for Sapporo and the summer Games for Tokyo.

After 1936 the country came increasingly under the control of military adventurers who were in much more of a hurry to obtain international success than Japan's sports bureaucrats. Tales of atrocities committed by the Japanese troops in China were shunted aside by cosmopolitan sports bureaucrats such as Avery Brundage, president of the American Olympic Committee, who declared that "sport transcends national boundaries," and, "Whether our Committee or athletes like or dislike Japan's military policy is beside the point." Then in July 1938 the Japanese cabinet announced the withdrawal of invitations to foreign athletes. The Games of 1940 would be "Japanese Olympics." The Finns had since 1912 used the Olympic Games to further their international stature and Helsinki was then designated as the site of the 1940 Olympics. Then the war of Finland with the Soviet Union forced the cancellation of these Games too. London had been for some time scheduled for the Games of 1944. Though the number of modern "Olympiads" had been maintained every four years since 1896, the war aborted all preparations for this international festival as well.

We can, for purposes of narrative simplicity, include the Olympic Games of 1948 through 1956 in a general discussion. None of these festivals was significantly advanced in its techniques or festive trappings over the Winter and Summer Games in 1936. However important they were for the hosts and however tight the strain on the war-damaged economies, they were not grandly expensive and did not have major political consequences.

The Winter Olympics in St. Moritz and the Summer Olympics in London took place under conditions of general approbation, but with some austerity in 1948. The winter Games of 1952 in Oslo and in 1956 in Cortina d'Ampezzo as well as the Summer Games of 1952 in Helsinki and of 1956 in Melbourne indicated that the Olympics could take place rather far from the news-making capitals of Europe and America as far as well from the places of origin of modern sport. These festivals all provided cyclical high points for the sports news and sports equipment industries. They were stimulating to local economies. At least in one case—the introduction of winter tourism to the Italian Alps in 1956—the results were substantial and long lasting.

The sports programs and the audiences continued to grow. There were more events for boats and horses. Basketball was added in 1948. There were ever more events for women. Events for weight lifters, boxers, and wrestlers were increased by narrowing the weight classes. By 1956 large teams were coming from all over the globe. Olympic victors might return to exotic or unexpected places. For a while weight lifters came from Egypt, wrestlers from Turkey, gymnasts from Japan. The winner of the 1500 meter run in 1952 was a Luxembourger, Josef Bartel. There were some desperate moments shortly before his victory ceremony when the band on the site could not, at first, find a score for his national anthem. American blacks appeared in greater numbers at the festivals and broke ever more records. The appearance of large numbers of superbly trained African blacks was imminent.

Until 1956 in Melbourne, it appeared that the Olympic "incidents" (those little *contretemps* perceived and exploited by opportunistic journalists) would be confined to silly disputes over such matters as surreptitious advertising by "amateurs" for sports equipment (for this reason Avery Brundage always opposed the equipment-laden winter Olympics) or bad calls by referees. However in Melbourne in 1956, the distant city was provided a theater for the acting out of some playlets that reflected tensions elsewhere.

Some of the troubles in Melbourne were organizational. There were disputes over who—the IOC, the Australian government, the Australian Olympic Committee, various international and local sports federations—should get what portions of the substantial income from radio and film rights. There were fears that the main facilities would not be built in time. The Australian government's strict quarantine laws against importing horses required that the equestrian events be shifted to Stockholm.

More serious were the political and propaganda incidents. The episodes were in some cases illustrative of much larger troubles far from Melbourne. The Hungarian revolution against Soviet occupation was in its early stages when, to the astonishment of many, a hastily assembled Hungarian team appeared in Australia. At the opening ceremony the team marched, contrary to protocol, in two different sorts of uniforms and was the object of stormy demonstrations of sympathy. Disgust at the suppression of the Hungarians in Europe caused the Dutch Olympic Committee to withdraw from the Games because "events in Hungary had spoiled the festive Olympic atmosphere." Egypt and Lebanon boycotted the Games because of the military campaigns of Israel, France, and Britain in the Sinai Peninsula and Suez. The eagerness of the East Germans to be allowed to make known their ambitions as an athletic power compelled them to march together with the West Germans as one team. The Peoples' Republic of China (the Mainland) withdrew because the Republic of China (Taiwan) had been accorded official Olympic recognition and allowed to march and compete.

Relative to the sporting results of the 1956 Olympics, the great astonishments were the excellent performances of the best athletes from the Soviet Union. By all the scoring schemes to determine national rankings, the Soviet Union, in its second appearance at the Olympics, had excelled over the United States. The many gold medals of the Soviets in soccer, distance running (Vladimir Kuts set world records in the 5000 and 10,000 meters), boxing, weightlifting, and many womens' events in all sports exposed and justified the long-term commitment by Soviet authorities to high-performance sports that had had no organic basis in either the Russian Empire or Soviet society. The whole world saw the results of a belated emulation of those benefits the National Socialists had gathered from their determined and meticulous preparations for the Games in Berlin twenty years before. Though segregated by the aristocratic and conservative members of the IOC from competition in international contests until 1952, the Soviets had, late in the 1930s, embraced the forms of Anglo-Saxon sport. Soviet authorities have viewed sport as a means of improving the health of the nation, and for inspiring efficiency and accomplishment in the productive system, and therefore as too important to leave to haphazard development. But it was only beginning in 1956 that the Soviets would employ high-performance sports results to demonstrate to their people and to the world the superiority of the "socialist" system of government.

The Soviet success (like the even more remarkable successes of the East Germans later) was based on a many-sided approach to the achievement of results that had certain models elsewhere. The Soviet sports scientists far exceeded in care and determination the few biologists and engineers at American universities who for decades had watched sprinters' legs as they ran on treadmills, who studied blood oxygenation in endurance events, or who calibrated the efficiency of ski outfits in wind tunnels. After 1945 the Soviet Union was canvassed ever more carefully for children who fit previously specified physical and psychological "profiles" that suggested medal-winning potential in gymnastics, swimming, or any other (now traditional) Olympic sport. Learning from the rather timid and hasty (in retrospect) German example employed in the 1930s, potential athletes were quartered in certain sports "academies" that were really full-time training camps, and there were rationally prepared for those newspaper-reported, broadcast (later telecast) appearances that would be the climaxes of their lives. The 1956 Olympics clearly demonstrated that sporting results were manipulable in the long run. Sport battalions were objects to be obtained like panzer divisions or batteries of guided missiles. All were the products of political objectives to be realized by the application of short- and long-range planning to resources, scientific knowledge, and the particularly gifted members of society.

The Olympic Games of 1956 closed rather harmoniously. So many dissidents had left. Happily there had been only one confrontation between the Hungarians and the Soviets. At a water polo game attended by passionate partisans of the Hungarian team (Australia had many immigrants from Eastern Europe), Australian police barely maintained order as a Hungarian, Ervin Zádar, was forced to leave the water because of a split and bloody eyebrow. As they had in 1932, 1936, and 1952, the Hungarians won the gold medal—this time with a score of 4–0. But this setback for the Soviets was exceptional: As a whole they were triumphant.

A lot of people took this lesson earnestly. Sport at the international level became yet more earnest. The Australians and southern Californians became Soviet-like in their devotion to the scouting out and training of swimmers. The Canadians of the western provinces became analogously devoted to figure skaters. The French established some academies for fencers, skiers, and bicyclists. But the Soviet model was taken over most readily and wholly by other "socialist" nations under their protection. The East Germans had already had pre-war experience with state-fostered sport, which partially explains why their success, as we shall see, was most remarkable.

The steady evolution of the Olympic Games continued for the next three meetings of the winter Games at Squaw Valley in 1960, Innsbruck in 1964, and Grenoble in 1968 and of the summer Games at Rome in 1960, at Tokyo in 1964, and in Mexico City in 1968. It is perhaps an affront to go so lightly over the preparations of many thousands of devoted sports functionaries, financiers, artists, and athletes for these meetings, but these festivals can probably be justly discussed within the frame of a certain historical period. All of these great international festivals were major financial, political, and cultural undertakings for the host nations. The exception may be the winter Games of 1960 in California, for Americans do not give the Olympic Games the earnest attention that the Games receive elsewhere in the world.

The various national teams and the individual athletes on them performed in an ideologically and symbolically charged atmosphere. The athletic competitions, the rituals, the festivities proceeded rather smoothly, thus adding to the impression that these celebrations were venerable and had possibly acquired a sacred legitimacy. There were, of course, "incidents." But these mishaps, however critical for the reputations of the athletes or the teams involved, dramatically came to conclusions apart from the disrupting major international concerns of the time. The world's ruling elites were more concerned with the Cold War, the political turbulence in the Middle East and the wars in Indo-China. If one blurred his critical vision a bit, one could take an optimistic stance and predict for the Olympic Games an ever larger role as a peaceful forum for the demonstration of architectural originality, organizational virtuosity, the peaceful mingling of people, the steady improvement of human performance and—with all of these things—vivid, concrete demonstrations of one of the inspiring *Leitmotifs* of our age, the idea of progress.

The generally happy impression left by the Rome Olympics was due partly to the stunning beauty and classical evocations of that great city. Wrestling took place in the basilica of Maxentius, gymnastics in the baths of Caracalla, the course of the Marathon was a tour (whose evocations the runners could not enjoy) of the Capitol, several of the seven hills, and the arch of Constantine. Luigi Nervi, the virtuoso architect of reinforced concrete, the construction material of our time, executed a new large and a new small sports palace (called *"palazzo"* and *"palazetto"* respectively). The ideological task of the 1960 Games, which was to demonstrate to the universe of sports readers or listeners or viewers that the Italians had cleansed themselves of fascism, did not prevent the Italians from employing Mussolini's *Foro italico* for the track-and-field and the swimming events.

Less redolent of history, yet even more artistically impressive, were the facilities in Tokyo in 1964. Here again the building material was spectacularly used reinforced concrete. Avery Brundage, a pope of the international rituals, called Kenzo Tange's swimming stadium a "cathedral of sports." The Games of 1964 were so statistically presented, so organizationally efficient and were so marked by generosity on the part of their hosts that they did indeed communicate to those who viewed the spectacle either in person or by means of telecommunications that the defeat of 1945 had been obliterated by an Asian nation that was powerful but nonthreatening, artistically refined and very up-to-date.

The lavish facilities provided for the Winter Olympics four years later in Grenoble were more obviously staged to present a certain picture to the world. France had since 1959 been ruled by General Charles de Gaulle who saw as his duty the restoration of France's pre-eminence among nations and, if possible, the accretion of some *gloire*. The French teams at the Olympic Games of 1960 in Rome had produced little evidence of distinction. Some newspapers called the results for France "a debacle." The results in 1964 were also scanty. De Gaulle declared all this a "national scandal." Grenoble, an old town near the French Alps, was to be a showplace for French *élan*. Three-quarters of the enormous budget, almost all of it provided by the central government, went for the modernization of the city. And sure enough, the French won many medals and along the way produced a hero of international renown and, it followed, of national value. Jean-Claude Killy won three medals in Alpine skiing and went from there to an easy multi-million-dollar career as a giver of his illustrious endorsement to improved varieties of expensive winter sports equipment.

The Winter Olympics of 1972 in Sapporo were yet more costly and, despite the isolation of this site on the northernmost island of the Japanese Archipelago, were yet more broadly, if only electronically, observed. Order in communications was maintained by an elaborate computer network. The broadcasting facilities in Japan simultaneously sent out thirteen different programs during the ten-day festival. This cold and isolated city looked attractive and so did the Japanese. The generosity of the Japanese was once again successfully communicated to the whole world. At Sapporo, the press, radio and television personnel made up a total of about 3000 and for the first time at a sports festival, outnumbered the athletes two-to-one.

We must go back a bit. The summer Games of 1968 in Mexico City were the first since 1896 to take place in a nonindustrialized nation. The costly and disruptive effort to maintain the expected standard of pomp and festivity was possible only because Mexico was still, at the time, a rather politically efficient one-party state. Nevertheless, the preparations did not go as smoothly as hoped, but were marred by some opposition groups. Many Mexicans felt that such outlays might be better devoted to social reform. Some thought a pretty picture of Mexico was a false picture. Some young leftists believed they could use the wide-reaching publicity apparatus concentrated in the capital to demonstrate old and suppressed grievances. In any case, a climax was reached ten days before the opening ceremonies when 10,000 protesters, many of them students, demonstrated in the great Zocalo before the cathedral and the national palace. A unit of the Mexican army fired on the crowd, killing some 250 and wounding another 1000. Resistance to the preparations was crushed. Further political demonstrations in Mexico City were small and led by non-Mexicans.

Almost needless to say, the number of nations entering the Olympic Games grew. There were 67 teams at the Summer Olympics of 1956, 94 teams at those of 1964, and 124 teams at the 1972 Games. There were steadily more events. Volleyball was added for men and women in 1964. A "super-heavyweight" division for freestyle and Greco-Roman wrestling was added in 1972. Paralleling the vogue for women's rights in politics, the women's program grew at a faster rate than the men's program did. By the late 1960s participation was indeed world-wide. Small, statistically verifiable championship weightlifters and wrestlers were coming from Indonesia and the Philippines. African runners were setting records and winning gold medals in the longer foot races. They thus brought immense prestige to their new nations and, along the way, destroyed the myth that dark-skinned people were not amenable to the long-term discipline or severe effort required for a distance event. The political utility of an Olympic hero in the modern age was comparable to the situation in the ancient Olympic Games when a victor gained immense symbolic value for the political entity that sponsored him.

As in ancient times, the world-class athletes tended to be splendidly beautiful or otherwise impressive persons whose training and isolation made them awesome personalities even though their only allowable expression of individualism was often their particular sports event. The ideological utility of the Olympic Games was avilable only through the instrument of nation states. An individual had to compete as the member of a nation or not at all. One recalls the terrific *brouhaha* in Mexico City in 1968 when a few American black sprinters slightly altered and disrespectfully used their appearance at the stylized victory ceremonies and raised their fists as a gesture (they explained later) favoring justice for American Negroes. One is reminded of such earlier desecrations as profaning the host or mutilating the flag. The International and American Olympic Committees banned the youths forever from

international competition. Some measures of the rapidly solidify-
ing power of Olympic "ritual" are that the conceivably noble ges-
tures of the young sprinters live in infamy and that the fates of
250 or more protestors slaughtered before the Mexican Olympics
are eased out of the history books.

With the Munich Games of 1972, the Olympic Games reached
an organizational, popular, artistic, and tragic climax. At this writing, it appears that circumstances allowing the creation of such a
festival will never arise again. There were several factors that encouraged the Federal (West) Germans to prepare carefully and lavishly for their first laying of the feast since their total collapse and
partition in the mid-1940s. The Munich Games were intended to
obliterate some durable impressions left by the Berlin Games of
the Nazis. The 1972 Games were planned as a forum for demonstrating the genius, taste, vigor, wealth, and power of a nation that
was negligible militarily. In the light of the factors cited above,
the Federal Germans were especially pleased to have a forum from
which to demonstrate their ascendency over their brother republic, the Soviet-dominated Democratic (East) Germans. Significantly, in the course of the long preparations after the I.O.C. gave
the 1972 Games to Munich in 1966, there were only the merest
peeps domestically against the enormous outlays and local disruptions that the preparations required. The architecture was almost
all new. The *pièce de resistance* was the stadium (seating only 70,000
it should be well noted) which had a swooping canopy of translucent plastic. There was also a vast new apartment complex almost
ironically called the "Olympic Village" and another new apartment complex that had yet more luxurious quarters for the journalists. Munich had no 2000-meter lake for the rowing events. In
the course of seventeen months a new one was dug up and correctly equipped in nearby Oberschleissheim for five days of use.
It cost an enormous sum to construct and was almost useless once
the Games were over. Preparations (as those for the earlier festivals in Grenoble and in Sapporo) included a transformation of the
"infrastructure" of Munich which got new hotels, renovated monuments, new multilaned highways, and a new subway system. The
perfection-oriented Federal Germans were especially proud of the

Olympic computer, dubbed "Golem," which stored and retrieved, among thousands of other things, the *vitas* of all the journalists on the site, traffic conditions, current attendance conditions, the status of various construction projects and, of course, almost any conceivable statistic on the past performances of all the athletes who were scheduled to appear.

A figure at the Games who was nearly unknown, but was very much in evidence was a certain Otl Aicher, a professor of design who was the czar of color in Munich. Aicher arrived too late on the scene to plan the architecture (which was, in any case, universally praised for its appearance and function, if not for its economy), but he was empowered to integrate all the visual aspects of the 1972 Games into a purposeful, logical scheme. Aicher was a dictator regarding all the posters for internal and external use, the uniforms of functionaries, the banners flapping over the site, catalogs for the accompanying art exhibitions—in short all the *surfaces* in any way connected with this at once particularly German and generally international festival. He even "invented" six new colors, two blues, two greens, and two yellows, which had never existed in history or nature for the surfaces in Munich. Quite significantly, Aicher and the German organizers shunned red—the color of revolution, of totalitarianism, and of the Nazis. This festival of the prosperous, generous, good Germans was seen at the outset as the anti-Nazi Olympics.

Visually there were more indications of the festival's universality and altruistic embrace. Aicher imposed on the Games a stark, rounded typeface called "Univers" that was the very opposite of the painfully reminiscent black letter of Wilhelmian Germany and the one imposed by Hitler. The designer's "team" (he had a staff of about thirty) devised "pictograms" or a system of readily recognizable symbols (comparable to the coordinated traffic symbols all over Europe's roads) for athletic events. All those on hand speaking only Russian or Urdu or Swahili could readily differentiate swimming from cycling or, as the system expanded, a men's room from a resfreshment stand. However, the euphoric creativity that pervaded the site affected the pictograms' designers too. This system of visual Esperanto (which both symbolized and furthered the loosening of the refinement and distinctions of language) also had signs for saunas, baby sitting and car washes. The pictograms, like modern sport, were to be universally applicable.

That the stadium was relatively small and the journalists (of which this writer was one) had grander facilities and more reliable services at hand than the athletes did are matters worth dwelling on. The organizers made deliberate, though little publicized, efforts to keep tourists out of Munich and out of Germany, which could not handle even a fraction of the world's travelers who would have liked to have been on the spot. Though the athletes were essential for the tightly programmed sporting competitions and a certain number of spectators were necessary to lend credence to the notion that this was a public festival as well as to embody a happy community, the intended participators for the grand show were far from the site. This audience was composed of some 500 million to 1 billion television viewers who would see seductively appealing performances of the new universal heroes of specified individualism, the new beautiful gods and goddesses of selfless preparation and symbolic accomplishment. As the postwar Germans gave the supreme public demonstration of our time of organization, efficiency, and achievement, they also (by the use of the air waves and of the press) demonstrated that they had effaced their regretted past and were now supreme in positive contributions to high culture. Along the way the new Germans would demonstrate that they were peaceful and rich. For hundreds of millions of have-nots in the world in 1972, the Olympic Games of Munich were a seductive demonstration of European power and creativity.

The Olympic Games now required a whole day of fanfares, concerts, parades, mass escapes of doves, balloon flotillas, passing of flags, oaths, congratulations, and lighting of flames. Contrived though it all may have been, the ritual did begin a magnificent festival of organizational wizzardry and affirmative competition. The athletes and the journalists of the world mingled hopefully and the world chimed in delightedly for only eight days. For late in the night on September 4 some men who were not awed by the expensive preparations for staging a peaceful *tour-de-force* took ruthless advantage of the communications network provided for others. Some Palestinian terrorists killed an Israeli weight lifter (machine gun bullets cut his body in half) and seized ten Israeli athletes. The thousands of journalists on hand observed and eagerly communicated the ensuing drama. The terrorists had intended to dramatize their rage over the existence of the modern Jewish state. In a bloody and grossly mishandled shoot-out, 13 more people died at the Fürstenfeldbruck airport. All the world watched.

A certain affirmative momentum of the Olympic Games was halted. It was as though some madman had desecreated the host, urinated in the holy water, blasphemed the holy. Attempts by mourners on the site who were stunned by the sacrilege to cancel the remaining events were successfully opposed by the shaken, but firm priests of modern sport. It had been a terrible transgression. The whole world watched as the organizers tried to regain the earlier impetus. There was a hastily contrived funeral ceremony in the main stadium where the Munich Philharmonic played Beethoven's "Creatures of Prometheus" overture. Then the schedule resumed, a day late.

There were several heroes of the 1972 Games. Mark Spitz was an inarticulate, but handsome American swimmer, who inspired deep yet sympathetic envy. Spitz posed for photographers with seven gold medals suspended by ribbons around his neck and wearing the merest nothing of a bathing suit. He had reasons for smiling. His hard work had paid off. He had alread pledged his future advocacy of certain consumer products to the William Morris Agency, the largest theatrical agency in the world. A senior executive estimated that the gold medals were worth about $5 million. A heroine was the tiny (84-pound) Soviet gymnast, Olga Korbut. Korbut was a splendid and courageous performer, but was neither the conventionally prettiest nor the very best of the supremely accomplished Soviet gymnasts. However, this junior officer in the Soviet army (such was the cover that permitted her to devote her life to training) once wept while observed by television zoom lenses. She had just failed at an especially daring maneuver on the high bars. Olga Korbut eventually won gold medals in the floor exercises and the high beam, but also won (because of a most exceptional revelation of human weakness) the hearts of hundreds of millions.

The profanation by the heathen-opportunists at the Munich Games of 1972 caused the proceedings to close a day late, on September 11, 1972. Despite the dreadful setback, the organization held, the periodicity was reaffirmed, the affirmative power of sport brilliantly made manifest for the world-wide audience. The new Federal Germans did succeed in demonstrating that they had overcome their regretted recent past.

The Munich Games were expensive. Indeed they were much more expensive than the planners in 1966 had foreseen. The total bill came to somewhere between $600 million and $1 billion. Such sums can buy a lot of schools, care for the aged, and other more concrete, urgent, and less artistically manipulable government services. But Munich got a great deal of modernization, the West German state gained immeasurably in prestige and international status. That lives were lost and some injustices were done were not part of the planning. However expensive the Olympic Games in the summer of 1972 were, they still cost less than a large, modern aircraft carrier, of whose ugliness and uselessness there can be little doubt.

By 1972 festively presented high-performance sport was thoroughly integrated into the cultural affairs of most industrial nations and was at least known everywhere else. World-class sport was an affair worthy of mobilizing vast economic resources, long-term political energies and, as was so vividly demonstrated in the events at Munich, vulnerable to opportunistic interference.

So the evolving grandeur of the Olympic movement faltered. The privilege of offering the Winter Games of 1976 had been given to Denver, the large, isolated American city nestled against the eastern slope of the Rocky Mountains. The organizers, largely retired advertising executives and local bankers and land speculators, advanced their plans quickly and with some confidence. It was expected that spectators and journalists would indeed strain the city's infrastructure. Some new construction, particularly the instllation of a regulation bobsled run, would require the "redoing" of some mountain scenery. Nevertheless, the boosters of the Denver Olympics were convinced that the universal attention drawn to the area would lead to accelerated growth, particularly in the winter tourist industry. They assumed general approbation. They reckoned without the anti-progressivists and the environmentalists of that troubled time. Determined opponents eventually got the issue on the state and city ballots for November 1972. The voters rejected the use of any tax revenues for the Olympic Games.

The 1976 Winter Olympics quickly found a new berth in Innsbruck, where facilities still existed from the Games of 1964, where they had taken place to the satisfaction of almost everyone. The Austrian government and the city of Innsbruck had assumed that the existing facilities and their experience would make the presentation simple and relatively cheap. They were brought up sharp. The new standard of hospitality required the provisions for an enormous media population.

The usual annoyances caused by athletes attempting to parlay their media exposure into the advertising of sports equipment was especially nettlesome. From the beginning it had remained a principle of the Olympics that the privileges of gaining and spending at the lavish Olympic presentations were to be barred to the athletes. The bill covered by the Austrian government came to more than twice what had been originally planned for.

Money became a serious issue again in the preparations and presentation of the 1976 Olympics in Montreal. The first estimates in 1972 were that the Games would cost $310 million and would be covered by lotteries and the sale of souvenirs. The costs for certain items of architecture eventually doubled and quadrupled the first estimates. In the light of the terrorism at Munich, security was tight and expensive, costing an estimated $100 million or $12,500 for each of the 8000 athletes there. The "velodrome," a splendid building for cycling and swimming events, cost $62 million. Total costs went out of control, exceeding $1.5 billion.

Political issues with dangerous implications dogged the organizers from the beginning. Nowhere in North America were the Games regarded with the nearly universal approbation that greeted them in Europe. The Games and the money surrounding them were tempting targets for a variety of dissidents. The huge city of

Montreal was the only part of the French-speaking province of Quebec that had a large English-speaking population and was and would remain a stage for the acting out of Francophone resentment against the Anglophone national government in Ottawa and the powerful banks in Toronto. The ambitious organizational and construction requirements for the 1976 Olympics quickly exhausted the supply of competent, honest politicians and contractors. Costs escalated to the point that the city was burdened with public debts it would never dispose of. The deficit for the Games of 1976 for the province of Quebec and the city of Montreal was more than $1 billion, or more than the 1972 Olympics cost all together.

There were annoying international political complications. The Canadian government, under pressure from the mainland Chinese, would not admit the team from Taiwan, since the politicians in Taipai demanded that they march and be celebrated as the citizens of the Republic of China. Many African heads of state used the forum of the Olympic Games to denounce South Africa and to keep their teams at home.

In many details and even as a whole the festival was badly managed and, contrary to the hopes of the organizers, was probably damaging to Canada's domestic harmony and her international prestige. Some of the architecture, in particular the much heralded stadium, though usable, was never finished. Its computer-regulated translucent top remains in storage. Pampered foreign super-athletes from the sports academies, where they had been accustomed to tender care, were annoyed when they were quartered ten or more to a room in the Olympic Village.

In the midst of the tumult in Munich in 1972, the IOC had awarded the summer Olympics of 1980 to Moscow. This was an acknowledgment of the earnestness and in fact the success with which the nations in the Soviet bloc had promoted sport. The Soviets had long since surpassed the Americans in the medal-gathering at the Olympic Games. Indeed, in the light of the susceptibility of the Games to ideological gangsters (as in 1972), many westerners believed that because of the new standards of Olympic staging, the gigantic, complex Games could only be successfully presented by a tightly controlled, totalitarian state. Moscow already had several large sport complexes ready for use and the rest of the arrangements went forward without a hitch. "Mischa," a cartoon version of a Russian bear, would be the mascot. In America, the National Broadcasting Company (NBC) paid almost $100 million for the exclusive American television rights.

But then, in December 1979, reasons of state caused the Soviets to install 30,000 troops in Afghanistan. The American President, eager to punish politically short of war, organized an American boycott and induced the West Germans, the Japanese, and several other nations to boycott as well. As it turned out the program remained complete, though the participation was truncated. As the days of the festival went on, there were the inevitable accusations of dishonest judges and annoyance at inadequate facilities, but the contests proceeded. The world missed the tense confrontations, loaded with dramatic and ideological significance, between the USA and the USSR on the one hand and that of the Germans of the Federal Republic and those of the Democratic Republic on the other hand.

At this writing the summer Olympics are scheduled for 1984 in Los Angeles and the organizers are faced with the reluctance of American governments to provide financing. If national or state financing should materialize, it would be a major departure in American policy toward sport. Further meetings of the Olympic Games are scheduled. No one would doubt that the sports demonstrated at the Olympic Games are gathering significance and nearly universal adherence. But the optimistic momentum has been lost. Long before the modern Olympic Games could be a century old, they have acquired an importance that their structure cannot support.

[13]

SPORT AND SOCIETY IN THE LATER TWENTIETH CENTURY

We have seen how the foundations of modern sport have offered fresh possibilities for forming heroes, allowed innovations in popular theater, promoted the mobilization and harmonization of public opinion and, for some, facilitated the making of money. I have proposed that modern sport had two fairly distinct areas or milieus of origin and has continued to evolve in two different though ever less separate ways. One tradition had remote origins in venerable philosophical debates concerning educational theory and found its earliest fruition in Enlightenment Germany. I have repeatedly used the terms "ideological," "political," and "directed" to describe the directions taken by modern sport in this tradition. Continuing this heritage, sport has continued to develop in Central and Eastern Europe.

Modern sport also had separate origins in the novel material and cultural conditions that were also the bases for the origins and development of industrial production in England and the United States. The innovators in this tradition continue to be entrepreneurs or individuals seeking profit or approbation from the world's leisured, moneyed masses.

These traditions are becoming ever less distinct geographically and culturally. As examples: the highly centralized states of Central Europe without a democratic heritage have sought and will continue to seek popular support and fame in particular contests or competitions that originated and evolved elsewhere but which have been accepted into the Olympic program. And sport for ideological and educational purposes continues to find its effective limits (as do other sorts of political impositions) when the masses of citizens refuse to participate or observe. On the other hand, while it is true that the United States remains the place of origin of most innovations in sport (for example, the frisbee and popular participation in long-distance running) sport at all levels of education becomes increasingly repressive and performance oriented. And it seems unlikely that legislators in Washington much longer will resist appeals to regulate the independent national associations overseeing amateur and professional sport. American legislators may not be able to resist indefinitely public pressure to promote American prestige by subsidizing sports academies on the Soviet model.

I will dwell here on the development and geographical extension of modern sport under the direction of persons, usually ideologically or politically motivated, who have assumed that sport is just too useful or too important to be allowed haphazard evolution. If my tone is sometimes ironic or pessimistic it is because I am generally skeptical about the benefits accruing to mankind as a result of large-scale political idealism in recent decades. The next chapter will be more sunny in mood.

It might at the outset be useful to give a very brief and belated history of the word sport. The conquest of sport has been rapid, though scarcely noticed, and world wide. Some evidence can be seen in the career of the word itself. Though derived from Norman French, "sport" in English meant mostly hunting and horse racing until the late nineteenth century. By the early twentieth century it had assumed its present meaning in America. The word had also reentered French by way of the English pastimes. German linguistic purists at the end of the nineteenth century tried to confine "sport" to games and recreations of distinctly foreign origin, but popular culture overtook them. "Sport" now covers more activities in German than in any other language. Few Germans are now aware that "Sport" (along with "Training," and "Rekord") are so new to their language and culture. And so it goes. The noun has gone unchanged into all the Romance, Scandinavian, and Slavic languages as well as into Hungarian and Finnish. Modern Hebrew uses "sport" as do various varieties of Arabic, Japanese, and many languages in India and Africa. Other words are formed from the root, "sport," and these words in other languages are subject to the traditional grammatical rules. This is linguistic evidence that the complex of modern sport has not really evolved much, but rather has been new wherever it intruded.

I observed in the Preface that, Bero Rigauer, critic of modern sport and modern industrial society has listed some characteristics that modern sport shares with industrial employment and urban society: Discipline, authority, competition, accomplishment, rational objectives (*Zweckrationalität*), organization and bureaucracy. That modern participator and spectator sports have strengthened and progressed so in numbers taking part and in area covered is owing to ideological and political empathy between the psychological adaptations necessary for modern social life and the ideology implicit in sport.

But we must return to a historical narrative. The spread of modern sport, well underway when World War II intervened, continued through the decades of peace and world wide modernization afterward. Sport has almost always been associated with modern production and modern social and political life. The spread and integration of sport is thus one aspect of a world-wide desire to improve living standards. Certainly part of sport's rapid evolution in the twentieth century has been due to its adaption by the modern state.

The Soviet Union, that state which suffered most in World War II, can serve as a salient and influential illustration. The Soviet Union was isolated diplomatically and internationally from 1918 to 1939. During that period Bolsheviks condemned and attempted to subvert what they considered capitalist governments. Pride and fear of discovery of their weakness kept the Communists out of Olympic and other international sports competitions. The determined forcing of mass and high-performance sport after 1945 is due to several changes. The postwar Soviets felt that participation in the international community was necessary for their security. The Soviet Union had certainly learned from the examples of Fascist Italy and Nazi Germany that festively presented, high-performance sport can provide, among other things, inspiring heroes, useful distractions, and international fame.

In any case, Soviet sport became not only imitatively, but also innovatingly, modern after the war. There was no indigenous sports tradition acceptable for the vast empire of many cultures, so the Soviets adopted all those sports that since 1896 had been steadily integrated into the Olympic program. The thorough recruiting of potential stars, the scientific investigation of principles of movement and performance, the refinement of apparatus and training that had characterized American and then Japanese and Nazi sport were pushed much further. Fitness exercises were introduced at all levels of education and even on the job. Sports academies and scientific sports institutes were set up to prepare specialists in sport from gymnastics and sprinting (which had some tradition in Russia) to yachting and dressage—quintessentially the sports of decadent capitalism. Almost immediately after the war the Soviets began a diplomatic campaign to have a member on the International Olympic Committee and to have their teams admitted to Olympic competitions. Accordingly, Soviet teams participated modestly at the 1952 Olympics in Helsinki, successfully at the Melbourne Olympics of 1956, and outstandingly thereafter. They proved to an audience consisting of the whole world that sports heroes, sports records, and sports victories were not confined to race or political system and that all these desirable entities could be obtained in a rather short time by the rational and diligent application of time, energy and money.

The ambitious and idealistic sports bureaucrats of the leading Communist state did not keep their ambitions or their methods to themselves. Like the Soviet advocacy of the fine arts and intensive, universal education, sport was encouraged in all the republics of the Soviet Union. Furthermore, even before the international success of Soviet high-performance sport was apparent, the Soviets strongly encouraged the forcing of modern sport on the client states of Romania, Bulgaria, Czechoslovakia, Poland, and the German Democratic Republic.

All of these states proved to themselves and to the world that

sport is immensely useful. But nowhere was the calculated building of a sports establishment ever more determined and more
triumphant than in East Germany. The explanation of the East
German sports story may be based on some long-term factors. The
East Germans remembered and were able to build upon pre-war
Germany's remarkable sports successes, which then wore different
ideological clothing. Perhaps the utter futility of any sort of effective political life and the boredom of cultural life the eastern part
of Germany have diverted available talent and energy to the creative
possibilities of sport.

The leaders of the German Democratic Republic, frustrated from
using the conventional diplomatic institutions, innovatingly and
successfully employed the international sports federations and most
especially the International Olympic Committee to acknowledge
that the small country (it has eighteen million people—that is, it
is one-third the size of Poland and one-fourth the size of the Federal Republic of Germany) had a right to its own flag, national
hymn, and independent national teams. In successive international
sports meets, the exquisitely prepared athletes served as nonbelli-
cose troops assuring the nation's territorial integrity and political
distinction.

Because the competition for attention may be so weak, sport
figures large in public and, consequently, spiritual life in East Germany. There the newspapers have little worth reading. The politically imposed journalism of orthodox Marxist rhetoric, paranoia
regarding the West, and relentless optimism regarding the regime
makes for deadly boring reading and so the newspapers are little
read. The separately published sports newspapers may have lots
of ersatz news, but the facts are verifiable and the tales of struggle
and triumph are lively and usually true.

As we know, in the capitalist countries sports journalists are
circumscribed by the lack of novelty to report and by stultifying
rhetorical conventions. The political and crime reporters have all
the fun. In East Germany politics are stultified and local crime is
not admitted to exist. The sports reporters have prestige and some
are even allowed to travel abroad.

It may be useful to look more closely at a central institution that
has advanced the earnestness and success of high-performance sport

THE LATER TWENTIETH CENTURY 267

not only in East Germany and in eastern Europe, but elsewhere. The *Deutsche Hochschule für Körperkultur* (German College for Body Culture—hereafter D.H.f.K.) in Leipzig is not original in concept. Much of the distinction of American collegiate and professional athletes in the first half of this century was due to the notorious American espousal of calculation, engineering, and long-term planning to attain verifiable, especially technical, accomplishments. For decades Americans were almost the only people to apply technology systematically to the desire to attain superior sports accomplishments in many varieties of athletic activites.

During the Weimar Republic the Germans had had a sports college in Berlin. But its self-assigned task was to promote mass-participation by training teachers for various school systems. The triumphs of the German athletes at the Berlin Olympics of 1936 are best attributed to an intense campaign—almost a Blitz—of recruitment, training, and psychological preparation.

The D.H.f.K., founded in 1952 while Leipzig was still in ruins, was methodical and took the long view. The institution grew to enormous size with its own 100,000-seat stadium (erected while almost all of the East German churches, libraries, and opera houses were rubble), boarding schools for pupils of all ages, lecture halls, research institutes and, of course, training facilities. There are now dormitories for thousands of athletes ranging in age from six to thirty. There are all sorts of fenced or otherwise secured experimental laboratories. The D.H.f.K. does indeed prepare many teachers of physical education, but it is not a "college" in the usual sense. It can be more correctly compared with something preparing a valuable product—like General Motors Proving Grounds in Detroit.

The Soviet Union trained some of the first German "sports scientists" (*Sportwissenschaftler*), but some Soviet trainers now complain that they are denied their socialist colleagues' findings concerning such things as ideal psychological profiles for specific types of high-performance athletes, new plastics for kayaks, the racing performance results of removing body hair from swimmers, and the long-term results on performance of amphetamines, anabolic steroids, birth control drugs, and testosterone.

The recruitment and isolation of East German athletes begins early. All four to six year olds are measured, sometimes X-rayed, and otherwise objectively examined and meticulously observed to single out such things as the optimal tennis shoulder, the gymnasts' thighs, or the platform diver's granite composure. The socialist German researchers have established norms (always subject to revision, of course) for these and thousands of other traits indicating superior athletic potential.

It is now essential for the automobile and computer manufacturers of France, West Germany, Japan, and the United States to defend themselves from industrial espionage. It is also essential for the world's great sporting nations, especially those in the socialist world, to protect themselves from sports espionage. There are sports spies who attempt to steal proven drug formulas or particularly effective workout routines. The sports academy as an institution has spread all over the world. In America, career athletes are still prepared in the large state universities and at a few private tennis, golf, or bowling camps. But even Luxembourg has a sports academy and it does not even have its own currency. In order for a nation to be a nation given today's prevailing and unquestioned concepts, it must have a supply of materiel incontrovertibly its own to put into its sports pages.

Ideological, purposeful sport on the new statist model had, by adapting the sports of the international Olympic program, taken on the *appearance* of Anglo-Saxon sport, but the purposeful underpinnings make it much different. That state supported and proclaimed sport has been so much envied and imitated is the result of its intimate association with aggressive and successful foreign policy. Even before the spectacular utility of Soviet and East German sport was apparent, these nations were sending as goodwill ambassadors, teams of athletes and coaches to the insecure nations of the so-called "Third World"—especially in Africa. It needs to be reemphsized here that to leaders who are eager to modernize, the appeal of modern sport is not emotionally superficial, but is based on an appreciation of the deeper content of modern sport. We can list a few of these appeals: Festively presented performances having no history within a developing country can foster the creation of national heroes as opposed to local or tribal ones. The concepts of the record and of long-term training declare and celebrate rational supra-local concepts of time and accomplishment. These are essential ideals for disciplined market production as opposed to local, subsistence economic activity which is extremely difficult to organize for purposes of taxation. Publicly and nationally touted sports contests compete with and destabilize tribal rituals which celebrate parochial mystery and independence.

Until the appearance on the world scene of large numbers of superior African athletes in the 1960s it was accepted as fact that blacks could not achieve distinction in distance running (as it still is assumed for swimming). An early outstanding sensation was the tall Ethiopian, Abebe Bikila, who won the Olympic marathon twice: barefoot in Rome in 1960 and shod in Tokyo in 1964. At the Olympic Games in Mexico in 1968 there were victors from Ethiopia, Tunisia, and from Kenya. The Kenyan Kipchoge Keino, victor in the 1500 meters in Mexico, was a winner in the 3000 meter steeplechase in Munich four years later. Keino and other Kenyan runners were in the sports pages thereafter. While generally strengthening black self-confidence everywhere, the superior Kenyans boosted their country's international prestige, diplomatic standing, and very likely its political stability as well. By the late 1970s many African states were recruiting and training natural athletes who subsequently became domestic and international heroes.

The prizes for which these athletes and the others they have inspired to struggle are valuable to many others besides themselves. The gambles are costly and risky, but somehow or other the international rules of amateurism must ostensibly be observed. The full-time, socially responsible athletes of Kenya or the Ivory Coast must pose as dilettantes. As the full-time and well-compensated Romanian gymnasts often are nominally army officers, and the full-time sprinters of the GDR are nominally machinists, the African track-and-field stars usually are nominally police officers or teachers in a police academy.

The trappings of modern sport have been useful to the new African states in other ideological ways. We have noted that mass sport is in its origins and by definition democratic, and the high-performance sports of the present are quintessentially meritocratic. South African *Apartheid*, an abomination to leaders in the

270 THE LATER TWENTIETH CENTURY

Third World, extends to participating in and watching sport in South Africa. Third world leaders, revolted by *Apartheid*, have been able to punish the white leaders of South Africa by keeping their teams from international sports festivals. This shame is deeply felt in South Africa and modern sport continues to serve as the cutting edge of the tentative erosion of *Apartheid* carried out by ideological and practical sportsmen. In the United States, idealistic modern sport has been employed for decades against institutionalized racism.

Since 1945, along with tourism, transistor radios, literacy teachers, and industrial salesmen, sportsmen, both administrators and performers, have served everywhere to delocalize and to modernize. In their aid to underdeveloped nations, the Americans have preferred to give or sell high-technology agriculture, public health advice, or military equipment. Smaller, but still wealthy nations have added to this sport help (German: *Sporthilfe*) in the form of touring exhibition teams, donations of training or spectating facilities, equipment, and what is often most welcomed: long-term loans of high-performance trainers.

African leaders have been especially grateful for sport help. In the 1970s Dr. Hastings Kamazu Banda, the "President for Life" of small and poor Malawi, encouraged help from not only the archrival two Germanys, but also from the USSR, France, England, and Israel. This assistance and the athletes so discovered probably emboldened Banda to send Malawi's first Olympic team to Munich in 1972. Perhaps so many novelties offered to the Malawian athletes confused them. They *looked* like athletes, but once on the scene in Munich, the team of 30 Malawians performed more modestly than the athletes of any other nation. A Malawian team has not appeared at the Olympics since. However, the longer term work of track-and-field coaches has produced superior athletes in many other countries. Such nations as Algeria, Cameroon, and the Ivory Coast have for some time been producing soccer teams of the very highest caliber. The Algerian national team was outstanding in the World Cup competition of 1982.

After stressing the increasing extent and growing earnestness of modern sport, it may be useful to focus on the critical recruits and trainees in this cultural endeavor. Everywhere, proven evidence of superior ability in accepted sports is a precious commodity. There were some pre-war precursors of the valuable, charismatic athlete of the present. Jack Dempsey earned well as a boxer and then ran a prosperous restaurant in New York named after himself. He was often there on Broadway to shake customers' hands. Joe Louis earned (but did not keep) a fortune. Max Schmeling, as his nation went to war, kept himself away from the fighting fronts and after the war manipulated himself into a lucrative Coca-Cola distributorship. With the ending of the war and the growing spending power of media audiences increasing to many millions and occasionally billions, this quaint protoera of sport heroism was ended.

"Pelé" (Edson Arantes do Nascimento, born 1940), a remarkably charming, tough, and adept soccer player, is one of the very few Brazilians of international renown (Carmen Miranda is another). His best years as a footballer were in the late 1960s. However, by attracting really enormous crowds of paying spectators, he earned for the promoters who managed him somewhat more than the $4.5 million they paid him to tour the United States in 1975. When asked to comment on the large sum, Pelé remarked, "I could have had that much money to play in many places. In Brazil, probably. But this is where I could do the most for soccer."*

Franz Beckenbauer's remarkable talents were carefully developed and then exercised at a rare degree of supremacy in the Federal Republic of Germany. His fame is so great that it extends far beyond the stadium. In addition to his rewards for his play, his agents are able to command for him splendid sums for his public appearances and for his widely publicized declarations that he favors some beers and automobiles over others. Most moralists would find it difficult to accept that he merits lifetime earnings that are several times those of any German civil servant (including the Chancellor or the President), artist, scientist, or teacher.

In the United States, professional golfers who have won substantial tournament prizes earn far more by posing for commercial photographers in name-brand clothing. Pro football players, on an average, earn more than Supreme Court justices and university presidents. Unionized baseball players of second or third rank earn much more than airline pilots who are also unionized and much

*Sports Illustrated. July 21, 1975, p. 49–52.

more than district attorneys and civil engineers who are not. The average salary of a professional basketball player in 1981 was over $200,000 a year. Gary Carter, a catcher for the Montreal Expos, earned over $2 million in the 1982 season. All this is known by almost everyone and tends to raise further the charisma of the star athlete and, consequently, to demean those equally disciplined, skilled individuals in responsible, socially constructive occupations. It does little to make the nonathletes feel better about themselves that the bosses of and providers for these athletes have reliable statistics showing that highly paid athletes usually earn their wages by attracting lucrative media audiences.

Athletes outside the capitalist orbit also expect exceptional rewards that are less spectacularly capitalistic, but which are notorious all the same. Soviet sport heroes are allowed to travel abroad and obtain large new apartments without long waits. East German Olympic medalists get formal public attention (almost no one else does), cash bonuses under the table, and sporty automobiles. Unlike capitalist athletes whose high earnings cease abruptly when their supremacy and, consequently, public appeal ceases, aging socialist athletes are kept in the public eye as patriotic heroes and enjoy rich state pensions comparable to those given to military officers.

I have mentioned a few of a larger number of stars who occupy positions for which there are many contestants. The notorious rewards obscure the sadness of the vastly more numerous candidates who fail—usually utterly. This deception for black Americans is socially retarding and for many no doubt tragic. A pathetically tiny number of black athletes (as well as popular musicians) earn lifelong adequate wages. Nevertheless, these heroes inspire large numbers of children to dedicate their lives to the attainment of supreme physical excellence and composure which nature and the apparatus for exploiting fame have confined to a very few. Youthful energy, precious years, whole lives are wasted.

The above observation about the popular deceptions inherent in sport inspiringly presented on television and on the sport pages can be extended to the intensifying earnestness in American intercollegiate sport. All but a few of the best private universities have been unable to resist pressures by alumni and state legislators to offer lavishly presented sports festivals featuring efficiently recruited and scrupulously prepared athletes who perform at them. The process that takes place at State U. is comparable to what takes place in Bulgaria or Kenya. Time, energy, and money are devoted to isolated athletes so they can scientifically train full time. Ever more in North America "student-athletes" are housed apart from other students, fed well, and trained to exhaustion. The American colleges and universities with the best teams do not expect their athletes to become liberally or professionally educated or even to graduate. Amateur rules and various intercollegiate watchdog organizations assure that the athletes who are able to manipulate cash subsidies for themselves are able to get only small ones. In many ways the athletic programs of some American universities have become academies for many thousands of deceived and isolated young men and women. Only a few dozen per year can expect lifetime wages as athletes. This is the most corrupt aspect of American higher education. The American establishment magazine, *Sports Illustrated*, even attacked this scandal, the nature of which is almost common knowledge. The edition of May 19, 1980 had on its cover, "Rip Off: The Shame of American Education: The Student-Athlete Hoax," which sums up the lead article in that issue.

If American sport were more subject to political influence, the "shame of American education" might be subject to a traditional American tendency aggressively to legalize justice. But almost all of American sport continues to evolve by the action of entrepreneurs seeking profit and power wherever they can be found. It is worth interjecting here the reminder that though supremely skilled athletes and record performances can occur in Belgium or New Zealand or Kenya or anywhere else, new sports never do. Innovations in sports broadcasting, sports showmanship, or sports coruption almost always appear first in the United States.

Americans, for example, are rather unencumbered if they wish to experiment with performance-enhancing drugs. To be sure, the socialist sports scientists have been exposed. For example at the Montreal Olympics in 1976, a journalist remarked to their coach that some teenaged girl swimmers from East Germany had unusually large shoulders and deep voices, indicating the administration of the performance-enhancing male hormone, testosterone. The coach replied, "They are here to swim, not sing!" (*"Die sollen swimmen, statt singen!"*) And a West German attempt to increase the buoyancy of male swimmers by pumping their large intestines full of air was unsuccessful due to the failure to devise a retainable cork. But the many experiments with drugs in Europe and especially in the Eastern bloc have as their object to improve performance *without damaging the athlete.* As of this writing in 1983 there was a steady tendency in Eastern Europe to use fewer drugs ever more carefully. Though illegal and reprehensible, amphetamines are used in dangerous amounts in American colleges and even in high schools. Not many coaches prescribe the anabolic steroids which can have devastating long-term physical effects. However, the steroids are employed by most American shot putters, weight lifters, and body builders by their own choice for purposes of individual success. The individual athlete just cannot be controlled. Painkillers further the maiming of many hockey players and professional football players. The 1973 novel (later a film) by Peter Gent about professional football players, *North Dallas Forty*, uses pain killers as fateful, destructive themes in the story. In America, it seems, the drug-ruined athlete is expendable.

Americans continue to innovate in employing various sports as consumer attractions in the telecommunications industry. And they continue to alter certain sports. We have already noted the scheduling of time-outs and other intervals in professional and collegiate football and basketball, for purposes of inserting television commercials. Among the masses traditional baseball continues to slip in favor of contact team sports, which are more technological, brutal, lively, and otherwise telegenic.

Americans retain a great deal of leadership. Nowhere else are sport rhetoric and sports cosmology more integrated into public life. Advertising employs athletes to proclaim the virtue of particular consumer products. Business executives inspire their underlings by emphasizing the "team," "team playing," "winning," establishing sales "records," being "number one," "rankings" with competitors and other teams. These images or other sports metaphors which almost all Americans have long accepted still sound ridiculous in most other languages. However, it does seem likely that such rhetoric and cosmology will probably work their way into the culture of other nations as sport becomes more deeply established.

English sport and then later, and more profoundly so, American sport were more or less haphazard, natural adaptions to their respective social conditions. And they remain so. As we stated in chapter 11, President Richard Nixon was a peculiarly intense sports fan. As a strong leader he attempted fundamental government changes that were almost *coups d'état*. However, Nixon never considered instituting any sort of a national sports policy. There is no American sports policy. Unlike many nations, the United States has no equivalent of a Minister of Sport. The bulk of financing for American international competitions continues to come from private sources.

Elsewhere in the world sport advances in public life with some comparable characteristics. Sport everywhere is seen as "modern" or as an essential and perhaps inseparable element in modern life and material progress. Almost always the effective promoters are politicians or intellectuals who are altruistic and ambitious for their people. Modern sport depends on and promotes such characteristics of modern life as a growing landless, literate population, money wages, cheap long-distance transportation, large cities, and a meritocratic, democratic ideology.

Some points regarding the *Guinness Book of Records* may be instructive here. The first edition contained largely sports statistics and was published in 1955 by the great Irish brewing house to settle arguments in Irish bars. It sold briskly. An American edition was published in 1956. Soon there were much expanded, yearly editions and it became the most frequently consulted (and stolen) reference book in all libraries where English was spoken. It is one of the biggest best-sellers of all time. The first translations were in French and then German. Subsequent translations have almost exactly followed the order that peoples have accepted dramatized, high-performance sport. By 1977 it had been translated fourteen times and had sold 27,000,000 copies. The point is that the order of the translations was the same as the chronological order in which masses of people have advocated a democratic ideology, urban life, and disciplined industrial labor.

The record as a talisman for modern life has extended far beyond the statistically specifiable aspects of sport. It is an appealing symbol of modernity. The original book of records became the foundation of a publishing empire. There are now more than twenty Guinness record books including *The Guinness Book of Superstunts and Staggering Statistics*, *The Guinness Book of Dazzling Endeavors*, and some books especially for children. In English the sports statistics are now mostly confined to *The Guinness Book of Sports Records* and the *Guinness Book of Sports Spectaculars* though there is also a *Guinness Book of Women's Sport Records*.

The record as a general concept is a spiritual monument to the well-established achievement principle. Each particular record adds testimony to the idea of progress—for each record is an improvement and, one assumes, will itself be improved *ad infinitum*. There are records for the mile run, records for high school girls in the 100 yard dash in South Carolina, and batting averages in Cuba. Each individual athlete may have his or her "personal best" and there are "track" and "meet" records. There are verified existing records for Volkswagen packing, flagpole sitting, parachute jumps in a 24-hour period, number of deaths in airplane crashes, and domino toppling. Frank Freer of Woolcott, New York in 1980 obtained a continuous peel, 1568½ inches long, from a single apple. We are approaching a two-hour marathon, but the record for the 100 meter dash may stay for a while at or very near 9.95 seconds (James Ray Hines, Mexico City, October 14, 1968).

The sports record, then is the most specifiable aspect of a complex and protean system of symbols, slogans, rituals and ideas that continues its conquest of the world. And this system, though dynamic and difficult to describe at any one time or place, continues to compete with older rituals and forms of play.

The forms of modern sport may be evolving, but sport is not evolving much outside of these forms. The extremely narrow Olympic gymnastics program has been exploited to produce exquisite performances that are almost literally incredible to observers. But the precisely prescribed four events for women and the six events for men have displaced almost all the various national gymnastics, the rope climb, and routines with dumbbells and other apparatus. One no longer sees the tug-of-war. Some few regional forms of European field sports (for example, the Scottish log toss) and wrestling are surviving thanks to the efforts of local antiquarians. These competitions and some others are regular features of annual festivals called "Highland Games" that date from the nineteenth century in certain parts of Canada and since 1956 in North Carolina near Grandfather Mountain. Modernization has taken its tolls of the immense variety of Chinese and Japanese ceremonial recreations. A great deal of original and fresh physical virtuosity can still be seen in the American, European, and Chinese traveling circuses. The summer of 1982 was the occasion for the first completed quadruple somersault from the aerial trapeze. But the circuses and their performers are decreasing in number.

The advance of modern sport might be compared to the advance of other aspects of modern life. Homogenization and progress have taken a toll in the variety of nature. In North America hundreds of plants and animals have become extinct; more are "endangered." Industrialization has had a devastating ecological impact on Europe and Japan. The Parthenon is eroding away. The tiger will probably not be saved in India; nor the gorilla or elephant in Africa. The modernization of the Philippines and the Amazon basin have wiped out hundreds of integrated human cultures. More will go. And so modern sport is just part of a pattern of advance that brings with it prosperity, increase in numbers, synchronization, civilization and, alas, destruction. Almost all the losses mentioned above have been noticed and well-documented. While apparently irrepressible, they have inspired some moral outrage. What is so peculiar about the conquest of sport is that it has so few critics—a subject that merits, and will receive, more attention below.

I have repeatedly claimed that the package of modern sport contains a system of public rituals, rhetoric, and symbols providing affirmative support for the forces making modern life possible. Modern sport contains intrinsic ideological messages favoring merit, democracy, and verifiable accomplishment. But of course, the realization of these last-named ideals has not worked out—either in modern life or in modern sport.

The disharmonies may not be obvious even where sport has evolved most freely, in the United States. Access to positions allowing the public display and recognition of the very best performances may be meritocratic; almost nothing else is. In North

America the very rich sail large boats, enjoy sport horses that they own but that are maintained by others, and fish, hunt, or ski with costly equipment in places that are time-consuming and dear to get to. The lower classes bowl, attend baseball games or horse races, or otherwise pay cash to enjoy facilities owned by the rich. Everybody, however, absorbs televised sport.

In much of the capitalist world one can continue to place a person socioeconomically by his or her participating and spectator sports. Large tracts of land in West Germany or Japan are far more expensive than they are in North America and so golf serves there as an emphatic indication of wealth and therefore high position. Everywhere soccer hooliganism requires and is indeed fostered by no possessions at all and so is a festive undertaking of male teenagers of the urban, unskilled working (or nonworking) class.

In the (newly) great sport nations in the Soviet orbit, sports performances and sports access have little to do with wealth. A great deal depends on merit and ambition. But still, an athlete's state-supported sports career can depend on his or her connections in the bureaucracy. Reliability and especially political reliability are crucial. A Comecon athlete suspected of disaffection will not be allowed to compete abroad because of the fear of defection—an abominable crime in the view of the party apparatus.

The socialist nations and many capitalist European nations publish statistics showing how very many of their people belong to sports clubs or otherwise indicate active interest in sport. But, except for male adolescents almost all over, nowhere in the world does a big proportion of any large defineable sector of a population actively, with muscle and sweat, participate in sport. Physically active recreation has always been and will remain a special taste. Of course, everywhere, much of the time almost everyone (but most especially mature males) watches televised sports or, minimally, reads the sports pages or listens to the radio.

What about the social critics and sport? The critics make much of the violence in sports. Some of them may actually be protesting that sport is not performing its civilizing function efficiently enough. Wars, street crime, and auto traffic are far more costly in suffering and cash. The worst victory riots in Columbus, Ohio or in Pittsburgh have resulted in some overturned cars and smashed plate glass. Drunken and vociferous Scottish soccer fans terrify the regular riders of the London Underground. Equivalent performances revolt the sensibilities of responsible citizens in Montevideo, Leningrad, and Nairobi. But it may be far more remarkable that so little property or personal damage occurs when disparate people assemble at truly enormous sports meetings such as the Maccabbi Games in Israel, the Pan American Games, the World Cup matches, and the Olympic Games.

What about crime and sport? Drugs, dishonest judges, violations of amateur regulations, and broken bodies may be consequences of the high monetary stakes in big-time capitalist sport. Large sums of money and an atmosphere of credulity in modern sport attract criminals. Gambling of any sort leads to efforts to fixed results. Here again, American *laissez faire* attitudes and all the money around provide fertility for the most interesting innovations. But crime in sport is not much different than crime elsewhere.

It is only to be expected that the pervasiveness of modern sport would provoke social critics. The sort of criticism being introduced here is not that sports-page man-chat about the performers and tactics that produced disappointing performances. Rather what is meant is the critical or moral examination of modern sport as a creative force in society. Almost everyone who has examined the problem of sport criticism (see the Bibliographical Essay) are struck by naïveté or paucity of the modern critiques of sport.

Simple critiques of sport are everywhere and common: too many people observe what they should be practicing. Sport has not led to the well-being of the masses. International sport has not led to the brotherhood of peoples. Interracial sport has not led to the attenuation of racism. High-performance athletes (contrary to the maxim *mens sana in corpore sano*), are overwhelmingly ordinary, dull people. The above faults in modern sport are not meant to be encompassed in a search for a social or moral critique of sport.

Although very many, perhaps most, twentieth-century social critics have included sport in their analyses of society (see the discussion of John Hoberman's brilliant survey cited in the Bibliographical Essay), few seem aware of what sport might be. In the great sports nations of Eastern socialist Europe, sport is intimately integrated into official political policy. Therefore sport, like the existing political situation, can only be praised, not examined, much less criticized. However, the orthodox Marxists do launch rather elementary polemics at the sports programs of their capitalist enemies for being so capitalistic. If there is a critic or a group of sports critics in the developing nations they have not made themselves known.

It is yet another indication of the naturalness of American sport (I hope my readers will allow me yet again to make this point) that a critique of American sport has been so feeble. Surely American sport is, among other things, disruptive of some good traditions, the preserver of some bad ones, vulgar, ruinous to some lives, a diversion from the earnestness of life, expensive, and morally equivocal. But few protest.

For a while in the late 1960s and the early 1970s, when almost all American institutions were under attack, there were a few attempts at analyzing and criticizing American sport. Jack Scott, a young physical education teacher published two books significantly entitled *Athletics for Athletes* (1969) and *The Athletic Revolution* (1971). He encouraged the publication of the candid memoirs of a couple of disaffected professional football players and track stars. Scott also inspired a few other exposés and polemics. Some of these publications employed neo-Marxist or anarchic rhetoric. But the complaints were rather specific and more or less as follows: Sport was owned by monopoly capitalists. Coaches were authoritarian. Athletes were misused and underpaid. American sport is best compared with the Roman circuses. The 1960s cultural upheavals of which Scott's criticism was a very minor part lost some of their impetus in the middle 1970s, and Jack Scott's career took other directons. American sports analysis once again became and remains overwhelmingly descriptive and approving.

There has been one place where there have regularly been intelligent, skeptical people who have posed the statement and asked the question, "Sport must mean something. What?" As was stated in chapter 8, sport has always been subject to critical analysis in Germany. Whole portions of this book, including much of this chapter, are indebted to German scholarship and criticism.

There were plenty of alert, young social critics in Germany when the expensive and disruptive preparations began for the 1972 Olympics in Munich. The great freedom of intellectual life in West Germany and its corresponding ease of publication encouraged the presentation of a stimulating analysis of modern sport. Often these critiques are put in the jargon of academic social science and sometimes that of exhortatory revolutionary optimism. The rather deterministic philosophical anthropology of neo-Marxism limits the imagination of a few of these critics and almost all of these young and well-educated critics focus rather narrowly on a historical analysis of German sport (not excluding a retrospective analysis of Nazi sport). However, their Marxism does not prevent them from being equally critical of the hothouse flowers of statist sport in East Germany. In more recent years and most particularly in the writing of the most brilliant analyst of them all, Henning Eichberg, the critique of modern sport is part of a pro-ecology, populist movement whose leaders call themselves "the Greens" (*die Grünen*). The German tradition of sports analysis gets ever richer. The rest of the world stays in unnecessary ignorance because these works remain untranslated.

Elsewhere sport is becoming less of an academic's or an intellectual's taboo. For a few intellectuals, at least, sport is not completely a refuge from a problematic world where all the other cultural institutions and manifestations are subject to analysis. Sport, too, can be examined, perhaps explained and understood. There are now a few careful English historians who are investigating the origins of sport in the country where it all began. There are some American psychologists who are illuminating significant small problems regarding the individual athlete's motivations and the social forces in a team. The financing of big time sport is better understood than ever before. The victimization of the bulk of American collegiate athletes is ever less of a secret. There are a couple of solid, warts-and-all biographies of American boxers and of Babe Ruth. Allen Guttmann's solid biography of Avery Brundage has recently appeared. At least some aspects of the vast, protean spectacle of modern sport are being caught and held for careful examination. In the future we will know more about what is going on.

[14]

JOYOUS SPORT,
BEAUTIFUL SPORT

At the limits of their power, six strong young men approach the string along the finish line. The swiftest of them breaks the cord, detonating the release of joyous empathy among the thousands in the stadium. This massed satisfaction raises yet further the ecstatic self-satisfaction of the victor. His sweaty face cracks with happiness and he shouts joyously, adding to the tumult. He runs about in tight circles as the losers—envious of his accomplishment—respectfully slap his back. They are noble. They tried as hard as he did. Next time one of them may produce the minute piece of extra power to certify supremacy. They all participated in one of the fine, festive moments that is a well-observed sports victory.

This is an accurate if abstract portrayal of the climax of a blessedly frequent ritual that characterizes and reinforces many distinct aspects of modern life. Such a stirring piece of sport theater need not be confined to a foot race, but could just as well be a moment during an international competition for figure skaters in Ottawa or a local basketball tournament in a suburb of Montevideo. Comparable, theatrically staged sports meets are high points of our popular culture. They are joyous celebrations of democratic opportunity, bureaucratic organization, verifiable supremacy, and physical beauty. Sports contests now take place thousands of times a day. Such moments are best planned for and most observed where modern industrial society has been most wholeheartedly accepted—where social mobility based on merit is most assured, where wealth is most evenly distributed, where specialized production and regular work are most efficiently organized and least criticized.

It is jaundiced and reprehensible to stress too much those dark, inefficient, opportunistic, aspects of sport that were the topics of the previous chapter. The integration (I use the word literally to mean "integral" that is, an indispensable, essential part of the whole) of sport in modern life is also liberating, inspiring, beautiful, and possibly morally just. Here I hope to establish the dynamic creativity lying within sport.

Modern sport encourages and demonstrates the democratic achievement principle. Indeed it is now incontestible (as it never was before our time) that measurable, superior accomplishment (and nothing else) ought to be the basis of material reward. It is a principle of democratic societies that opportunities to strive for rewards should be equally accessible to each person at birth. The idea that results should be apportioned on the basis of equal access to opportunity is as natural to us as were such previous notions as the inevitability of slavery for the majority of persons and that compensations were to be had in heaven and only there for moral earnestness. Modern sport's ideology supports democracy, meritocracy, and the rational application of time, energy, and money. Sport industry, sport art, sport myth, and sport ritual are almost inseparably integrated into our public and spiritual lives.

Another brief treatment of the sports record and the sports hero may be in order here. As we observed in chapter 7, the sports record had its origin in English social conditions in the eighteenth century. The sports record came to maturity there in the later nineteenth century whereupon Americans refined and elaborated it. In chapter 13 in a discussion of the *Guinness Book of Records*, I offered some circumstantial evidence for the correlation and perhaps mutual dependence of the progress of the sports record and the advance of democratic ideology and industrialism—in other words, modern life.

Before the acceptance of standardized, precisely measurable, abstract accomplishment that was accessible to all and theatrically or publicly performed apart from the world of work, there were heroes such as the determined pedestrian "Captain" Barclay, or the strongman "Sandow." These early names of sport's protohistory are curious figures. Their renown while living was perhaps due more to the fact that they were actors and conceivably even freaks who were unselfconscious enough to perform dramatically (but not precisely—or measurably) before large numbers of noncognescenti. They were, then, more like the jugglers and rabbit-out-of-a-hat performers who have always existed. Records (and, I claim, sports heroes, as well) in our sense, were only possible with the demand for and development of nonindustrial metering devices for distance such as the measuring wheel and the stopwatch. We date formal track-and-field records from the Oxford–Cambridge track meet of 1863. In the decades before 1890, there were famous wrestlers, cricketers, baseball players, archers, weightlifters, yachtsmen, and oarsmen who merited journalistic attention and some popular respect. However, a sports hero who fits the modern mold perfectly was Charlie Murphy, the bicyclist discussed in chapter 9 who first pedaled his wheeled steed at the pace of sixty miles an hour on June 30, 1899.

At the time, the recently developed "safety" bicycle was, for the millions able to afford it, one of the most liberating (in the sense of convention-destroying) inventions yet experienced. It affected women's costumes, sexual morality, and by extending commuting distances the look of large cities. Charlie Murphy, a professional athlete, had employed one of these machines to seize the holy grail of the epoch—the mile-a-minute. He later teamed up with "Major" Taylor, a remarkably handsome black cyclist and one of the first internationally famous athletes of his race, to form a vaudeville act. Both also performed on the many recently built competition cycling tracks in America, Europe, and Australia. But Murphy's special fame (which declined as the charisma of the fine bicycle was overwhelmed by that of the racing automobile) was due to a verifiable, repeatable and—this is the crucial point—*im-*

provable accomplishment of a standard distance in a record period of time. Now Charlie Murphy's salient accomplishment, if it had been stageable in one of the new stadiums of the time, might have inspired rapturous approbation on the spot. The essence of the verified event was that it established a new frontier for a widely recognized distance for an appealingly stated period of time. This mile-a-minute separated ordinary humans from supreme (and inspiring) super-accomplishers. In fact, Murphy's accomplishment has been improved upon. At this writing, cyclists are attempting to cycle a mile-a-minute *without* a windbreak. The "state-of-the-art" machines are enclosed in lightweight aerodynamic pods.

Subsequent remarkable records—Babe Ruth's 60 home runs in 1927, Kitei Son's first sub 2:30 Marathon in Berlin in 1936, Bob Beamon's long jump of over 29 feet in Mexico in 1968—were all accomplished before well-prepared throngs (we envy them their presence at a "historic" event) in theatrical settings. On the other hand, Roger Bannister, a big New Zealander, ran the first sub-four-minute mile at the Iffley Road Track at Oxford on May 6, 1954. There were few spectators; but even if there had been 100,000 on hand, the verifiable distance on the track and the verified positions of the hands on stopwatches were the essential witnesses to this modern "heroic" accomplishment.

The accomplishments of Charlie Murphy, Babe Ruth, Kitei Son, Bob Beamon, Roger Bannister, and some hundreds of others are ritually heroic and have been absorbed into the mythology of dynamic, democratic life.

There was a curious attempt in 1935 on the part of the Soviets to mythologize and make heroic something that does not lend itself to ritualization: hard work. Early in 1935, Alexei Stakhanov, a 22-year-old coal miner trained in a technical institute, decided to apply intelligence and exceptional energy to the task of removing coal from underground seams. With the help of some "proppers," he quickly doubled the daily norm and then set "records": 100 tons in a day; 200 tons; 250. A maximum of 310 tons was moved by an emulating competitor, Artukhoff, who worked with three proppers. Without doubting the veracity of these accomplishments, we know that these were the occasions for major campaigns of the Ministry of Propaganda. The Soviets invented

"Stankhanovism" and ceremoniously awarded medals and cash bonuses to "Stakhanovites" in other branches of work that also lent themselves to analagously precise measurement and new records. Similarly (if less precisely), the Maoist Chinese in 1964 elevated to heroic stature a modest worker, a certain Lei Feng, who claimed that in the progressive, political transformations in which he was playing a part, he wished only to be considered a "rust-proof screw" of the revolution. (In the debunking period of 1976–77 the whole campaign was exposed as a set-up by idealogues—but no matter.)

Despite the massive efforts to make inspirational heroes of Alexei Stakhanov and Lei Feng, in the end the movements were shrugged off by socialist citizens and snickered at abroad. After 1945, Joseph Stalin and his successors energetically promoted training for the high-performance games and sports then internationally practiced. These had no organic history outside of the Anglo-Saxon world. Like the accomplishments of Stakhanov, sports performances were to be officially praised as inspirations for long-term planning and high-performance work. Similarly, both domestically and internationally, the Chinese have supported high-performance ping-pong and other sports. No one, anywhere, snickers at Valeri Borzov, the fastest sprinter at the Olympic Games of 1972 and 1976. Sports heroes such as the Romanian gymnast Nadia Comaneci and the big teenage female swimmers of East Germany, all of whom are state supported and state advertised, are heroic upholders of the democratic accomplishment principle the world over. The accomplishments of all these high-performance athletes, and those representatives of Western capitalism as well, are intrinsically worthless. As reinforcements of the modern status quo—wherever it is—these sports heroes and their performances are immensely valuable—perhaps irreplaceable.

This leads us to the claimed role of competitive sport in promoting international harmony. That modern high-performance sport is often politically inspired and politically committed goes without saying. No one accepts without crossing his fingers the official myth that the Olympic Games take place on politically hygienic ground. But even many pessimists admit that international tensions may be defused or at the very least that confrontations are delayed by the mutual pitting of national finances, national bureaucracies, national communications networks at the Olympic Games or at the various World Cup competitions. These and thousands of less tensely viewed games or meets are intense experiences for athletes and trainers. But perhaps vastly more important, spectators on the spot or spectators as media recipients are led to understand the universality of pain in effort, fear before trials, disappointment at defeat, and joy at triumph. Surely international aggression was *not* promoted by the Germans' admiration of Jesse Owens in 1936 or by the enduring impression made by Olga Korbut when, watched by television cameras, she wept at the Olympic Games of 1972 in Munich. The world view of American television watchers must surely be broadened by the sights of the superior soccer techniques of Hans Beckenbauer and Pelé.

Democratic, accomplishment-oriented, cosmopolitan sport (but more specifically the bureaucrats of sport who are held by its ideology) can be an instrument for imposing aspects of liberal morality on nations whose internal policies do not harmonize with these qualities. Because of the sanctions imposed by international sports bodies, the racist leaders of South Africa have been exposed to additional shame. As in America much earlier, some integration is underway in South African sport. The ideology of modern sport appears to be on a higher moral level than that of corporate directors and ministers of foreign affairs.

As well as being publicly useful, high-performance, theatricalized sport can be ideologically inspiring. Athletes—whether well-observed or not—celebrate, ritually reinforce, and make vividly concrete an immensely consequential creation of the eighteenth-century philosophers which has gained force since then. The idea of progress has until rather recent times been an assumption or an inspiration to very few. Traditional elitists, authoritarians, and cultural pessimists at all times would have us freeze the social system and the technology that supports it. They have claimed that mankind and the universe are constants not to be tampered with, that progress as most of us see it is not progress at all. The pessimists about human or social improvability point to the likelihood of an atomic holocaust or ecological disasters already underway. Sport metaphorically refutes them. Sports participation and the joy it brings are everywhere increasing. Records continue to improve. Perhaps they are indefinitely improvable. The sports historian can find evidence that the 2:30 Marathon was once considered a "natural" limit as were such frontiers of accomplishment as the four-minute mile and the fourteen-foot pole vault.

Sports participation is now very widely spread and spectator devotion if well-mannered is almost universally praised. The integration of sport has taken place so smoothly in industrial-professional, mobile, modern society that sport has not needed and consequently has not found many historians, careful analysts, or dispassionate critics.

If sport has been progressive—an enrichment or an inspiration in modern society—can we push the case of moderate advocacy yet further? What has sport had to do with the advancement (or lack of it) of high culture? The problem so posed will call for an unusual survey of the fine arts.

In the visual arts, certain long-existing play and ritual activities we now generously and retrospectively sum up with the word "sport" have consistently provided themes for pictorial representation. The Mayans, Aztecs, and Incas left many pictures of wrestlers and ball players on their pottery and stone carvings. Persian miniaturists devoted predictably exquisite attention to the maneuvers of polo players. The pre-Meiji Japanese artists produced large editions of wood block prints of archers and the practitioners of some of their finely differentiated martial arts. Some large prints of Sumo wrestlers even contain indications of the bobbing heads of an enthusiastic, critical audience. The artistic conventions governing these pictures of performing athletes and of attentive onlookers are no different than those for other topics we could not call "sports" subjects. Similarly, in the pre-contemporary, Western tradition, pictures of Dutch ice skaters, German fencers, French tennis players, or the first American baseball players, the conventions in pictorial art are not distinguished from other types of instructional illustrations, genre pictures, or pretty scenes.

In self-conscious "fine" European art since the Renaissance in Italy, some powerful painters and sculptors established a momentum in which their painted scenes or sculpted figures were not merely pretty pictures or decorative objects, but were endowed by the producers, patrons, and subsequent collectors with semi-sacred qualities. The status of certain art objects was henceforth raised above that of merely precious or pretty things. Such titans as Michelangelo, Raphael, and others of their times enthusiastically employed as a theme the athletic physique which, it was assumed, had already been established as an ideal by the Hellenistic sculptors. Naked, massive sprinters and wrestlers once again were established as the ideal types of symbolic depictions of power and nobility. Bernini, Canova, and indeed most European artists of major rank retained the convention of heroic (and athletic) nudity throughout the nineteenth century. Many of the innovative painters of the last century painted male models of classically heroic proportions. However, some, such as Theodore Géricault or Gustave Courbet, painted athletes so devoid of heroic posture or trappings that they look like mere chunks of living meat softened perhaps by some pity.

The Impressionists such as Edouard Manet, Claude Monet, Pierre Auguste Renoir, and their followers expanded the domain that the critical consensus would consider fine art. Their obsessions with natural light and natural movement led many of them to paint quickly pictures of sport sailboats, rowers, and dilletante tennis players in sunlight. Very likely the immensely skilled and daring Edgar Degas (1834–1917) was challenged by racehorses and jockeys just as he was by ballet dancers. The motions of all of these appealing subjects are difficult to preserve attractively in painted pictures. Only a superb artist can do it. Degas succeeded very well. However, it would be difficult to call any one of these innovators at any stage in their careers a "sports" artist.

Is there such a thing as sports art? By the middle of the eighteenth century, some English painters such as George Stubbs (1724–1806) were already endowing the thoroughbred horse with an aura of magic splendor. That the taste for proto-modern sports and games was widely based and particularly English is suggested (perhaps proved) by the mass production between 1750 and 1850 of sporting prints which were meant to be framed as decorations for middle-class houses. The finest English prints were aquatinted, copper engravings. They were complicated conceptions of sport sailboat races, hunts by the gentry, derbies attended by thousands, and speeding scull races. The prints were also sold abroad. Fashionable merchants in St. Petersburg, Hamburg, or Buenos Aires might have these prints nicely framed for hanging in their studies, but the sports themselves remained for decades almost exclusively English. The less expensive prints by Thomas Rowlandson and others of boxing matches, smock races for women, or village football depicted specifically English pastimes that were not upper-class and so they remained in England.

American sporting art (if it can be ennobled by such usage) like the sports it depicted was at first imitative. However, American sport pictures became even more so a commercial response to a popular demand. American sporting prints of famous horses, steamboat races, and collegiate rowers were less carefully exe-cuted, and were published in larger, cheaper editions. We leave the fine arts and enter the area of popular culture when we discuss much of the objects created for commerce and inspired by Amer-ican sport. Popular items in the late nineteenth and early twen-tieth centuries were the highly colored portraits of baseball players first packed with cigarettes and later with slabs of bubblegum.

Europeans, and most particularly Frenchmen, had since the early nineteenth century been accustomed to rewarding public achieve-ment with medals of honor and certificates of merit provided by the state. Americans have long viewed sports participation and es-pecially sports distinction as publicly meritorious. Americans pi-oneered in the development and iconography of ephemeral sports trophy art. Many American families with a history of several gen-erations have attics holding dozens of these cheaply plated statues mounted on walnut or black plastic bases.

A few Americans stand out as makers of innovative sporting art. In the nineteenth century, in America as in Europe, the work of energetic persons acknowledged by critical opinion as pioneering artists was ever more endowed with near sacred status. Successful innovators could claim and receive homage (especially posthu-mously) as spiritual titans. Thomas Eakins (1844–1916) was one of the first American artists of established reputation to give dra-matic dignity and pathetic intensity to athletes. He did many fine paintings of rowers (*Max Schmitt in a Single Scull*, 1871), boxers

(*Salutat*, 1898) and wrestlers. Eakins was an innovating photographer of athletes, also. Another American, Eadweard Muybridge (1830–1904) was the first to attempt to analyze athletes in motion by means of his stop-action photographers. Later American painters were among the few modern masters who exalted boxers, baseball players, and sports audiences by making them the subject of ambitious oil paintings.

Even now, however, as this is written, it would be difficult to assemble an exhibition of first-rate modern painting, graphics, or sculpture all dealing with sport. Henri de Toulouse-Lautrec did some clever posters for bicycle manufacturers, but the drawing of the machines was, for him, very bad. Henri "Le douanier" Rousseau (1844–1910) painted an amusing picture of some soccer players. The German expressionists Max Liebermann (1847–1935) and Ernst Kirchner (1880–1938) tossed off some oil sketches of horse races and football games. Max Beckmann (1884–1950) painted a nice *"Rugby Player."* Oskar Schlemmer (1888–1943) did some cubistic paintings and drawings of static, muscular males which he called "athletes." An exhibition of the works of these artists that had sporting subjects would be nice, but it would not contain their best work.

The only European in the innovating modern tradition to analyze sport with some devotion is the Frenchman Robert Delaunay (1885–1941). In the 1920s, Delaunay painted some partly representational, brightly colored canvases preserving his impressions of the clashing uniformed players at a football game. These canvases and his pictures of some runners and boxers are successful attempts to see sport as something distinct, enchanting, and worthy of artistic transmutation.

It may be that artists of great ability and ambition have ignored sport as too common and too new for their attention; or it may be the case that fine original art is ipso facto expensive art which can be purchased only by those classes among whom sport (excepting possibly yachting and horse racing) is not to be encompassed in their view of high culture. The triumph of nonfigurative art in the European and American academies and in our high society has certainly hindered the development of sporting art. As subject matter, modern athletes, their equipment, festivities, and fans are too ordinary, too corporeal, and perhaps therefore too difficult or too uneconomic to preserve or interpret.

The upper-class biases favoring expensive, nonfigurative forms in our century have worked yet more effectively against the development of modern sports sculpture. Perhaps, paradoxically, the lingering classical tradition has been a hindrance, also. Well into the twentieth century, monumental sculptures of George Washington required that he be shown with the torso of a Hellenistic athlete. Auguste Rodin, whose accomplishments required that all who followed him use new types of surfaces in their marbles or bronzes, took as his subjects already established human passions and brutalities. His themes were not modern. That one of his seated, roughly molded small bronzes is called an "athlete" is merely incidental. An often cited and exhibited early example (1886) of three runners at a finish line by Alfred Boucher (1850–1934) turns out to be an allegory of the precariousness of human endeavor. Franz von Stuck's *Athlete* of 1889 (edited in bronze after 1906) is impressive, but is really a slick and cynical studio piece characteristic of that Munich society prince.

The French *animalier* sculptors such as Antoine Baryé (1795–1875) and Pierre-Jules Mène (1810–1879) and their followers made meticulous, energetic small bronzes of hunting dogs and race horses. The occasional nineteenth-century and early-twentieth-century sculpted representations of rowers, cricketers, football players, and runners are usually suggestive of that naïve clumsiness that still characterizes the small industry of sports trophy art.

The only sculptor of originality and conviction to produce an *ouevre* of sports art was the Canadian Robert Tait MacKenzie (1867–1938). Originally a physician specializing in the physiology of exercise, MacKenzie was enchanted by the euphoric grace of the ice skater, the physical wizardry of the pole vaulter under full power, and the agony of the finishing long distance runner. He calculated the mean measurements of hundreds of college athletes to sculpt a modern ideal of male beauty. In MacKenzie's reliefs and bronzes one rejoices both esthetically and sympathetically in the intensity of an athlete's supreme moments. This Canadian artist proved again and again that it can be be done.

Some isolated instances of sports sculpture deserve mention. Almost all are German. Max Schmelling's super masculinity and unaffected charm provided Berlin café society with a diversion in the late 1920s and so some chic artists such as Georg Grosz painted him and Ernesto di Fiori and Rudolph Belling sculpted him in boxing trunks with his mitts up. The sculptress Renée Sintenis (1888–1965) is mostly famed for her amusing bronzes of young animals. Her famous bronze of Paavo Nurmi (ca. 1930) proved that sport art is readily capable of accomplishment. The statue is anatomically incorrect. A distance runner's kicking foot is never that far from the ground. Still, the piece does communicate respect for that early hero of spiritual and physical power.

Commissioned sculptors produced tons of colossal marble statues of athletes for the Olympic Games of 1932 in Los Angeles, those of 1936 in Berlin and those of 1960 in Rome. From these clumsy errors—as from the thinly gilded bowlers, golfers, and tennis players that occupy the summits of hastily manufactured sports trophies—we turn away in embarrassment.

Pierre de Coubertin, the ideologue and promoter of the modern Olympic Games, had long hoped that the fine arts would be integrated into high-performance, international sports festivals. At last, there were international art competitions that were part of the Olympic Games of 1928, 1936, and 1948. For these competitions, artists everywhere produced hundreds of two or three dimensional, male and female gymnasts, sulkey drivers, football players, divers, cyclists and others. During these esthetically inclusive Olympic competitions, the writers for the sports pages ignored the art, and the art critics—as always—ignored what was not either already proven or chicly avant garde and therefore saleable. Art at the Olympic Games won ribbons, but we can assume that the best as well as the not so good things are all languishing the world over in the store rooms of provincial art museums.

Sports architecture is original, various, and numerous. With significant exceptions, the esthetic *éclat* is accidental. The architecture typically provides practical solutions for simple problems. Training or competing athletes need dependable playing surfaces, unimpeded spaces, and protection from disagreeable weather. One response was the modern "gymnasium" which evolved in nineteenth-century America after inspiration by the gymnastic programs of the nineteenth-century Germans and Swedes. Competition swimming and diving pose different technical problems that find ever more adequate solutions thanks to efforts of technically sophisticated plumbing engineers.

The modern stadium is more complex. Since stadiums encompass inspiring public activities viewed by vast concourses of taxpayers, they lend themselves to monumental treatment. A maximum number of spectators must be able to move quickly to—but more importantly from—their seats. Standing will not do. They must be as close as possible to the focus of action, for games that demand a large piece of usually urban (and therefore expensive) area. Here Americans have been the technical leaders. The huge football stadiums built around the turn of the century for Harvard and Yale and soon afterward for the "Big Ten" universities, as well as the stands surrounding the baseball diamonds of league teams, established norms in effect ever since.

Until heavy political wagering became built into Olympic Games after 1936, almost all sports buildings were technical responses to the need for performance and for sympathetic observation by the largest possible assemblages of fixed spectators. It can be noted here that modern sporting competitions have been the occasions for some of the largest public assemblies since the late Roman Empire. Tennis courts, football fields, natatoriums, more or less enveloped the games being played. (On the other hand, for decades the rules of basketball adapted to the gymnasiums at hand.) The architectural complex provided for the well-organized Olympic Games of 1912 in Stockholm were rather ordinary (according to the standards of the time) contiguous facilities. Their modern function was hidden by using the bricks, battlements, and crenellations of Nordic fortresses.

On the other hand, the *Reichssportsfeld* for the Berlin Games of 1936 was intended from the beginning to be not merely efficient, but also a well-publicized element in the propaganda for the new order. Then, as now, this most ambitious *completed* complex of Nazi architecture is both usable and esthetically as well as monumentally impressive.

After the war, there were more exciting Olympic complexes that were also intended to declare the cultural integrity and great wealth of their national sponsors. Various political leaders have assumed that international prestige can be purchased at the Olympic Games and have opened wide their treasuries for daring architects. Reinforced concrete may be the most challenging building material for use by original architects in our century. The possibilities of thin-shell concrete were well realized by the stadiums and various sporting halls designed by Luigi Nervi for the Rome Olympics of 1960 and also by Kenzo Tange's two main stadiums for the Tokyo Olympics of 1964. The grandiose swoops of acres of plastic tenting spanned over the main complex of the Munich Olympics of 1972 were impressive, playful, and outrageously expensive. The Benisch firm provided far more than an engineering solution to a practical problem. All of these radically innovative and splendid buildings were successful attempts to impress an international audience with the taste, genius, technology, determination and, especially, wealth of the modern nation-states which so demonstratively offered them up.

The awe-inspiring, multi-purpose "Astrodome" and "Superdome" erected, respectively, in Houston and New Orleans are in another category. These multi-purpose, megastructures devoted to entertainment and celebration emphatically meet some of the practical (dare one suggest "spiritual"?) needs of our time. As such they may be comparable to the Colosseum of Imperial Rome, the cathedrals of medieval Europe, and the houses of parliament and banks of the previous century. These computer-designed, computer-operated monuments to profit-oriented, high-performance, theatrically presented sport are some marvels of our epoch.

So at least one traditional art form, architecture, when inspired by and applied to sport, has found generous patrons, daring practitioners, and enthusiastic general approbation. Might comparable claims be made for literature? Now it is true that a vast number of words are written and published daily that describe or deal with sport. The most cursory survey of the lines in our daily newspapers and the sports magazines in our newsstands emphatically show us this. Since the first publication in 1857 of Thomas Hughes' *Tom Brown's School Days*, there has been a great deal of widely welcomed literature stressing that sports training and teamwork on the playing fields have built, respectively, good bodies and good characters. Every modern language has brought forth escape literature with wholesome sports heroes who are supposed to inspire hard work and patience in awaiting luck. The oldest and most numerous of the genre is the American baseball novel.

Baseball deserves further attention here, for in addition to its many trivializers, it is the only sport anywhere which has attracted writers acknowledged to be major artists. There are at least four ambitious American baseball novels: Bernard Malamud's *The Natural* (1952), Mark Harris' *Bang the Drum Slowly* (1956), Robert Coover's *The Universal Baseball Association, Inc., J. Henry Waugh, Prop.* (1968), Phillip Roth's *The Great American Novel* (1973). All of these were written by mature, innovating artists and all employ baseball's established rituals and myths. In the earliest and most richly symbolic of these, Malamud's *Natural*, Roy Hobbes, the nearly invincible pitcher, is a reincarnation of King Arthur. His bat, "Wonderboy," is discovered in a tree. The novel has classic conflicts of good and evil, fate, and free will. Malamud has masterfully, perhaps magically, combined the myths of big league baseball with the venerable forms of the legends of the Holy Grail— which in this case is a World Series victory. This richly symbolic American epic is, nevertheless, fast-paced, funny, and tragic. Its stature grows. Why is it almost alone?

It is also worth noting here that baseball is also the only sport anywhere to have attracted any competent historians (Harold Seymour and David Q. Voigt), some good biographers (who, however, have not gotten beyond the subject, admittedly heroic and tragic, of Babe Ruth), and some analytical essayists of literary refinement and broad culture (for example, Roger Angell, *The Summer Game*, 1972). Baseball was the topic for a successful Broadway musical, *Damn Yankees*, which opened in October 1955, ran for 1119 performances and then was the basis for a movie in 1958.

Here and there one finds that certain writers acknowledged as important have written on sport. Antoine de Saint Exupéry and Henry de Montherlant occasionally wrote about athletes and their contests. Wilfred Sheed and Norman Mailer have written charming if ironic tributes to Muhammad Ali. Thomas Mann's amusing short story of 1911, "The Fight Between Jappe and Do Escobar," is about an impromptu boxing match at a North Sea resort. It is filled with contempt for all parties connected with the affair. Robert Musil, the great Viennese writer, who was devoted to physical fitness, wrote some short pieces about his own sports, tennis and rope jumping, but they are filled with his characteristic, apologetic self-mockery. All of these items are occasional pieces not fitting into the body of work of these writers.

There may be some modern sport poetry that is more than mere versification. But it has not been noticed by me or by critical anthologists. An exception may be surfing poetry. Surfing poetry seems glorious and original to this writer, but since I have never before seen it authoritatively praised, my confidence withers and I will drop the case in this survey.

With the significant exceptions of large-scale architecture, the accepted art forms have, as yet, only occasionally been enriched by or contributed to modern sport, even though artists such as R. Tait MacKenzie and Bernard Malamud have proven that opportunities are readily available. However, outside the traditional forms, the enormous appetite of the world's masses at every level of society have provided opportunities for innovation in several varieties of human endeavor that we may call "sports festivity," but that could perhaps be thought of as mass participation sports theater. The great variety of staged sports events are still too much in flux to consider them as formal or institutionalized. They are the visible efforts of ideologues and impressarios to give comprehensible structure, dramatic intensity, rhythmic continuity, esthetic focus, symbolic meaning, and ritualistic assurance to modern sport.

We recall that Pierre de Coubertin felt from the outset that modern sport (which he assumed was an unalloyed good thing) was naturally appealing only to upper-class Anglo-Saxon males. The rest of the universe had to be "seduced" (he used that word) by means of parades, music, oratory, flags—in short the traditional trappings of patriotic civic festivity. Some of the ceremonies subsequently adopted by the Olympic Games may have precursors in the ceremonies invented by the German turners and the Scandinavian gymnasts whose larger assemblies were always presented with slogans, songs, and banners in order to deepen the devotion of the comrades to each other and to the fatherland. During his tours of America in the 1890s, Coubertin observed the haphazardly designed paraphernalia of collegiate football: the school colors, mascots, scoreboards, and marching bands. The impresarios of sports festivity have all been tolerant, opportunistic eclectics.

In any case, it may have always been known, if not stated outright, that games and competitions that evolve solely out of the players' or competitors' experience (such as long distance running or squash) are not appealing to a broad (or nonparticipating) audience. The organizers of Spanish bull fights (and their precursors since Minoan times) have always known this. Who wants to see an animal merely killed? It must be prolonged, predictably ceremonialized. The innings of cricket, the halves of a soccer game, the quarters of a basketball game are like the acts of a play or the intervals of a socially affirmative ritual. Games with expected intervals of tension and release lend themselves to festive (that is intrinsically irrelevant as far as sport is concerned) ornamentation and slow anticipatable rhythms to heighten dramatic intensity.

The very newness of sport and the obstinate aloofness of traditional intellectuals have permitted shallow publicists to supply and evolve the iconography of various opening ceremonies, oaths, marchings in and out, and assorted other entertainments. Carl Diem simply invented the now "traditional" Olympic torch run for the Games of 1936. The symbolic binding of the Games of antiquity and those of the present is reassuring, enjoyable, and bogus. I, who went to the Olympic Games of 1972 quite purposely as a cynical sports critic, recall my deep, near mystical transports which I experienced during the long and varied opening ceremonies at that magnificent stadium on a cool sunny afternoon in August 1972. I subsequently learned that everyone on the site felt comparable, nearly ecstatic, emotions. The obvious (though we deny it) silliness of the halftime ceremonies at American professional football games assuredly heightens the pleasure of the spectators. Clearly, festivities need not be rooted in tradition or even well done in order to be satisfying. Lots of room for further creativity here.

The most original and still far from exhausted art of the twentieth century is the cinema. One stunning and very early exception prevents one from deploring the distance between the cineastes and sport. This monument, as we have seen, is Leni Riefenstahl's *Olympia* of the Berlin Games of 1936. The film was not a "documentary" as she insisted after the war, but an artistic contrivance from its earliest conception to the final editing. Certainly Riefenstahl's platform diving sequence is one of the supreme artistic accomplishments ever.

Another is the stunningly beautiful (if uneven) collective work by eight international directors done at the 1972 Olympics and titled *Visions of Eight*. Yet another is the technically accomplished, sentimental tale of British athletes at the 1924 Olympics in *Chariots of Fire* (1981).

Here again I must refer to the independent, almost rootless originality of the surfers. Surfing movies were probably inspired by the older cottage industry of American ski movies that were made by ski bums who, beginning about 1950 or so, took their travelogues about for a paying audience who listened to their spoken jargonized commentary. Surf movies evolved later along with the technology of fast color films, long lenses, and watertight cameras that could be mounted on the boards themelves. Bruce Brown's commercial film of 1966, containing lots of footage of fine waves and of handsome surfers on them and held together by a transparently simple story, was called *The Endless Summer*. Some self-indulgent, but, we come to feel, essentially spiritual, youths set out on a round-the-world quest to find the perfect wave. It matters little that at last they found a long, high, dependable roller with a perfect curl on the eastern coast of South Africa. The characters were appealing, their adventures enviable, the cinematography and sound track irresistible. Is it art? One looks in vain for many other films about sport that come close to it.

Yet again to the surfers. They are the most numerous, innovative and craftsmanlike sports photographers. Like the surf filmers, they urge and quickly seize upon novelties in technology and push them yet further with risky developing, cropping, and blowups. They plan methodically, wait for a piece of luck and shoot rapidly. The American surfing magazines arrange contests. A sensitive and critical audience applauds the best, which are often published in large editions as surfing posters. All this seeking and propagating of beauty takes place utterly outside the art world and indeed apart from the enormous and diffuse industry of sports journalism.

Some artistically inspired sports photo-journalists have their work more conventionally published. The well-financed, establishment weekly, *Sports Illustrated,* has been supportive here. The editors frequently publish color shots of yachts, hang gliders, skiers and horse races which indicate the possibilities. Dan Baliotti shot and cropped the photographs for a picture book on professional ice hockey. The text by Stan Fischler of *This is Hockey* (Englewood Cliffs, New Jersey: Prentice-Hall, 1975, 234 pp.) is inconsequential, but almost all of the photographs are meticulously considered quasi-abstractions of great power. All, while esthetically impressive, are intense, almost cruel revelations of this frequently demeaning (to players and spectators alike) show.

In Europe, there are contests for sports photographers. Some French, and more successfully, German professional photographers have been experimenting with deliberately slow exposures, highly selective focusing, or moved cameras to suggest athletes in action. One is tempted to employ the word "impressionistic" to describe the deliberate revealing of high-performance photography's technology as well as the esthetic object of the photographer on the viewer. In Germany, these deliberately fuzzy (*verwischt*) shots render the subjects unidentifiable and so the pictures (which are often of considerable dramatic power) can be freely sold to publishers or advertisers without paying the athlete-models a legitimate fee.

We will stretch the usual categories of art a little. Some of the loveliest byproducts of modern sport are the essential objects used in competitions and games. The contemporary, conventional, and historical conception of what is art perhaps should be expanded. The racing bicycle, an archer's bow, a world-class scull, or a competition sloop are objects that invite us to stroke them and be dazzled by their sculpted, colored, and polished surfaces. For these objects, their purpose is their explanation. They are only incidentally intended to be lovely. Their visual and tactile qualities are byproducts of a concentrated focusing of their designers on concepts and tiny details that might increase the chances of their users for superior performance. Even soccer balls, baseball mitts, hockey player masks, lacrosse sticks, ice axes, stop watches (the list could be greatly extended) are all characterized by a craftsmanship and strength that has almost disappeared from ordinary consumer goods. For modern consumer goods are not designed with verifiable performance in mind. However, innovation based on new technical possibilities heightens the chance of supremacy in sports performance. And victory in sport, as we have seen, can produce substantial rewards.

Sports equipment has almost no history—witness the very rapid evolution of skateboards and running shoes. There is a chasm between the community that makes and uses the finest sports equipment and the equally cosmopolitan universe of high-markup galleries and art critics. Exceptions were the 1962 exhibition, "Design for Sport," at the Museum of Modern Art in New York and the modest "Technology in the Olympic Games" held as part of the Munich Olympics in 1972. Another large exhibition took place in Baden-Baden in 1981.

There are esthetes (though they might object to the appellation) who slaver over surfboards too seductively colored and shaped (and too costly) to be taken to menacing waves and scratching beaches. There are refined collectors of fishing tackle meant to be fondled and not used; pocket knives that will stay in their velvet-lined, leather cases. Some of us emphathize and may envy the man who pays a very large sum for the most exquisitely finished racing bicycle (the basic design and essential proportions of these machines have changed but little during the last half century) whose only frivolities are some carvings on the lugs or some witty striping on the bright metallic paint. These artifacts may be ridden sparingly or not at all—for they are too beautiful to soil. The equipment esthete hangs his Colnago against a matte white wall and illuminates it at night with a small spot.

Here again, a point has to be made. All of these objects evolved outside of the universities, the world of pure science, the social critics, the fine arts, and the intelligentsia. The very contrast, on the one hand, between the refinement and the popularity of sports objects, and, on the other, with sport as subject matter in the arts as conventionally conceived, suggests the extent to which modern sport is socially harmonious and, paradoxically, academically ignored.

If we shift our view somewhat, we might consider the proposition that the most important and beautiful products of modern sport are the participators themselves. There are millions of them. Their numbers continue to increase. The modern sportsman may almost be considered a new type of being. The healthy person rejoicing in his or her body has always existed. The classical Greeks extolled them, and thereby established artistic canons still in effect. Even aside from their art conventions, no subsequent high culture has been so frank in its physicality, save our own, and our situation is very new. Without debating whether Christianity has opposed innocent physical pleasure, all the Christian churches opposed activities not directed at the afterlife. Even the durable ideals of the rationalist eighteenth century proposed as erotic models the pale lady and the wan lover.

As was mentioned earlier, some nineteenth-century artists painted or sculpted well-made, physically fit male and female models who were clearly athletes and who then and forever after remained nameless. They were merely meat as pretty as a glaucous wine goblet, as neutral as a split steer's carcass. Well into the twentieth century, healthy human bodies remained excuses to do near abstract studies of mass, balance and proportion—not of human values. The curiously cool female nudes of Aristide Maillol come to mind here.

As the twentieth century draws to a close, it is rapidly becoming obvious to millions (for they act on this assumption) that sport is too happy an invention to be the possession of high-performance athletes and the industry surrounding them. Ever more, the publicity heroes and heroines of sport are not merely objects of eroticized fantasies, but become inspirations for happier, fuller, more physical lives. The pleasure of Franz Beckenbauer, Jean-Claude Killy or Pelé in moving and testing the limits of their superb bodies is an inspiration for our more prosaic, yet very modern indulging in very good health, and the spiritual alertness and optimism that it brings.

The well-observed climbs to prominence and riches by Joe Namath or Muhammad Ali are (not unequivocal) inspirations for the democratic achievement principle and pleasure in existence. A child born socially disadvantaged may indeed have a slender chance of finding such fame and fortune, but, as was suggested earlier, sports heroes can be models for ambition and hard work that produce personally treasured or socially useful results in other areas of endeavor.

But it is wrong to focus on stars in this discussion of what is meant to be a survey of joyous sport. The millions of participants in Sunday football games, the affectionately chatting long-distance runners, the wind surfers, the amateur cyclists polishing their lovely machines, the self-involved body builders, the leisurely golfers, the pensive back packers—the list could be longer—are investigating and indeed using possibilities for harmless and conceivably constructive pleasure that simply were not known before our time.

All these pastimes are blessed by authorities and encouraged by local and national governments. Indeed sports participation gets approbation by the very atmosphere around us. Now it is true as the neo-Marxist critics claim that a healthy, happy citizen is a better worker, taxpayer, and insurance risk and that fitness is of positive military value. In the 1970s there were several lavishly advertised and subsidized government campaigns to encourage sports participation (read fitness) in Europe. One example the *Trimm Dich* movement in Western Germany.

There were others in Belgium, the Netherlands, and elsewhere. These and other governments are rarely able to prove that direct increases in mass sports participation are due to official efforts. The advocacy of fitness may be nearly omnipresent and evidence of deeper forces that encourage all of us constructively to pursue our limits in self-realization. Almost no one doubts that sports participation and even mass sports theater leads to an increase in the general level of happiness.

Would not life in the various censored, restrictive, in-a-hurry-to-modernize, single-party states in Eastern Europe be yet more stultifying and boring, if the populations were not inspired by the successes of their internationally acknowledged sports heroes, entertained by ambitious sports theater and distracted by the lively writing in sports newspapers? Modern sport provides not only for physical release. Modern sport is a force for spiritual assurances as well. The creative possibilities are far from being exhausted.

For when broadly considered, very little of modern sport is violent. The myths, the rules, the epic literature, the organization, the exhortatory ideology—all are means of channeling and controlling aggression, idleness, and insecurity harmlessly for private pleasure and community solidarity. That the creative potential contained in modern sport has remained largely in the hands of shallow profiteers, ignorant sensation seekers, and opportunistic politicians cannot continue indefinitely.

The complex organizations and the inspiring ideology of modern sport continue to captivate the eager bodies and spirits of millions of participants and the allegiance of billions of spectators. We can be sure that sport will evolve constructively and will gather ever greater mythic force.

BIBLIOGRAPHICAL ESSAYS

PREFACE

This essay, the first of fifteen, will discuss some surveys and general or comprehensive collections. As will be the case throughout, I will exclude journalism, memoirs, and other such ephemera and include only items of earnestness with some lasting value.

Some general and particular observations first. Sport has only recently been viewed as meriting analysis; almost all the good literature is not old. That most of the solid literature is in German is probably a reflection of the fact that in Central Europe sport has never been widely separated from physical education which has always been a matter of intense concern to politicians, intellectuals, and scholars. This connection will receive due attention in the narratives for chapters 8 and 13. The research for the survey is based on English and French works as well. I suspect that the book's claims may be slightly weakened because I cannot use Russian and Japanese authorities in the original.

The literature of sport is uneven in its coverage. The well-surveyed epochs are classical Greece, modern Germany and, less so, early industrial England. That we know a lot about some aspects of Egyptian sport is thanks to the work of one young scholar. There is one exception to the observation that almost no one has bothered to determine how American sport came to be or what is happening now. Baseball has a rich analytical and even poetic literary tradition. Outside of these subjects, there is not much.

Not unexpectedly, the first careful survey of sport was in German. It is a collective work assembled and edited by G. A. E. Bogeng, a German bibliographer who owes his greatest fame to his editing of Voltaire's letters. The two-volume work is grandly comprehensive; the word "sport" in German encompasses many more recreational activities than it does in English. The *Geschichte des Sports aller Völker und Zeiten* (Leipzig: E. A. Seemann, 1926, 2v. 784 pp.) is dependent upon the community of German scholars Bogeng and his subeditors could induce to contribute. It is strong on ethnography and European sports, but even in these areas it has been superseded by later, special studies.

The next ambitious history of sport is also broadly comprehensive and in German. Carl Diem (1882–1962) was a great sports prosyletizer and sports festival organizer. Alas, he was not a trained or critical historian. His *Weltgeschichte des Sports* (Stuttgart: Cotta, first edition, 1960, 1224 pp.) (Spanish translation) was hastily written and drew upon dozens of student theses which he supervised as the director of the world's most prestigious school of physical education before and after World War II. It is uneven, uncritical, and lacks documentation for its many provocative claims.

Horst Ueberhorst is a third German to attempt comprehensiveness. His *Geschichte der Leibesübungen* (Berlin: Bartels und Wernitz, 1972+) reflects the cosmopolitanism of the postwar Western Germans and draws on contributing scholars from all over the world. Articles are in German, English, and French. As of 1983, five volumes had been published and the future of the project was uncertain. Ueberhorst has given his contributors of 40 to 100 page articles great independence. Since the work lacks a controlling tone or thesis, it will not be discussed further here, but several of the sections will be in later essays of this sort.

Jean le Floc'hmoan has written a racy survey, *La genèse des sports*

(Paris: Payot, 1962, 184 pp.) which appears to be based upon careful research but which is unfortunately undocumented. The volume *Jeux et sports* (Paris: Gallimard, 1967, 1826 pp.) of the *Encyclopédie de la Pléiade* was edited and partly written by the great philosopher of play, Roger Caillois. The section on sport covers pages 1185–1697. The articles on sport are more technical than historical.

There are several encyclopedias of sport. By far the most useful for historians is the *Oxford Companion to Sport and Games* (London: Oxford, 1975, 1143 pp.) The editor is John Arlott. The longer historical articles (e.g., "Football", "Pelota") have brief bibliographies of literature in English.

The solid historical journals everywhere are no longer reluctant to publish well-researched, provocative articles on sport. Many of these articles will be cited in later essays in this book. Recently two journals have been established which seek and publish sport-historical articles. *Stadion* (1975 +   ) is edited by several historians based at the Institut für Sportgeschichte at the Deutsche Sporthochschule in Cologne and publishes solid research in several languages. *The Journal of Sport History* (1974 +   ) is sponsored by the North American Society of Sport History which is, in turn, run by physical educators, not historians.

This essay is deliberately exclusive. Serious readers would only be misled, if I were to list much of the vast amount of literature in English or other languages which purports to be historical, but which is instead derivative, opportunistic and ephemeral.

1. SPORT BEFORE HIGH CULTURE

This chapter deals with three problems traditionally considered separate. One is the problem of examining the play element in human nature. The second is concerned with the interpretation of the descriptive literature of play and sport by observers of primitive societies. A third touches on a major problem of this book: to what extent are play, games, and recreation in primitive societies comparable to sport in modern, industrial society? In none of these areas is there an extensive or authoritative bibliography.

The most important and possibly most exciting work on play is

Johan Huizinga's *Homo ludens* (first published 1938) (many translations). English edition (London: Routledge, 1949, 256 pp.) Huizinga, a Dutch historian of the Middle Ages wrote this work while
dismayed at the prospects for European culture. He provocatively
(and, for many, convincingly) posits the playfulness of mankind
as the essential experimental and creative force in human development. The book has stimulated and even inspired a grand array
of theologians and culture critics. Unfortunately, the very little
that Huizinga wrote on modern sport is wrong and condemning.

Huizinga did inspire, among others, a French philosopher who
attempted to distinguish or classify various types of play, games,
contests, and sports. Roger Caillois's *Man, Play and Games* (New
York: Free Press, 1961, 208 pp.) (First French edition, 1958) is
one of the noblest efforts to determine what sport is or is not and
to distinguish the various types and characteristics of play. Another profound examination of play is by Friedrich Georg Jünger,
Die Spiele: Ein Schlüssel zu ihrer Bedeutung (Frankfurt am Main:
V. Klostermann, 1953, 236 pp.). The introductory chapter, "Play,
Games, Contests, Sports" (1–14) in Allen Guttmann's *From Ritual
to Record* (New York: Columbia University Press, 1978, 198 pp.)
is a tight survey of the problem of play and has good bibliographical notes.

The anthropological literature dealing with play, contests and
games is vast in extent and coverage. I can best be of service by
referring to some careful surveys and bibliographies. Gerhard Lukas is an East German historian whose stern Marxism helped him
to make one of the most rigorous attempts ever to see recreations
and play as reflections and reinforcements of a society's basic economic structures. The Anglo-Saxon world would benefit from a
translation of Lukas' *Die Körperkultur in frühen Epochen der Men-
schheitsentwicklung* (East Berlin: Sportverlag, 1969, 193 pp.). He
provides good notes and bibliographies. Horst Ueberhorst's chapter "Ursprungstheorien" (15–36) in the first volume of his multi-
volumed, in-process *Geschichte der Leibesübungen* (vol. 1, Berlin:
Bartels und Wernitz, 1972, 263 pp.) is a fine, well-documented
survey. Another German survey with good bibliographical citations is H. Damm, "Vom Wesen sog. Leibesübungen bei Natur-
völkern: Ein Beitrag zur Genese des Sports," *Studium Generale*

(Berlin, 1960) 13(1):1–10. Guttmann's notes, in the chapter cited above, provide a more up-to-date bibliographical survey and cite (alas, only cite rather than evaluate) useful French and English literature.

But was sport before modern times anything like sport as we know it? The small universe of sport scholarship is now and is likely to remain in a productive debate. That debate centers around the recent work of a brilliant, original sociologist, Henning Eichberg, who has used his own anthropological observations and his splendid philosophical and historical knowledge to support his claims that the games and sports of any society (and most particularly our own) are so particular to that society as almost to obliterate the meaning or significance of other than superficial similarities. Eichberg's first book, *Der Weg des Sports in die industrielle Zivilisation* (Baden-Baden: Nomos, 1974, 172 pp.) marks a new critical rigor and a major theoretical departure in sports scholarship. A subsequent book, *Leistung, Spannung, Geschwindigkeit* (Stuttgart: Klett-Cotta, 1978, 353 pp.) discusses the foundations of modern European sport in the context of other changes of social behavior and ideology that took place in proto-industrial Europe. Henning Eichberg has also written on spectator sports and gambling in Sumatra. His writing is marred by a neglect of English and American scholarly literature that would buttress his claims and (perhaps paradoxically) a sociological jargon derived from American sociologists. But his work is original and, for some, convincing. He has already been a major influence on Allen Guttmann (see above) who has attempted to identify the distinctly modern characteristics of modern sport.

2. SPORT BEFORE THE GREEKS

The essay for this chapter would be misleading, if it were long. With the possible exception of the discussion of Egyptian sport, the claims of the chapter are modest—as they must be. For most of the societies before classical Greece, the evidence of activities offering comparisons with our sports is scant; the conjectures based on that evidence are fanciful. The reader should beware of the attempts of amateur sport historians to legitimize their undertakings by finding continuities from the distant past to the present. Much of the discussion in this chapter is based on general reading on cultural history. Much of the approach of this volume (and particularly this chapter) has been bolstered and tempered by the courageous summary by William McNeill, *The Rise of the West* (Chicago: University of Chicago Press, 1963, 829 pp.). The *Cambridge Ancient History* (Cambridge: Cambridge University Press, 12 vols., 1923–1939) (third revised edition, 1970 +) has been most useful.

The outstanding exception to the admonition urging modesty in the areas under discussion is due to meticulous analysis of one young German, Wolfgang Decker. His body of work (which is still underway) began with the publication in 1971 of his dissertation, *Die physische Leistung Pharaos* (Cologne: Historisches Institut der Deutschen Sporthochschule Köln, 271 pp.). Since then Decker has steadily published articles, bibliographies and documents—for example *Quellentexte zu Sport und Körperkultur im alten Ägypten* (Sankt Augustin: Hans Richarz, 1975, 123 pp.)—that stress the suitability of the games, competitions, and public festivals of the Egyptians to their social structure, political system, and cosmology. Decker is young and his work goes on.

Less substantial, but with lots of pretty pictures, is A.D. Touny and Steffen Wenig, *Sport in Ancient Egypt* (Leipzig: Edition Leipzig, 1971, 119 pp.) (German edition, Leipzig: Olympic Editions, 1969, 123 pp.).

In his *Leibesübungen bei Homer* (Schorndorf bei Stuttgart: Karl Hofmann, 1969, 71 pp.) Klaus Willimczik presents Homer's texts dealing with games and contests. His introduction is critical and offers useful bibliographical apparatus. The first three chapters of E. Norman Gardiner's *Athletics of the Ancient World* (Oxford: Oxford University Press, 1930, 246 pp.) deal, respectively, with sport in the ancient East, Crete, and in Homer.

3. GREECE

When dealing with the sport of the ancient Greeks we have, relatively, bibliographical riches. The scholarly tradition is old and is still vigorous. There is solid literature in the major languages and much of the literature is accessible. The rigor that characterizes this area, of course, is just part of the high critical standards that govern all scholarship on the classical Greeks.

Here again, however, the best literature is often German. A German scholar, Johann Heinrich Krause, was the first to sort through the literary sources for Greek exercises and athletic festivals. One can consult Richard D. Mandell, "The Modern Olympic Games: A Bibliographical Essay," in *Sportwissenschaft* (1976) 6(1):89–98, for more on Krause. Germans were the first (beginning in 1875) to do systematic excavations at ancient Olympia and these excavations have continued intermittently into the present. For more on this one can consult the illustrated and annotated catalog done for a fine exhibition at the 1972 Olympic Games, *100 Jahre deutsher Ausgrabung in Olympia* (Munich: Prestel, 1972, 136 pp.). It may be useful to note here that the most comprehensive encyclopedia of the ancient world, *Paulys Realencyclopädie der klassischen Altertumswissenshaft* (G. Wissowa *et al.* eds., 34 volumes plus 13 supplemental volumes, Stuttgart: Druckenmüller, 1893–1973), contains many articles useful to the sports scholar. The articles are difficult to find, but have been indexed by Karl Lennartz in his bibliography, *Olympische Spiele* (Bibliographie: Geschichte der Leibesübungen, V [Cologne: Seminar für Leibesübungen der Pädagogischen Hochschule Rheinland Abteilung Köln, 1971, 150 pp.]).

An especially useful and well-documented work is Ulrich Popplow's *Leibesübungen und Leibeserziehung in der griechichen Antike* (Schorndorf bei Stuttgart: Karl Hofmann, 1959, 200 pp.). A useful collection of literary fragments is in Rachel Sargent Robinson, ed., *Sources for the History of Greek Athletics* (Cincinnati: Published by the author, 1927 [reprinted 1955], 289 pp.)

The connection between the ancient and the modern Olympic Games is based only on sentiment and nomenclature, but the connection has inspired some good historical literature. Examples are Heinz Schöbel, *The Ancient Olympic Games* (Princeton: Van Nostrand, 1966, 163 pp.) (German edition, *Olympia und seine Spiele* [Berlin (East) Sportverlag, 1955]), and Hans-Volkmar Herrmann, *Olympia: Heiligtum und Wettkampfstätte* (Munich: Hirmer, 1972, 269 pp.). E. Norman Gardiner, *Athletics of the Ancient World* (1930, cited in full in the previous chapter) remains useful. H. A. Harris in his *Greek Athletes and Athletics* (London: Hutchinson, 1964, 244 pp.) stresses literary sources and linguistic evidence to dispute the claims of previous scholars about the sports techniques of antiquity. One can also use Harris' *Sport in Greece and Rome* (London: Thames and Hudson, 1972, 288 pp.). Yet another useful survey (which, however, lacks bibliographical apparatus) is M. I. F. Finley and H. W. Pleket, *The Olympic Games: The First Thousand Years* (London: Book Club Associates, 1976, 138 pp.). Pleket wrote a well-documented article, "Games, Prizes, Athletes and Ideology: Some Aspects of the History of Sport in the Greco-Roman World," *Stadion* (1975) 1(1):49–89.

The brevity of this essay is not meant to diminish the accomplishments of hundreds of other researchers who worked on problems discussed in this chapter. Their efforts are to be applauded because, as in many other areas of classical scholarship, the evidence is scant and equivocal. Their publications can be located by using the works cited above and with the help of standard bibliographical tools. However, I am probably not alone in wishing that many of them, particularly those who re-did work already accomplished reasonably well, had worked as carefully on other, waiting problems in sport history.

4. SPREAD OF THE TASTE

The subjects of this chapter lie within a well-defined and much researched period of social and cultural history. The topic is the spread of Greek culture and the changes in culture over time in various economic and political circumstances in the Mediterranean world. The scholarly tradition as a whole is venerable and productive. Though a lot of literature illuminates the topics of this chapter, little of it deals specifically with sport.

Especially useful for this chapter were the books by William McNeill (cited in the essay for chapter 2) and the splendid biography, *Alexander the Great* (London: Penguin, 1973, 568 pp.) by Robin Lane Fox. Books on sport that were useful here that were also cited in previous essays are those by Lukas (chapter 1), Gardiner (chapter 2) and Finley and Pleket (chapter 2).

There are some useful, rather specific monographs. Two books on the history of ideas are Eberhard Mähl, *Gymnastik und Athletik im Denken der Römer* (Amsterdam: B. R. Grüner, 1974, 83 pp.) and Alois Koch, *Die Leibesübungen im Urteil der antiken und frühchristlichen Anthropologie* (Schorndorf bei Stuttgart: Karl Hofmann, 1965, 134 pp.). Koch's book is well annotated. Michael Grant's *Gladiators* (London: Weidenfeld and Nicolson, 1967, 128 pp.) is accessible, lively, and has a short bibliography on p. 125. The best discussion so far on the horse in ancient times is Paul Vigneron, *Le cheval dans l'antiquité gréco-romaine* (Nancy: Faculté des lettres et des sciences humaines . . . , 1968; Vol. 1, 338 pp.; Vol. 2, 105 plates). Vigneron supplies detailed, annotated bibliographies.

The usefulness of some short or specialized pieces makes them worth citing here. An unusual and helpful article is Charles Homer Haskins, "The Latin Literature of Sport," in *Studies in Medieval Culture* (New York: Friedrich Ungar, 1958) 107–20. A young German has illuminated several traditional scholarly topics by examining the sources for Hellenistic sport in the Middle East. One can consult the articles by Manfred Lämmer: "Eine Propaganda-Aktion des Königs Herodes in Olympia," *Kölner Beiträge zur Sportwissenschaft*, 1 (Schorndorf bei Stuttgart: Karl Hofmann, 1973), 160–73 and "Griechische Wettkämpfe in Jerusalem und ihre politischen Hintergründe," *Kölner Beiträge zur Sportwissenschaft*, 2 (Schorndorf bei Stuttgart: Karl Hofmann, 1973) 182–227.

5. SPORT IN PRE-INDUSTRIAL HIGH CULTURE

The claims in this chapter are modest and so, of necessity, are the claims of this essay. But there is something additional to keep in mind. It is quite possible that some of my assertions or even my modesty itself could be refuted. There may exist solid literature that has remained obscure to me because of language problems.

However, I must state that almost all sport-historical literature that appears outside of a scholarly or critical tradition is suspect. There is almost a pathetic tendency for beginners in sport history to attempt to legitimize by establishing the continuous history of their topic. They stress continuities from the past to the present and tend to confirm the ancient foundations of modern sport on the basis of flimsy evidence. In such cases, sport history is employed as patriotic propaganda or to justify certain political programs. Two examples of what I mean are the attempts of some Mexicans to see evidence of modern team sports in the Aztec and Mayan ball courts and the propaganda from Maoist China stressing the sportiness of the ancient and modern Chinese.

Those interested in reading further on some subjects touched in this chapter might consult, warily, Carl Diem's *Weltgeschichte*. . . . (discussed after the preface). Diem's *Asiatische Reiterspiele* (Berlin: Deutscher Archivvertrag, 1942, 291 pp.) discusses the varieties of horse sports in the Near and Far East and is much more rigorous than Diem's many other works.

Useful for this chapter was the article by Kohsuke Sasajima, "History of Physical Exercises and Sport in Japan," in Horst Ueberhorst, ed., *Geschichte der Leibesübungen* (Berlin: Bartels und Wernitz, 1972) 4:190–214. Sasajima's References (pp. 213–14) list the translated titles and transliterated authors of some Japanese works on Japanese sport. Another article with useful bibliographical notations is Arnd Krüger and Akira Ito, "On the Limitations of Eichberg's and Mandell's Theory of Sports and their Quantification in View of Chikaraishi," *Stadion* (1977) 3(2):244–56.

When completed, Horst Ueberhorst's multi-volumed *Geschichte der Leibesübungen* will have chapters dealing with several topics surveyed in this chapter.

The standard bibliographies dealing with Latin American archaeology list lots of speculative literature on the evidence for sport (if it was that) in the pre-Columbian period. Roman Pĭna Chan, *Games and Sport in Old Mexico* (Leipzig: Edition Leipzig, 1969, 72 pp.) (German edition, 1968) has good illustrations, but is light.

6. EUROPE 500–1750

This chapter covers a grand span is history, encompassing much of what is traditionally conceived of as the history of Western civilization. There are vast amounts of literature that touch on the topics of this chapter, but little that is specifically concerned with sport as I am trying to describe it.

Alan Cameron, *Circus Factions: Blues and Greens at Rome and Byzantium* (Oxford: Clarendon Press, 1976, 364 pp.) is careful and both cites and discusses all previous literature. One can also consult his *Porphyrius the Charioteer* (Oxford: Clarendon Press, 1973, 286 pp.). Paul Vigneron, *Le cheval dans l'antiquité* . . . . (cited and praised in the essay for chapter 4) summarizes the theories about the origin of the big horse.

Martin Hahn, *Die Leibesübungen im mittelalterlichen Volksleben* (Langensalza: Hermann Beyer, 1929, 104 pp.; reprint, Walluf bei Wiesbaden: Martin Sändig, 1972) sees too much evidence for modern sport in ancient practices, but has excellent notes and bibliographies. Klemens C. Wildt, *Leibesübungen im deutschen Mittlealter* (Frankfurt am Main: Limpert, 42 pp.) is slight. One of the more splendid works I have encountered on sport is J. J. Jusserand, *Les sports et jeux d'excercise dans l'ancienne France* (Paris: Plon, 1901, 474 pp.). Jusserand is perhaps too eager to see precursors for modern sport in French history, but the book is an admirable effort to incorporate games, contests, and physical education into general cultural and intellectual history.

A work which merits great attention and praise is Joachim Rühl, *Die "Olympischen Spiele" Robert Dovers* (Heidelberg: Carl Winter, 1975, 261 pp.). This doctoral dissertation is an exhaustive discussion of a particular, regular festival in seventeenth-century England and may more correctly deserve listing after the next chapter. However, Rühl's chapter 2, "Vorgeschichte" (21–77) is a sober and yet witty survey, with meticulous apparatus, of a wide range of topics in medieval sport ranging from jugglers to the Puritans' attitudes toward competitions and games. Note, too, that several other books cited in full in the essay after the next chapter, particularly those by Kloeren and Dunning, were useful for this chapter.

The only book-length historical treatment of Italian civic sports is William Heywood, *Palio and Ponte: An Account of the Sports of Central Italy from the Death of Dante to the XXth Century* (London: Methuen, 1904, 267 pp.). Almost all other literature, particularly the large amount on the Palio of Sienna, is nonhistorical.

The intellectual origins of sport and education or physical education have a rich primary as well as secondary literature. The original writings of Vittorino da Feltre, Thomas Elyot, John Locke, Jean-Jacques Rousseau and other educational theorists are easy to obtain. Fred Eugene Leonard, *A Guide to the History of Physical Education* (Philadelphia: Lea and Febiger, 1923, 361 pp.) (many later printings and editions) is still sound. Diebold B. van Dalen and Bruce L. Bennett, *A World History of Physical Education: Cultural, Philosophical, Comparative* (Englewood Cliffs: Prentice Hall, second edition 1971, 694 pp.) is a college textbook with useful notes and bibliographies in English. A group of East Germans have completed a massive history of physical education and sport that is partly obfuscated by orthodox Marxist rhetoric and periodization. It is Wolfgang Eichel, et al. eds., *Die Körperkultur in Deutschland von den Anfängen bis zur Neuzeit* (East Berlin: Sportverlag, 4 vols., 1969–1973). The discussions of the Nazi period and of the political relations of the two postwar Germanies are not objective. Nevertheless, the survey's very completeness and care in documentation makes this work valuable and exceptional.

7. ENGLAND: LAND OF SPORT

This chapter is based on a lot of fine work dealing with a critically important problem and period in sport history. It is worth observing here that English sport arose so naturally out of English conditions that few English scholars have noticed its significance or have given sport much attention until very recently. That so many of the good works are German is largely explained by an old tradition that has been mentioned in previous essays and will be discussed again in the text of chapter 8.

As general background for this chapter, I must mention a magnificent synthesis *not* about sport, David S. Landes, *The Unbound Prometheus: Technological Change and Industrial Development in Western Europe from 1750 to the Present* (Cambridge: Cambridge University Press, 1969, 566 pp.). Landes' general subject is the Industrial Revolution, but his judgments are so acute and his range so broad that this brilliant survey can be urged as basic reading for almost any topic dealing with modern Europe. The bibliographical notes should serve as models for responsible scholars.

A brief and stimulating, but undocumented book is Herbert

Schoeffler, *England, das Land des Sportes: Eine kultur-soziologische Erkläring* (Leipzig: Tauchnitz, 1935, 86 pp.). Schoeffler's dissertation student, Maria Kloeren, provided lots of supporting anecdotes and documentation for Schoeffler in her *Sport und Rekord: Kultursoziologische Untersuchungen zum England des sechzehnten bis achtzenhnten Jarhunderts* ("Kölner anglistische Arbeiten") (Leipzig: A. Tauchnitz, 1935, 294 pp.). Another useful examination of English sport is U. Hirn, *Ursprung und Wesen des Sports* (Berlin: Weidmannsche Buchhandlung, 1936, 167 pp.). Gerhard Schneider, *Puritanismus und Leibesübungen* (Schorndorf bei Stuttgart: Karl Hofmann, 1968, 138 pp.) covers our period and is broader than the title suggests. Another book which offers far more than the title suggests is Joachim Rühl, *Die "Olympischen Spiele" Robert Dovers* which was praised previously.

Henning Eichberg, who was discussed in previous essays, believes that sport arose out of new and broadly European conditions of the eighteenth century. One can (perhaps should!) consult his provocative articles, "Auf Zoll und Quintlein: Sport und Quantifizierungsprozess in der frühen Neuzeit," *Archiv für Kulturgeschichte* (1974) 56:141–76 and "Zur historisch-kulturellen Relativität des Leistens in Spiel und Sport," *Sportwissenschaft* (1976) 6(1):9–34.

An anecdotal survey that is still enjoyable is Joseph Strutt, *The Sports and Pastimes of the People of England* (London: Tegg, 1801, 384 pp.) (many subsequent editions). Dennis Brailsford, *Sport and Society: Elizabeth to Anne* (London: Routledge, 1969, 279 pp.) focuses on debates among theologians and moralists. Montague Shearman, *Athletics and Football* (London: Longmans, Green, 1886, 410 pp.) (subsequent editions) emphasizes techniques and organizational history in the nineteenth century. The article "Athletic Sports" in the *Encyclopedia Britannica* (Eleventh edition, 1911, 2:846–49) is still of use for historians. Peter McIntosh, *Physical Education in England since 1800* (London: Bell, 1952, 259 pp.) has a useful emphasis. Eric Dunning, *Barbarians, Gentlemen and Players: A Sociological Study of the Development of Rugby Football* (New York: New York University Press, 1979, 321 pp.) includes substance that was in his earlier, brilliant articles on the origins of football. This is another valuable and exciting book that goes way beyond the subject matter indicated in the title. Dunning provides good bibliographical assistance. Less substantial, but still very good is James Walvin, *The People's Game: A Social History of British Football* (London: Allen Lane, 1975, 201 pp.).

Lilly C. Stone, *English Sports and Recreations* ("Published by the Folger Shakespeare Library") (Ithaca: Cornell University Press, 1960, 29+ pp.) is light, but has helpful "Suggested Readings" (28–29) and illustrations.

I must cite a fine, annotated bibliography, Peter Lovesey and Tom McNab, *The Guide to British Track and Field Literature, 1275–1968* (London: Athletics Arena, 1969, 110 pp.). Lovesey and McNab cite and discuss lots of literature that otherwise would remain unknown.

8. INDUCED SPORT

For the subjects covered in this chapter there is a lot of good existing literature. However, the remarks made before about the dominance of German scholarship are especially relevant here.

There are two good American textbooks. The text by Fred Eugene Leonard was previously cited in chapter 6. Deobold B. Van Dalen and Bruce L. Bennett, *A World History of Physical Education: Cultural Philosophical, Comparative* (Englewood Cliffs, New Jersey: Prentice Hall, 1971) 694 pp., is responsible, but has an American bias and cites only English literature.

There is a superb French survey that is also relevant to the subject matter of the last pages of chapter 6. Jacques Ullmann's *De la gymnastique aux sports modernes: Histoire des doctrines de l'éducation physique* (Second edition, Paris: J. Vrin, 1971) 430 pp., ignores organizational and eventful history. The book is, in fact, part of a series, "Bibliothèque d'histoire de la philosophie." Ullmann has excellent, comprehensive notes and bibliographies citing literature in the European languages. Pages 97–348 deal with Europe since the Renaissance. That this book remains untranslated is a loss for sport scholars.

However detailed they may be, the German works devoted to the problems in the chapter are not comprehensive, but are concerned with German history. The great East German survey of physical education and sport deserves a complete citation here: The title is *Geschichte der Körperkultur in Deutschland* (East Berlin: Sportverlag, 1967–1973). The editor-in-chief (*Vorsitzender*) is Wolfgang Eichel. For the four volumes I list the period covered and pagination, respectively: 1, *Von den Anfängen bis zur Neuzeit*, 227 pp.; 2, *Von 1789 bis 1917*, 439 pp.; 3, *Von 1917 bis 1945*, 309 pp.; 4, *Von 1945 bis 1961*, 309 pp.

A book that surveys its problem while listing and criticizing all the previous literature is Hajo Bernett, *Die pädagogische Neugestaltung der bürgerlichen Leibesübungen durch die Philanthropen* (Schorndorf bei Stuttgart: Karl Hofmann, 1960), 123 pp. A symposium in Berlin in 1978 on Friedrich Ludwig Jahn led to the publication of a series of papers covering topics on physical education and sport in German history. The papers were published as Volume 4 (408 pp.) of *Stadion* in 1978.

The literature on Germany is part of an old and rich tradition. To survey the bibliographical riches here is impossible. Readers who wish to probe further can best consult the bibliographies in Ullmann, Eichel (ed.), and Bernett cited above.

In contrast, the literature on physical education in countries inspired by the earlier German developments is very sparse and undependable. The few pieces of historical literature in English, German, or French are clumsily or not at all annotated. All of the patriotic sports movements were so passionately ideological that, despite their very great political significance, they developed rapidly in an atmosphere that precludes the documented analysis the historian expects. However, my observations above are also suspect because I cannot use with any confidence many of the relevant Slavic and Scandinavian languages.

One fine article, Hartmut Becker, "Die Jüdische Turnbewegung. Ihr Verhältnis zum Zionismus," *Judaica* (June 1975) 31(2):71–84 shows how intimately sport was integrated into the early phases of the Zionist movement. Mass sport, high-performance sport, sports festivals, and sport myths have remained so intimately integrated with Zionism and the history of modern Israel, themselves topics of passionate partisanship, that it may be vain to hope for objective studies.

Clearly, a lot of good work remains to be done.

9. AMERICAN SPORT TO THE 1920s

Nowhere else is there such a vast contrast between the great amounts of readily available provocative material and pathetic use made of it. Sources for studying the development are in scrapbooks, newspaper files, archives, and special libraries—including those in halls of fame. There are even enormous quantities of published materials. What is lacking is a desire to view American sport as a historical topic like any other.

Sport has been called "an academic taboo," but the taboo extends far beyond academia. Sport in America may be a refuge from the cruel criticism and the relentless logic of public life. Sport may be a semi-sacred reservoir of myth, diversion, and hope.

This essay will attempt to deal only with exceptions to the claims above. I will concentrate on the solid accomplishments; the signs of better things to come.

We must begin with a salient exception. John Rickards Betts died before he could finish his book *America's Sporting Heritage* (Reading, Mass.: Addison-Wesley, 1974, 428 pp.). Betts used more sources, particularly early newspapers and magazines, than any other historian. Sport's evolution in his narrative is very closely related to major changes in technology, transportation, communication, and ideology. The book has a coolness in style and a specificity about dates, people, and turning points that a reader has learned to expect in other areas of cultural history, but which are almost never encountered in American sport history.

Though Betts died in 1971, he apparently used very few sources dating from after 1950. And the book was completed after his death by his son Rickard Betts and by Guy M. Lewis. Alas, the bibliographical apparatus is undependable and for many stimulating claims Betts provided no bibliographical sources whatever.

After reading James A. Michener's *Sports in America* (New York: Random House, 1976, 466 pp. one knows more than before, but Michener is mostly interested in the origins in the recent past of present moral problems. Some books deserve to be listed that deal responsibly with the problems stated in their titles: Jennie Holliman, *American Sports: 1785–1835* (Durham, N. C.: The Sieman Press, 1931, 222 pp.), Foster Rhea Dulles, *America Learns to Play:*

A History of Popular Recreation, 1607–1940 (Gloucester, Mass.: Peter Smith, 1940 441 pp.); Dale A. Somers, *The Rise of Sports in New Orleans 1850–1900* (Baton Rouge: Louisiana State University Press, 1972, 320 pp.); Gerald Redmond, *The Caledonian Games in Nineteenth Century America* (Rutherford: Farleigh Dickinson University Press, 1971, 146 pp.).

Benjamin G. Rader's *American Sports* (Englewood Cliffs: Prentice-Hall, 1983, 376 pp.) is more profound and more comprehensive than any of the books cited above. Alas, it came into my possession too late to be incorporated into the book at hand.

If a metaphor might be allowed, baseball is an oasis of happiness. There are at least two large responsible histories. A good narrative is David Quentin Voigt. *American Baseball, 1 From Gentleman's Sport to the Commissioner System* (Norman, Oklahoma: University of Oklahoma Press, 1966, 336 pp.), *2 From the Commissioners to Continental Expansion* (Norman, Oklahoma: University of Oklahoma Press, 1970, 350 pp.). More analytical and less documented than the above is Harold Seymour, *Baseball, 1 The Early Years* (New York: Oxford University Press, 1960, 373 pp.), *2 The Golden Years* (New York: Oxford University Press, 1971, 492 pp.). Seymour was planning further volumes. An inspiring piece of research which is solid, and profound is a reworked doctoral dissertation, Steven A. Riess, *Touching Base: Professional Baseball in the Progressive Era* (Westport, Conn.: Greenwood Press, 1980; 268 pp. Two brilliant, documented essays deserve to be cited here: Allen Guttmann's, "Why Baseball Was Our National Game," in *From Ritual to Record* (New York: Columbia University Press, 1978), 91–116; Gunther Barth, "Ball Park," in *City People* (New York: Oxford University Press, 1980), 148–91. There is even a responsible warts-and-all biography of Babe Ruth: Robert W. Creamer, *Babe: The Legend Comes to Life* (New York: Simon and Schuster, 1974) 443 pp. Much of the other accurate, statistical, or lyrical literature of baseball is cited in the above works.

The contrast with other American sports is striking and dismal. For college and university sports of all kinds, professional football, basketball, or hockey there is little of substance. A recent biography, Randy Roberts, *Jack Dempsey, the Manassa Mauler* (Baton Rouge: Louisiana State University Press, 1979, 310 pp.)

discusses Dempsey's career only to 1927. However it is sage and scholarly and indicates that improvements may be ahead.

Many have responded to one aspect of the most obvious failure of American ideals and have written about the Negro in sports. The literature is voluminous, admonitory, heroic, and usually inaccurate. It is curious that the best analysis of the problem is a published German dissertation, Egon W. Steinkamp, *Sport und Rasse: Der schwarze Sportler in den USA* (Ahrensburg bei Hamburg: Czwalina, 1976 269 pp.) The book is well annotated and the bibliography, pp. 252–67 is useful.

There are no existing, solid bibliographies of American sport nor libraries that have been especially devoted to this area. I must cite a useful, though hidden work which cites and evaluates many other bibliographies: Melvin Leonard Adelman, "An Assessment of Sports History Theses in the United States, 1931–1967" (Unpublished Masters' thesis in Physical Education, University of Illinois, 1970, 230 pp.). For a further critical view of American sports scholarship one can read Adelman's essay, "Academicians and Athletics: Historians' Views of American Sport," *Maryland Historian* (1973) 4(2):123–37.

10. THE MODERN OLYMPIC GAMES

I have dealt with the bibliographical problems posed in this chapter in "The modern Olympic Games: A Bibliographical Essay," *Sportwissenschaft* (1976) 6(1):89–98. In the article, I stress the fact that until 1936 or so the Olympic Games were rather modest, local festivals. I also praised the bibliographical usefulness of a major work that deserves to be cited here again: Hans Lenk, *Werte, Ziele, Wirklichkeit der Modernen Olympischen Spiele* (Schorndorf bei Stuttgart: Hofmann, 1964) ("Verbesserte Auflage", 1972, 376 pp.).

There is another useful bibliography for the early period: K. Brown, "The Modern Olympics: An Informal List of Material in the New York Public Library," *New York Public Library Bulletin* (May 1939) 43:405–31.

The pre-history of the modern Olympic Games is treated in an interesting set of documents edited by Karl Lennartz: *Kenntnisse und Vorstellungen von Olympia und den Olympischen Spiele in der*

Zeit von 393–1896 (Schorndorf bei Stuttgart: Hofmann, 1974) 224 pp. One can read my own *First Modern Olympics* (Berkeley: University of California Press, 1976) 194 pp. John J. MacAloon, *This Great Symbol: Pierre de Coubertin and the Origins of the Modern Olympic Games* (Chicago: University of Chicago Press, 1981, 359 pp.), focuses on Coubertin's ideas. Both books have good bibliographical notes.

Each "Olympic" year (I believe this terminology may be employed) several books appear in each major language that purport to survey the history of the Olympic Games from antiquity to the near present. They stress heroes, incidents, records, and statistics. Two of these, though undocumented, rise above the rest. They are: Walter Umminger, *Die Olympischen Spiele der Neuzeit* (Dortmund: Olympischer Sportverlag, 1969, 397 pp.) and Lord Killanin and John Rodda, eds., *The Olympic Games: 80 Years of People, Events and Records* (New York: Macmillan, 1976 272 pp.)

There are great stores of official reports, scrapbooks, and pictorial material awaiting diligent historians seeking topics that lend themselves to lively writing. Very little has been done on the Olympic movement between 1900 and 1932. An exception is Karl Lennartz, *Die VI. Olympischen Spiele Berlin 1916* (Cologne: Carl-Diem-Institut an der Deutschen Sporthochschule Köln, 1978), 215 pp. That there still has appeared no solid literature on the 1932 Olympic Games in Los Angeles is one of the wonders of modern scholarship.

II. AMERICAN SPORT IN RECENT TIMES

This essay will be an amendment and continuation of the essay for chapter 9. Though the previously mentioned survey by John Rickards Betts is useful for the period only to 1950, the accomplishment merits praise again.

Several well-written and comprehensive appraisals by disillusioned or skeptical sports journalists deserve citation here. All reflect the social-critical atmospheres of their publication dates. They are: Paul Gallico, *Farewell to Sport* (New York: Knopf, 1938, 346 pp.); Leonard Schecter, *The Jocks* (New York: Bobbs-Merrill, 1969, 278 pp.); Robert Lipsyte, *Sportsworld: An American Dreamland*

(New York: Quadrangle 1975, 292 pp). The various collected writings of "Red" (Walter Wellesley) Smith (1905–1982), are readily available or traceable.

There have been several recent collections or anthologies of careful writing on American sport that were designed for college course work. These collections were conscientiously done and all supply good bibliographies. Some of them are: John W. Loy, Jr. et al., eds., *Sport, Culture and Society* (Philadelphia: Lea and Febiger, 2nd ed., 1981, 376 pp.); George H. Sage, ed., *Sport and American Society: Selected Readings* (Reading, Mass.: Addison-Wesley, 3rd ed., 1980, 395 pp.); M. Marie Hart and Susan Birrell, *Sport in the Socio-Cultural Process* (Dubuque, Iowa: William C. Brown, 3rd ed., 1981, 521 pp.); D. Stanley Eitzen, ed., *Sport in Contemporary Society: An Anthology* (New York: St. Martins, 1979, 467 pp.)

In their survey of the recent North American scene, John W. Loy, Barry D. McPherson, Gerald Kenyon, *Sport and Social Systems: A Guide to the Analysis, Problems and Literature* (Reading, Mass.: Addison-Wesley, 1978, 447 pp.), provide comprehensive, but unannotated bibliographies.

More specialized good books that survey the topics mentioned in their titles are the following: John F. Rooney, Jr., *A Geography of American Sport* (Reading, Mass.: Addison-Wesley, 1974, 306 pp.), Roger G. Noll, ed., *Government and the Sports Business* (Washington, D.C.: Brookings Institution, 1974, 445 pp.), William P. Lineberry, ed., *The Business of Sport* (New York: H. W. Wilson, 1973, 220 pp.). All of the above provide useful, if unannotated and unevaluated bibliographies.

Those interested in the background for Australian sport can look at Keith Dunstan, *Sports* (North Melbourne: Cassell, 1973, 367 pp.)

12. THE OLYMPIC GAMES, 1936–1980

For good histories of the modern Olympic Games the reader can consult the surveys by Lenk, Umminger, and Killanin and Rodda that are cited in the essay for chapter 10. Mandell's bibliographical essay in *Sportwissenschaft* was published in 1976 and covers literature until that date.

There is a documented survey of the 1936 Olympics in Berlin: Richard D. Mandell, *The Nazi Olympics* (New York: MacMillan, 1971, 316 pp.). There has been an American paperback and Norwegian, Hebrew, German, and Japanese translations. Arnd Krüger, *Die Olympischen Spiele 1936 und die Weltmeinung* (Berlin: Bartels und Wernitz, 1972, 255 pp.) is better on the political background.

Columbia University Press has recently published *The Games Must Go On*, Allen Guttmann's archivally based biography of Avery Brundage (1887–1975), the most prominent bureaucrat in American amateur sport and President of the International Olympic Committee, 1952–1972. Richard Espy's *Politics of the Olympic Games* (Berkeley: University of California Press, 1979) (Paperback, "With an Epilogue, 1976–1980," 1981, 238 pp.) is intelligent, but uses sources available only in the United States and only in English. A sport survey of some political problems from a British point of view is Richard Thompson, *Race and Sport* (London: Oxford University Press, 1964, 73 pp.). Jean Meynaud is a French Canadian. His *Sport et politique* (Paris: Payot, 1966, 321 pp.) is more theoretical than narrative and deals with more than the Olympic Games. His "Orientation bibliographique" (315–318) lists lots of relevant literature not cited elsewhere. There are other solid works in progress on the modern Olympic Games that will surely improve on all of the above.

There are three types of literature that merit discussion, if not bibliographical detail, here. One type is the vast amount of official and ephemeral literature published on the occasion of an Olympic meeting. The problems of preserving, locating, and employing this material are discussed in Mandell's essay mentioned earlier and cited in full in the bibliographical essay for chapter 10. Related to this is the polemical literature connected with each Olympic Games. The output of the sort was especially revealing and provocative on the occasion of the 1972 Olympics in Germany. But this literature is more interesting for its contemporary and ideological, than its historical, content and some of these essays have been discussed and cited elsewhere in these essays. A final category of Olympic literature worth mentioning, but not listing in detail, consents of those compendiums of statistics on performance either separately published or appended to the readily available, up-to-date surveys of the Olympic Games. As with other aspects of modern sport, what *happened* is easy to determine. What it might all *mean* is a different matter entirely.

13. SPORT AND SOCIETY IN THE LATER TWENTIETH CENTURY

There are no surveys that cover even wide expanses of the area covered in this chapter. There are, however, some skeptical treatments of modern sports that deserve more than mere mention. One is Philip Goodhart and Christopher Chataway, *War Without Weapons* (London: W. H. Allen, 1968, 163 pp.) which examines international sports competitions as tools in modern diplomacy. The content is less sensational than the title suggests, but there are lots of statistics and anecdotes, all of which are, alas, undocumented. For a recent sour view of American sport in its social context, one can look again at several books, but especially those by Robert Lipsyte and Leonard Schecter discussed in the essay for chapter 12. Another interesting essay is the chapter "The Degradation of Sport" (pp. 100–24) in Christopher Lasch's much discussed *The Culture of Narcissism* (New York: W. G. Norton, 1978, 268 pp.).

Alex Natan (1906–1970) was a world-class sprinter, a German and a Jew who was consequently barred from competition in Germany after 1933. He later edited two remarkable collections of essays that examine the darker aspects of modern sport. They are: *Sport and Society: A Symposium* (London: Bowes and Bowes, 1958, 208 pp.) and *Sport-Kritisch* (Bern: Hallweg, 1972, 224 pp.). The critics Natan includes are not ideologically unified or equally adamant—a rarity in sports-critical literature.

The most fruitful critique of sport is that that has come from young, leftist social critics. A salient essay was that by Bero Rigauer, *Sport und Arbeit*, which, happily, has been translated by Allen Guttmann as *Sport and Work* (New York: Columbia University Press, 1981, 110 pp.). Much of the critical literature on German sport was inspired by the disruptive preparations for the 1972 Olympic Games in Munich and has been well appraised and cited by Franz Begov, "Olympisches und Antiolympisches in neuren historischen und soziologischen Veröffentlichungen," *Sportwissenschaft*, (1972/3) 3:182–89.

There are three French leftist critiques of sport that are not very substantial, but which still deserve to be cited. They are: *Sport, culture et repression* (Paris: F. Maspero, 1972, 172 pp.); *Le sport en questions: Les responses des communistes* (Paris: Editions sociales, 1976, 188 pp.); Jean-Marie Brohm, *Critiques du sport* (Paris: Christian Bourgois, 1976, 240 pp.).

Sport where it is most vigorous and newest, in Eastern Europe, has not inspired indigenous, critical literature. There are, however, some sober Western critics. The title of Dieter Voigt's, *Soziologie in der D.D.R.* (Cologne: "Wissenschaft und Politik," 1975, 335 pp.) is deceptive. It is really about sport and recreation in the modern German Democratic Republic. Voigt has a fine, though unannotated "Literaturverzeichnis," 235–308. A West German journalist, Willi Knecht, has written a lot on East German sport. Some of his interviews with defected athletes are in an edited work (pp. 149–254), *Amateur '72* (Mainz: Hase und Koehler, 1971, 368 pp.). The weekly news magazine *Spiegel* also had a well-researched series, "Fussball auf dem Spielfeld der Politik," on East German sport that ran in three issues from May 20 through June 3 in 1974.

An early book on sport in the USSR is Henry W. Morton, *Soviet Sport: Mirror of Soviet Society* (New York: Collier Books, 1963, 221 pp.). Much more detailed, documented and based on intimate knowledge of Soviet sources is James Riordan, *Sport in Soviet Society* (Cambridge: Cambridge University Press, 1977, 435 pp.). Riordan's *Soviet Sport* (Oxford: Basil Blackwell, 1980, 172 pp.) repeats much of what was in his earlier book. Many Western readers may be astonished at Riordan's admiration of the Soviet system and his sympathy with the view that sport is just too important to be allowed haphazard development. Riordan also edited *Sport under Communism* (London: C. Hurst, 1978, 177 pp.) which contains essays on various countries, including Cuba. The material is factual and sympathetic. Jonathan Kolatch, *Sport, Politics and*

Ideology in China (New York: Jonathan David, 1972, 254 pp.) is intelligent, but is dated.

Achôt Mélik-Chakhnazarov, *Le sport en Afrique* (Paris: Présence africaine, 1970, 206 pp.) emphasizes deeds and statistics. There is nothing else worth citing about sport in Africa, South America or in the Third World.

Two unusual books deserve more than mention here. Edouard Seidler, *Le sport et la presse* (Paris: A. Colin, 1964, 269 pp.) concentrates on France, but is exemplary in its historical analysis of the sports pages. Lothar Quanz, *Der Sportler als Idol* (Giessen: Focus, 1974, 174 pp.) has some interesting analyses of the sports reporting in *Bild-Zeitung*, the widely circulated West German tabloid.

At this writing, a manuscript by John Hoberman on sport and ideology is expected to be published in early 1984 by the University of Texas Press. Hoberman has done some careful digging and analyzing that is long overdue.

14. JOYOUS SPORT, BEAUTIFUL SPORT

The best yea-saying survey of sport is the large survey by Carl Diem that has already been discussed and criticized in the bibliographical essay for the preface.

There is some good literature on art and sport. The article by Henriette Heiny, "Die Sportdarstellung in der Malerei des 20. Jahrhunderts, aufgezeigt am Beispiel des Fussballsports," *Kölner Beiträge zur Sportwissenschaft* (1973) 2:138–54 is useful. Heiny's *"Anmerkungen"* (152–54) cite lots of other literature. There have been many exhibitions of sport art. Almost all have platitudinous texts and no documentation.

One can consult Sisto Favre, *Civiltà, arte, sport* (Rome: Società Editrice Dante Alighieri, 1970, 602 pp.). Favre provides 97 plates and an unannotated "Bibliografia" (561–71).

Sport in der Kunst (Munich: Bruckmann, 1972, 125 pp.) is a catalog with splendid illustrations of an exhibition arranged for the 1972 Olympics. More illustrations are in *Sport in der Kunst* (Leipzig: E. A. Seemann, 1969, 46 illus., unpaged).

Since 1959 there has existed a small privately funded "National

Art Museum of Sport," which was located in Madison Square Garden in New York from 1961 to 1978. The catalog of the museum's most ambitious exhibition is *The Artist and the Sportsman* (New York: Renaissance Editions, 1968, 95 pp.). The present home of the museum is in West Haven, Connecticut.

Much more substantial and provocative is the catalog, *Sport und Design* (Stuttgart: Nationales Olympisches Komitee für Deutschland und Design-Center, Stuttgart, 1981, 158 pp.) edited by Otl Aicher. Aicher was the dictator of taste at the 1972 Olympic Games. The catalog was of a large exhibition of sports equipment and sports architecture arranged for the eleventh Olympic Congress in 1981 in Baden-Baden. The heavily illustrated catalog is itself a beautiful thing and the text (in German, French, and English) is intelligent and stimulating.

Andrew J. Kozar's, *R. Tait MacKenzie* (Knoxville: University of Tennessee Press, 1975, 118 pp.) is well illustrated, annotated, and inspiring to read and behold.

Regarding the various designers of sports architecture, they and their works are easily traceable in the usual art indexes.

Regarding sport and literature, there is no survey or bibliography. Neil David Berman, *Playful Fictions and Fictional Players: Games, Sport, and Survival in Contemporary American Fiction* (Port Washington, New York: Kennikat Press, 1981, 112 pp.) is narrowly focused but has helpful bibliographical notes and a "Select Bibliography (pp. 108–10). Christian Messenger's *Sport and the Spirit of Play in American Fiction: Hawthorne to Faulkner* (New York: Columbia University Press, 1981, 389 pp.) provides brave analyses, fine details, and exemplary bibliographical precision and evaluations. Karl Schwarz, *Dichter deuten den Sport: Auslandische Dichter* (Schorndorf bei Stuttgart: Karl Hofmann, 1967, 126 pp.) is a collection of translated excerpts with some discussion and bibliographies.

Regarding the suggestion that sport itself has offered new esthetic possibilities, a curious and stimulating essay is Pierre Frayssinet, *Le sport parmi les beaux arts* (Brussels: Dargaud, 1968, 128 pp.). Regarding the possibility that the modern athlete could him- (or her-) self be considered a new type of creation, this problem has been faced most courageously by the body builders. A book that rises above masses of popular literature on the body builders is Charles Gaines and George Butler *Pumping Iron* (New York: Simon and Schuster, 1974, 221 pp.).

The whole physical fitness movement of which the long-distance runners are the most visible manifestation is maintaining its momentum. But we are still too close to it to have produced solid literature. Clearly, there is lots of room for thought and diligence.

INDEX